Distance Education and Languages

NEW PERSPECTIVES ON LANGUAGE AND EDUCATION
Series Editor: Professor Viv Edwards, *University of Reading, Reading, Great Britain*
Series Advisor: Professor Allan Luke, *Nanyang Technological University, Singapore*

Two decades of research and development in language and literacy education have yielded a broad, multidisciplinary focus. Yet education systems face constant economic and technological change, with attendant issues of identity and power, community and culture. This series will feature critical and interpretive, disciplinary and multidisciplinary perspectives on teaching and learning, language and literacy in new times.

Other Books of Interest
Beyond the Beginnings: Literacy Interventions for Upper Elementary English Language Learners
 Angela Carrasquillo, Stephen B. Kucer and Ruth Abrams
Bilingualism and Language Pedagogy
 Janina Brutt-Griffler and Manka Varghese (eds)
Continua of Biliteracy: An Ecological Framework for Educational Policy, Research, and Practice in Multilingual Settings
 Nancy H. Hornberger (ed.)
Language and Literacy Teaching for Indigenous Education: A Bilingual Approach
 Norbert Francis and Jon Reyhner
Language Learning and Teacher Education: A Sociocultural Approach
 Margaret R. Hawkins (ed.)
Language Strategies for Bilingual Families
 Suzanne Barron-Hauwaert
Language Minority Students in the Mainstream Classroom (2nd edn)
 Angela L. Carrasquillo and Vivian Rodríguez
Learners' Experiences of Immersion Education: Case Studies of French and Chinese
 Michèle de Courcy
Trilingualism in Family, School and Community
 Charlotte Hoffmann and Jehannes Ytsma (eds)
Making Sense in Sign: A Lifeline for a Deaf Child
 Jenny Froude
Multilingual Classroom Ecologies
 Angela Creese and Peter Martin (eds)
A Parents' and Teachers' Guide to Bilingualism
 Colin Baker
Power, Prestige and Bilingualism: International Perspectives on Elite Bilingual Education
 Anne-Marie de Mejía
Second Language Students in Mainstream Classrooms
 Coreen Sears
Understanding Deaf Culture: In Search of Deafhood
 Paddy Ladd

For more details of these or any other of our publications, please contact:
Multilingual Matters, Frankfurt Lodge, Clevedon Hall,
Victoria Road, Clevedon, BS21 7HH, England
http://www.multilingual-matters.com

NEW PERSPECTIVES ON LANGUAGE AND EDUCATION
Series Editor: Viv Edwards

Distance Education and Languages
Evolution and Change

Edited by
Börje Holmberg, Monica Shelley
and Cynthia White

MULTILINGUAL MATTERS LTD
Clevedon • Buffalo • Toronto

Library of Congress Cataloging in Publication Data
Distance Education and Languages: Evolution and Change/Edited by Börje
Holmberg, Monica Shelley and Cynthia White.
New Perspectives on Language and Education
Includes bibliographical references and index.
1. Language and languages–Study and teaching. 2. Distance education. I. Holmberg,
Börje. II. Shelley, Monica. III. White, Cynthia. IV. Series.
P53.2967.D57 2005
418'.0071–dc22   2004012870

British Library Cataloguing in Publication Data
A catalogue entry for this book is available from the British Library.

ISBN 1-85359-776-7 (hbk)
ISBN 1-85359-775-9 (pbk)

Multilingual Matters Ltd
UK: Frankfurt Lodge, Clevedon Hall, Victoria Road, Clevedon BS21 7HH.
USA: UTP, 2250 Military Road, Tonawanda, NY 14150, USA.
Canada: UTP, 5201 Dufferin Street, North York, Ontario M3H 5T8, Canada.

Typeset by Archetype-IT Ltd (http://www.archetype-it.com).
Printed and bound in Great Britain by the Cromwell Press Ltd.

Contents

Preface

Distance education is attracting much attention at the beginning of the 21st century – considerations of it can be based on a wealth of research reports, studies of various aspects and comprehensive works on its evolution, character and problems. However, few studies of its application to special subject areas have been published. This book is about distance education as applied to language learning and includes papers by distance educators from various parts of the world.

The basic concerns of distance education influence the teaching and learning of languages as much as other areas and play an important part in the contributions to this volume. The two main constituents of distance education, subject matter presentation and interaction (between students and tutors and peer-group interaction) are investigated here. The use of computer communication plays an important part in facilitating such interaction through e-mail, the chat function and other applications of online learning. Dialogue contributing to rapport between the parties involved in the learning process is discussed. So are metacognition and the pervasive problems of student autonomy and individualisation.

While, for instance, most distance education allows – and encourages – students to pace their study as it suits them and study individually, there are other types of approach common in distance-teaching universities which expect students to keep to a common time-table and even – particularly in American university distance education – to belong to 'classes' (a concept rejected by several pioneers in distance education who insist that each student constitutes a class of his own). These and other differences of approach are mirrored in the presentations in this book. So are a number of other general distance education concerns which serve as background to the more specific problems of teaching and learning foreign languages at a distance, such as linguistic theory and teaching and learning methodology. The need of theory on which to base practice is recognised and has led to contributions to theory building.

The editors of this volume hope that it will inspire further thinking and debate, not only among distance educators, but also others engaged in the teaching of foreign languages.

Börje Holmberg

Introduction

MONICA SHELLEY and CYNTHIA WHITE

This edited collection of work from all over the world is devoted to an examination of research in the field of teaching languages at a distance, both from the point of view of the learner and of the teacher of languages. The emphasis in this book is on a critical examination of current issues, and on recent developments within the field. While some contributions come from practitioners who have been active in this field for some years, others come from institutions where teaching languages at a distance is at a relatively early stage of development. The contexts, institutional and educational requirements and higher education systems within which the authors of these chapters are operating are diverse and subject to a range of pressures for change. There are, however, sufficient commonalities between the distance teaching contexts to provide new ideas and generate reflections on research and practice, and this variety of experience provides a particularly fruitful and illuminating aspect for readers.

The book is divided into six different sections to reflect different themes. There is, as one might expect, a good deal of common ground between the themes, with the difference in many cases more a matter of emphasis than discrete treatment of topics. While readers may prefer to concentrate (initially, at any rate) on those subject areas of most immediate interest to them, all chapters cover much that is of general interest and a broader perspective on the field will be gained by exploring the book as a whole.

The six sections are:

- Learner autonomy
- Learner perspectives and support
- Development of intercultural competence
- Methodology and course design
- Learning environments
- Language teacher development.

Learner Autonomy

All three of the chapters in this section are based in the UK; they deal with markedly different aspects of learner independence and autonomy, the discussion of which underlies much of the debate about the function and operation of the distance teaching of languages.

Stella Hurd provides an overview of autonomy, reviewing various interpretations of the concept and its place within the field of distance language learning and teaching. She spells out how language teaching at a distance has developed at the Open University, UK (OUUK), and debates whether autonomy has a part to play in the highly structured system in place there. Affective factors, such as motivation, learning style and previous learning experience, are related to autonomy, as are metacognition and self-regulation. Hurd draws on the Open University experience to discuss how autonomy may be promoted via computer-mediated communication (CMC) – while warning that technology-mediated learning is not problem-free.

The next contribution is from Linda Murphy, drawing on the work she has done with students of French, German and Spanish at the OUUK. She explores how students approach distance language study, and whether a range of support materials developed by tutors is effective in increasing learner autonomy. She concludes that there is strong evidence of learner control and active engagement with the study materials, except in the case of writing skills development, and that overall students demonstrated critical analysis and reflectiveness. Gaining insights into the tutor perspective was an important part of this research, and Murphy notes how this process raised the tutors' appreciation of the importance of helping their students to develop language learning strategies.

The last chapter in this section, by Alex Ding from the University of Nottingham in the United Kingdom, focuses on the role of a virtual self-access centre (VSAC) in the promotion of collaborative learner autonomy. The language being taught in this example is English for Academic Purposes. Ding concludes on the basis of his experience that, despite the dichotomy between theory and practice that he encountered when setting up his VSAC, it is essential that theory should be used as a basis for informed decision-making in this area. He expounds on the relevance of the theory of intersubjective collaborative autonomy and demonstrates how he has employed such theory in his work. Ding is realistic about the success of the VSAC, and looks forward to learning more from the research which still remains to be done in this area.

Learner Perspectives and Support

The second section of this book emphasises the importance of the learner as the centre of the process of successful distance language learning. Contributions about learners from three very different parts of the world are included here.

This section begins with the introduction of a learner-based theory of distance language learning. Cynthia White from Massey University in New Zealand draws on her research into the ways in which learners conceptualise the process of distance language learning to elaborate on the notion of the interface which develops between the learner and the learning context in the course of learning experiences. The different dimensions of the theory are explored, together with the purposes which the interface serves for distance language learners. Commentaries given by learners provide a valuable link between the theory and realities of distance language learning. The emphasis on theory development with learner perspectives as the starting point is in marked contrast to the evolution of theory in distance education, which is also traced in this chapter. White concludes that the learner-context interface theory provides a starting point for further research and theory construction in the field.

The learner is also centre stage in the chapter by Cristina Ros i Solé and Mike Truman from the OUUK, where the two authors focus on feedback in distance language learning. The importance of students' active involvement in the process of the provision of feedback is emphasised, and examples given from the authors' work in the Spanish programme at the Open University. The role of feedback in the development of student autonomy is spelt out and discussed. Readers who are engaged in the development of assessment for distance language learning courses will be familiar with the long-term debate over formative and summative assessment – and this is illustrated here via the outcomes of research conducted among students enrolled on a Spanish course. Views as to the types of fault which students make, and recommended ways of dealing with them, are discussed, with the help of specific examples. Finally, Ros i Solé and Truman look forward to the development of new assessment strategies and formats to enhance the experience of distance language learning.

The third chapter in this section comes from South Africa and looks at what seems, at first sight, to be a fairly limited situation, the support of students studying English via a mixed-mode delivery system. But Carisma Dreyer, Nwabisa Bangeni and Charl Nel soon make it clear that they are having to deal with problems familiar to educators around the world – dropout and failure rates, and institutional accountability. Their description of how to profile students provides a useful framework for drawing up criteria and priorities for new courses. The management of change in South Africa forms the background to Dreyer, Bangeni and Nel's research project, which identified at risk and successful student profiles, and the support the different kinds of student required. A particularly useful aspect of this chapter is the outline of a framework for learner support provision model, which locates different types of support, when and where the support will be needed and who might provide it.

Development of Intercultural Competence

The first chapter in this section, by Monica Shelley and Uwe Baumann of the OUUK, looks at a range of student-oriented issues, but focuses for the main part on the acquisition of intercultural competence by distance learners of German. Reviewing the nature and role of assessment in language teaching and, more particularly, the function of assessment in distance language learning, they conclude that the written and spoken assessment in the German course under review reflected the acquisition of those skills, attitudes and knowledge which go towards the development of intercultural competence in the language being learnt. Shelley and Baumann compared the outcomes of the student assessments with the results of a questionnaire administered to students at the beginning and end of their study, which made a basic measurement of knowledge gain over the duration of the course, and also assessed whether students' attitudes had changed at all. They concluded that, typically, their adult students began their courses already possessing a fair degree of cultural competence, but that this increased during their period of study.

The focus of the contribution from Richard Fay (University of Manchester, UK) and Leah Davcheva (British Council, Bulgaria) is very different from the previous chapter, though still centred on the acquisition of intercultural communicative competence. In this instance the two authors reflect on the lessons learnt from two programmes for English language teachers and translator/interpreters being presented in Bulgaria in collaboration with the University of Manchester in the UK. Distance education is a relatively recent arrival in Bulgaria, and the group responsible for the two programmes was anxious to ensure that culturally appropriate distance learning methodology was employed in their implementation. The authors demonstrate how different definitions of intercultural communication fit with areas of language education. They present a tentative model of professional intercultural communicative competence, which subsumes the cognitive, affective and behavioural dimensions of intercultural learning. Realistically, they admit that 'it is very difficult to keep a firm eye on all these [diverse] elements at the same time within the constraints and opportunities of real projects'.

Methodology and Course Design

This section contains two contributions which both reflect the main theme, albeit from different perspectives. The first chapter is from Börje Holmberg, formerly of the FernUniversität in Germany, and offers a definition and discussion of the theoretical aspects of foreign language teaching at a distance. Starting with a brief history of the discipline, he summarises the various theoretical considerations which need to be examined. He discusses the significance of behavioural thinking in relation to language teaching, concluding that cognitivism and constructivism are more useful approaches today. Holmberg illustrates this with the use of examples based in different methodological frameworks and discusses the value of a combination of the learning of principles and imitative practice. The teaching of pronunciation is another thorny area for distance education, and Holmberg picks up on some problems and inconsistencies. Finally, he concludes that the judicious use of the mother tongue is best employed in contrastive analysis, and that explicit explanations have great value for distance language learners.

The other chapter in this section has been contributed by Cecilia Garrido of the OUUK and studies the development of the suite of Spanish courses. Starting from a discussion of the decision-making with regard to course design, assessment and student support in the Spanish team at the OU, she lists the various priorities which were adopted to serve as a basis for the syllabus of the Spanish programme. Once the initial challenges had been surmounted, new ones arose, which she defines as evolving mainly from the implications of teaching language and culture in an integrated manner, and from the opportunities and threats of the information age. Touching briefly on the significance of teaching for intercultural competence, Garrido highlights the difficulties presented by the formulation of evaluation and assessment criteria with regard to intercultural communication. She also discusses the challenges of cultural diversity, with particular reference to the number of standard varieties of Spanish in the Spanish-speaking world.

Learning Environments

A number of examples of different learning environment are presented in this section. They have been chosen to reflect the very diverse and varied approaches being taken, and also to illustrate different solutions which have been found.

The first chapter is from the United States of America. Donald Weasenforth, Christine Meloni and Sigrun Biesenbach-Lucas have collaborated in this contribution to discuss their use of course management software (CMS) to improve the English language proficiency of international students. Emphasising that their aim is to demonstrate that the technologies available to distance teachers can be most effective in fostering language autonomy, they show how CMS enabled their students to work without supervision, to become teachers and researchers, to exercise choice and to benefit from feedback other than the 'right answer'. Finally, they touch on issues which may mitigate against success in the use of CMS.

Vincenza Tudini, from the University of South Australia, concentrates on the use of a chatline by *ab initio* learners of Italian without teacher supervision. How far can this replace classroom interaction? What skills can such learners gain from the use of this medium? Tudini summarises the research on chatlines, concluding that they have several proven benefits, including opportunities for the negotiation of meaning. Most of this research, however, was done with more advanced learners, so Tudini's work with *ab initio* learners has particular value. Looking at the various opportunities available for distance students in South Australia to develop speaking skills, very few offer a high level of interactivity, so the introduction of chatlines was welcome. On the basis of her research project, Tudini concludes that her study demonstrated that it is worth including chatlines as a learning tool when setting up language programme for complete beginners learning at a distance. They are particularly useful in providing an opportunity for students to establish connections with each other in a colloquial, non-threatening way.

Andreas Schramm, from Hamline University in the USA reports next on the ethnographic strategies he employed when transforming several courses of an on-campus ESL teacher education programme to an interactive online format. He asks the question: How can an interactive, student-centred classroom experience be moved to the Web? Schramm focuses on the importance of establishing an agreed set of standards for Web-based courses so as to assess their success – or otherwise. In addition he emphasises the importance of what he terms the ethnographic approach, which is employed in the initial analysis and in the modes, types and means of interaction involved in the construction and delivery of Web-based courses.

Based in the Hong Kong University of Science and Technology, John Milton has focused on the creative use of online tools to generate authentic language. The need to be creative is especially important, since learning in South East Asian classrooms has been more imitative than creative in the past. When first researching different possibilities among the commercial course delivery systems available, Milton was forced to conclude that, despite the promise of Internet technology, ' . . . no ready-made content delivery system seemed to offer the range of activity types and tools that meet the Web's potential to create and deliver courses for dynamic language learning'. Working with a small team of students, he developed a tailor-made system to meet the students' needs which provided asynchronous voice messaging, online data-driven language learning, feedback on student writing and online role plays. The tools he describes have been incorporated into an online course development system that supports several online EFL courses aimed at various groups of learners.

Finally in this section, Mirjam Hauck and Regine Hampel from the OUUK describe their progress in the introduction of online tutorials for all language courses using an Internet-based audio-graphic conferencing system. This began with pilot projects, and progressed to the introduction of tutorials 'online only' in a mainstream language course in German. The Lyceum learning environment used has three main components: the audio-graphic conferencing client, a website and e-mail. Students and tutors work together in Lyceum in real-time inputting both audio data and information presented on the screen. Developing the tasks for the online tutorials presented a particular challenge, in that while the designers wanted to make optimal use of the new environment, they knew from the pilot work that the activities needed to allow learners to familiarise themselves gradually with the various tools available. Feedback provided the designers with useful guidance for revising the structure of the programme so as to provide more flexibility, and to ensure that groups were kept small. The ways in which the role of the Lyceum tutor changes from that of the classroom teacher are explored and the next steps in this exciting project are outlined.

Language Teacher Development

The first of the three chapters in this final section comes from Sweden: Heidi Hansson (Umeå University) and Elisabeth Wennö (Karlstad University) discuss their experience with the development of a distance training course for teachers of different practical subjects who wanted to add English. By comparing a group of students taking more or less the same course face to face with the group of distance learners, Hansson and Wennö concluded that the results from the distance learners were at least as good as those who learned in the classroom. They compared the two groups on the basis of increase in the level of language proficiency and degree of interaction; student views were also taken into consideration. The authors argue that they have demonstrated clearly that the factors which are important for successful distance learning are little different from those considered vital in any learning process. Distance is not really the issue, but rather the available time and energy of the students (and teachers).

A very different project is described in the chapter by Franca Poppi and Marina Bondi (University of Modena and Reggio Emilia in Italy) and Lesley Low from the University of Stirling in the UK. This project arose from a Europe-wide initiative to extend the teaching of foreign languages to primary age pupils by training more teachers to cater for this new demand. Different European countries responded to the initiative in a huge variety of ways, but a joint project located in Italian and Scottish institutions of higher education led to the development of the PLEASE website (Primary Language teacher Education: Autonomy and Self-Evaluation). This had the general aim of helping primary school teachers to recognise and overcome any dependencies they might feel and encouraging them to become more active as language learners and users, and as agents for their own development. More specifically, the website provides a resource pool of ideas, activities and references which require a direct contribution from the learners and can act as stimuli for group discussion and project work. The website includes online grids and checklists for language assessment and needs analysis; online papers on classroom language and an exchange conferencing area. A particular feature is the provision of a content Webmaster, who acts as an online motivator and adviser.

Last but not least, Do Coyle from the University of Nottingham in the UK assesses the development of a pilot network of Teaching and Learning Observatory (TLO) sites which can be used to enhance the pre- and in-service training of foreign language and bilingual teachers. The need which had been identified was for trainee modern language teachers to have a greater variety of school-based experience than could be provided in their immediate locality. The TLO was set up to link ten secondary schools with a training institution using video conferencing and interactive technology. While the original plan had been to offer trainee teachers the opportunity to observe experienced teachers in action, and for tutors to be able to observe and co-reflect on lessons taught by trainees, the TLO has developed into a powerful learning, teaching, training and research tool. Coyle discusses how this evolution has come about, and highlights features of the project which deserve particular attention. She emphasises that learning to accept that innovative practice can be uncomfortable, and to balance realism with vision in terms of what can be achieved has been an ultimately positive aspect.

The Future

Our aim in assembling these contributions in one volume has been to make the work encapsulated here available to a wide audience, and to encourage the establishment of collaborative links between practitioners in different institutions and around the world. We hope that this book will serve as the basis for fruitful co-operation and inspire more related research in the future to guide our understanding and reflection on evolution and change within the field.

Chapter 1

Autonomy and the Distance Language Learner

STELLA HURD

Introduction

Autonomy is a multidimensional concept now firmly rooted in mainstream literature and practice relating to language learning and teaching. However, while there are a number of theoretical descriptions of autonomous language learning, a single, universal theory has yet to emerge. The implications for a theory of autonomy are arguably even more complex in the case of distance language learning, where highly structured course materials and fixed assessment points would appear to run counter to notions of choice and responsibility. Taking as its point of reference the experience of distance language learning at the Open University (UK), this chapter examines the various dimensions of autonomy, in particular its relationship with affective aspects of learner differences and with metacognition. In conclusion, the chapter looks ahead to the potential of new technologies to create learning communities in which autonomy is promoted through social interaction, learner empowerment and reflection.

Interpretations of Autonomy

Despite the proliferation of research and publications over the last two decades, autonomy is a concept that remains elusive, particularly in relation to language learning and teaching. First, there are questions to do with definition, degree and application. Is it the 'ability to have and to hold the responsibility for all the decisions concerning all aspects of this learning' (Holec, 1981: 3) or is it a 'capacity for detachment, critical reflection, decision-making, and independent action' (Little, 1991: 4)? Is it an attribute that signifies 'organic independence' (OED online) or does it also imply interdependence? Does it entail complete freedom and responsibil-

1

ity on the part of learners, or does it come with constraints? Is it something that can be taught, or even imposed on learners, or is this a 'contradiction in educational terms' (Holec, 1985: 169)? There are also important issues to do with the role and timing of autonomy in learning. Is it a precondition for successful learning or an outcome of certain modes of learning, for example self-instruction?

Definitions

While there are no easy answers to any of these questions, there does appear to be almost universal acceptance of the development of autonomy as an 'important, general educational goal' (Sinclair, 2000: 5), and that autonomy can take a variety of different forms depending on learning context and learner characteristics. Where there are differences, it is not always a question of favouring one definition or interpretation over another. For example, the 'capacity' of Little and the 'ability' or 'skill' of Holec are not opposing constructs. Benson (2001: 49) argues that 'Little's definition is complementary to Holec's', in that it makes explicit the cognitive processes underlying effective self-management of learning, and thus adds 'a vital psychological dimension that is often absent in definitions of autonomy'. Benson (2001: 47) prefers to use the term 'control' over learning, because such a construct allows for easier examination than 'charge' or 'responsibility'. Others define autonomy in terms of what it entails or implies, hence, 'self-regulation' (Schunk & Zimmerman, 1998; Wenden, 2001) or 'self-direction' (Candy, 1991; White, 1999). Another approach is to describe what autonomy is not (Little, 1991). The main priority, according to Benson (2001: 48) is 'that we are able to identify the form in which we choose to recognize it in the contexts of our own research and practice'.

Social interaction, interdependence and reflection

The psychological dimension of autonomy has attracted a great deal of attention over the last decade, largely as a result of renewed interest in the work of the Soviet psychologist Vygotsky and his emphasis on interdependence in learning. According to Vygotsky (1978), we do not learn in isolation, but through our interactions with others. His 'zone of proximal development' is the gap between what learners can achieve on their own and what they can achieve in collaboration with others. Both Kohonen (1992) and Little (1996) view the idea of collaborative learning through social interaction as essential for the reflective and analytic capacity that is central to autonomy. Kohonen's (1992) experiential language learning model, based on Kolbian experiential learning principles, involves a cyclical process moving through concrete experience, reflection, abstract conceptualisation and action. The reflective (inner) process interplays with the experiential and active (social) processes to bring about deeper awareness of the self in relation to language learning. Collaboration with others through sharing the insights of reflection can enhance knowledge and lead to deeper understanding. Little (1996: 211), in line with Vygotskian thinking, also claims that 'the development of a capacity for reflection and analysis [. . .] depends on the internalization of a capacity to participate fully and critically in social interactions'.

For some, the social, human element is seen to have particular significance for language learning. Warriner-Burke (1990: 131) maintains that 'many experienced foreign language professionals think that language and language learning are deeply human experiences' and that 'perhaps it is this human factor that distinguishes foreign language learning from other knowledge . . . '. Little's view (2001: 32), however, is that learning is the product of a complex interplay between both social and reflective processes and warns that 'in stressing the importance of the social-interactive dimension [. . .], it is important not to underplay the importance of the individual-cognitive dimension'. He cites Ackermann (1996: 32) who states that, 'without connection people cannot grow, yet without separation they cannot relate' and talks of learning as 'a dance between diving in and stepping out' (1996: 32). In other words, reflection (stepping out) is as important as social interaction (diving in) for cognitive development and autonomy.

Developing reflection

Reflection is thus an integral part of the process of exercising autonomy, yet for most learners it does not come naturally and needs to be developed. Strategy or learner training programmes, either embedded in the materials or as stand-alone elements, can be effective. However, language 'advising' or 'counselling' is becoming a more widespread and popular option in universities in the UK operating self-access language learning systems (Mozzon-McPherson, 2001). Following an individual needs analysis, the student is shown over a period of time how to develop awareness and reflect on learning through the use of learning logs or diaries, given advice on strategy use, and encouraged to engage in self-evaluation as part of control over learning.

In some institutions teachers take on a timetabled adviser role; in others the advisory service is a separate unit operating in conjunction with teachers. Whatever the particular organisational structure, the shift in the locus of control from teacher to learner, which is central to an autonomous approach, involves a profound change in role, and can bring feelings of insecurity, uncertainty and discomfort (Little, 1995). Nevertheless, teachers in all educational contexts are the human interface between learners and resources and cannot therefore expect or help their learners to develop a capacity for critical reflection unless they have this capacity themselves. In this sense, learner autonomy is dependent on teacher autonomy. In a distance context, the challenges may be greater and the problems intensified, as the social interaction or 'pedagogical dialogue' Little (1995) regards as the 'decisive factor' in the development of learner autonomy can be infinitely more difficult to achieve. Dialogue can to a certain extent be promoted through the materials, but it is perhaps tutor feedback, paper-based or online, that can best create the conditions for learners to become good critical reflectors and develop self-management strategies. But what are the assumptions behind the nature and timing of autonomy within language learning?

Prerequisite or outcome?

Is autonomy a precondition for successful language learning, or a product or goal that emerges from learner exposure to certain contextual influences in language learning? Benson (2001: 9) highlights a common assumption among those working in self-access centres that 'self-access work will automatically lead to autonomy', and, from the producers of self-instructional and distance learning materials, that 'autonomy will be one outcome of these modes of learning'. These are false assumptions if applied generally. As argued in Hurd (1998a: 72–3), '[. . .] if learners are not trained for autonomy, no amount of surrounding them with resources will foster in them that capacity for active involvement and conscious choice, although it might appear to do so'. Little (2001: 34) also maintains that 'the pursuit of autonomy in formal learning environments must entail explicit conscious processes; otherwise we leave its development to chance'. Some studies into distance learning (Hurd, 2000b; White, 1995, 1999) have cited the importance of the context itself as a key factor in the development of autonomy in the learner: 'A self-instruction context for learning does not automatically equate with learner autonomy, but autonomy may arise and develop within the learner as a response to the specific demands of a self-instruction context' (White, 1995: 209). The distance learning context requires a certain degree of autonomy in order for a learner to function at all, which ties in well with Little's assertion (2001: 35) that 'essentially, the only way of becoming autonomous is to be autonomous'. The British Open University has over 30 years of experience in addressing these issues. How does it structure its materials and support for language learners?

Open and Distance Language Learning at the Open University (UK)

In the 1980s, Holmberg's idea of distance learning as a 'guided didactic conversation' in which a relationship is established to 'involve the student emotionally so that he or she takes a personal interest in the subject and its problems' (Holmberg, 1983: 117) became widely accepted as a basis for writing materials for distance learners. Specially written open and distance materials play a central role in all OU courses as the *teaching voice*, the link between teacher and learner. In other words, they carry out all the functions of a teacher in a more conventional setting. Derek Rowntree (1990: 11) sums these up as: 'guiding, motivating, intriguing, expounding, explaining, provoking, reminding, asking questions, discussing alternative answers, appraising each learner's progress, and giving appropriate remedial help'. Particular attention is paid to the design of print materials, both academic and visual, so that they are easy to follow and attractive to work with. Any audio-visual input is carefully researched, designed and produced to work with the other materials, so that the overall course is an integrated whole. A structured and supported approach ensures that students know what they are expected to do and at what point. In OU language courses, each activity or sequence of activities is introduced by an 'organiser' that gives a brief rationale for each activity or activities. This is designed to help students understand why they are being invited to take part in particular activities and how these fit into the wider structure, so that they can become more aware of the language learning process, begin to set their own goals and learn to monitor their own progress.

Courses, students and materials

The Centre for Modern Languages at the Open University (OU), renamed the Department of Languages in 1999, was set up in 1991 and offers a Diploma in French, German or Spanish that students may count towards a BA or BSc Open degree or one of the named degrees in Modern Language Studies, Humanities, European Studies or International Studies. There are around 7000 students registered on one or more of the 13 language courses currently available, making the OU the biggest language provider in the UK university sector. Since November 2003, students have also been able to study at beginners' level. A beginners' course plus the next stage together make up the Certificate at Level 1.

Students register from all parts of the UK and from Continental Western Europe (CWE). The typical distance language learner at the OU is in the 35–50 age range, in work and with family commitments. The University is 'open' in that there are no prerequisites to courses. Students may, if they wish, take advantage of the Self-Assessment Tests offered in all three languages, to help them determine their level of proficiency. Course materials include course books and recorded video, audio and CD extracts. There are also print support materials in the form of course and study guides, transcripts, study charts and supplementary notes, and a web-based guide to OU study containing general information and study tips. Assessment consists of Tutor Marked Assignments (TMAs), some formative, that assess both written and oral skills, and are submitted on a regular basis to the tutor for marking and feedback. On some courses there are also Student Marked Assignments (SMAs), which allow learners to assess grammatical and semantic knowledge themselves as they progress through the course. Detailed feedback is given to help students understand and correct their mistakes, analyse and address more serious errors, and develop the skills of self-correction and self-monitoring. A two-part written and oral examination completes the assessment for the year.

Learner support

For those who choose or have no option but to study at a distance the demands are great: 'distance learners must regulate and oversee the rate and direction of their learning to a much greater degree than classroom learners' (White, 1994: 12–13). But support is available to those who want it. First, there is Student Services, a dedicated unit that operates in all the 13 OU regional centres across the UK, using staff trained to advise on a range of issues concerning academic study. Second, each student is assigned to a designated tutor in their region, who can be contacted at agreed times for advice, and who conducts regular tutorials and the occasional dayschool at one of the regional centres. Tutorials are optional and are conducted either face-to-face, online or by telephone, depending on the particular course and personal circumstances of individual students.

In such a highly structured set-up it is reasonable to ask if autonomy has any role to play at all. Hurd *et al.* (2001: 344) raise just this question: 'How can we reconcile two notions clearly at opposite ends of the spectrum: learner autonomy and highly structured and rigid instructional pro-grammes?' The solution adopted by the OU is 'to turn those constraints and limitations imposed by a distance teaching and learning medium into opportunities for students' (2001: 349). This is achieved by taking specific aspects of autonomy and building them into activities in the course materials. Thus students are offered activities to promote reflection, to self-assess and monitor progress, to identify gaps and solve problems. They are also provided with examples of how to transfer the knowledge and skills they have acquired to other contexts, which, as Little (1991: 4) maintains, is one of the ways in which the capacity for autonomy is displayed. The contention is that even in such a structured and supported mode of learning, autonomy can be promoted through specially designed materials, which are varied and flexible enough to cater for a range of learner differences.

Individual Differences: Affective Factors and their Impact on Autonomy

Individual differences refer to the different factors or variables that characterise learners, such as age, gender, aptitude, intelligence, personality, learning style and previous learning experience. Learners also come to learning with their own individual beliefs, attitudes, expectations, anxieties, motivations and strategies. Whether classified as cognitive or affective, such variables are generally considered to have some bearing on the ways in which a learner is likely to interpret, relate and respond to the learning materials.

For the distance language learner, it is perhaps affective variables – beliefs, motivation and anxiety – that are of greater relevance, because their effect on learning may be intensified in an independent context, and because of their capacity for modification and change. According to Oxford (1990: 140), 'the affective side of the learner is probably one of the very biggest influences on language learning success or failure'. Results from studies carried out with undergraduate language learners in the late 1990s into affect in language learning have supported 'substantial links among affective measures and achievement' (Gardner *et al.*, 1997: 344).

Beliefs and expectations

According to Cotterall (1995: 195) and many others writing in the field, learner beliefs are said to have a profound influence on the learning behaviour of language learners. She argues further that 'the beliefs learners hold may either contribute to or impede the development of their potential for autonomy' (1995: 196), thus making explicit a link between beliefs and autonomy. Her view is that through investigating learner beliefs, teachers can assess learners' 'readiness' for autonomy and give appropriate support. White (1999: 444), in writing about distance language learners, makes a similar point: 'attention to expectations and beliefs can contribute to our understanding of the realities of the early stages of self-instruction in language'.

The growing cultural diversity among distance learners has prompted a closer look at the nature and extent of cultural influences on beliefs and expectations with regard to language learning. Culture is said to influence both the learning process and its outcomes (Dunn & Griggs, 1995) and cultural behaviour is 'always and inevitably culturally conditioned' (Little, 2002: 3). While there is evidence to suggest that the idea of autonomy as an educational goal is shared by diverse cultures (Aoki & Smith, 1999; Yang, 1999), it is important to recognise that the emphasis on an autonomous approach may be inappropriate for those whose cultural background brings with it expectations of language learning in which the teacher has sole responsibility for directing learning activities, setting goals, assessing work and measuring progress. In China, for example, the idea of self-management is at odds with the philosophy of learning that is deeply rooted in Chinese culture (Hurd & Xiao, 2004). The risk of cultural inappropriateness, or worse, the charge of cultural imperialism, through attempting to impose Western practices on other cultures, has to be taken seriously and addressed sensitively.

Researchers into the effects of cultural difference (Dunn & Griggs, 1995; Horwitz, 1999; Sanchez & Gunawardena, 1998), while underlining the importance of understanding the beliefs and values of different ethnic groups, nevertheless argue that in addressing cultural difference we should not lose sight of the individual differences to be found in all cultural groups. Horwitz' (1999: 575) study finds that 'within-group differences' are likely to account for as much variation as the 'cultural differences' and that 'there is not strong evidence for a conclusion of cultural differences in learner beliefs' (1999: 576). Sanchez and Gunawardena (1998) maintain that while it is important not to make generalisations about individuals based on evidence from particular culturally defined groups, distance teachers and writers should provide a variety of methods, strategies and activities to accommodate a wide range of affective and cognitive needs and preferences.

For all learners, the power of beliefs, whether grounded in cultural background, psychological make-up or personal experience, is such that they can enable or seriously disable language learning. According to a survey done for the European Year of Languages (2001), 22% of the EU population do not learn languages because they believe they are 'not good' at them. Materials writers and teachers face a significant challenge when it comes to addressing such disabling beliefs and encouraging learners to change them through developing the ability to reflect critically. As Benson (2001: 74) points out, 'there is considerable anecdotal evidence in the literature that learners are capable of reflecting on their learning experiences and changing their beliefs or preferences in ways that are beneficial to learning'. The distance language learner who is denied the classroom experience and regular face-to-face contact with other learners has fewer outside factors to influence her or his beliefs and must rely to a greater extent on personal resources. White's study (1999: 449) underlines the adaptive nature of beliefs among distance language learners through engagement with the materials: '[. . .] learners are influenced in new ways by the solo learning context, to extend and develop their learning skills and knowledge about themselves as learners. Obviously this is one indicator of recognition of metacognitive growth'. Beliefs and expectations can have an effect on motivation, another powerful affective factor.

Motivation

Extensive research carried out over three decades has consistently underlined the importance of motivation as in many instances the best overall predictor of language learning success (Dörnyei, 2001; Gardner & Lambert, 1972; Naiman *et al.*, 1978; Oxford & Shearin, 1994; Ushioda, 1996). For distance language learners, motivation has a special and direct role. In many cases it is the determining factor in whether to study or not in the first place, and it remains crucial for enjoyment, goal-setting and retention throughout the course of study. Motivation, at least in the early stages, is largely intrinsic, although extrinsic elements may come into play as aspirations to achieve higher qualifications begin to emerge. Maintaining motivation levels is a particular challenge at a distance. The demands of self-instruction, together with the shift of control from teacher to learner can be overwhelming for many students. Some have difficulty in coping with the amount and range of material that makes up the course, particularly at the start. For others, perceived inadequacy of feedback, frustration at unresolved problems, and lack of opportunities to practise with others and share experiences can have an adverse effect on motivation levels. In many cases, these difficulties diminish or are resolved as students become more skilled in self-management, learn to use their tutor as a key resource, and take the initiative in forming or joining a self-help group.

Dickinson (1995: 168) finds a strong link between motivation and autonomy, in that the two constructs share certain key concepts: 'these are learner independence, learner responsibility and learner choice. Incorporated within these, or entailed by them are other concepts such as decision-making, critical reflection and detachment, all of which are important in cognitive motivation'. He quotes Deci and Ryan (1985: 13) who, in describing self-determination and learner locus of control as key features of intrinsic motivation, are citing the very elements that also characterise autonomy. Ushioda (1996: 2) states unequivocally that 'autonomous language learners are by definition motivated learners'. In terms of a causal link, Ellis (1999) warns that 'we do not know whether it is motivation that produces successful learning, or successful learning that enhances motivation'. Gardner and MacIntyre's original socio-education model of second-language acquisition (1993: 2) 'explicitly proposes reciprocal causation'. The results of Yang's study (1999) suggest a cyclical rather than a uni-directional relationship between learners' beliefs, motivation and strategy use. Larsen-Freeman (2001: 20) argues that 'it is conceivable that as we search for an advanced conceptualisation of learner factors, we will also find that they are not only mutable, but that they also vary in their influence, depending on the learner's stage of acquisition', and, arguably as important, on the context in which they are learning.

Anxiety, introversion and extraversion

Often implicated in motivation as a negative influence, anxiety is increasingly seen as a powerful factor in language learning. According to Oxford (1999: 59), anxiety 'ranks high among factors influencing language learning, regardless of whether the setting is informal or formal'. With regard to language learning, Horwitz *et al.* (1986: 128) argue that 'probably no other field of study implicates self-concept and self-expression to the degree that language study does'. Research has focused on a type of anxiety termed language anxiety that is related specifically to language situations (Gardner & MacIntyre, 1993: 5), and is not connected with general ('trait') anxiety. Its effects are described as pervasive and subtle (MacIntyre & Gardner, 1994: 283) and are also associated with 'deficits in listening comprehension, impaired vocabulary learning, reduced word production, low scores on standardised tests, low grades in language courses or a combination of these factors' (Gardner *et al.*, 1997: 345). Anxiety is said to be strongly associated with low self-confidence (Cheng *et al.*, 1999) and with introversion. Introverts tend to have higher anxiety levels than extroverts and take longer to retrieve information. On the more positive side, however, they are more accurate and show greater cognitive control (Dewaele & Furnham, 1999). While extrovert students worry less about accuracy and have a tendency to take risks with their language – both of which are assets when it comes to communicative oral competence – the potential for introverts to become autonomous in their learning through their capacity to self-regulate may be a distinct advantage in distance language learning.

Metacognition, Self-regulation and Autonomy

Self-regulation, self-direction and autonomy are often used synonymously in the literature, and while this does not necessarily lead to confusion, a useful distinction might be to interpret being autonomous as an attribute of the learner, self-direction as a mode of learning and self-regulation (a term borrowed from cognitive psychology) as the practical steps taken by learners to manage their own learning. Learning a second language is generally perceived by learners to be 'different from learning other subjects, and to involve more time, more practice and different mental processes' (Victori, 1992, cited in Cotterall, 1995: 202). Distance creates a further difficulty. Sussex (1991: 189, cited in White, 1994) maintains that 'languages are more difficult than most subjects to learn in the distance mode because of the complex combination of skills and information required for language mastery'. The knowledge and skills most needed by those learning a language, particularly in the distance context, are those that entail self-awareness and self-management, in other words metacognition. Metacognition is about the management as opposed to the process of learning. Chamot and O'Malley (1994: 372) argue that on the basis of information to date, it 'may be the major factor in determining the effectiveness of individuals' attempts to learn another language'.

Metacognitive knowledge

Flavell (1976: 232) identifies two components of metacognition: (1) metacognitive knowledge, which is 'the knowledge concerning one's own cognitive processes and products or anything related to them'; and (2) metacognitive strategies or skills, which refer to 'the active monitoring and consequent regulation and orchestration of these processes', in other words the ability to carry out the planning, monitoring and evaluation that constitute self-regulation. Wenden has written widely on the subject of metacognitive knowledge, which she terms the 'neglected variable' (2001), and its critical role in the self-regulation of learning. She makes an explicit link between metacognitive knowledge, self-regulation and autonomy: 'a recognition of the function of metacognitive knowledge in the self-regulation of learning should contribute to a clearer understanding of learner autonomy [. . .]. The realization of this potential (to develop autonomy) for language learners is in part dependent on their ability to self-regulate or self-direct their learning' (2001: 62). In an earlier work, Wenden (1999: 437) gives two examples of how metacognitive knowledge can influence self-regulation: (1) task analysis in which students call upon their metacognitive knowledge to identify what they need to do and how; and (2) monitoring: 'the regulatory skill that oversees the learning process that follows the initial planning. It is the basis for determining how one is progressing, and it is what constitutes the internal feedback, i.e. the state of awareness which lets the learner know that he/she has encountered a problem'. Little (2001: 35) finds a link between motivation, metacognition and autonomy: '[. . .] the pursuit of autonomy engages the learner's intrinsic motivation and stimulates reflectivity. In other words, the development of learner autonomy brings the motivational and metacognitive dimensions of learning into interaction with each other'. The regulatory skills that characterise an autonomous approach are widely considered to be dependent on the use of appropriate learning strategies.

Learning strategies

The research into learning strategies, both cognitive and metacognitive, is extensive and varied (Cohen, 1998; Dickinson, 1990; McDonough, 1995, 1999; O'Malley & Chamot, 1990; Oxford, 1990; Wenden, 1991). Cohen (1998: 15) contends that 'learning strategies do not operate by themselves, but rather are directly tied to the learner's underlying learning styles and other personality-related variables (such as anxiety and self-concept) in the learner'. Dickinson (1990: 200) also talks of a likely 'relationship between cognitive style and preferred learning processes and strategies in language learning'. Ellis' case study of two adult German *ab initio* learners (1992: 174–89) suggests that learners do benefit if the instruction suits their learning style but asks: 'Are learning styles fixed or do they change as acquisition proceeds?' A consensus has yet to emerge, though there is some evidence (Cohen, 1998; Oxford, 1990; O'Malley & Chamot, 1993; Skehan, 1998) that preferences and styles can change as learners gain proficiency, or in response to pedagogical intervention in the form of strategy training. Little (2002: 2–3) remains sceptical, contending that 'the benefits of teaching learners strategies have still to be demonstrated'. He favours an approach in which learners are encouraged to explore alternatives to find what works for them personally.

Given the particular need for self-management skills in the distance learning environment, it is perhaps unsurprising that studies into the use of strategies in distance language learning have shown distance learners make more use of metacognitive strategies than do classroom learners (White, 1995: 211). Hurd (2000a: 46) also found that women tend to use more metacognitive strategies overall than men. While some learners do succeed in developing many of the features of autonomy through the experience of learning in distance mode, they are unlikely to do so without appropriate support and intervention, and we 'cannot make any assumptions or expectations about learners' willingness or ability to become autonomous learners' (Hurd, 1998b: 222), just because they are adults and have chosen for whatever reason to learn at a distance. For distance learning, any attempts at pedagogic intervention to promote autonomy through the use and transfer of strategies must take place via the materials and tutor feedback on assignments, as attendance at tutorials is optional and cannot therefore be guaranteed. For this reason, all Open University language courses contain sections on learning strategies and study skills, language awareness activities and practical guidance in the development of specific language skills. Students are also encouraged to experiment with a range of strategies to determine which work best for them (Hurd *et al.*, 2001). This approach ties in well with Sanchez and Gunawardena's view (1998: 61) that in a distance learning environment 'variety itself becomes the solution'. An important strand of the variety necessary to support student diversity is the increasingly significant contribution technology is making to language learning.

The Role of Technology: Promoting Autonomy through Computer-mediated Communication (CMC)

The potential of the Internet to facilitate exchanges among learners in the foreign language is increasingly recognised and exploited in universities in the UK. Sophisticated software and growing expertise in the use of CMC for language learning make it possible today for language learners to communicate not just with one other person asynchronously through e-mail, but with groups of other learners either asynchronously or synchronously, through bulletin boards, text chat, audio-video conferencing or Multi-user Object-oriented domains (MOOs), as part of a virtual community.

E-mail tandem learning

Early attempts to include Internet-based activities in language programmes concentrated largely on tandem exchanges between native speakers of two different languages who were studying each other's mother tongue. One-to-one e-mail tandem learning, set up at Sheffield University UK in the mid-90s, following successful pilots in face-to-face tandem learning, is now an integral part of the modern languages programme. There are today many such schemes worldwide (Kötter, 2002) and the International E-Mail Tandem Network is now well established. The potential advantages lie in 'its combination of immediacy with asynchronicity [. . .] it can be used at any time of day or night; no external constraint governs the frequency of an exchange of messages, or their content (Lewis *et al.*, 1996: 113). It 'can offer genuine interpersonal and intercultural communication' and is 'an ideal tool for the autonomous learner' (1996: 117) in that the medium encourages learners to take control over their own learning.

Advantages of online communication: Text-based and voice-based

Most practice and research is in text-based CMC, as an extension of rather than a substitute for classroom-based learning. The advantages are in both the cognitive and affective domain. Students working asynchronously have time to attend to grammar and develop their linguistic accuracy. The text-based mode allows them to pause and reflect while interacting, thus creating a 'special relationship between interaction and reflection' (Warschauer, 1997: 5). In an online environment, learners feel less inhibited as they are out of the spotlight, and peer support can have a positive impact on attitudes towards learning. Levels of participation are also found to be much greater and more equal in online as opposed to face-to-face discussion (Hudson & Bruckman, 2002; Warschauer, 1997). For distance learners, online communication 'can provide a sense of "presence"'. CMC in general offers the opportunity to communicate and socialize with other learners' (Shield, 2002). At the OU, an increasing number of language courses offer online tuition through Lyceum, an audio-graphic Internet-based conferencing system. Early findings from research studies (Hampel, 2003; Shield *et al.*, 2000) confirm that a voice-based as opposed to a text-based CMC is just as successful in supporting and engaging learners, reducing social isolation and anxiety and enhancing motivation. The combination of different modes that Lyceum offers – visual (through graphics), verbal (through writing and text chat) and acoustic – allows 'a choice between modes to suit the task in hand, as well as catering for different learning styles' (Hampel, 2003: 25). It also helps to address the well-known drawback of learning a language at distance – the development and practice of oral skills. In addition, it has the potential to promote autonomy through empowering learners to manage their own interactions, choosing and negotiating between options and gradually increasing their ability to take responsibility for their own learning, not only during online tutorials but at any time with other learners.

Critical reflection on both language (cognitive, form-focused) and learning (metacognitive), is also strongly encouraged as an integral part of successful online activity. For distance language learners, however, this is by no means automatic. Lamy and Hassan (2003: 54) in their study of what influences reflective interaction in distance peer learning, warn that 'distance learners cannot easily be persuaded to undertake either solo or interactive reflective work if task presentation is not completely explicit in its expectation that they do so' and suggest that task writers 'might encourage reflection by building in psychological and conversational "space" in which learners can be responsible for 'task-management as "themselves".'

Challenges

It would be naive to suggest that technology mediated learning is problem-free. While a major advantage is seen to be the reduction in social isolation for geographically dispersed and/or shy learners, others dislike what they see as a lack of a human dimension. Moreover, while a CMC environment can be motivating and confidence boosting, without proper guidance the reverse can occur and, far from reflecting empowerment and expertise in self-direction, 'student work may become unfocused, unbalanced and trivial' (Schwienhorst, 1998: 119). Other difficulties are the level of technical expertise needed, the danger of information overload and the absence of paralinguistic elements such as body language. Some students and teachers simply find the medium depersonalising, fragmentary and lacking the humanity and intimacy that the face-to-face environment affords. There is still a major job to be done in convincing many actual and potential users of its benefits.

Conclusion

According to a recent working definition from Little (2002: 1), 'the practice of learner autonomy requires insight, a positive attitude, a capacity for reflection, and a readiness to be proactive in self-management and in interaction with others'. For distance language learners, this is just the starting point. 'Capacity' and 'readiness' need to become actualised rapidly as abilities and skills. Distance learning students are no more homogeneous than classroom learners, but they are by definition less accessible. This presents a real challenge to all course designers, task writers and tutors to devise ways of supporting their learners at a distance in developing the skills of self-management and self-regulation that are central to autonomy. Strategy development embedded in the OU course materials offers more than just the basic tools, and is constantly being improved and extended. The use of CMC programmes can enhance the potential for autonomy by giving greater freedom of control, a choice of mode, tasks and activities that promote reflection and intercultural awareness, and a communicative environment which is non-threatening and supportive. What is important is that, in the effort to address the specific challenges of the distance language learning context, and the exciting potential of new technologies, we do not lose sight of the human dimension of language learning. Future research also needs to address the issue of transfer of language skills developed online, and to what extent the development of autonomy, equal participation and increased levels of self-confidence can translate to the real world in which language interactions are spontaneous, unpredictable, and conducted face-to-face.

References

Ackermann, E. (1996) Perspective-taking and object construction: Two keys to learning. In Y. Kafai and M. Resnick (eds) *Constructionism in Practice: Designing, Thinking and Learning in a Digital World* (pp. 25–35). Mahwah, NJ: Lawrence Erlbaum.

Aoki, N. and Smith, R.C. (1999) Learner autonomy in cultural context: The case of Japan. In S. Cotterall and D. Crabbe (eds) *Learner Autonomy in Language Learning: Defining the Field and Effecting Change* (pp. 19–27). Frankfurt am Main: Peter Lang.

Benson, P. (2001) *Teaching and Researching Autonomy in Language Learning*. Harlow: Pearson Education Limited.

Candy, P.C. (1991) *Self-direction for Lifelong Learning*. San Francisco: Jossey-Bass.

Chamot, A.U. and O'Malley, J. (1994) Language learner and learning strategies. In N.C. Ellis (ed.) *Implicit and Explicit Learning of Languages* (pp. 371–392). London: Academic Press Limited.

Cheng, Y., Horwitz, E. and Schallert, D. (1999) Language anxiety: Differentiating writing and speaking components. *Language Learning* 49 (3), 417–6.

Cohen, A.D. (1998) *Strategies in Learning and Using a Second Language*. New York: Addison Wesley Longman Limited.

Cotterall, S. (1995) Readiness for autonomy: Investigating learner beliefs. *System* 23 (2), 195–205.

Deci, E.L. and Ryan, R.M. (1985) *Intrinsic Motivation and Self-determination in Human Behaviour*. New York: Plenum Press.

Dewaele, J-M. and Furnham, A. (1999) Extraversion: the unloved variable in applied linguistic research. *Language Learning* 49 (3), 509–44.

Dickinson, L. (1990) Self-evaluation of learning strategies. In R. Duda and P. Riley (eds) *Learning Styles* (pp. 199–206). France: Presses Universitaires de Nancy.

Dickinson, L. (1995) Autonomy and motivation: A literature review. *System* 23 (2), 165–74.

Dörnyei, Z. (2001) *Teaching and Researching Motivation*. Harlow: Pearson Education Limited.

Dunn, R. and Griggs, S.A. (1995) *Multiculturalism and Learning Style: Teaching and Counselling Adolescents*. Westport, CT: Praeger.

Ellis, R. (1992) *Second Language Acquisition and Language Pedagogy*. Clevedon, UK: Multilingual Matters.

Ellis, R. (1999) *Understanding Second Language Acquisition*. Oxford: Oxford University Press.

European Year of Languages survey (2001) – Online document: http://europa.eu.int/comm/education/languages/lang/eurobarometer54_en.html

Flavell J. (1976) Metacognitive aspects of problem solving. In B. Resnick (ed.) *The Nature of Intelligence* (pp. 231–35). Hillsdale, NJ: Lawrence Erlbaum.

Gardner, R. and Lambert, W. (1972) *Attitudes and Motivation in Second Language learning*. Rowley, MA: Newbury House.

Gardner, R. and MacIntyre, P. (1993). A student's contributions to second-language learning. Part II: Affective variables. *Language Teaching* 26 (pp. 1–11). Cambridge: Cambridge University Press.

Gardner, R., Tremblay, P. and Masgoret, A-M. (1997) Towards a full model of second language learning: an empirical investigation. *The Modern Language Journal* 81 (iii), 344–62.

Hampel, R. (2003) Theoretical perspectives and new practices in audio-graphic conferencing for language learning. *ReCALL* 15 Part 1, 21–35.

Holec, H. (1981) *Autonomy and Foreign Language Learning*. Oxford: Pergamon Press for the Council of Europe.

Holec, H. (1985) On autonomy: Some elementary concepts. In P. Riley (ed.) *Discourse and Learning* (pp. 173–90). London: Longman.

Holmberg, B. (1983) Guided didactic conversation in distance education. In D. Sewart, D. Keegan and B. Holmberg (eds) *Distance Education: International Perspectives* (pp. 114–122). New York: Croom Helm.

Horwitz, E. (1999) Cultural and situational influences on foreign language learners' beliefs about language learning: A review of BALLI studies. *System* 27, 557–76.

Horwitz, E., Horwitz, M. and Cope, J. (1986) Foreign language classroom anxiety. *The Modern Language Journal* 70 (ii), 125–132 – Online document: http://www.lang.ltsn.ac.uk/resources/goodpractice.aspx?resourceid=416

Hudson, J.M. and Bruckman, A.S (2002) IRC français: The creation of an internet-based SLA community. *Computer Assisted Language Learning* 15 (2), 109–34.

Hurd, S. (1998a) Too carefully led or too carelessly left alone? *Language Learning Journal* 17, 70–4.

Hurd, S. (1998b) Autonomy at any price? Issues and concerns from a British HE perspective. *Foreign Language Annals* 31 (2), 219–30.

Hurd, S. (2000a) Helping learners to help themselves: The role of metacognitive skills and strategies in independent language learning. In M. Fay and D. Ferney (eds) *Current Trends in Modern Language Provision for Non-specialist Linguists* (pp. 36–52). London: The Centre for Information on Language Teaching and Research (CILT) in association with Anglia Polytechnic University (APU).

Hurd, S. (2000b) Distance language learners and learner support: Beliefs, difficulties and use of strategies. *Links and Letters* 7: *Autonomy in L2 learning*, 61–80.

Hurd, S. and Xiao, J. (2004) Distance learning at the Central Radio and TV University, China and the Open University, UK: A cross-cultural perspective. In preparation.

Hurd, S., Beaven, T. and Ortega, A. (2001) Developing autonomy in a distance language learning context: issues and dilemmas for course writers. *System* 29 (3), 341–55.

Kohonen, V. (1992) Experiential language learning: Second language learning as cooperative learner education. In D. Nunan (ed.) *Collaborative Language Learning and Teaching* (pp. 14–39). Cambridge: Cambridge University Press.

Kötter, M. (2002) *Tandem Learning on the Internet*. Frankfurt am Main: Peter Lang.

Lamy, M-N. and Hassan, X. (2003) What influences reflective interaction in distance peer learning? Evidence from four long-term learners of French. *Open Learning* 18 (2), 39–59.

Larsen-Freeman, D. (2001) Individual cognitive/affective learner contributions and differential success in second language acquisition. In M. Breen (ed.) *Learner Contributions to Language Learning* (pp. 12–24). Harlow: Pearson Education Limited.

Lewis, T., Woodin, J. and St John, E. (1996) Tandem learning: Independence through partnership. In E. Broady and M-M. Kenning (eds) *Promoting Learner Autonomy in University Language Teaching* (pp. 105–20). London: Association for French Language Studies (AFLS) in association with the Centre for Information on Language Teaching and Research (CILT).

Little, D. (1991) *Learner Autonomy: Definitions, Issues and Problems*. Dublin: Authentic Language Learning Resources Limited.

Little, D. (1995) Learning as dialogue: The dependence of learner autonomy on teacher autonomy. *System* 23 (2), 175–82.

Little, D. (1996) Freedom to learn and compulsion to interact: promoting learner autonomy through the use of information systems and information technologies. In R. Pemberton *et al.* (eds) *Taking Control: Autonomy in Language Learning* (pp. 203–18). Hong Kong: Hong Kong University Press.

Little, D. (2001) How independent can independent language learning really be? In J. Coleman, D. Ferney, D. Head and R. Rix (eds) *Language-learning Futures: Issues and Strategies for Modern Languages Provision in Higher Education* (pp. 30–43). London: Centre for Information on Language Teaching and Research (CILT).

Little, D. (2002) Learner autonomy and second/foreign language learning, *Good Practice Guide*. LTSN Subject Centre for Languages, Linguistics and Area Studies – On line document: http://www.lang.ltsn.ac.uk/resources/goodpractice.aspx?resourceid=1409

MacIntyre, P. and Gardner, R. (1994) The subtle effects of language anxiety on cognitive processing in the second language. *Language Learning* 44 (2), 283–305.

McDonough, S. (1995) *Strategy and Skill in Learning a Foreign Language*. London: Edward Arnold.

McDonough, S. (1999) Learner strategies. *Language Teaching*, 32, 1–18.

Mozzon-McPherson, M. (2001) *Beyond Language Teaching Towards Language Advising*. London: Centre for Information on Language Teaching and Research (CILT) in association with the University of Hull.

Naiman, N., Frohlich, M., Stern, D. and Todesco, A. (1978) *The Good Language Learner*. Canada: Ontario Institute for Studies in Education.

O'Malley J. and Chamot, A.U. (1990) *Learning Strategies in Second Language Acquisition*. Cambridge: Cambridge University Press.

O'Malley, J. and Chamot, A.U. (1993) Learner characteristics in second-language acquisition. In A. Omaggio Hadley (ed.) *Research in Language Learning: Principles, Processes and Prospects* (pp. 96–123). USA: Lincolnwood (Chicago).

Open University (2002) *Learning with the OU: Your Guide to OU study* – Online document: http://www.open.ac.uk/learning/induction/undergraduate/index.htm

Oxford, R. (1990) *Language Learning Strategies: What Every Teacher should Know*. Boston, MA: Heinle & Heinle.

Oxford, R. (1999) Anxiety and the language learner: New insights. In J. Arnold and H. Douglas Brown (eds) *Affect in Language Learning* (pp. 58–67). Cambridge: Cambridge University Press.

Oxford, R. and Shearin, J. (1994) Language learning motivation: Expanding the theoretical framework. *The Modern Language Journal* 78 (i), 12–25.

Rowntree, D. (1990) *Teaching through Self-instruction: How to Develop Open Learning Materials*. London: Kogan Page.

Sanchez, I. and Gunawardena, N. (1998) Understanding and supporting the culturally diverse distance learner. In C. Campbell Gibson (ed.) *Distance Learners in Higher Education: Institutional Responses for Quality Outcomes* (pp. 47–64). Wisconsin: Atwood Publishing.

Schunk D. and Zimmerman, B. (eds) (1998) *Self-regulated Learning: From Teaching to Self-regulated Practice*. New York: Guilford Press.

Schwienhorst, K. (1998) Matching pedagogy and technology: Tandem learning and learner autonomy in online virtual environments. In R. Soetaert, E. De Man and G. Van Belle (eds) *Language Teaching On-Line* (pp. 115–27). Ghent: University of Ghent – pdf version.

Shield, L. (2002) Technology-mediated learning, *Good Practice Guide*. LTSN Subject Centre for Languages, Linguistics and Area Studies – Online document: http.//www.lang.ltsn.ac.uk/resources/goodpractice.aspx?resourceid=416

Shield, L., Hauck, M. and Kötter, M. (2000) Taking the distance out of distance learning. In P. Howarth and R. Herrington (eds) *EAP Learning Technologies* (pp. 16–27). Leeds: Leeds University Press.

Sinclair, B. (2000) Learner autonomy: The next phase? In B. Sinclair, I. McGrath and T. Lamb (eds) *Learner Autonomy, Teacher Autonomy: Future Directions* (pp. 4–14). Harlow: Pearson Education Limited.

Skehan, P. (1998) *A Cognitive Approach to Language Learning*. Oxford: Oxford University Press.

Ushioda, E. (1996) *The Role of Motivation*. Dublin: Authentic Language Learning Resources Limited.

Vygotsky, L. (1978) *Mind in Society: The Development of Higher Psychological Processes*. Boston: Harvard University Press.

Warriner-Burke, H.P. (1990) Distance learning: What we don't know can hurt us. *Foreign Language Annals* 23 (2), 131.

Warschauer, M. (1997) Computer-mediated collaborative learning: Theory and practice. *Modern Language Journal* 81 (4), 470–81.

Wenden, A. (1991) *Learner Strategies for Learner Autonomy*. Hemel Hempstead: Prentice Hall Europe.

Wenden, A. (1999) An introduction to metacognitive knowledge and beliefs in language learning: Beyond the basics. *System* 27, 435–41.

Wenden, A. (2001) Metacognitive knowledge in SLA: The neglected variable. In M. Breen (ed.) *Learner Contributions to Language Learning* (pp. 44–64). Harlow: Pearson Education Limited.

White, C. (1994) Language learning strategy research in distance education: The yoked subject technique. *Research in Distance Education* 3, 10–20.

White, C. (1995) Autonomy and strategy use in distance foreign language learning. *System* 23 (2), 207–21.

White, C. (1999) Expectations and emergent beliefs of self-instructed language learners. *System* 27, 443–57. Online document: www.lang.ltsn.ac.uk/resources/goodpractice.aspx?resourceid=1409

Yang, N-D. (1999) The relationship between EFL learners' beliefs and learning strategy use. *System* 27, 515–35.

Chapter 2

Critical Reflection and Autonomy: A Study of Distance Learners of French, German and Spanish

LINDA MURPHY

Introduction

Perspectives on language learning and distance education are evolving in response to a variety of pressures. In a post-modern world characterised, according to Edwards (1997: 16), by rapid, unpredictable change, uncertainty and ambivalence, Benson (2001: 19) suggests successful learners are seen increasingly as those who can construct knowledge directly from experience of the world, rather than those who respond well to instruction. Research in the areas of learning theory, language learning theory and student autonomy indicates the significance of critical reflection, active involvement and conscious choice in effective learning and language learning. In the UK, higher education is placing increasing emphasis on the development of independent, autonomous learners. 'Learning to Learn' is one of the Key Skills the National Committee of Inquiry into Higher Education (Dearing, 1997) recommended should be developed within the UK HE curriculum (recommendation 21). The UK Quality Assurance Agency benchmark statement for Languages and Related Studies states that a graduate in this discipline will be expected to be 'an effective and self-aware independent learner' (2002: 13, section 6.3).

But what does it mean to be an *independent* and *autonomous* learner? How does one achieve this state? Distance learners are often assumed to be autonomous, so perhaps this mode of language learning represents a good way to respond to these pressures; but how autonomous *are* distance language learners? To what extent do they engage in critical reflection and take control of their learning? Might this be enhanced? This chapter presents findings from an investigation involving part-time language learners in the South Region of the UK Open University (OU) that explored how they approached their study. Students were offered supplementary materials designed to develop their use of critical reflection and the metacognitive strategies involved, and to promote an autonomous approach to learning. The findings are derived from an analysis of interviews carried out with a sample of students who used the materials and those who did not. The chapter concludes by considering some changes needed in teaching/course design and staff development if distance language learning is truly to support the development of autonomous learners.

Research Background

The role of critical reflection and active engagement in learning, language learning and autonomy has been emphasised by many researchers. A brief summary of some key aspects of this research is presented here as background to the investigation.

Critical reflection in learning theory

Kolb's model (1984) of a reflective learning cycle/spiral whereby 'concrete experience' is subjected to 'reflective observation', leading to 'abstract conceptualisation', and further 'active experimentation' now underpins many programmes of learning across all sectors. Boud *et al.* (1985) suggested two main stages in reflective observation, i.e. 'returning to the experience' and 'attending to feelings' before 're-evaluating the experience'. Their aim was to avoid a rush to action without due consideration of the original experience and to promote recognition of the need to recognise and accept feelings generated by it, which may block learning.

To be effective, it is argued that reflection must be a conscious process and result in decisions or choices about further action. Schön (1983) writes of two different kinds of thinking involved in reflection. The first he calls 'reflexiveness' ('the mind's conversation with itself', Thorpe, 2000: 82), the purpose of which is to become aware of existing knowledge, skills, attitudes and assumptions. The second is referred to as 'critical analysis' where assumptions, judgements, applications of models and theories are questioned. This questioning is important if we are to learn from experience and avoid what Langer (1989, quoted in Ridley, 1997: 30) terms the 'mindlessness' that characterises much adult behaviour. This refers to habitual ways of thinking or acting: for example, from a language learner's point of view, continuing to learn vocabulary in a certain way 'because I've always done it that way', rather than considering how well it works and whether there might be other, more effective ways.

Researchers argue that the capacity for reflection can be developed (see, for example, Boud *et al.*, 1985; Race, 1993; Thorpe, 2000). However, learning to challenge one's assumptions or change one's approach can be difficult in any context and for the distance learner working in isolation in particular. Some researchers suggest it is very difficult for any learner to engage in critical reflection on his or her own. Brockbank and McGill (1998: 56) argue that dialogue is a key requirement. They distinguish between internal 'conversation' and 'dialogue' between individuals, stating that 'without dialogue, reflection is limited to the insights of the individual' (1998: 58). Boud *et al.* (1985) also highlight the importance of dialogue with others in raising awareness, questioning assumptions and developing new approaches, i.e. the 'critical analysis' aspect of reflection.

Apart from dialogue, Moon (1999: 166–70) states that learners need time and space for reflection to legitimise the activity within the learning programme, a clear explanation of the purpose of reflection and likely outcomes and support or strategies to guide them through the process. These are essential if learners are to develop the capacity for conscious, critical reflection and the metacognitive strategies involved in the reflective learning cycle: monitoring and evaluating, goal-setting, planning and implementing. The question is how best to achieve these conditions within a distance learning context? The investigation described here is based on an attempt to create such conditions for distance language learners, offering a framework to support them in developing the capacity for critical reflection.

The role of critical reflection in language learning and autonomy

For many years, the influence of the communicative approach in language teaching led to an emphasis on spontaneous communication rather than reflection on performance – a reaction against the strong focus on language form in grammar-translation methods (Tarvin & Al-Arishi, 1991). More recently, language researchers have suggested the need to prompt learners to develop selective attention and reflect on or 'notice' the language forms they encounter or produce (Ellis, 2001; Lightbown & Spada, 1993; Long, 1996; Schmidt, 1994). In their classic study of the 'good language learner', Naiman *et al.* (1996) emphasise the importance of self-awareness, reflection on performance and active involvement. These themes are picked up by others such as O'Malley and Chamot (1990) and Oxford (1990) who highlight the significance of the metacognitive strategies referred to above for effective language learning.

Critical reflection and active engagement are also seen to be crucial in the development of autonomous language learners. The definition of autonomy widely used by language learning researchers is 'the ability to take charge of one's own learning' (Holec, 1980: 3). The concept of knowing how to learn is central to this definition, underpinned by the same metacognitive skills of goal-setting, planning, implementing, monitoring and evaluating. Cotterall (1995: 199) sees the link between autonomous and successful learners as their capacity for self-monitoring and self-assessment. Other researchers (e.g. Hurd *et al.* 2001; Wenden, 1998) also highlight the importance of self-assessment in successful autonomous learning.

As already noted, however, learners find critical reflection challenging and difficult, and these aspects in particular may be contrary to their previous experience of language learning. Candy (1991: 221) suggests learners find taking greater responsibility or responding to encouragement to question and take decisions about their learning to be a 'challenging and unsettling transition'. This can be particularly evident where learners are asked to engage in self-assessment (Broady, 1996: 223). Researchers such as Nunan (1996) have suggested how students in classroom-based language programmes may be helped to self-monitor and self-evaluate, but these strategies also need to be developed in the distance learning context. The supplementary materials devised for this study represent one possible approach to the development of these metacognitive skills.

Autonomy and distance language learning

As indicated above, distance learners are often assumed to be in control of their own learning. Indeed, they choose when, where and how they learn. A comparative study by White (1995) found that distance language learners demonstrated higher levels of metacognitive language learning strategy use, particularly self-management. In a later study of learners' beliefs about distance learning and how these changed with experience (White, 1999), she found that those who struggled with the distance context were those with a low tolerance of ambiguity and an expectation that the teacher should direct their learning. Hurd *et al.* (2001) describe how UK OU distance language courses constrain autonomy, due to their highly structured nature. That structure is, as they describe it, an attempt to reduce potential ambiguity in a situation where course writers are unable to predict the exact nature of students' previous experience and have to anticipate a variety of levels and learning styles.

One way of identifying the extent to which distance learners take control of their learning is to examine what they actually do with the materials supplied. In one of the limited number of studies of this kind carried out in a distance language learning context, Rowsell and Libben (1994) explored the behaviour of independent language learners who were working from course materials only. They distinguished between the ways in which learners took pedagogical and functional control in their studies. In terms of *pedagogical* control, they examined the extent to which the learners deleted, repeated, transposed or otherwise changed the set tasks presented in the materials. In terms of *functional* control, they examined the extent to which learners created meaningful forms of interaction or contexts for their learning over and above the activities presented in the course materials. Rowsell and Libben found little evidence of pedagogical control, but did discover that successful distance learners demonstrated considerable functional control, engaging in a variety of practice activities of their own. Ramsden (1992: 58) suggests a focus on meaning makes study more satisfying; learners engage in more activity, see more evidence of progress, and are motivated to do more. This investigation set out to discover the extent to which OU language learners took pedagogical and functional control in their learning and to assess the impact of any functional practice in relation to self-assessment, self-evaluation and critical reflection.

A desire or intention to develop independent, autonomous learners has to be matched by programmes and tuition that actually allow learners to develop the capacities and skills described above, and encourage critical reflection, conscious decision-making and active engagement. Biggs (1999: 11) suggests that 'constructive alignment' of all aspects of the learning environment is essential if this is to be achieved. This study brought into focus the issue of alignment between language teaching materials, tuition and assessment on OU language courses.

In summary, the investigation described here set out to explore how a sample of UK OU distance language learners actually approached their study. It examined the extent and nature of their pedagogical and functional control, their use of critical reflection and their responses to a framework of supplementary material designed to develop reflection and self-direction at a distance. It prompted consideration of the extent to which the teaching materials, tuition and assessment supported the development of independent, autonomous learners.

The Investigation

The learners and the project materials

The project was carried out in the UK OU South Region. (See Notes 1 and 2 at the end of the chapter for information about the students and courses involved.) Special materials were developed to encourage language learners to reflect on their performance, needs, strengths and weaknesses in order to make informed decisions about what and how they learn within a distance learning context. To achieve this, at intervals throughout the course learners were invited to carry out specific tasks linked to their assignments and in conjunction with their normal study activity. These materials were adapted from generic materials (based on Kolb's Learning

Cycle) piloted as part of a project *Supporting Key Skills Achievement in Higher Education* and published *as Key Skills: Making a Difference* (Open University/DfEE, 1998). They consisted of (see Note 3):

a skills audit   which summarised the range of skills that might be needed to complete an assignment. Students were encouraged to identify the skills required for a specific assignment; reflect on previous learning, strengths and weaknesses in these skills; select one or two priorities to work on and draw up an appropriate action plan.

a self-assessment sheet   which asked students to reflect on the work they had done, to share their priorities with their tutor and to assess the extent to which they felt their goals had been achieved. Students were encouraged to complete a self-assessment sheet and send it in with each assignment.

a reflection sheet   which invited students to study and summarise their tutor's feedback and use it alongside their own judgements, the skills audit and the next assignment task in order to review their priorities, set new goals and decide how best to achieve them.

a tips sheet   which advised students on what to do when an assignment was returned. It helped students to 'return to the experience' and 'attend to feelings' (Boud *et al.*, 1985) before moving on, making active use of the feedback.

skills sheets   which offered advice on developing specific skills (reading, listening, writing, speaking and vocabulary extension) as well as referring students to other sources of help. They were made available by tutors to students who needed them.

The tasks were to be repeated for each assignment. In this way students were encouraged to engage in the different stages of Kolb's Learning Cycle. They moved from 'reflective observation' on their language learning and performance, i.e. their 'concrete experience', into 'abstract conceptualisation' formulating new priorities and action plans ready for 'active experimentation' and further 'concrete experience' in the next assignment. Apart from the skills sheets, all materials were bilingual, although students could complete them in English or the language they were studying. Particularly at Level 2, tutors felt it was important to give students the language to talk about skills and strategies during tutorials without switching to English. Feedback from students indicated that they were keen to have bilingual versions, even if they usually completed the sheets in English.

Following an initial pilot of these materials, 17 tutors working across the French, German and Spanish programmes offered by the OU at the time, volunteered to introduce and support the use of these materials in their tutor groups in 1999. (Details of the numbers of students involved are given in Note 2.) These tutors worked on the design of the materials. They also discussed methods of introducing them, devised language activities in French, German and Spanish to encourage students to think about and exchange experience of language learning strategies and refined guidelines for ongoing use of the materials. Student use of the materials was optional.

Data collection and analysis

At the end of the course, a questionnaire was sent to all students in the tutor groups involved. The aims were to find out who had used the project materials, the reactions and priorities of users and the reasons for non-use. Respondents were asked to say whether they were willing to talk about their experience in an interview. Eighty-seven users and 43 non-users returned the questionnaire. A sample including students of each language and level of study, male and female, was selected for interview on the basis of their replies (extremely positive or negative, or indicating interesting avenues to follow up) and their availability. Similar numbers of users (17) and non-users (15) of the project materials were selected for interview. The aim in sampling was to explore a variety of experience. Statistical sampling was felt to be inappropriate both because of the number of students involved and, as Ashworth and Lucas (2000: 300) suggest, because the experience of each individual would be different. Interviews were also carried out with all the participating tutors to explore their view of the way students used the materials and how the project materials impacted on their tutoring.

The experience of the sample groups of students and the tutors was explored via in-depth, semi-structured telephone interviews. These were recorded with the permission of the participants, transcribed and analysed using NUD*IST (QSR, 1997). Students were encouraged to talk about how they worked through the course materials and tackled assignments, where they felt more or less confident, how they worked on aspects of particular skills such as speaking or listening and what they did to consolidate or extend their vocabulary or knowledge of grammar. Students who had used the project materials were asked for their reactions to them. Tutors were asked about their contact with students, how their students responded to the project materials and how they and their students used the materials during the course. They were also asked how they responded to the self-assessment sheets from students and whether they made any changes to their teaching as a result of working with these materials.

Responses were analysed in a number of ways. Oxford's classification of language learning strategies (1990: 18–21) was used to categorise the strategies students had adopted to develop their language skills. This classification was chosen because it gives equal recognition to strategies used in oral performance and in written contexts and recognises both social and affective strategies. The extent to which students took an _active_ approach and made decisions about their own learning was examined, including actions by which they took pedagogical or functional control or activated language beyond coursework and created their own learning tasks (Rowsell and Libben, 1994). Their responses were examined for evidence of critical reflection and choice or decision-making, awareness of alternative strategies and self-awareness. Tutor responses were examined in terms of the perceived impact of the project materials on their relationship with students and on other aspects of student learning. They were also examined for evidence of practice supporting student use of the materials, self-direction and student choices, and for their awareness of the impact of affective factors on learning.

Findings: Evidence of Learner Control and Active Engagement

As mentioned above, the findings are derived from interviews that covered the broad range of student behaviour and experience during their course of study, not simply their reaction to the specially devised, supplementary materials.

Pedagogical control

As in Rowsell and Libben's study (1994), there was little evidence of students taking pedagogical control by making changes to the set tasks. The main changes reported were to skim or read through activities rather than actually doing them, or to leave them out completely, usually due to lack of time. Extensive viewing or listening with the audio-visual materials was the only other significant alteration to the prescribed study patterns. Students reported watching or listening to longer sections of these materials than the course writers had suggested for individual activities and often listened to or watched them right through. Sometimes this was to gain an overview, to fill in on activities they had missed out, or because they found them particularly interesting and wanted to know what happened next.

Functional control and active engagement

In terms of functional control, however, the picture was very different. When examining the strategies students adopted to develop their language skills, it was clear the majority made considerable efforts to use the target language in situations beyond the course and were actively involved in creating meaningful practice opportunities. This applied to both groups of students.

As White (1995) found, these distance language learners used meta-cognitive, social and affective strategies to a considerable extent in seeking opportunities to practise their speaking and listening skills. They sought out native speakers, joined language clubs and circles, made use of family and friends or workplace opportunities, and they valued tutorials and got together with fellow students wherever possible. They tuned into radio and TV stations or played and replayed tapes and videos from the course and elsewhere. As well as using these situations to produce the target language actively or develop their comprehension, it was clear students also used them to monitor and measure their own performance. How well did they cope? Were they understood? At the same time, they gained tremendous encouragement, satisfaction and motivation from such encounters. 'Yes, I *can* manage this! [. . .] I get an enormous amount of pleasure from it' (French student, Level 2). 'I was very encouraged because practically everybody understood what I said to them' (Spanish student, Level 1). 'The German TV stations [. . .] are quite difficult to understand [. . .] but you feel very pleased when you understand some of it' (German student Level 2). It was also clear that they were very much focused on overall meaning in such situations. Few talked about making any note of individual words or phrases, though they might notice something they could use another time, or realise how they could express themselves better. 'I only jot down if there's a phrase I really like' (German student, Level 2). A similar picture emerged when students talked about reading beyond the course materials, as they would read in their own language, focusing on topics of interest and generally not worrying about words they hadn't met before. 'Some words you think, oh, that's a nice word . . . and you can use it yourself, then I probably would [make a note]' (French Student, Level 2).

When it came to developing their vocabulary, students deployed a wide range of active memory and metacognitive strategies and regularly used association and context techniques. They grouped items in various ways and sought opportunities to use them. Many were aware of the conditions that enhanced their vocabulary development. They had realised the importance of interest in a topic or personal relevance, the importance of context, and were aware of alternative strategies, though they had not always tried them out. For example, several students mentioned mind mapping, but only one had used this extensively. 'I know that really worked for me sort of in topics [. . .] you could show the relationships [. . .] I prefer that sort of diagram to a long list of things' (French student, Level 1). Beliefs about the decline of memory with age influenced some students' approaches. For some, their beliefs prevented them from trying anything new, while for others, they were spurs to trying a wide range of different strategies, 'Anything I can do to remember things [. . .] the biggest problem is fear [of forgetting], you see' (German student, Level 2). Students might benefit from support to experiment more with memory strategies. Generally similar strategies were deployed in relation to grammar development, but there was less evidence of active techniques. This was probably due to the fact that many felt reasonably confident in this aspect of language learning. The age profile of the sample is likely to have had a bearing on this and their concerns about memory (see Note 2).

Writing skills development: The odd one out

Writing skills were the one area where very few students appeared to take functional control or adopt an active approach. Students generally reported writing only in relation to activities in the course, assignments or notes they made for their own reference. Very few completed any course activities requiring a piece of continuous prose, other than the assignments. This contrasted markedly with the efforts they made to practise oral skills and was at odds with some students' acknowledged need to develop this skill, as written assignments carry 50% of the course marks. The reasons for this contrast appear to lie in a number of factors. There was concern that distance study offered more limited opportunity for development of oral skills and therefore this required more effort. When asked about their motivation for study and interest in the language, the majority spoke about their desire to communicate with people and their interest in the culture. Writing was viewed simply as a way of practising and consolidating the mechanics of the language. Increasing use of electronic communication may change this view of writing in the longer term as more students become involved in email contact with target language users, or take part in tandem learning programmes via the internet. Another reason was lack of time. Students felt they didn't have time to sit down and write a long piece of prose even when they had identified a need to develop their writing skills. 'If time was very short, I'm afraid that was always one of the first things to go' (German student, Level 2). However, behind these reasons appeared an unease about or lack of experience in self-assessment, since such activities would be checked by the student against a model rather than by a teacher. 'Without the feedback, you wonder if you're just compounding mistakes' (French student, Level 2), 'having written it [. . .] I've only got my own judgement as to whether it was good or not' (French student, Level 2). Only one student in the entire sample gave an example of written functional practice. This Level 1 Spanish student regularly wrote short pieces about a variety of topics of interest. However, she then got this work checked by native speakers. Responses indicated a need for much more development and practice in self-assessment to be built into the courses and tutorials and a greater awareness of the potential difficulties of developing writing skills at a distance. Distance language learning relies on the presentation of models and solutions to activities, yet on examination of the courses concerned it was found that they gave relatively little advice, guidance or practice on how to make the best use of these models and solutions. Student responses indicate that ability to do this should not be assumed. It also became clear that when students talked about checking their work, they were almost entirely concerned with grammatical accuracy. Few talked in terms of fulfilling the task or the appropriateness of language used for the intended audience.

With the exception of writing skills, these students displayed a considerable degree of functional control and active involvement in their learning. They focused on meaningful communication in areas of interest to them and gained considerable satisfaction and motivation in the process. They certainly appeared to confirm the view that engaging in meaningful use of the target language makes study more interesting and satisfying, resulting in increased activity, more evidence of progress and enhanced motivation.

The impact of assessment

However, the situation changed dramatically once students spoke about the way they tackled assignments. Oral assignments had involved students recording themselves speaking onto an audio-cassette for a certain length of time according to task guidelines. Both written and spoken tasks had involved listening to, or reading some prescribed stimulus material. The oral assignments were found to be nerve-wracking, due to the need to record and time themselves and focus on the task, not to mention accuracy, etc., all at the same time. 'I was just so worried about making a fool of myself, I realise that my difficulties were caused by anxiety and inability to relax' (French student, Level 2). There were comments about how this destroyed the ability to speak spontaneously, yet students are penalised for preparing and reading from a script. 'In France I don't find it too difficult to communicate because in that context, I'm focusing on the message' (French student, Level 2). In practice many did read as they found this the only way to cope. 'That was something I found incredibly difficult not to write out [...] even though my conversational abilities were reasonably strong [. . .] to cram it into the time, that was the problem' (French student, Level 2). Prescriptive task guidelines and the time limit meant that students also felt unable to express their own ideas or be more creative. Yet the task guidelines are intended to ensure that the task is unambiguous and the time limit should restrict the amount of work the student has to do.

In the written assignments, although the situation was less extreme, there was a sense of playing safe, a focus on detailed points required and word- or sentence-level production and accuracy. The need to extract points from unseen listening material, worries about memory and possibly missing something, led students to virtually transcribe in some cases, rather than trusting in their ability to extract key points. All this might be seen simply as evidence of an 'achieving' or 'surface' approach (Biggs, 1988), but the degree of dissatisfaction and tension caused suggests a group of people who resented being forced into this approach, as predicted by Ramsden (1992: 58). Biggs (1988: 134) argues that the volume of content, lack of time and lack of opportunities for individual contribution promote a surface or reproducing approach, and this appears to have happened here. Van Patten (1990, 1996, quoted in Ellis, 2001: 8) suggests that learners have limited attention capacities and that different aspects of comprehension and language production compete for these capacities. Robinson's (2001) discussion of 'cognitive complexity' also supports this view. It seems that when writing course assignments course designers need to look for ways of capitalising on the students' meaning-focused approach and willingness to take functional control while continuing to test mastery of linguistic forms. Assignments need to be 'constructively aligned' (Biggs, 1999: 11) to recognise, promote and reward critical reflection, active engagement and a meaning focus if independent, autonomous learning is the goal. Otherwise, they are likely to produce the opposite effect, as appeared to be the case for many of the learners in this study.

Findings: Evidence of Critical Reflection

Reflexiveness

Both users and non-users of the project materials demonstrated a degree of critical reflection. They spoke about their knowledge, skills, attitudes and assumptions in ways which indicated 'reflexiveness' (Schön, 1983). They were able to describe how they approached their learning and were aware of what helped them to learn. For example, students described the importance of personal relevance or context, their need to write out examples or to have visual images, their preferred learning strategies, and their fears and ways of avoiding difficulty as well as the experiences they found inspiring.

Critical analysis

However, the user group appeared to show greater evidence of 'critical analysis' (Schön, 1983) in the way they were able to identify specific priorities and changes to their approach to study during the course. They appeared to have begun to question some of their assumptions about language learning and had developed metacognitive strategies involved in critical reflection. All students were asked about their priorities, the areas where they felt reasonably confident and what they particularly needed to work on. Reflection on priorities was encouraged by the *skills audit* and it was evident that students who had used this had identified very specific priority areas to work on, whereas others talked more about a general desire for improvement, or interests, or even simply 'completing the course'. Working through the audit had given these students the language and tools to carry out their analysis. Identifying priority areas enabled students to plan and focus activity on them. Students shared their priorities with their tutor when submitting an assignment (if they had not done so earlier and sought advice on how to achieve their goals), and indicated how successful they thought they had been. In other words, they engaged formally in a process of monitoring, self-assessment and self-evaluation. They were able to comment on progress in specific areas, whereas non-users could only identify progress in more general terms. When asked to talk about any changes in the way they tackled their studies, those who used the project materials were able to refer to specific techniques and strategies, while the other students talked less specifically about the general progress they had made.

Reactions to the materials

When asked about experience of using the materials, the *skills audit* appeared to have been the most useful, prompting students to set targets, give more thought to key areas (not just grammar), and focus their efforts. The *self-assessment sheet* was more problematic. As might be anticipated from the work of other researchers (e.g. Broady, 1996; Candy, 1991), a number expressed unease or a lack of confidence in this activity. There were particular concerns about saying what they had done well. Leaving aside any possible cultural tendency to play down success, there is the difficulty of committing oneself to a judgement with which a perhaps unknown tutor may or may not agree. Nevertheless, having tried it, students acknowledged that their tutor was often able to confirm their assessment or reassure them. Tutors, too, commented on how accurate the students' perceptions generally were, though with a tendency in some quarters to play safe by presenting a rather negative view of their work. In effect, these students were learning to self-assess, since, for the most part, they had little previous experience of this and examination of the courses concerned had indicated little or no explicit teaching or practice in this process. They were beginning to reflect critically on their learning and make decisions about further activity. The communication with their tutor could perhaps be seen to represent, at a distance, a form of the 'dialogue' seen as so vital for critical reflection by Brockbank and McGill (1998). Tutors commented on the way in which the self-assessment sheets increased their contact with students in a way that frequent exhortations to get in touch had otherwise failed to achieve.

Relatively fewer students completed the *reflection sheet*, though some worked through it without writing formal plans for the next stage of their work. However, it was apparent that students who used the project materials took a more active approach to engaging with their tutor's feedback.

A significant theme to emerge from all the interviews with students was the impact of affective factors, the feelings aroused when an assignment is returned and how students deal with these at a distance. This applies not only to the grades achieved, but also to the ways in which an isolated student may interpret comments from a tutor. 'Always I felt quite ill with fear' (French student, Level 2). 'When I got the first comment about my accent, it stopped me talking for a while' (French student, Level 2). Distance learners generally do not have anyone to turn to at the moment when the assignment drops onto the doormat. A Spanish Level 1 student described how he put it on one side until he felt strong enough to tackle it. Several students in the non-user group admitted that they never looked at the tutor's feedback or listened to the tutor's commentary on their cassette: 'I find it impossible to accept criticism; I find it very depressing. I probably wouldn't continue, so the poor tutor's comments never got looked at' (German Level 2 student). Those who had engaged with the self-assessment activity and communicated with their tutor in this way appeared less likely to be overwhelmed by feelings of despair or frustration. This might have been due to the increase in dialogue and perhaps because the gap between expectations and reality was reduced through the self-assessment process. The project materials also encouraged students to 'return to the experience' and 'attend to feelings' (Boud *et al.*, 1985). When asked what advice they might give to new students, it was noticeable that users of the materials commented on the satisfaction and enjoyment that was to be gained from studying the language, whereas no such comments were forthcoming from the non-user group. Thus, for a number of reasons, the development of the capacity for self-assessment and self-evaluation seems even more crucial in a distance context than in conventional settings.

Findings: The tutors' perspective

The tutors involved in this investigation were enthusiastic about the project materials and the ideas behind them. They were particularly appreciative of the self-assessment sheets (in contrast to the students) and felt these enabled them to give more relevant and focused feedback. 'I found that enormously helpful' (French tutor). There was considerable disappointment where few students had decided to use them. Tutors described generally low levels of contact from students (also reported by students) apart from at tutorials, where attendance was often irregular. In this context, they welcomed an additional means to promote dialogue around assignments, the one assured point of contact with all students. They valued this dialogue not only because it enabled them to give better support to their students, but also because it gave them reassurance about their feedback. They, too, were concerned about writing feedback at a distance to people they hardly knew, making assumptions about their needs and circumstances which could all too easily prove to be wrong. Tutors commented that the self-assessment sheet allowed students to 'get things off their chest' (French tutor), acknowledging negative feelings about the task or their performance. There were frequent references to dealing with negative feelings, reassurance, opportunities to motivate and encourage via feedback, indicating tutors were well aware of the affective factors at play in completing an assignment and receiving feedback as well as in giving it. Increasing dialogue via such materials as were used in this project appears to be important in managing affective aspects for both parties.

Tutors indicated that they had seen tutorials as primarily opportunities for language practice and had not previously highlighted the development of language learning strategies. As a result of participating in the project, some tutors had begun to incorporate awareness-raising activities and opportunities to try out learning strategies into their tutorials and to make reference to such issues in their assignment feedback. In this way, they had begun to encourage students to make choices and decisions about their own learning, but gave few other examples of practice that promoted conscious decision-making. Only one tutor had included any activity to develop self-assessment and self-evaluation in tutorials. Although the project materials were felt to be very valuable, little direct use was made of them. Tutors gave out the materials, explained them and encouraged students to use them. Like the course writers, they too made assumptions about the students' abilities to handle these processes.

Tutors were very concerned about student workload (having seen many struggle in the past) and worried that the materials could appear to increase the burden, rather than helping students to work smarter. They were aware of the number of issues competing for time in early tutorials and of students' expectations that tutorials would focus on target language performance. Therefore tutors' positive view of the materials was countered by a number of concerns that limited the amount of time they devoted to them. This may have helped to reinforce student views about an optional extra that would take up too much time. This lack of time was the most common reason given for not using the materials, both in the interviews and on the questionnaire. Both student and tutor responses confirmed the need to incorporate such materials and activities into the course materials with a clear rationale. Tutors alone cannot be responsible for transforming a situation where coursework and assessment send the message to students that the institution 'values dependency, identification and representation', despite avowed intentions to develop critical reflection and autonomous learning (Brockbank and McGill, 1998: 30).

Conclusions

The findings indicate that these distance language learners exercised a considerable degree of functional control in their learning. They sought ways of becoming actively involved and creating opportunities for interaction in the target language. They did this while focusing on meaningful communication, interest and personal relevance, enhancing their motivation and gaining tremendous satisfaction at the same time. However, the assessment process appeared to bring about completely the reverse situation. Further research is needed to explore how the assessment process might be adjusted in order to maintain enthusiasm and reduce tension and frustration. The responses of students in this sample indicated a lack of alignment between the nature of the assessment tasks and the goal of developing independent, autonomous learners. Assessment tasks are needed which focus on meaning and foster critical reflection. Where students are unable to express their more complex ideas in the target language, more use of their first language may be necessary. This may be particularly important for adult learners. Their interests, enthusiasm and knowledge of the world enable them to derive tremendous encouragement and motivation for learning the language from engaging with ideas in meaningful communication. Language learning will always involve attention to detail and accuracy. The issue is how to balance these demands and ensure that a focus on accuracy in assessment in the early stages does not drive out attention to meaning in assessment in the longer term.

The findings also indicate that these learners engage in critical reflection but may need to be helped to prioritise, make decisions and develop the capacity for 'critical analysis', self-assessment and self-evaluation at a distance. Students in the sample were able to demonstrate a considerable level of self-awareness about what helped their learning, but those who used the project materials showed greater evidence of these capacities, demonstrating the effect of a supportive framework, as suggested by Moon

(1999). In this study, the project materials provided a framework but it was an optional extra, not part of the course materials, and was rejected by many who were worried about the additional time it might take.

Thorpe (2000) points out that techniques to develop reflection have to be underpinned by a rationale that pervades the learning programme and is supported by development for tutors, both in terms of the tutorial support which they offer and the feedback which they give on assignments. Similar materials and activities could be built into courses, but the findings suggest that even more explicit development, support and practice opportunities for self-assessment and self-evaluation also need to be included in both course materials and tutorials. Developing these resources should also help in managing some affective aspects of study at a distance. Encouraging students to prioritise gives them a basis for decisions about which parts of the course they may choose to skim, or which activities they really must do. It offers a way of personalising the highly structured nature of distance language courses catering for all eventualities but has considerable implications for tutor development.

Overall, these OU distance language learners exercised considerable functional control; they were self-aware and deployed a variety of strategies and techniques to develop their language skills. However, to develop their capacities for reflection and self-direction further, they would be helped by having an explicit framework, clear rationale, encouragement, support and practice within the course materials, all backed up by their tutor.

Notes
1. The investigation was carried out with part-time, distance language students registered with the Open University in the South. This is one of 13 regions the University operates across the UK and Western Europe. It covers the counties of Buckinghamshire, Oxfordshire, Berkshire, Hampshire, Dorset, part of Wiltshire, the Isle of Wight and the Channel Islands. Students may be any age over 18. Their educational experience is very varied due to an open entry policy and may range from no formal qualifications to a higher degree. Students are offered self-assessment tests to enable them to register for a course at the appropriate level. Their previous language learning may have taken place informally while living abroad or through family ties, but many have attended formal classes in adult, further or higher education, as well as having learned the language at school. Their previous language qualifications range from no formal qualifications to a degree in another language.
2. In 1999, the Open University offered the following courses: Level 1: A course in French, German or Spanish rated at 30 credit points (tutorial groups in the South Region: French 10; German 4; Spanish 6). Level 2: A course in French or German rated at 30 credit points (tutorial groups in the South Region: French 5; German 3). Level 2: A course in French or German rated at 60 credit points (tutorial groups in the South Region: French 6; German 4). The standard tutor:

student ratio is 1: 20 except for the Level 2 60 point courses where it is 1: 15. Students on a 30-point course completed four spoken and four written assignment tasks; on a 60-point course they completed seven spoken and seven written assignment tasks. Tutors from each of these courses in the South Region opted to become involved in the investigation, 17 in total who between them tutored just over 300 students. Tutors estimated that approximately 100 students used the materials. 130 returned the questionnaire. The interview sample shown below included 11 male and 21 female students from each of these courses, both users and non-users of the project materials. Their ages ranged from 21 to 75, with an average age of 50.

	Users of project materials			Non-users of project materials		
	French	*German*	*Spanish*	*French*	*German*	*Spanish*
Level 1	2	2	3	2	1	2
Level (30 points)	3	3		3	1	
Level 2 (60)	2	2		4	2	

All students have a personal tutor. The role of Open University Language tutors is to facilitate students' study of course materials designed and prepared by a course team. They mediate the course materials and develop students' ability to use the language they are studying via a limited number of optional tutorials (once a month at most) and through written and spoken feedback on the students' assignments at regular intervals. They are also responsible for grading those assignments. Tutors are expected to check on students' progress from time to time and to respond to questions or concerns about the course and its content. Assignment feedback is the only form of contact tutors have with all their students.

3. Copies of or further information about the specific project materials are available from the author (L.M.Murphy@open.ac.uk)

References

Ashworth, P. and Lucas, U. (2000) Achieving empathy and engagement: A practical approach to the design, conduct and reporting of phenomenographic research. *Studies in Higher Education* 25 (3), 295–308.

Benson, P. (2001) *Teaching and Researching Autonomy in Language Learning*. Harlow, Essex: Pearson Education Ltd.

Biggs, J. (1988) The role of metacognition in enhancing learning. *Australian Journal of Education* 32 (2), 127–138.

Biggs, J. (1999) *Teaching for Quality Learning at University: What the Student Does*. Buckingham: Society for Research into Higher Education and Open University Press.

Boud, D., Keogh R. and Walker, D. (1985) Promoting reflection in learning: A model. In D. Boud, K. Keogh and D. Walker (eds) *Reflection, Turning Experience into Learning* (pp. 18–40). London: Kogan Page.

Broady, E. (1996) Learner attitudes towards self-direction. In E. Broady and M. Kenning (eds) *Promoting Learner Autonomy in University Language Teaching* (pp. 215–36). London: CILT.

Brockbank, A. and McGill, I. (1998) *Facilitating Reflective Learning in Higher Education.* Buckingham: Society for Research into Higher Education and Open University Press.

Candy, P.C. (1991) *Self-Direction for Lifelong Learning: A Comprehensive Guide to Theory and Practice.* San Francisco: Jossey-Bass.

Cotterall, S. (1995) Readiness for autonomy: Investigating learner beliefs. *System* 23 (2), 195–205.

Dearing, R. (1997) *Higher Education in the Learning Society* (The Dearing Report). Norwich: HMSO.

Edwards, R. (1997) *Changing Places? Flexibility, Lifelong Learning and a Learning Society.* London: Routledge.

Ellis, R. (2001) Introduction: Investigating form-focused instruction. *Language Learning* 51 (1), 1–46.

Holec, H. (1980) *Autonomy and Foreign Language Learning.* Strasbourg: Council of Europe.

Hurd, S., Beaven, T. and Ortega, A. (2001) Developing autonomy in a distance language learning context: Issues and dilemmas for course writers. *System* 29 (3), 341–55.

Kolb, D.A. (1984) *Experiential Learning: Experience as the Source of Learning and Development.* New Jersey: Prentice Hall.

Lightbown, P.M. and Spada N. (1993) *How Languages are Learned.* Oxford: Oxford University Press.

Long, M.H. (1996) The role of the linguistic environment in second language acquisition. In W.C. Ritchie and T.K. Bhatia (eds) *Handbook of Second Language Acquisition* (pp. 413–68). San Diego: Academic Press.

Moon, J.A. (1999) *Reflection in Learning and Professional Development.* London: Kogan Page.

Naiman, N., Froehlich, M., Stern, H.H. and Todesco, A. (1996) *The Good Language Learner* (2nd edn). Toronto: Ontario Institute for Studies in Education.

Nunan, D. (1996) Towards autonomous learning: some theoretical, empirical and practical issues. In R. Pemberton, E.S.L. Li, W.W.F. Orr and H.D. Pierson (eds) *Autonomy in Language Learning* (pp. 13–26). Hong Kong: Hong Kong University Press.

O'Malley, J.M. and Chamot A.U. (1990) *Learning Strategies in Second Language Acquisition.* Cambridge: Cambridge University Press.

Open University (1998) *Key Skills: Making a Difference.* Kent: Thanet Press Ltd.

Oxford, R.L. (1990) *Language Learning Strategies: What Every Teacher Should Know.* New York: Newbury House.

Quality Assurance Agency for Higher Education (QAA) (2002) *Academic Standards: Languages and Related Studies.* Gloucester: QAA.

Qualitative Solutions and Research Pty Ltd. (QSR) (1997) *Non-numerical Unstructured Data Indexing Searching and Theorising.* London: Sage.

Race, P. (1993) Never mind the teaching feel the learning. *SEDA* 80.

Ramsden, P. (1992) *Learning to Teach in Higher Education.* London, Routledge.

Ridley, J. (1997) *Reflection and Strategies in Language Learning.* Frankfurt am Main: Lang.

Robinson, P. (2001) Task complexity, task difficulty and task production: Exploring interactions in a componential framework. *Applied Linguistics* 22 (1), 27–57.

Rowsell, L.V. and Libben, G. (1994) The sound of one hand clapping: How to succeed in independent language learning. *Canadian Modern Language Review* 50 (4), 668–87.

Schmidt, R. (1994) Deconstructing consciousness in search of useful definitions for applied linguistics. *AILA Review* 11, 11–26.

Schön, D.A. (1983) *The Reflective Practitioner*. London: Temple Smith.

Tarvin, W.L. and Al-Arishi, A.Y. (1991) Rethinking communicative language teaching: Reflection and the EFL classroom. *TESOL Quarterly*, 25 (1), 9–27.

Thorpe, M. (2000) Encouraging students to reflect as part of the assignment process: Student responses and tutor feedback. *Active Learning* 1 (1), 72–92.

Wenden, A.L. (1998) Metacognitive knowledge and beliefs in language learning. *Applied Linguistics* 19 (4), 515–37.

White, C. (1995) Autonomy and strategy use in distance foreign language learning: Research findings. *System* 23 (2), 207–21.

White, C. (1999) Expectations and emergent beliefs of self-instructed language learners. *System* 27 (4), 443–57.

Chapter 3

Theoretical and Practical Issues in the Promotion of Collaborative Learner Autonomy in a Virtual Self-access Centre

ALEX DING

Introduction

A number of recent publications (e.g. Dudeney, 2000; Oakey, 2000; Warschauer & Kern, 2000; Windeatt *et al.*, 2000) outline the role of the Internet as an important means of facilitating language learning. While many articles analyse online language learning courses, materials and the roles of students and learners online, few publications focus specifically on the potential of Virtual Self-access Centres (VSACs) to facilitate learner autonomy. The aim of this chapter is to explore the possibilities for promoting collaborative learner autonomy within VSACs.

The first section outlines a theory of collaborative autonomy, based on intersubjectivity, which provides a theoretical foundation for the creation and running of VSACs. In addition, examples of pedagogical practices that exemplify this version of autonomy are briefly described. The second section examines the evidence from the research literature dealing with self-access language learning (SALL) and online learning to assess the feasibility of promoting collaborative autonomy within the framework of a VSAC. It is argued that there is sufficient evidence from the literature to justify the creation of VSACs for language learning. Section three describes and evaluates the attempts I have made at Nottingham University to implement the theory and practice of collaborative learner autonomy in a VSAC for English for Academic Purposes (EAP). A number of problems have arisen in the promotion of collaborative autonomy, and two pilot projects that attempt to deal with these issues are described briefly. The final section highlights the large gap between theory and practice in the

40

fostering of learner autonomy in an online environment. However, it is argued that despite this gap it is essential to be guided by theory – at least in part – in order to make informed and coherent decisions about learners and learning. Whether the version of collaborative autonomy proposed here is an adequate model to serve as a basis for practical decisions remains subject to further, more rigorous investigation.

Outline of an Intersubjective Version of Collaborative Autonomy

There is widespread agreement in the literature (Benson & Voller, 1997; Broady & Kenning, 1996; Pemberton, 1996; Tudor, 1996) that terminology relating to autonomy is confusing. The confusion and profusion of terms (e.g. 'autonomy', 'independence', 'empowerment', and 'self-directed learning') demonstrates the complexity of issues involved in promoting autonomy. If autonomy is understood as a 'movement' (Crabbe, 1999: 3) that contains 'concepts in transition' (Benson & Voller, 1997: 12) it is perhaps not surprising that there are different interpretations and versions of autonomy. This section explores the version of collaborative autonomy that provides the theoretical foundation for the creation of the VSAC.

Holec (1981: 3) has defined autonomy as the 'ability to take charge of one's own learning'. Holec's definition of autonomy is probably the most quoted and referred to in the literature (e.g. Benson & Voller, 1997; Esch, 1996; Nunan, 1997; Sinclair, 2000; Victori & Lockhart, 1995). There have been modifications and extensions of Holec's definition (e.g. Dam, 1995; Littlewood, 1997; Sheerin, 1997) although there is general acceptance that taking charge of one's own learning lies at the heart of autonomy. The version of autonomy adopted here accepts Holec's basic premise on learner control but emphasises collaborative learner autonomy much more explicitly.

Intersubjective collaborative autonomy is defined as a version of autonomy that not only stresses the 'virtues' of collaboration as a means of facilitating autonomy but also argues that promoting autonomy necessarily entails complex relations of interdependence. These relationships with others are at the core of learner autonomy, and it is these relationships (with institutions, teachers, students, native speakers, friends, etc.) that help determine – along with individual factors – the extent to which learners take control of their learning. Intersubjective collaborative autonomy can be argued for both theoretically and pedagogically. Benson and Voller (1997: 2) argue that there is no 'canon for concepts such as autonomy and independence in the field of applied linguistics'. So theoretical justifications for autonomy come from other domains, such as philosophy, adult education, politics, and psychology. The main theoretical arguments for intersubjective collaborative autonomy come from the works of Crossley (1996), Husserl (1991), Kojéve (1969), Mead (1967) and Merleau-Ponty (1962). These philosophers and social theorists have different visions of intersubjectivity; however, all have contributed a powerful explanation of self and group identity and, more specifically, have defined how concepts such as self-hood, communication, power and community can be understood.

It is beyond the scope of this chapter to examine intersubjectivity in any detail other than to sketch some of the central arguments. Intersubjectivity emphasises the social and dialogic nature of knowledge and thought. Thoughts and experience are interwoven and are not the property of individuals, but are shared. Human speech, identity and action are necessarily social, and meaning is derived from social contexts. If one accepts the basic argument that humans are fundamentally interconnected in terms of thought, language and identity, this will have some important effects on how autonomy is to be both theorised and developed in language education.

Pedagogical examples of collaborative autonomy

Accepting an intersubjectivist account of collaborative autonomy does not require reinventing the wheel. There are sufficient examples of pedagogical practices in the literature that are compatible with an intersubjectivist account of autonomy. Benson's approach to autonomy – which is highly compatible with the political implication of intersubjectivity – is best summed up as follows:

> Greater learner control over the learning process, resources and language cannot be achieved by each individual working alone according to his or her own preferences. Control is a question of collective decision-making rather than individual choice. Yet collective decisions are also arrived at by individuals achieving consensus and acting in concert. (Benson, 1996: 33)

Building on a wide range of literature from child development (including Vygotsky and Bruner) and first language acquisition, Little (2000) situates the essence of autonomy in terms of interdependence. The pedagogical implications of understanding autonomy as interactive interdependence is that one cannot, always, isolate the promotion of an individual's autonomy from that of the group. Little argues this point as follows:

... learning can only proceed via interaction, so that the freedoms by which we recognize learner autonomy are always constrained by the learner's dependence on the support and cooperation of others.(Little, 2000: 204)

Other practical examples of how intersubjective collaborative autonomy can be fostered are to be found in the work of Carpenter (1996), Esch (1997) and Ho and Crookall (1995). Esch provides an excellent example of learner training for autonomy. The guiding principle behind the training is that it should be 'critical, conversational and collective'. What is particularly interesting is the collaborative, group-directed nature of the training: students are treated as valuable sources of advice and knowledge, and have complete control over the content of each session. Carpenter (1996) offers an interesting example of peer teaching in which pairs of students take responsibility for a 3-hour class. This experiment in peer teaching would appear to offer very strong support for the provision of learning experiences in which learners are responsible for themselves and for others. In Ho and Crookall's (1995) experiment in promoting experiential autonomy, students participated in a large-scale, worldwide computer-mediated simulation of international relations. After completing the simulation Ho and Crookall (1995: 242) concluded that it resulted in strong group identity, motivation, sense of responsibility, involvement, and collaboration.

The essence of intersubjective collaborative autonomy lies in the emphasis and importance placed on creating opportunities for learners to exercise as much collective control over all aspects of learning as possible. Adopting an intersubjective approach to learner autonomy entails the belief that autonomy is not a 'method' with step-by-step pedagogical actions to be taken (Little, 1999), but is rather an educational approach to learning in which numerous pedagogical configurations and practices could contribute to learner autonomy in a variety of learning environments. The implications of fostering intersubjective collaborative autonomy within a virtual self-access centre are examined in the next section.

From Self-access to Virtual Self-access

One of the striking features in the literature on self-access language learning is the perceived efficiency of self-access centres (SACs) to cater effectively for individual differences. Individual differences are often categorised in terms of learning styles, learning strategies, willingness and disposition to learn autonomously, learners' specific needs, levels and objectives. If SACs are organised to cater for individual differences in language learners, then the logical conclusion is that promoting collaborative autonomy may not be very effective in a self-access environment. An alternative explanation is that we know too little about how to organise self-access to facilitate collaborative autonomy. The few published accounts of promoting collaborative autonomy in SACs indicate a lack of experimentation and development in this area.

Despite collaborative learning having 'often been given short shrift' in SALL (Martyn, 1994: 76) there are a number of reasons why collaborative autonomy may be promoted in this environment. Individualised learning does have a role in SALL, albeit potentially far more limited than generally thought. Little argues:

> Of course, not all learning can be done collaboratively. Just as learners need regularly to step back from the process of learning in order to reflect on what they have achieved, so they need as individuals regularly to step back from the group and do some learning on their own. (Little, 2000: 21)

Individualisation does have an important role, however. Little's claim reveals a significant shift in the justification for individualisation. Sometimes necessary for learners to collaborate more effectively together, individualisation operates as an effective support for collaborative learning but not as a pedagogical end in itself, as might be assumed from reviewing the literature on SALL.

Many of the tasks and activities carried out in SACs are performed on an individual basis. Counselling sessions are often carried out individually; learner contracts are drawn up individually (Or, 1994); training advice sheets address learners as individuals (Sinclair, 1996: 158); logs or learner diaries are completed individually (Martyn, 1994); and SAC evaluations are carried on an individual basis (Thomson, 1996). Many of these activities could profitably be carried out in pairs or groups. In addition, collaborative project work (in which learners provide mutual support for the completion of a task which might be beyond any of the group members' linguistic or [meta-] cognitive skills), peer teaching, group writing tasks (negotiation of content and meaning), and concordancing to examine target language texts collectively or to analyse student errors would seem useful tasks to perform in SACs.

Unfortunately there is a lack of research indicating the potential for collaboration in a number of these areas. In theory, at any rate, counselling could benefit from the insights and advice of other learners, and pairs or groups of learners could decide on a collective learning contract to carry out SALL together (thus gaining insights into strategies used by other learners). Learners could be addressed as a group to encourage them to experiment collectively with learning to learn techniques, and collective evaluations of SALL would enable learners to compare and share learning insights. In addition, there is some evidence that learners could be given a prominent and active role in SACs.

Involving learners in self-access

Studies reveal learners can successfully be involved in SACs at various levels. They can be directly involved in the design, management and running of SACs to ensure the centre respects the educational culture of learners (Jones, 1995). They can also select, catalogue and describe learning material (Benson, 1994), produce leaflets and reports for users (Aston, 1993), and select authentic material for use in the SAC or classroom (Dam, 1995). Although this is not an exhaustive list of how learners could be involved in the life of the SAC it does demonstrate that learners can participate effectively at all levels in the running of a SAC. How far the learners might be involved in the running of the centre is likely to be determined by factors such as the willingness of teachers to involve them and their own willingness to become involved, the number of learners using the centre, whether the educational institution encourages and expects student participation, and the degree to which learners feel they belong to the centre.

Having argued that intersubjective collaborative autonomy is a viable version of autonomy and that, at least in theory, this form of learner autonomy could be fostered within SACs, the question remains as to the feasibility of transferring SACs online to create VSACs and whether intersubjective collaborative autonomy can be fostered effectively in an online environment. The next section examines the potential of the Internet to promote collaborative autonomy in a VSAC.

Promoting collaborative autonomy in virtual self-access centres

Research often focuses on the collaborative nature of online learning (Cezec-Kecmanovic & Webb, 2000; Coverdale-Jones, 1998; Ragoonaden & Bordeleau, 2000; Söntgens, 1999). In particular, e-mail has been researched extensively in terms of potential for collaboration. E-mail is ideal for promoting collaboration because it provides easy access to group knowledge (Brown, 1997), thus facilitating sharing of ideas and work (Coverdale-Jones 1998). Collectively, learners have a greater role in managing and controlling online discourse in terms of asking questions, steering conversations, requesting information, expressing opinions and querying teachers than in traditional classrooms (Warschauer, 1997). Peer-correction and editing (Söntgens, 1999) have been found to benefit from e-mail discussions. E-mail discussions may, depending on the circumstances and learning environment, lead to greater (quantitative) learner participation than in classroom discussions (Brown, 1997; Ortega,

1997), partly because this environment is less threatening and reduces the psychological pressure of making mistakes (Chun, 1994). This helps facilitate compromise and improves social learning and co-operative skills (Ragoonaden & Bordeleau, 2000; Wolff, 1997). Shy students speak out more, resulting in more equally distributed communication (Brown, 1997). It has also been found that females tend to participate more in e-mail than classroom discussions (Coverdale-Jones, 1998).

Synchronous communication is considered potentially beneficial for the development of oral communication in that synchronous communication is dynamic and interactive and corresponds more closely to oral interaction than to written communication (Pellettieri, 2000; Schultz, 2000). Users key in, send and receive text messages almost instantaneously, requiring users to react quickly to others. Communication breakdowns can be observed and repaired immediately thus facilitating language awareness through the negotiation of meaning (Pellettieri, 2000). The interactive nature of synchronous communication means peers offer mutual support in the creation of a learning dialogue (Schwienhorst, 1998).

A large body of research analyses the potential of the WWW to promote effective language learning mainly through the provision of web-based courses (Felix, 1999; Orsini-Jones, 1999). There appears to be general agreement that web-based learning enables learners to take control of their learning:

- the web provides exposure to and experience of other cultures (Chen, 1999; Felix, 1999), which can improve motivation and attitudes to the target language (Felix, 1999);
- the web provides exposure to a wide range of communication styles and a rich array of resources (Brown, 1997);
- learners can take control of their learning (Gordon, 1996) by choosing materials and resources (Herrington & Oliver, 1997), discovering new materials for themselves (Brown, 1997; Motteram, 1997), devising their own ways of handling information (Gordon, 1996), controlling navigation (Brown, 1997), choosing the order in which they tackle activities (Fox, 1998), and working at their own pace (Herrington & Oliver, 1997) and when they wish to (Motteram, 1997);
- through working online learners become more confident and more able in their research skills (Wolff, 1997).

This section has examined the ways in which the WWW and computer-mediated communication (CMC) might support collaborative autonomous learning. There is a significant body of research indicating that CMC can effectively promote collaborative autonomous learning. The

WWW can also contribute effectively to learner autonomy by providing an environment for learners to work on language skills together, access and exploit all types of authentic material and publicly produce their own work. The following section analyses an attempt to put some of the potential the Internet offers for collaborative autonomy into practice.

The Centre for English Language Education, University of Nottingham VSAC

The VSAC was created in 2001 to:

- provide online EAP (English for Academic Purposes) support for in-sessional students (international students studying at undergraduate and postgraduate level), particularly those unable to attend classes;
- provide a framework for students to experiment in collaborative autonomous learning;
- act as a guide through the enormous quantity of EFL websites available to students;
- provide support for tutors to recommend sites/activities for individuals and groups of students;
- act as a means of communication with tutors for advice;
- act as a means of communication between international students to create an international student online community;
- provide advice on strategies to use the Internet for language learning; and
- provide an environment for tutors to explore and experiment with online provision for in-sessional students, identifying student needs, interests, strategic competence (in using online materials and communication tools), measuring the degree of support necessary to enable students to work effectively online.

The VSAC is a simple low-tech website requiring little maintenance and involving only a limited investment in time and resources to design the site. This was done to avoid investing too much time designing a site that is essentially experimental and subject to significant change (following observations and evaluations of student and tutor use of the VSAC). The simplest possible navigation system was adopted to enable students to find what they want quickly and with little assistance/training. The site tries to reflect the way in which students understand language learning. The VSAC is divided into discreet skills sections (grammar, vocabulary, listening, etc.) and offers the possibility of communicating both synchronously and asynchronously with tutors and international students.

External links have been selected carefully to try to cover the most common student needs for general English and EAP (English for Academic Purposes).

The VSAC has been operational for almost three years and is used by approximately 200 university students per month. In an average week, online tutors receive up to 35 e-mail requests from students. Despite encouragingly large numbers of university students using the VSAC on a regular basis, and regular requests for advice and positive feedback in questionnaires, the VSAC has failed to achieve a number of important objectives. The most significant failure is to provide a truly effective means of supporting collaborative autonomy. In discussions with students, a number of reasons have emerged for the lack of student collaboration. These factors should be treated with caution as they are only now beginning to be subjected to more rigorous research. The first reason is that students do not necessarily identify very strongly with the label 'international student'. Being identified in this way is not, it appears, a strong enough bond to create an active online community with others. Other bonds such as being in a particular faculty or department, or being a member of a nationality or language group seem to create much stronger ties among some students. A number of students revealed they did not want other students to see their requests for help and advice. They did not want it to be public knowledge that they appeared to be struggling. Students also explained they visited the VSAC only when necessary, and that time constraints meant they had little time to help themselves, never mind offer advice to other students. Many students do not see themselves as sources of information and knowledge and are reluctant to voice an opinion. The tutor is perceived as being the sole expert and source of information. A few students hold the view that the university environment is a competitive one and that helping other students might indirectly affect their own chances of success. Lastly, most students have little or no experience of using the Internet for educational purposes and a number of students stated they were unsure what was expected of them in terms of collaboration and the degree of control they could have in the VSAC. In order to address the problem of lack of collaboration two pilot projects have been set up.

The pilot projects

One of the themes to emerge from discussions with students was a lack of experience and understanding of how the Internet and CMC could support collaborative language learning. A pilot module, *ICT and Language Learning,* has been created to provide pre-sessional students (international students who take an intensive EAP course before they join their academic departments) with classroom experience of using the WWW and CMC for EAP. This 15-hour face-to-face module helps prepare students for when they start their academic studies and have far less language support available to them. The *ICT and Language Learning* module employs a collaborative task-based approach to exploring some of the ways in which the Internet can support language learning. The module is divided into units and each unit explores a different aspect of the Internet. Units presently on offer include an introduction to the web and CMC, data-driven web-learning, independent learning on the web, communication with others, evaluation of web resources, and listening on the web. Throughout the module, a discussion forum and chat room are available for students to explore online communication. Resources and external links are provided to encourage students to investigate further sites that may be of interest to them, and students share sites they have found interesting. Questionnaires have been designed to provoke reflection on how the Internet might be beneficial for language learning. Students are required to provide feedback on the module continuously and are provided with their own web space to explore online writing.

The second measure taken to address the issue of student collaboration has been to set up a pilot project with a group of 13 international students studying on the same academic course. International students studying for an MA in English Language Teacher Development were asked to volunteer to participate in this online collaborative project. The aim of this project is to try to encourage collaboration by means of group-directed discussions on issues arising from their academic studies. The website framing this discussion includes a thread-based discussion forum, a chat room, a resources section (links to online journals, associations, worldwide discussion forums, and EAP resources), questionnaires (one of which aims to measure attitudes to online collaboration, autonomous learning and learning styles), web space for writing, technical help, key dates, and an outline of the objectives of the pilot project, in addition to what is expected of participants.

Every two weeks three students 'take over' the website to lead a discussion on a theme chosen by a group. It is the responsibility of each group of students to animate and maintain a discussion on their chosen topic, suggest readings, and provide summaries of discussions. Each group of students leading the discussion is encouraged to ensure that all members of the class participate.

One of the main reasons for setting up this pilot project was to explore the idea that students might feel more comfortable working in small groups (maximum 15), on subject-related issues (language or academic), and with others who share the same set of interests and perhaps the same

problems. The VSAC attempts to create an online community of international students who share nothing more than being non-native speakers,
whereas this project attempts to create a community through shared
academic interests. If this project is a success, then one of the outcomes
might be to maintain the main VSAC as a drop-in centre for individual
language study and to develop satellite faculty-based VSACs for collaborative subject-specific language and academic work.

The Gap Between Theory and Practice of Collaborative Autonomy in a VSAC

The first section of this chapter outlined a theory of collaborative autonomy
based on the idea that we are interconnected in a number of inescapable and
fundamental ways. The potential of applying a theory of collaborative
autonomy to pedagogical practices in a VSAC was then explored. Network-based language learning appears to be a promising means of promoting
collaborative learner autonomy. A large gap is clearly noticeable between
theory and practice in promoting collaborative autonomy in a VSAC. The
observations made in this chapter thus far could lead to a number of conclusions. First, the modest degree of student collaboration taking place in the
VSAC might indicate the theory is inadequate to provide a framework for collaboration and effective language learning and, consequently, needs to be
modified or dropped. Second, the VSAC is ill designed to promote collaborative autonomy: the pedagogical design of the VSAC does not facilitate
collaboration effectively. Third, the context in which the VSAC has been
created (EAP) does not lend itself well to collaboration; in short, students do
not want or perceive the need to collaborate with other students online.

Any or all of these conclusions may be drawn by readers. However, the
two pilot projects described in the previous section may, eventually,
provide more precise and rigorous explanations of how collaborative
autonomy can be facilitated effectively online. In addition, creating a VSAC
that is informed by theory, however imperfect, does have advantages.
Following Benson (1997), it could be argued that:

> every aspect of a self-access centre – its architecture and interior
> design, the selection and lay out of resources, the allocation of space to
> users and staff, the availability of advice and counselling, classification
> and cataloguing systems, handouts, notice boards and so on – forms
> part of a system that communicates something about the nature of
> language and language learning. (Benson, 1997: 73)

If Benson is correct, it is important that any VSAC be informed by theory, as
every icon, message, resource, link, text, can - potentially - illustrate a particu-

lar ideology or view about learners and language learning. Not having an explicit model of virtual self-access language learning may lead to conflicting messages and ideas being sent to learners, ineffective learning, and confused and confusing creation and selection of resources and tasks. It is also arguable that the potentially rich benefits from effective learner collaboration in an online environment deserve to be investigated further and more rigorously.

The future success of the VSAC at Nottingham University lies in probing and researching the potential for collaboration among students in a variety of pedagogical configurations. Some of the research questions that need to be explored include:

- Are there other models of autonomy that could provide a better foundation for VSACs?
- To what extent (and how) do learning styles, learning strategies and the degree of learner autonomy influence the effectiveness of online collaboration? Does learning online require substantially different skills from the classroom or SAC for collaborative autonomous learning to take place?
- Does previous experience of using the Internet for 'infotainment' and educational purposes influence collaboration? If so, how?
- Does the educational environment support collaborative learning? Does previous experience of collaboration influence online collaboration? If so, how?
- What are the students' motivations to use or not use the VSAC?
- Under what conditions would students view online collaboration as being useful and effective?

This research will undoubtedly never generate clear guidelines for the setting up of a definitive VSAC with set pedagogical practices. However, the hope is that with continued research and development of the VSAC, a much clearer picture of the adequacy of the theory of collaborative autonomy will emerge, as will the pedagogical practices that support this aim.

If this chapter exemplifies anything, it is the struggle to promote learner autonomy. Students will not necessarily take collective control of their learning and it is difficult to pinpoint the most favourable conditions to enable them to do this. It also reinforces the constant need to reassess how and why we promote autonomy to reduce the gap between theory and practice and to enable our students to exercise as much control over their learning as they wish.

References

Aston, G. (1993) The learner's contribution to the self-access centre. *ELT Journal* 47 (3), 219–27.

Benson, P. (1994) Self-access systems as information systems: questions of ideology and control. In D. Gardner and L. Miller (eds) *Directions in Self-access Language Learning* (pp. 3–12). Hong Kong: Hong Kong University Press.

Benson, P. (1996) Concepts of autonomy in language learning. In R. Pemberton, E. S. L. Li and H. D. Pierson (eds) *Taking Control: Autonomy in Language Learning* (pp. 27–34). Hong Kong: Hong Kong University Press.

Benson, P. (1997) The semiotics of self-access language learning in the digital age. In V. Darleguy, A. Ding and M. Svensson (eds) *Educational Technology in Language Learning: Theoretical Considerations and Practical Applications* (pp. 70–78). Lyons: National Institute of Applied Sciences.

Benson, P. and Voller, P. (1997) Introduction: Autonomy and independence in language learning. In P. Benson and P. Voller (eds) *Autonomy and Independence in Language Learning* (pp. 1–12). London: Longman.

Broady, E. and Kenning, M-M. (eds) (1996) *Promoting Learner Autonomy in University Language Teaching*. London: Association for French Language Studies/CILT.

Brown, A. (1997) Designing for learning: What are the essential features of an effective online course? *Australian Journal of Educational Technology* 13 (2), 115–26.

Carpenter, C. (1996) Peer teaching: a new approach to advanced level language teaching. In E. Broady and M-M. Kenning (eds) *Promoting Learner Autonomy in University Language Teaching* (pp. 23–38). London: Association for French Language Studies/CILT.

Cecez-Kecmanovic, D. and Webb, C. (2000) Towards a communicative model of collaborative web-mediated learning. *Australian Journal of Educational Technology* 16 (1), 73–85.

Chen, H-J. (1999) Creating a virtual language lab: An EFL experience at National Taiwan Ocean University. *ReCALL* 11 (2), 20–30.

Chun, D.M. (1994) Using computer networking to facilitate the acquisition of interactive competence. *System* 22 (1), 17–31.

Coverdale-Jones, T. (1998) Does computer-mediated conferencing really have a reduced social dimension? *ReCALL* 10 (1), 46–52.

Crabbe, D. (1999) Defining the field: introduction. In S. Cotterall, and D. Crabbe (eds) *Learner Autonomy in Language Learning: Defining the Field and Effecting Change* (pp. 3–10). Frankfurt: Peter Lang.

Crossley, N. (1996) *Intersubjectivity: The Fabric of Social Becoming*. London: Sage.

Dam, L. (1995) *Learner Autonomy 3: From Theory to Classroom Practice*. Dublin: Authentik.

Dudeney, G. (2000) *The Internet and the Language Classroom: A Practical Guide for Teachers*. Cambridge University Press: Cambridge.

Esch, E. (1996) Promoting learner autonomy: Criteria for the selection of appropriate methods. In R. Pemberton, E.S.L. Li and H.D. Pierson (eds) *Taking Control: Autonomy in Language Learning* (pp. 35–48). Hong Kong: Hong Kong University Press.

Esch, E. (1997) Learner training for autonomous language learning. In P. Benson and P. Voller (eds) *Autonomy and Independence in Language Learning* (pp. 164–76). London: Longman.

Felix, U. (1999) Exploring the web for language teaching: Selected approaches. *ReCALL* 11 (1), 30–7.

Fox, J. (1998) Breaking down the distance barriers: Perceptions and practice in technology-mediated distance language acquisition. *ReCALL* 10 (1), 15–26.

Gordon, J. (1996) Tracks for learning: Metacognition and learning technologies. *Australian Journal of Educational Technology* 12 (1), 46–55.

Herrington, J. and Oliver, R. (1997) Multimedia, magic and the way students respond to a situated learning environment. *Australian Journal of Educational Technology* 13 (2), 127–43.

Ho, J. and Crookall, D. (1995) Breaking with Chinese cultural traditions: Learner autonomy in English language teaching. *System* 23 (2), 235–44.

Holec, H. (1981) *Autonomy in Foreign Language Learning*. Oxford: Pergamon.

Husserl, E. (1991) *Cartesian Meditations*. Netherlands: Kluwer Academic Publications.

Jones, J.F (1995) Self-access and culture: Retreating from autonomy. *ELT Journal* 49 (3), 228–34.

Kojéve, A. (1967) *Introduction to the Reading of Hegel*. New York: Cornell University Press.

Little, D. (1999) Learner autonomy is more than a western cultural construct. In S. Cotterall and D. Crabbe (eds) *Learner Autonomy in Language Learning: Defining the Field and Effecting Change* (pp. 11–18). Frankfurt: Peter Lang.

Little. D. (2000) Learner autonomy and human interdependence: Some theoretical and practical consequences of a social-interactive view of cognition, learning and language. In B. Sinclair, I. McGrath and T. Lamb. (eds) *Learner Autonomy, Teacher Autonomy: Future Directions* (pp. 15–23). London: Longman.

Littlewood, W.T. (1997) Self-access: Why do want it and what can it do? In P. Benson and P. Voller (eds) *Autonomy and Independence in Language Learning* (pp. 79–92). London: Longman.

Martyn, E. (1994) Self-access logs: Promoting self-directed learning. In D. Gardner, and L. Miller (eds) *Directions in Self-Access Language Learning* (pp. 65–78). Hong Kong: Hong Kong University Press.

Mead, G.H. (1967) *Mind, Self and Society*. Chicago: Chicago University Press.

Merleau-Ponty. M. (1962) *The Phenomenology of Perception*. London: Routledge.

Motteram, G. (1997) Learner autonomy and the web. In V. Darleguy, A. Ding and M. Svensson (eds) *Educational Technology in Language Learning: Theoretical Considerations and Practical Applications* (pp. 17–24). Lyon: INSA National Institute of Applied Sciences.

Nunan, D. (1997) Designing and adapting materials to encourage learner autonomy. In P. Benson and P. Voller (eds) *Autonomy and Independence in Language Learning* (pp. 192–203). London: Longman.

Oakey, D. (2000) An EAP module via the Merlin internet learning environment. In P. Howarth and R. Herington (eds) *EAP Learning Technologies* (pp. 115–28). Leeds: Leeds University Press.

Or, W.W.F. (1994) Helping learners plan and prepare for self-access learning. In D. Gardner and L. Miller (eds) *Directions in Self-Access Language Learning* (pp. 45–58). Hong Kong: Hong Kong University Press.

Orsini-Jones, M. (1999) Implementing institutional change for languages: Online collaborative learning environments at Coventry University. *ReCALL* 11 (2), 61–73.

Ortega, L. (1997) Processes and outcomes in networked classroom interaction: Defining the research agenda for L2 computer-assisted classroom discussion. *Language Learning & Technology* 1 (1), 82–93.

Pellettieri, J. (2000) Negotiation in cyberspace: The role of chatting in the development of grammatical competence. In M. Warschauer and R. Kern (eds) _Network-based Language Teaching: Concepts and Practice_ (pp. 59–86). Cambridge: Cambridge University Press.

Pemberton, R. (1996) Introduction. In R. Pemberton, E.S.L. Li and H.D. Pierson (eds) _Taking Control: Autonomy in Language Learning_ (pp. 1–8). Hong Kong: Hong Kong University Press.

Ragoonaden, K. and Bordeleau, P. (2000) Collaborative learning via the internet. _Educational Technology & Society_ 3 (3), Online document: http://ifets.ieee.org/periodical/vol_3_2000/d11.html.

Schultz, J. M. (2000) Computers and collaborative writing in the foreign language curriculum. In M. Warschauer and R. Kern (eds) _Network-based Language Teaching: Concepts and Practice_ (pp. 121–50). Cambridge: Cambridge University Press.

Schwienhorst, K. (1998) The 'third place' – virtual reality applications for second language learning. _ReCALL_ 10 (1), 118–26.

Sheerin, S. (1997) An exploration of the relationship between self-access and independent learning. In P. Benson and P. Voller (eds) _Autonomy and Independence in Language Learning_ (pp. 54–65). London: Longman.

Sinclair, B. (1996) Materials design for the promotion of learner autonomy: How explicit is explicit? In R. Pemberton, E. S. L. Li and H. D. Pierson (eds) _Taking Control: Autonomy in Language Learning_ (pp. 149–166). Hong Kong: Hong Kong University Press.

Sinclair, B. (2000) Learner autonomy: The next phase? In B. Sinclair, I. McGrath and T. Lamb (eds) _Learner Autonomy, Teacher Autonomy: Future Directions_ (pp. 4–14). London: Longman.

Söntgens, K. (1999) Language learning via e-mail – autonomy through collaboration. In _Proceedings of the Computer Support for Collaborative Learning (CSCL) 1999 Conference_, C. Hoadley and J. Roschelle (eds) Stanford University, Palo Alto, California. Mahwah, NJ: Lawrence Erlbaum.

Thomson, C.K. (1996) Self-assessment in self-directed learning: Issues of learner diversity. In R. Pemberton, E.S.L. Li and H.D. Pierson (eds) _Taking Control: Autonomy in Language Learning_ (pp. 77–91). Hong Kong: Hong Kong University Press.

Tudor, I. (1996) _Learner-centredness as Language Education_. Cambridge: Cambridge University Press.

Victori, M. and Lockhart, W. (1995) Enhancing metacognition in self-directed language learning. _System_ 23 (2), 223–34.

Warschauer, M. (1997) Computer-mediated collaborative learning: Theory and practice. _Modern Language Journal_ 81, 470–81.

Warschauer, M. and Kern, R. (eds) (2000) _Network-based Language Teaching: Concepts and Practice_. Cambridge: Cambridge University Press.

Windeatt, S., Hardisty, D. and Eastment, D. (2000) _The Internet_. Oxford: Oxford University Press.

Wolff, D. (1997) The use of e-mail in foreign language teaching. In V. Darleguy, A. Ding and M. Svensson (eds) _Educational Technology in Language Learning: Theoretical Considerations and Practical Applications_ (pp. 136–45). Lyon: National Institute of Applied Sciences.

Chapter 4

Towards a Learner-based Theory of Distance Language Learning: The Concept of the Learner–Context Interface

CYNTHIA WHITE

Introduction

The developments in new technologies, the emergence of virtual learning environments and the demand for lifelong flexible learning opportunities have given rise to a marked increase in language learning through distance education – both in terms of new providers and new participants. While at one time distance education struggled for recognition, the viability of distance environments for language learning is now well established. A number of important avenues for research into distance language learning have been pursued, focusing on such issues as the development of interactive competence (Kötter, 2001), knowledge gain of distance language learners (Baumann & Shelley, 2003), social presence in mediated learning environments (Tammelin, 1999), and learner strategies (White, 1995, 1997). More recently a number of research projects relating to distance language learning in specific contexts have been documented (see for example Catterick, 2001; Curtis *et al.*, 1999; Fox, 1998; Garing, 2002; Grosse, 2001; Hauck & Haezewindt, 1999). These have played an important role in contributing to the professional background of language teachers and knowledge development within the field. What is still lacking, however, is a central theoretical framework to inform both research and practice in the broad range of contexts and experiences for distance language learning.

The need for further theory building reflects the wider situation within the field of distance education as a whole and is a recurrent theme in recent writings (Chu, 1999; Garrison, 2000; McIsaac & Gunawardena, 1996). The situation is all the more acute since innovations in technology and practice have outstripped theory development in distance learning. As a result, the use of technology in learning environments has tended to be technology-led rather than theory-led (Ravenscroft, 2001). At the same time, a degree of conceptual confusion exists 'with the advent of new technology (virtual, open, distributed and distance education), new technologies, new programme demands, new audiences, and new commercially competitive providers' (Garrison, 2000: 1). The absence of a central theoretical framework limits the extent to which it is possible to inform, explain and shape new practices, and its existence would contribute to research and debate concerning virtual learning environments in the larger educational community.

Theory development is well advanced within the field of second language learning: in recent years the focus has been on such areas as the role of input and interaction, cognitive approaches to second language learning and socio-cultural perspectives informed in the main by research carried out in face-to-face classrooms. Important contributions to the mainstream literature on second language learning have been made by distance education researchers mainly in relation to learner autonomy (e.g. Hurd *et al.*, 2001), online critical reflection (e.g. Lamy & Goodfellow, 1999) and the development of learner beliefs (e.g. White, 1999). However, these contributions remain limited and there has been relatively little theory building in relation to distance language learning. This chapter first aims to trace the evolution of different theories within distance education, and then to propose a learner-based theory of distance language learning that centres on the notion of the learner-context interface.

Evolution of Theory in Distance Education

The earliest form of theory development involved attempts to define the important and unique attributes of distance education as part of a wider search for recognition and credibility for what was a less conventional form of learning. McIsaac and Gunawardena (1996) identified the following three key contributions: the distance learner is someone:

- who is physically separated from the teacher (Rumble, 1986);
- who has a planned and guided learning experience (Holmberg, 1986);
- who participates in a two-way structured form of education distinct from the traditional form of classroom instruction (Keegan, 1988).

The limitations of a specific focus on issues of definition were recognised as attempts to articulate a theory were being made. The following extract from Keegan (1983: 3) reflects this position:

A theory is something that eventually can be reduced to a phrase, a sentence or a paragraph and which, while subsuming all the practical research, gives the foundation on which the structures of need, purpose and administration can be erected. A firmly based theory of distance education will be one which can provide the touchstone against which decisions – political, financial, educational, social – when they have to be taken, can be taken with confidence. This would replace the *ad hoc* response to a set of conditions that arises in some 'crisis' situation of problem solving, which normally characterizes this field of education.

Four of the most influential theories – to be found in the work of Holmberg, Moore, Peters, and Garrison – are reviewed here. While distinctions can be drawn between distance education and distance learning – with distance learning perceived as a more learner-centred term – for the purposes of this chapter they can be considered as synonyms.

Holmberg: The conversational model of distance education

Börje Holmberg, a pioneering theorist in distance education and in distance language learning (Holmberg, 1986, 1989a, 1989b), developed a philosophy that was influenced by humanism and andragogical theory. He called for theory development to focus on the notions of independence, learning and teaching (Holmberg, 1989a), and argued that distance learners should be *helped* to achieve independence. While learner independence was seen as a key characteristic of distance education, Holmberg challenged the position adopted by many distance institutions that 'base their work on the assumed prevalence of students' capacity to work independently' (Holmberg, 1986: 88). Holmberg placed his view of learner independence within a context of ongoing conversation between the teacher and the learner, underpinned by various support mechanisms. Independence is seen as an ideal that needs to be deliberately fostered by the institution through support that should be present in, and central to all forms of provision.

The emphasis in his work is on the content and conversational character of course materials as a means of fostering learner independence. He argues that *guided pedagogic conversation* can be fostered by well-developed self-instructional materials; it is the responsibility of the course developer to create a simulated conversation with the learner through the materials. Holmberg's theory drew attention to the importance of learner support and encouragement within clearly organised instructional programmes. He was the first theorist to focus on the importance of interpersonal aspects within distance education, and the role of empathy as an essential ingredient in teacher-learner interactions (Holmberg, 1986, 1989a). The teaching style of distance education should, he argued, be informed by an empathetic approach on the part of the teacher to the context, situation and characteristics of each student. The guided conversational model of distance education and the importance of an empathetic approach have informed many of the innovations in course design and in teacher-learner interactions.

Moore: Transactional distance theory

Michael Moore's theory of transactional distance, introduced in the early 1970s, marked one of the earliest moves away from a concern with the physical separation of the teacher and the learner. He focused on the nature of 'distance' within distance education, and its effect on the teaching-learning relationship; transactional distance refers to the communicative and psychological distance between learners and teachers – and this is seen as more significant than the physical separation of teacher and learner. Transactional distance is a function of two variables: dialogue (purposeful, constructive interaction, valued by each party, towards improved understanding), and structure (the rigidity or flexibility of course objectives, strategies and forms of evaluation or assessment). In any teaching-learning relationship, the degree of transactional distance depends on whether students are left alone with their materials or whether they can communicate with their teacher (dialogue), and on the degree to which the programme is pre-planned and prescribed (structure).

Moore also related transactional distance to the dimension of learner autonomy (Moore, 1993; Moore & Kearsley, 1996), arguing that autonomy may be enhanced by both high and low transactional distance, depending on the preferences of the learner. According to Moore's view, learner autonomy is at its greatest when learners determine their own aims, and learning paths, and where they are not restricted when learning either by dialogue or a prescribed structure. Moore also argued that the autonomous learner is in no way 'an intellectual Robinson Crusoe' (Moore, 1972: 81), but someone who is constantly challenged to adapt to influences within his/her learning environment. In an editorial written in 1994 entitled 'Autonomy and Interdependence' Moore emphasised the importance of the educational transaction between the learner and the teacher within distance education, as a means of developing individual autonomy:

> Distance educators still face the important challenge of engaging with individual students in ways that build on and develop personal learning autonomy . . . Equally exciting is the process of developing

and engaging interdependence among individuals in distant groups, developing group interdependence within a total system, and developing distant-group autonomy. (Moore, 1994: 2)

Moore's comments reflect a shift in the debate on autonomy towards a focus on educational relationships. In his view, autonomy is part of the potential for distance education to be both personalised and to encompass many forms of interdependence (tutor-learner, learner-learner, learner-learning group).

Peters: The industrial model of distance education

Otto Peters' main theoretical contribution was the representation of distance education as an industrialised form of teaching and learning (see, for example, Peters, 1967, 1989). Here he emphasised that distance education was characterised by the division of labour and the development of instructional units that could be mass produced and distributed with standardised delivery, thus achieving economies of scale. Distance education processes were conceptualised, developed, delivered and supported by an entire team of specialists; the end product was an educated student. This was thought by some to be a controversial and somewhat reductionist view of distance education, essentially limited in that it did not address important issues relating to communication and interaction within educational experiences. A number of critical evaluations and responses to this theory have been advanced, showing how the advantages of these structures, from the point of view of educational policy and organization, are also connected with important educational disadvantages. Garrison (2000), for example, noted the theory was not a theory of teaching or learning, but an insightful contribution to ideas about the organisation of distance education. The focus on structural and organisational issues within distance education has had a major impact on further research and theory and the way distance education is conceptualised.

Peters subsequently addressed the issue of the role of distance education in post-industrial society (Peters, 1993, 1998, 2000). He has argued that distance education is in line with post-industrial tendencies in terms of the dislocation from the classroom, self-direction, social interactions among students, and has an affinity with electronic media. According to this view the dominating goal in education will be self-realisation, and autonomous groups will become the main constituent of the learning process. Peters extended this argument when he envisaged all universities would be transformed into institutions of self-study and distance teaching (Peters, 2000) in response to the possibilities offered by the new technologies and the demands of lifelong learning.

Garrison: The theory of collaborative control

The theory of control put forward by Garrison and Baynton (1987) challenged the conception and practice of distance education as a private form
of learning based on self-instructional texts. An excessive concern with
independence as a desirable goal for distance education, it was argued, has
seldom been balanced against a concern for support and recognition of the
demands placed on the learner. Garrison's approach reflected an emerging
emphasis on direct communication between teachers and students, and
interaction between groups of learners and the teacher. Interaction is the
means by which control is developed and maintained by the learner.
Control does not require a form of self-reliance that excludes all external
interaction and resources. Rather, through communication the learner and
the teacher can negotiate the degree of control each has over the learning
process; control is essentially collaborative, in that it is dependent on both
the teacher and the learner, though it exists separately from either of them:

> Control is not transferred automatically to a student solely by giving
> freedom of choice as to time and place of learning without consider-
> ation of the student's abilities and resources. Control is *negotiated*
> continuously through sustained interaction. (Garrison, 1989: 33)

The aim of this communication is to enable the learner to negotiate and
develop control through ongoing collaboration.

The theoretical work of Garrison and his co-researchers marked a watershed
in the field. It moved away from a concern with organisational issues to what
Garrison (2000) called 'transactional issues' relating to sustained interactions
at a distance which take place within a community of learners. The theoretical
work of Garrison also addressed the relationship between the development of
theory and different paradigms of distance education. He (1997) noted that
alongside the dominant paradigm in distance education that has emphasised
independent learning carried out principally through self-instructional
materials, there is what can be called an emerging paradigm of distance
education. This paradigm places much greater emphasis on interaction and
the construction of knowledge, and is aligned with constructivist approaches
within distance education. Given that in reality programmes of study frequently incorporate elements from both paradigms of distance education, the
challenge for theory is to encompass the range of practices developing in the
wide variety of contexts that exist for distance education.

Developing a Theory of Distance Language Learning

Generating theories about distance education necessitates critical evaluation of the basis for theory development. In any search for a theory, a

number of fundamental questions arise about the phenomenon under study, including: What is the reality of distance language learning? Where and how do we investigate it? Is it based on concerns located within the institution and with the teaching staff, or is it a complex, individual, unique phenomenon? How do we gain access to the process?

The essential components of distance learning identified in early theories – namely the physical separation of the teacher from the learner, and of the learner from the learning group, with interpersonal communication mediated by technology – represent a focus on structural and systems-based concerns as the defining hallmarks of distance learning. When wider perspectives are acknowledged, these theoretical explanations appear essentially limited since the students' attitudes to and involvement in the distance learning process have largely been overlooked. In addition, in earlier theories the influence of the individual contexts in which the learning takes place did not figure as a significant variable. Of course, a more contextualised approach to understanding distance language learning is difficult to develop and research since many aspects of the learning context are remote and individual.

A distinction drawn by Tudor (2001) between ecological perspectives and technological perspectives on language learning is useful here. A technological perspective focuses on potentialities, and is based on the idea that the technology of language teaching will 'lead in a neat, deterministic manner to a predictable set of learning outcomes' (Tudor, 2001: 9); it tends to be positivist in orientation. Ecological perspectives, on the other hand, look at language teaching within the totality of the lives of the participants involved, and focus on the realities of language learning as they are lived out in particular contexts. Such a perspective does not assume 'that the effects of educational technology can be predicted confidently from the inner logic of the technology alone, as this inner logic inevitably interacts with the perceptions and goals of those involved in using it' (2001: 9). The ecological/technological distinction is particularly relevant to research into distance language learning where the focus has tended to be on the setting up of systems, since projects are developed on a technology driven basis. With the possibilities offered by the new learning environments, interest has also tended to focus on course development rather than the complexities associated with ongoing, sustained course delivery. Much less research and commentary has been provided focusing on actual learner needs and responses to the new learning environments, and how learning can proceed within these systems.

Part of the critical evaluation of the basis for theory development in distance language learning also involves an acknowledgement of the limitations associated with an approach in which the researcher adopts an 'outside-in' perspective. White (2003) argues that since any understanding of distance education is rooted in experience and our interpretations of experience, it remains partial, not absolute: the learner's experience is different from the teacher's, and the researcher's contribution also reflects his/her particular perspectives. To develop a more complete understanding of the nature of distance learning, we need to explore different conceptions of the phenomenon. This argument for a more inclusive approach to understanding distance education is not new. Harris (1987), for example, contended that the individual student in distance systems tends to be seen in rather abstract terms, which was influential in highlighting the need to investigate learner understandings of their experience of distance learning. Jegede (1992) extended this argument by suggesting that the different views of distance education held by researchers, administrators, teachers, and students foreground the need for more information in the practice of distance education from different perspectives.

In this chapter I focus on the insider's perspective, that is the learner's perspective, experience and articulation of experience as the starting point for a complementary theory of distance language learning: a user-based perspective of what distance language learning means and what characterises it. Developing a learner-derived theory of distance language learning is particularly appropriate since we know relatively little about the reality of distance language learning from the point of view of those who are most involved, the learners. The importance of insider insights within this overall approach is that it brings us closer to the experience of distance language learning and how it is conceptualised by learners. Such a theory would include the kinds of requirements for any theory of language learning, which are identified by Mitchell and Myles (1998: 2–3) as:

> a *theory* is a more or less abstract set of claims about the units that are significant within the phenomenon under study, the relationships that exist between them, and the processes that bring about change . . . Theories may be embryonic and restricted in scope, or more elaborate, explicit and comprehensive.

The theory I propose here is embryonic, and derived from learner conceptualisations of the process of distance language learning; it is further informed by teachers' perspectives on distance language learning and by research findings (see White, 2003). It is aligned with an ecological approach to distance language learning that focuses on the perspectives of participants – how they perceive the distance learning process, the affordances within their learning context (that is, the opportunities as well as constraints, basically what the context affords them), and their role and identity within it.

The Learner-context Interface Theory

The learner-context interface theory is derived from a detailed, longitudinal five-phase study that investigated the conceptions developed by students in relation to distance language learning. For details of the study see White (1999, 2003). Students conceptualised distance language learning as based around the development of an interface that each learner constructs as s/he interacts with the learning context, and that informs future learning. This view formed the basis for the theory. Distance language learning is seen as an individual process in which learners develop and assume control of a personally meaningful and effective interface between themselves and the learning context. The learner-context interface theory is based on the premise that a meaningful theory of distance language learning must view the contribution of the learning context and the contribution of the learner as integral and reciprocal constructs. The importance of developing the learner-context interface that can inform and guide learning experiences is underlined in a number of studies: the research of Barty (1999) and Harris (1995) carried out in diverse contexts for distance language learning provide just two examples.

Karin Barty (1999) worked with high school students of German in a distance programme and noted the extent to which those students were reliant on the mediating role of the teacher to orient them to undertaking language tasks, and to help them respond to the requirements of the learning context. The fact that they were provided with a rich learning environment with many opportunities for interaction did not mean the students were willing or able to take advantage of the learning opportunities. More specifically, Barty observed that the presence of the teacher had a direct influence on the complexity of the target language material they could access: 'students often reported not understanding what the material was about whereas in linked sessions, with teacher guidance, the same material did not seem especially difficult' (Barty, 1999: 30). Affective elements were important too: students reported they felt 'overwhelmed' and 'uncertain' when working online with no teacher there to structure the session, offer guidance, advice and support. Four months into the course Barty observed that students had made considerable adjustments to the course-learning environment: they initiated questions, were positive about continuing on the online course and were more proficient at managing their learning. These adjustments can be seen as catering to the development of an interface with the learning context that made it possible for the students to participate in the learning opportunities while taking a more independent role as distance learners.

Claire Harris (1995) carried out detailed research with distance learners of English in the Adult Migrant English Programme in Australia, focusing on issues of study inhibition, progression and persistence. The course provided high levels of support, and learners reported a positive response to the materials, but only half completed the course. Harris found those who managed to remain motivated were able to match features within the course with their own self-supporting strategies. More specifically, they were able to match the level of the course, the learning sources within the course and the teacher support with their own learning strategies and needs, and the learning environment they created in their homes. They actively created for themselves a study-nurturing environment – which they saw as similar to the learning environment a teacher would develop within a face-to-face language class. This self-supporting strategy was a crucial element in maintaining study impetus. It is another expression of the importance of the individual distance learner's capacity to establish and maintain an effective interface with the learning context.

In both these cases it was essential for distance language learners to develop an effective interface with what was, initially at least, a new, and relatively inert learning context. We see a pattern of individual learners engaging with the learning context – with teacher support – in an attempt to create or alter an external environment for learning. Learners who are studying at a distance need to be able to develop an interface that will guide their learning, in accordance with their personal characteristics and the affordances of the learning context.

Dimensions of the theory

To return to the Mitchell and Myles (1998) definition of a theory, it is important to ask: What are the 'key units' in the theory of distance language learning? Essentially the theory has three dimensions: the *learner*, the *context* and the *interface* established between each learner and their individual context(s). These are represented in Figure 4.1.

To illustrate features of the theory I have included reports given by learners in the longitudinal study reported by White (1999, 2003).

The *learner* dimension includes individual attributes, conceptualisations, affects, skills and needs, all of which influence how each learner approaches, interprets and experiences distance language learning. Learner factors – including beliefs, motivation, affect – have a bearing on how learners interpret, relate and respond to the learning context and the kind of interface they are able to construct with the learning context. That interface, and how they act at the interface, in turn influences individual learner attributes and affects and the kind of identity s/he develops as a distance language learner. The following comment is from a learner of Spanish after eight weeks experience of distance language learning:

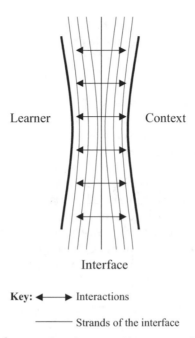

Figure 4.1 Model of the interface between learner and context (White, 2003: 91)

> Now I have begun to work more with the video – I relate a lot of what I learn now to the video. It has made me focus more on speaking and I feel more confident than before. I use it in different ways and now the speaking is driving my learning. This has been quite a breakthrough for me.

The learner is thus seen as a dynamic individual who both constructs an interface with the distance learning context and who changes in response to the ongoing learning experiences which take place at that interface.

The context dimension comprises the features of the distance language course (e.g. resources, course work and assessment, and opportunities for interaction, support, and learner control), access to other target language sources, and features of the different sites in which learning is carried out. Context includes more than the externally observable features of the course or the learning sites within which they operate; it includes the affordances and constraints to which individual learners perceive and respond in different ways. This report is from the same learner in Week 8:

> I now see how useful the video is. At the start I couldn't really see how the video could fit in with the way I work. It was there and I used it a bit

but it did not really figure as very important for me. Now it is quite central – that and the assessment tasks are really important for me. It is hard for me to get access to the VCR at home – so I get up early and work on the video.

The *interface* is an abstract notion that can be defined both as the place at which and the means whereby learner and context meet and affect each other. The interface is developed as the learner interacts with the learning context, and develops awareness of his/her own requirements, abilities, preferred means of working and so on. The interface is *constructed* – it does not merely represent the overlap between learner attributes and the affordances of the learning context. The quality and effectiveness of the interface developed by each learner then inform each future language learning experience – both in the way in which the individual learner perceives, engages with and respond to that experience, and the way it contributes to the nature and structure of the interface. The following is from a learner of Japanese in Week 5:

I have built up a way of studying over the past 5 weeks – it has taken a lot of time and effort. Getting an idea of how best to study, and seeing what works slowed me down a lot at the start. Now I know how to work with the materials – and I guess that may change as the language gets more difficult, and as I learn a lot more about what works best. I'm looking forward to checking things out at the contact course – I'll get some idea of how I'm going, and I might need to change things a bit.

The interface is thus a coordinating concept; it is not conceived as a static phenomenon, but as the result of the interplay between personal and contextual influences. The notion of the interface is central to the theory that reflects a belief in the primacy of the unique dynamic established between the learner and the context in the process of distance language learning.

Purposes of the interface

The development of the interface serves three broad purposes. First it serves to inform the construction of a learning environment in accordance with the needs, preferences and abilities of the learner, and in response to the affordances of the learning context. In the distance context the learner must take responsibility for this process, since the teacher is by and large remote from the site of much of the learning. Construction of the learning environment requires an ability to identify, select and incorporate meaningful learning experiences into one's learning environment, which meet one's particular learning needs. This involves a degree of self-awareness on the part of the learner, and an awareness of the affordances and requirements of the context, as well as the ability to match those two dimensions.

Second, the construction of the interface is related to the development of metacognitive knowledge and beliefs. The construction requires learners to draw on their metacognitive knowledge and skills, which they identify as relevant to the context and experience of distance language learning. As learners identify, select and engage with opportunities for interaction in the distance learning context – including learner-content interaction – those same interactions contribute to the development of the interface and enhance metacognition. When the interface is established and working effectively for an individual learner, external activities within the learning context and the internal reflective dimension are fused, and each supports the other.

Third, the construction of the interface is the means by which learners adjust and adapt themselves to new roles and develop an identity as a distance language learner. As part of this process, it is necessary to establish congruence between individual attributes, the distance learning context, and one's social, personal and work environment. Some learners may struggle to establish a viable interface between themselves and the learning context. A number of barriers – situational, practical or academic – may affect the degree of engagement and involvement in the distance learning environment, both of which are necessary to develop an effective interface.

A dynamic view of the learner

While the idea of the learner being active is not new, the idea of the learner as constructing an interface with the learning context that is then used to inform and develop further learning experiences is new. Learners both construct and operate at the learner-context interface, according to their own needs, preferences and beliefs, and also in response to the demands and requirements of the learning context. The demands and requirements of the distance learning context may be implicit, as in the need to assume more control for their learning than they have previously been used to; they may also be *explicit* as in assessment tasks, or requirements for participation in virtual environments. They are also influenced by the affordances of the particular learning environment.

The learner-context interface theory is aligned with constructivism in that it is based on the idea that each learner makes his/her own personal sense of the learning context and of tasks within that context, based on the kind of interface s/he has managed to construct with the context. Each learner is active in constructing an interface with the context that both informs and develops in response to the experiences undertaken by the learner.

Further questions

One way in which the development of theory in distance language learning can be advanced is to pose questions, which may also be a starting point for further research. Important questions to ask of the learner-context interface theory include:

- How can the theoretical framework guide research in distance language learning?
- What areas of further enquiry are revealed by the theory?
- How does the theory fit with current realities of distance language learning?
- How do learners experience the construction of the interface?
- How does the theory fit with current concerns within the field?
- Which factors facilitate or inhibit the development of the interface?
- What are the implications of the theory for research and practice?
- What challenges to the theory can be identified?
- What are the limitations of the theory?

Providing answers to these questions is beyond the scope of this chapter, but the questions themselves suggest a number of ways forward for developing and critically evaluating this learner-derived theory of distance language learning.

Conclusion

Distance language learning contexts make demands of a different order on learners. The learner-context interface theory presented here is concerned with how learners establish their learning environment and negotiate meaning and come to new understandings in the distance context. It points to the fact that distance language learning is a highly complex endeavour requiring the learner to develop an interface with the learning context that can both guide and be informed by meaningful learning experiences that in fact become the substance of the course for each individual learner. It places the relationship between the learner and the learning context at the centre of the process of distance language learning. The theory challenges the notion that the learning context is identical for each learner and that it is a fixed entity. Similarly 'the course' is realised differently by each learner and changes according to the interface developed by the individual learner. The concept of the interface also emphasises the importance of the relationship and interaction between learner and learning context in the process of distance language learning. The aim of this chapter has been to provide a starting point for theory construction in the field – I look forward to further frameworks that will guide us in understanding the essentials of distance language learning.

References

Barty, K. (1999) Developing an understanding of on-line course provision for secondary students. *Open, Flexible and Distance Learning: Challenges of the New Millennium. 14th Biennial Forum of the Open and Distance Learning Association of Australia, Deakin University 27–30 September 1999* (pp. 28–33). Deakin: Deakin University Press.

Baumann, U. and Shelley, M.A. (2003) Adult learners of German at the Open University: their knowledge of, and attitudes towards Germany. *Open Learning* 18 (1), 61–74.

Catterick, D. (2001) An academic writing course in cyberspace. In L.E. Henrichsen (ed.) *Distance-learning Programs* (pp. 83–94). Alexandria, Virginia: TESOL.

Chu, C.T. (1999) The development of interactive distance learning in Taiwan: Challenges and prospects. *Educational Media International: Journal of the International Council for Educational Media* 36 (2), 110–14.

Curtis, S.A., Duchastel, J. and Radic, N. (1999) Proposal for an online language course. *ReCALL* 11 (2), 38–45.

Fox, M. (1998) Breaking down the barriers: Perceptions and practice in technology-mediated distance language acquisition. *ReCALL* 10 (1), 59–67.

Garing, P. (2002) Adapting and developing e-learning courses: The challenge of keeping the quality. *Conference Proceedings DEANZ April 2002. Evolving e-learning* (pp. 77–85). Wellington: New Zealand.

Garrison, D.R. (1989) *Understanding Distance Education: A Framework for the Future.* London: Routledge.

Garrison, D.R. (1997) Computer conferencing: The post-industrial age of distance education. *Open Learning* 12 (2), 3–11.

Garrison, D.R. (2000) Theoretical challenges for distance education in the 21st century: A shift from structural to transactional issues. *International Review of Research in Open and Distance Learning* 1 (1) – Online document: http://www.irrodl.org

Garrison, D.R. and Baynton, M. (1987) Beyond independence in distance education: The concept of control. *The American Journal of Distance Education* 1 (3), 3–15.

Grosse, C.U. (2001) 'Show the Baby', the Wave, and 1,000 thanks: Three reasons to teach via satellite television and the Internet. In L.E. Henrichsen (ed.) *Distance-learning Programs* (pp. 39–50). Alexandria, Virginia: TESOL.

Harris, C. (1995) 'What do the learners think?': A study of how *It's Over To You* learners define successful learning at a distance. In S. Gollin (ed.) *Language in Distance Education. How Far Can We Go?* Proceedings of the NCELTR Conference Sydney: NCELTR

Harris, D. (1987) *Openness and Closure in Distance Education.* Lewes: Falmer Press.

Hauck, M. and Haezewindt, B. (1999) Adding a new perspective to distance language learning and teaching – the tutor's perspective. *ReCALL* 11 (2), 46–54.

Holmberg, B. (1986) *Growth and Structure of Distance Education.* London: Croom Helm.

Holmberg, B. (1989a) *Theory and Practice of Distance Education.* London: Routledge.

Holmberg, B. (1989b) *Distance Teaching of Modern Languages.* Hagen, Germany: Zentrales Institut für Fernstudienforschung, Fern Universität.

Hurd, S., Beaven, T. and Ortega, A. (2001) Developing autonomy in a distance language learning context: issues and dilemmas for course writers. *System* 29 (3), 341–55.

Jegede, O.J. (1992) Constructivist epistemology and its implications for contemporary research in distance education. In T. Evans and P. Juler (eds) *Research in Distance Education Vol. 2* (pp. 21–129). Geelong: Deakin University Press.

Keegan, D. (1983) *Six Distance Education Theorists.* ZIFF. Hagen, Germany: Zentrales Institut für Fernstudienforschung Fern Universität.

Keegan, D. (1988) Problems in defining the field of distance education. *American Journal of Distance Education* 2 (2), 4–11.

Kötter, M. (2001) Developing distance learners' interactive competence – can synchronous audio do the trick? *International Journal of Educational Telecommunications* 7 (4), 327–53.

Lamy, M.-N. and Goodfellow, R. (1999) 'Reflective conversation' in the virtual language classroom. *Language Learning and Technology* 2 (2), 43–61.

McIsaac, M.S. and Gunawardena, C.N. (1996) Distance education. In D. Jonassen (ed.) *Handbook for Research on Educational Communications and Technology* (pp. 403–37). New York: Scholastic Press.

Mitchell, R. and Myles, F. (1998) *Second Language Learning Theories.* London: Arnold.

Moore, M.G. (1972) Learner autonomy: The second dimension of independent learning. *Convergence* Fall, 76–88.

Moore, M.G. (1993) Theory of transactional distance. In D. Keegan (ed.) *Theoretical Principles of Distance Education* (pp. 22–38). New York: Routledge.

Moore, M.G. (1994) Autonomy and interdependence. *The American Journal of Distance Education* 8 (2), 1–4.

Moore, M. and Kearsley, G. (1996) *Distance Education: A Systems View.* Wadsworth: California.

Peters, O. (1967) Distance education and industrial production: A comparative interpretation in outline. In D. Keegan (ed.) *Otto Peters on Distance Education. The Industrialization of Teaching and Learning* (pp. 107–27). London: Routledge Studies in Distance Education.

Peters, O. (1989) The iceberg has not melted: Further reflections on the concept of industrialisation and distance teaching. *Open Learning* 4 (3), 3–8.

Peters, O. (1993) Distance education in a post-industrial society. In D. Keegan (ed.) *Theoretical Principles of Distance Education* (pp. 220–40). London and New York: Routledge.

Peters, O. (1998) *Learning and Teaching in Distance Education. Analyses and Interpretations from an International Perspective.* London: Kogan Page.

Peters, O. (2000) The transformation of the university into an institution of higher learning. In T. Evans and S. Nation (eds) *Changing University Teaching: Reflections on Creating Educational Technologies* (pp. 10–23). London: Kogan Page.

Ravenscroft, A. (2001) Designing E-learning Interactions in the 21st century: Revisiting and rethinking the role of theory. *European Journal of Education* 36 (2), 133–56.

Rumble, G. (1986) *The Planning and Management of Distance Education.* London: Croom Helm.

Tammelin, M. (1999) . In T. Nikko and P. Nuolijärvi (eds). Talous ja kieli III. Seminaari 9–10.5.1996. Helsingin kauppakorkeakoulu. *Helsingin kauppakorkeakoulun julkaisuja* B–17, 57–70.

Tudor, I. (2001) *The Dynamics of the Language Classroom*. Cambridge: Cambridge University Press.

White, C. (1995) Autonomy and strategy use in distance foreign language learning: Research findings. In A. Wenden and L. Dickinson (eds) *System Special Issue on Autonomy* 23 (2), 207–21.

White, C. (1997) Effects of mode of study on foreign language learning. *Distance Education* 18 (1), 178–96.

White, C. (1999) Expectations and emergent beliefs of self-instructed language learners. In *Metacognitive Knowledge and Beliefs in Language Learning. System Special Issue* 27 (4), 443–57.

White, C. (2003) *Language Learning in Distance Education*. Cambridge: Cambridge University Press.

Chapter 5

Feedback in Distance Language Learning: Current Practices and New Directions

CRISTINA ROS I SOLÉ and MIKE TRUMAN

Introduction

Historically, the correction of faults in students' work and the provision of feedback have tended to be regarded as discrete processes. In the past, researchers have concentrated mainly on the nature of faults[1] and how to correct them (Corder, 1967, 1971); it is only recently that feedback and the interaction between student and teacher during the correction process have been studied more systematically and in greater depth (Anson, 2000; Straub, 2000). Attention has gradually turned from the fault itself to the players in the process, namely teachers and students (Fernández-Toro and Jones, 2001; Hyland, 2001; Kubota, 2001; Leki, 1990). Moreover, given the central role that feedback plays in the development of learner autonomy in general (White, 1999) and, more specifically, in the area of distance learning in languages, it is surprising that the number of studies devoted to this topic is so small (Hyland, 2001; Kubota, 2001; Macdonald, 2001).

The debate on how faults should be corrected has also changed over time, concentrating to an ever-greater extent on the context in which these corrections take place. Accordingly, interest in teachers' and students' beliefs about what form feedback should take and how learners should react has been growing (Hyland, 2001). Teachers and students alike are conditioned by their expectations of learning, their experience of language learning and the institutions in which they work or study, whether in the classroom situation (Anson, 2000; Straub, 2000), or the distance education context (Thorpe, 1998). It is important, then, to investigate the perceptions and experiences of both groups to identify which types of learning can be encouraged by corrections and feedback. To do this, we must first consider the different approaches that may be adopted.

72

It is increasingly recognised that students' active involvement in the learning process is beneficial. This implies the sort of teacher–learner dialogue that features so prominently in good classroom teaching. In distance education much of this teacher–learner interaction takes place when tutors provide students with feedback on assignments. In this context, however, more emphasis has tended to be placed on what to correct rather than the roles tutors and learners play in the process. This new focus on dialogue and on greater collaboration between learners and teachers reflects a radical shift in perceptions of how students learn, and of how the learning process and its outcomes can be influenced by the ways in which tutors and students interact through feedback. In this article we shall consider how these changing perceptions have affected practice in distance education by examining students' and teachers' views of this process, as well as the factors that have special relevance in this context. We will then discuss whether the more learner-centred approaches to feedback advocated by various researchers and practitioners can be applied to distance education. First of all, however, we must clarify some of the terminology. In this chapter we use *feedback* as a generic term that embraces three types of tutor intervention:

- the *correction* of faults in students' work;
- the *specific feedback* or guidance provided on particular faults or problems and their correction;
- *commentaries*, which are any general advice designed to help learners improve their overall linguistic performance or their ability to handle certain types of assessments. They may also deal with faults, but at a more general level, focusing on the actions students must take to eliminate certain broad categories of fault, suggesting follow-up or remedial work, sources of information, learning strategies, and so on.

Many of the examples in this chapter are drawn from our own experience at the Open University in the United Kingdom (OU), so to contextualise them we shall start by describing this institution's assessment policies and practices.

The Open University Context

The OU distance education programmes in languages attract large numbers of students, who are generally not specialist linguists, and who are interested in learning a language for personal or vocational purposes. OU-produced course materials (print-based, audio, video and online) are the main vehicles for teaching students. There is also some face-to-face teaching in the form of tutorials and residential schools. However, attendance at tutorials is not compulsory, nor may it be practicable for students who have work commitments, or for those who live far from one of the OU's study centres. At the time of writing, attendance at residential schools is compulsory for students on Level 2 (i.e. intermediate) courses.

Assessment methods

Two methods of assessment are used: Continuous Assessment, plus in the case of Level 1 courses, an End of Course Assessment (ECA), or for all other Levels, an examination. This chapter concentrates on the feedback provided in the Continuous Assessment component, so we shall now describe its main features.

Students on most OU language courses are required to complete two types of continuous assessment: Student Marked Assignments (SMAs) and Tutor Marked Assignments (TMAs). These are all sent to them at the beginning of the academic year, or in two batches, one at the beginning and the second one about half way through the year. Both types of assignment reflect the parts of the syllabus that students should have covered by that particular point in the year, and are closely linked to the learning materials.

The SMAs, as the title implies, are designed to be used as self-assessment exercises on grammatical points and vocabulary taught in the course, so the questions they contain follow a prescribed format (multiple choice, gap fill, ranking, etc.). They are also used to assess students' listening and reading comprehension skills. Students check their answers against a key, which provides them with immediate and unequivocal feedback on their performance.

The TMAs have a double function: they not only assess students' performance but also provide invaluable opportunities for learner-tutor interaction. In a typical TMA, students will be asked to read one or more texts, or listen to a recorded talk or conversation with a view to obtaining certain pieces of information. They will then use this information to produce the 'output', which is the work they will submit for assessment. This output could be, for example, a short talk or letter in which they will be expected to show they have understood the stimulus and also give a personal response to some aspect of it. The TMAs are marked by the student's own tutor, who records the marks awarded on a form, where he or she also has space to give a detailed _commentary_ on the work submitted. Considerable importance is attached to these _commentaries_. Along with the annotations on the scripts, they are an integral part of the learning process, and are the distance learning equivalent of the feedback that teachers in campus-based universities would give to their students in seminars or tutorials. In their _commentaries_, tutors are encouraged to refer students to the general assessment criteria and to explain why their work has been placed in a specific band. These criteria vary from level to level, and cover various aspects of student performance.[2] For each criterion there are five bands, each of which relates to a standard of performance specified in the relevant descriptor. The criteria are made available to students. TMAs can have either an oral or a written output. Students do not complete oral assignments in tutorials; instead, they record them on cassettes, which are then sent to the tutor for marking. Tutors can record their *commentaries* on the tape as well as in writing. *Commentaries* on TMAs with a written output are not taped, but given in writing on the form mentioned above. The oral ECA takes place in one of the final tutorials on the course. Although students are required to attend the tutorial in which the ECA is carried out, they are under no obligation to attend any others.

In this article we shall concentrate mainly on the feedback tutors provide on TMAs with a written output. In the section that follows we discuss the feedback students receive in tutorials and other forms of face-to-face tuition that are part of the OU's concept of supported distance learning.

Residential schools and other face-to-face tuition

As we have already explained, apart from tutorials, the other form of face-to-face tuition is the week that students spend at residential school, which is compulsory for all Level 2 students. The schools are held in the summer, either in a country where the target language is spoken, or in the UK. Their main aim is to provide students with opportunities for interaction in the target language. All the activities they undertake at the school (both the classroom-based tuition as well as the visits and social events) are designed to facilitate not only tutor-student interaction, but also interaction among the students themselves.

The online tuition that is playing an ever more significant part in OU provision offers further potential for student intervention and the provision of specific feedback. For this purpose the OU has adopted Lyceum, which provides an audio-graphic online learning environment (OLE) incorporating various shared graphics tools (whiteboard, 'concept map', and web browser), as well as shared document handling, synchronous text chat and multiple synchronous audio channels. Lyceum is very flexible, enabling the tutor to work with students as a group, or split them into small groups or pairs. The OU's move towards online provision could have important repercussions in open and distance learning (ODL), since students could benefit from the instantaneous, informal corrective feedback possible in networked environments. Indeed, online systems can also be used to facilitate the provision of peer-feedback and collaborative learning, which at the same time have the potential to meet the specific needs of ODL students (Macdonald, 2001; Thorpe, 1998).

Face-to-face Versus ODL Feedback

The bulk of the literature on approaches to language correction concentrates on techniques and strategies applicable to the classroom situation (e.g. Chaudron, 1983; Hamp-Lyons, 1990; James, 1998; Leki, 1990). Although many of these are relevant to supported distance education – especially when it incorporates an element of face-to-face teaching – the instantaneous, informal corrective reactions from teachers that can help students to deal with faults are much less of a feature here. In supported distance learning, most *fault correction* inevitably takes place when students' assignments (i.e. TMAs) are assessed by their tutor, rather than in tutorials or summer schools. As White (1995) reports, in distance education the roles of both learners and teachers are fundamentally changed. The teacher is not present to provide feedback straightaway when students encounter difficulties, nor is feedback available from other learners.

Feedback as part of the learning process

As in conventional face-to-face tuition, in the distance learning context *fault correction* is only one part of the assessment process. The other components – the *commentaries* and *specific feedback* that tutors provide for their students – are equally vital elements. As Hunt (2001) points out (referring to face-to-face provision), tutors not only need to be clear about what constitutes a fault, mistake or unacceptable deviation from the expected norm; they should also be able to give students feedback, which she defines as 'advice on how to close the gap between actual and desired levels of performance'. Both the tutor and the student know the aim of assessment is not only product-oriented (summative in its nature, and focusing largely on judging the student's work against a benchmark in order to assign a grade to it), but also process-oriented (in other words, it has a formative function, the aim of which is to improve students' performance by helping them identify and remedy shortcomings in their approach). In the DL context, these multiple functions of feedback are all the more apparent. For instance, Hyland (2001) discusses the various functions that feedback might have, evaluating their potential for fostering reflection and learner autonomy. She cites Jarvis (1978), who examined its range of functions, and identified three levels at which the marking of assignments could operate: '(1) marking as a means of assessment; (2) marking as a means of communicating knowledge; and (3) marking as a way of facilitating learning' (Hyland, 2001: 234). Jarvis (1978) suggests tutors should try to focus more on the third level and should try to stimulate a 'dialogue' between themselves and their students.

Let us now consider how these three levels can function in the context of supported distance language learning, of the kind provided by the OU. When a tutor points out and corrects faults, he or she is imparting knowledge (level [2] marking). His or her *commentaries* could be either level (2) or level (3) marking, depending on whether their purpose is to complement tutor intervention in fault correction, or to encourage self-correction on the part of the student. On the other hand, *fault correction, commentaries* and feedback all contain elements of level (1) marking, since they are all concerned with assessing student performance. At level (1) marking tends to be summative, but at the other levels – especially level (3) – it has much more of a formative function. This function and, in particular, how tutor-student dialogue might be stimulated in a distance education context will be discussed later. However, before doing so we must explore the role played by learner autonomy in distance learning.

Learner autonomy and feedback

In classroom-based learning, teachers are usually responsible for deciding *what* and *how* their students learn. Although in distance education the format and structure of the teaching materials will determine to some extent what is learned and how learning takes place, students can nevertheless exercise a significant degree of choice with regard to how they manage their learning. This makes them more aware of the learning process, which in turn allows them better to manage their own learning and to become more autonomous (White, 1995). It also implies that distance learners must rapidly develop strategies in order to achieve this. White (1995) offers evidence to show that distance learners use these self-management strategies more frequently than their classroom counterparts. Hyland (2001) points out that feedback in distance learning can indeed reinforce this type of strategy. For example, it can have an effect on how students revise their work and manage faults. As Powell observes, 'The capacity to identify and self-correct at least some of their faults is one of the key metacognitive skills that students must develop in distance learning' (Powell, 2001: 147–50). Such feedback, however, needs to engage both the tutor and the student in the learning process.

Self-correction can be encouraged by tutors. Indeed, in the distance learning (DL) context it might be more appropriate to focus not so much on the amount of knowledge transferred from the teacher to the learner, but on the cognitive and autonomous learning that feedback might foster. For example, the use of a marking code by a tutor might well encourage learners to identify and self-correct faults, making them less dependent on him or her. In a study on the effects of the use of a marking code on the methodology employed by tutors in the *correction* of distance learners' written assignments, Ros i Solé and Truman (2000a) found tutors using this technique had an increased awareness of which faults to correct and how to correct them. By using the code, tutors were more likely to decide which faults were important, when it was essential to provide *corrections* or *specific feedback*, and when they simply had to point faults out, confident in the knowledge that the student would be able to self-correct them.

Although there is much contradictory evidence in the literature about the amount and type of feedback to give to students and whether this facilitates learning, feedback that promotes self-correction can become an important tool that can help to empower learners. However, as White (1999) reports in her study of students' beliefs in their first 12 weeks of self-instructed learning, not all learners react favourably to the experience and acquire the necessary cognitive resources when they are placed in a distance learning context. In the next section we analyse how the players in the process view the functions of feedback.

Students' and tutors' perceptions

Students' and tutors' perceptions of the process of acquiring a second language are especially relevant in ODL as they are largely responsible for determining their expectations as to the purpose and the benefits of formative assessment. Commenting on the results of a survey conducted among 800 students enrolled on the OU Level 1 Spanish course, Ros i Solé and Truman (2000b) reported the vast majority of these students (over 80%) thought the assessment strategy enabled them to demonstrate the knowledge and skills they had acquired 'fairly well' or 'very well', and a similar percentage found the questions in the preparatory (non-assessed) sections in the TMAs fairly or very useful. They also considered student perceptions of feedback. A substantial majority of respondents (69%) felt their tutor did not indicate or correct mistakes without penalising them. This would seem to indicate students see fault correction as having a summative, rather than a formative function (Ros i Solé & Truman, 2000b).

Students' opinions were in sharp contrast to those of tutors, who viewed fault correction as formative. Differences in perceptions of the purpose of feedback also exist among tutors. In an analysis of a DL English language course in Hong Kong, Hyland (2001) found considerable variations in the patterns of feedback given by tutors to students, even though the tutors had all been given similar training on how to mark assignments. Her study revealed that although tutors, when interviewed, made frequent references to students' language problems, only 22% of the comments in their feedback addressed these concerns. There were also variations in the content of the feedback from tutor to tutor, with some tending to concentrate mainly on language issues and others on organisational features. Surprisingly, less than 17% of the feedback given dealt with learning processes. In-text interventions (corrections and comments written on scripts) showed disparities in approach: some tutors preferred to give complete corrections or reformulations, whereas others pointed out problems, but offered no specific advice on how to deal with them (Hyland, 2001: 238–39).

Our interim study into students' perceptions of the *fault correction* strategies used by language tutors in distance education (Ros i Solé & Truman, above) showed similar variations in approaches to feedback by tutors in several crucial areas. This led us to conclude that greater attention should be devoted to the treatment of faults to make it more effective and responsive to learners' real needs. At the moment, these disparate approaches suggest tutor interventions and feedback tend to reflect tutors' personal approaches and beliefs rather than a conscious and systematic effort on their part to provide students with feedback that encourages them to develop effective learning strategies.

These two studies highlight the need for further research into feedback and its role in distance learning in languages, in particular the differing perceptions of students and learners about its functions, the distinctions between the various types of feedback, how strategies for giving it can be developed, how it can foster learner autonomy and how it can be influenced by individual and contextual factors. In the next section we shall discuss changing views on the correction of faults and how they inform current thinking on feedback.

Approaches to Correction for the Distance Language Learner

The definition of faults in terms of the actions students need to perform to remedy them is especially important for distance learners, whose success as such depends largely on their ability to develop an autonomous approach to language learning as quickly as possible. It is therefore essential to distinguish between different types of faults and determine the role the learner can play in rectifying them. James (1998: 83), expanding on Corder's (1967) earlier distinction between errors and mistakes, has identified several categories into which faults can be sub-divided:

- *slips* are faults that the learner can detect and self-correct;
- *mistakes* are faults that can only be corrected by learners if they are pointed out to them (either in general terms or in the form of hints about their location and/or their nature); and
- *errors* are faults that can only be self-corrected once they have been pointed out to learners and the latter have undertaken further learning.

As we pointed out earlier, the capacity to identify and self-correct at least some of their faults is one of the key metacognitive skills that students must develop in distance learning (Powell, 2001: 147–50). Teachers, on the other hand, must be prepared to provide the support students require to develop this capacity. Using James's classification of faults, it is possible to identify three approaches tutors in distance learning might use to foster the development of self-correction strategies by students. Each approach is defined by the nature and extent of the 'remediation' implicit in it:

- *feedback* (informing learners that there is a fault and leaving them to discover and repair it themselves);
- *correction* (providing treatment or information that helps learners to revise or correct a specific instance of a fault without necessarily aiming to prevent the same fault from recurring later); and
- *remediation* (providing learners with information that enables them to revise or reject the wrong rule they were operating, thereby inducing them to revise their mental representation of the rule and avoid recurrences of this type of fault). (James, 1998: 236–7)

In James's scheme, the three levels of correction also reflect the degree of tutor intervention required. *Feedback*, for example, may be used to indicate that the learner's work contains faults, but responsibility for any follow-up action rests with the student. It would therefore be an approach suitable for correcting *slips*. *Correction* and *remediation*, on the other hand, involve a much greater degree of intervention from the tutor, so these are approaches more suited to the correction of *mistakes* and *errors*. *Remediation*, in particular, lends itself to the treatment of *errors*.

These three approaches to correction are widely used by OU tutors, as can be seen in the examples below, taken from assignments produced by students on the Level 2 Spanish course. The tutors' comments are given in square brackets together with other relevant information (e.g. translation into English, location of comment, etc.). The text written by the student is in italics.

Example of feedback

A pesar de la constitución, que declare que un 30% de presupuesto nacional se dedica a la educación, el gobierno ha reducido progresivamente su presupuesto de educación, y en 1998 la tasa de gastos educativos fue sólo 14,2%.
[Tutor's comment in margin: Repetición]

Example of correction

Había una vieja profecía azteca que prometía el volver [Correction written above last word: la vuelta] *de Quetzalcóatl.*

Example of remediation

... crear centros escolares donde los adultos y los jóvenes se sienten seguros y donde pueden demostrar y enseñar ...

[Remediation written in margin: Presente de subjuntivo: es hipotético – Present subjunctive: it's hypothetical]

Dialogue-based feedback

Up to now we have concentrated mainly on faults and their correction. However, in distance learning it must be remembered that the tutor usually provides two types of feedback – the type that refers to specific linguistic faults and suggests some ways of dealing with them, and more general advice or *commentaries*. The approaches identified by James (1998) – *feedback, correction* and *remediation* – tend to be geared to the treatment of specific faults, but *commentaries* perform an overarching function, enabling tutors to take a more global view of the student's performance in the assignment. They therefore lend themselves to the discussion of issues such as content. Although both approaches encourage the learner to reflect on his or her work, *specific feedback, correction* and *remediation* focus mainly on what the student has done wrong, whereas in *commentaries* the view is wider, with an emphasis on the medium- or long-term action he or she needs to take to close the gap between actual and desired performance. In *commentaries* the emphasis is, above all, on learning. In the last analysis, all these types of tutor intervention are, of course, concerned with faults and their elimination from students' work, but *commentaries* tend to be discursive, carefully tailored to individual students' needs and the context, and accentuate the positive features in assignments. *Specific feedback, correction* and *remediation*, on the other hand, tend to be less discursive, and standardised rather than individualised (through the use of marking codes, for instance). Perhaps the most striking difference between them, however, is that *correction, remediation* and, to a lesser extent, *specific feedback* are, despite some learner involvement, mainly teacher-centred, whereas *commentaries* tend to place the learner centre stage. Good *commentaries* provide the learner with an insight into how others respond to what he or she has produced in the target language in a very context-specific and personalised way. As Elbow states, 'The right or best comment is the one that will help this student on this topic draft at this point of the semester' (Elbow, 1999: 43, in Straub, 2000).

Below we reproduce two extracts from *commentaries* appended to students' assignments. Once again, the examples are taken from the OU Level 2 Spanish course. The first illustrates how the tutor has integrated two functions (*feedback* and *correction* [cf. James, 1998]) into the *commentary*. The second provides an example of *remediation* (cf. James, 1998). Our comments are given in square brackets. For the benefit of readers each extract is followed by a translation into English. (Note that at this level, tutors are expected to provide feedback only in Spanish.)

Extract 1
¡Excelente trabajo! Has presentado un informe claro y detallado.
Contenido (1): [This is one of the general assessment criteria – see section 2.1 'Assessment methods'] *En general, muy buena comprensión de las dos fuentes, la escrita y la oral. Una pena que tengas unos fallitos en algunos datos.* [Feedback]
Contenido (2): [This is one of the general assessment criteria – see section 2.1 'Assessment methods'] *Muy buena presentación y desarrollo de la información. Además las ideas están presentadas clara y coherentemente. Creo que te han faltado dos cosas:*
1 *utilizar conectores a comienzo de párrafo para presentar / introducir el contenido del párrafo* [Correction]
2 *hacer una clara distinción al presentar información / opinión que es tuya.* [Correction]

Translation
Excellent work! You have presented a clear and detailed report.
Content (1): In general, very good comprehension of the two stimuli, written and oral. Pity about the slight mistakes in some pieces of information.
Content (2) Very good presentation and development of the information. Ideas are clearly and coherently presented as well. I think there were two things missing from your work:
1 you could have used connectors at the beginning of a paragraph to present / introduce its contents;
2 you should have made it clear when you were presenting information / opinions of your own.

Extract 2
En español los sustantivos que terminan en 'ión' (ej. educación, dirección, población) son femeninos : la educación, la dirección, la población. Lo mismo para sustantivos que terminan en 'ema' (el sistema, el problema, el tema): estas palabras son masculinas. Ten cuidado también con la concordancia (ej. el porcentaje . . . alta → alto). [Remediation]

Translation
In Spanish nouns ending in 'ión' (e.g. educación, dirección, población) are feminine : la educación, la dirección, la población. The same applies to nouns

ending in 'ema' (el sistema, el problema, el tema): these words are masculine. Watch out for agreement as well (e.g. el porcentaje . . . alta → alto).

We have seen that *fault correction* (i.e. *specific feedback, correction* and *remediation*) and *commentaries* are not two separate functions requiring the tutor to adopt two completely different forms of behaviour. On the contrary, the two functions are normally intertwined in practice. The *fault correction* process usually precedes the drafting of the *commentaries* (Ros i Solé & Truman, 2000b), so the latter quite rightly bear the stamp of the former. Taken together, they can provide students with two different, but complementary perspectives on their work. However, it must be remembered that *fault correction* and *commentaries* are only part of the process. Equally important are the reactions of learners to them, yet it is only recently that researchers have begun to examine issues such as how students interpret this guidance, how teachers can structure their *commentaries* to facilitate learning, and the extent to which learning is enhanced by engaging students in a dialogue. These questions will be examined in greater detail in the sections that follow.

Negotiating and constructing meaning through feedback

In recent research, scholars have begun to re-examine language learning and *fault correction* from a socio-cultural perspective. In this approach it is assumed knowledge is not something handed down directly from teachers to students or assimilated by individuals in isolation, but is part of an interactive, socially constructed process (Leki, 1990; Murphy, 2000). This implies a need to take a more comprehensive view of feedback, so as to include not only the *corrections* and *commentaries* made by the teacher on the student's work, but also the responses of the learner to each of them: the way they view their faults, how they understand their tutor's interventions and how they act on them.

Learners are seen as active constructors of meaning, who contribute to the knowledge-construction process that occurs in the interaction between teacher and student (Brooks & Brooks, 1993; Jonassen 1991). Leki (1990) emphasises the importance of the student response, together with the need to consider the ongoing dialogue between student and teacher. She makes a plea for teachers to encourage students to make multiple drafts of their work and to make comments on these, as well as the final one, thus avoiding turning each assignment into a test. Above all, she stresses that the key factor is not so much the quantity of comments teachers make, but when and how they make them. This implies the development of a more sophisticated and intellectually balanced approach to faults in the classroom, especially in the relationship between instruction and response to students' writing (Anson, 2000).

In the distance education context, learners also benefit from taking a more active role in the feedback process if they are given increased access to information about the institution's assessment policy and practices. In Hyland's study (2001) students had access to tutors' assessment criteria and fellow students' work. Macdonald (2001) has evaluated the effect of disseminating marking schemes and model answers online to make the assessment process more transparent and ensure that students understand the task. She also described an experiment in online peer review of assignment scripts, concluding there was potential for integrating it into official assignment submission, perhaps by using it as an 'initial stage of iterative assignment development', with marks awarded for 'the reflective use of peer comment, as well as for the final script' (Macdonald 2001: 188). She points out, however, that innovations such as these would be unavailable to ODL students without the use of electronic networking as the delivery medium.

Much of the thinking behind dialogue-based feedback is already reflected in distance learning tutors' responses to learners' writing, as seen in *commentaries* on assignment feedback sheets, where they give students guidance on revising their work. This is a widespread practice in distance education, where the tutor establishes a kind of rapport with the student by mediating between the text and the learner. This goes beyond making generalised comments on his or her performance, and implies a much more individualised approach on the part of the tutor (e.g. by commenting on progress or pointing out remedial action), as well as the use of informal, non-threatening language, praise and encouragement, all of which invite the student to respond. Here are some examples of such approaches taken from commentaries by tutors on the OU Level 2 Spanish course, together with translations into English, as appropriate. As usual, our comments are in square brackets.

Example 1

¡Buen trabajo, [student's name]! *En la cinta te comento con detalle el error en la estructura. Espero que mis comentarios te ayuden. ¡Suerte con TMA 8 y 9!*

Translation

Good work, [student's name]. I've given detailed comments about the fault in the structure on the tape. I hope my comments will help you. Good luck with TMAs 8 and 9!

Example 2

De nuevo, [student's name], *enhorabuena. Has realizado un excelente TMA, pese a que la nota no sea tan buena como en el TMA anterior. Esto es debido a algunos fallitos que te comento a continuación . . .*

Translation
Once again, [student's name], my congratulations. You have produced an excellent TMA, even though your mark is not so good as the one you were given for your previous TMA. This is because of some slight mistakes, which I comment on below . . .

Tutors can also engage students in dialogue by asking them questions or making specific references to their previous work, although in the authors' experience spoken feedback tends to be the preferred medium for doing so. In the classroom context, the view that learner and teacher must negotiate meaning is one that is also espoused by proponents of the response theory. Straub (2000), for example, describes his 'responding practices' to successive drafts of a student's written work, distilling them into seven broad principles:

(1) Turn your comments into a conversation.
(2) Do not take control over the student's text.
(3) Give priority to global concerns of content, context, organisation and purpose before getting (overly) involved with style and correctness.
(4) Limit the scope of your comments and the number of comments you present.
(5) Select your focus of comments according to the stage of drafting and relative maturity of the text.
(6) Gear your comments to the individual student.
(7) Make frequent use of praise.

In the following sections we shall examine new feedback strategies and formats for assessment that can help facilitate student–tutor interaction, as well as fostering distance learners' ability to detect and self-correct faults.

New assessment strategies and formats
In current research there is a great deal of interest in the use of assessment to inform students and encourage them to reflect on their own learning. As mentioned in the previous section, much effort is being devoted to the development of other new forms of assessment that will foster such approaches. Several studies in distance language learning have also emphasised the importance for students of developing good self-correction strategies and learner autonomy (Hurd *et al.*, 2001; Kubota, 2001). Indeed, these skills are not only important in distance learning; they are of value to all kinds of learners. For researchers such as Gardner and Miller (1999), encouraging students to reflect on their learning is the key to

making them more effective and independent as learners. They advocate the use of assessments for the student's own information, pointing to the value of self-assessments or peer-assessments for this purpose.

Bisaillon (1992), however, points out that students often find it difficult to revise their writing on their own. She advocates the use of correction grids listing, by category, the most common faults in various types of texts. Initially, the teacher identifies individual faults, but thereafter encourages the student to take responsibility for this process. As the student's confidence and ability grow, the teacher ceases to point out individual faults, indicating instead only the sentences and then the paragraphs in which they occur. The grids are used by students to identify the corrective action needed in each case (Bisaillon, 1992). Fernández-Toro and Jones (2001) have also produced a practical guide designed to encourage learner involvement and self-assessment through the use of questionnaires and guidance on the evaluation of their performance. All these approaches have much in common, incorporating systematic revision routines (in particular the production of successive drafts of written work, together with critiques) and the development of self-assessment strategies. In a number of higher education institutions, new strategies have been embedded in innovative assessment methods. They include portfolio assessment, peer-assessment and self-assessment.

Portfolio assessment is becoming increasingly popular, since it can incorporate the types of approach described above. Paulson and Meyer (in Bailey, 1998: 216) propose the following definition of a portfolio:

> A portfolio is a purposeful collection of student work that exhibits the student's efforts, progress and achievements in one or more areas. The collection must include student participation in selecting contents, the criteria for judging merit, and evidence of student self-reflection.

Portfolio assessment is, indeed, learner-centred assessment *par excellence*, giving students a large degree of control over what material they choose to present, how many times they revise it and how they present it. However, in ODL portfolio assessment is not always possible, given the large number of students involved.

Peer-assessment can also be problematic in the ODL context, since it relies heavily on types of student interaction and collaboration that can only be achievable in the classroom. The sort of computer-supported collaborative learning environment described by Berings and van der Meijden (2001), or that provided by Lyceum, however, offer much scope for developing such activities or forms of assessment for distance learners, who can now interact with their peers in a virtual classroom. Peer-assessment, or – to be more precise, peer-feedback – can also be incorporated into face-to-face tuition. For instance, at the end of their week-long residential school, the OU's Level 2 Spanish students take part in a group activity that is very similar in format to the oral component of their end of course examination. Each tutorial group is divided into two sub-groups. While the first sub-group takes part in the activity, the second one observes it, using a feedback sheet to make notes, not only on individual performances, but also on how the group members interact in the discussion phase of the activity. The two sub-groups then change places and the process is repeated, with the second group undertaking the activity and the first one observing. At the end of the session, the two sub-groups discuss their observations and give each other feedback. The discussion is moderated by the tutor, who adds his or her own comments as appropriate. Surveys confirm this is one of the most popular activities in the residential school programme. When asked to rate this activity in terms of its effectiveness in providing them with opportunities to practise their speaking skills, 94% of respondents in the 2002 schools thought it was 'excellent' or 'good'[3]; 82% placed it in the same categories when asked whether they found it enjoyable. The corresponding figures for 2003 were 98% and 91% respectively.[4]

In distance learning, self-assessment can either be integrated into assignments (e.g. as non-summatively assessed preparatory activities or checklists designed to be completed before or after the student has completed the task) or can form part of the course materials. Bishop (2001), for example, has advocated the use of a rating system that gives ODL students an indication of the individual qualitative progress they are making, as opposed to their relative progress within a group. Thus, students measure their performance in a given assignment by comparing two ratings – one for quality features and one for accuracy – against the ones they received for previous work.[5] The system can also be used to give students frequency ratings for different categories of fault, making the feedback they receive very specific and individualised.

In these forms of assessment both learners and teachers must assume roles that differ radically from their traditional ones. In peer-assessment, students make judgements about, or comment on each other's work (Hunt, 2001b). In self-assessment, 'the learners themselves evaluate their language skills and knowledge' (Bailey, 1998: 227), whereas in portfolio assessment, teachers are invited to compare students' performances with those of other students, rather than against benchmarks. Typically, these three methods are combined with more traditional teacher-led assessments, with the latter making up the bulk of the overall mark or grade awarded. Their great strength is that they encourage learners to become involved and take responsibility for their learning within the assessment process, raising their awareness of how it works and giving individual learners insights into how they can improve their own performance. This means, in turn, that the process has to be absolutely transparent and that students must be clear about their own role in it. Bailey (1998), for example, found there can be a 'moderately strong correlation' between self-assessment and test scores, although she also reports that evidence obtained by other researchers is less conclusive. As Gardner and Miller (1999: 22) point out:

> Assessments conducted mostly for the learner's own information (i.e. for their own learning rather than assessment) are better administered as self-assessments or peer-assessments. [. . .] In this way assessments become a tool to facilitate reflection and ultimately development, rather than a tool to describe and categorise the learner.

In other words, these new assessment strategies and formats are best suited to formative types of assessment where the emphasis is on development of students' self-awareness and autonomy.

Conclusion

In distance learning, fault correction and the commentaries made on assignments provide tutors and learners with what is often their sole channel of communication. Far too often, though, little attention is paid to this function. As current theories of second language acquisition and language teaching point towards more collaborative approaches to language learning, feedback and the learner–teacher dialogue that it promotes assume greater importance than ever.

Ideally, the collaboration and social interaction achieved through feedback can be catalysts for effective language learning in the distance context, in which learner autonomy and control play a key role by empowering learners. Another crucial element in this is technology, which can break down many of the barriers that have prevented DL students from enjoying the benefits of collaborative approaches to learning, although it can be argued that in some respects it simply solves one set of problems by substituting others. Implicit in all of this is the need to re-examine the roles played by both tutor and student. This, in turn, implies that tutors must engage students in a dialogue and give them some degree of ownership over the feedback process. There must, however, be a clear distinction between the different roles feedback can play, whether it be to correct mistakes and errors, suggest repair strategies, or provide commentaries. Moreover, individual student needs and particular contexts need to be taken into account to achieve a fruitful, collaborative dialogue. DL tutors must engage with learners as individuals, helping them situate their newly acquired knowledge, skills and understanding in a framework of experience and abilities that students have constructed over the years.

For far too long assessment in distance education has tended to adopt models developed for traditional face-to-face tuition, yet we would argue that the specific needs of distance learners can only be met by new ones that put students at the heart of the process and recognise their role is not a passive, but an active one. These new models must have firm theoretical foundations in language learning methodology and take cognisance of the special characteristics of distance learners. We will then be able to make the assessment process into a channel for two-way communication, allowing feedback to play a more sophisticated role and assume greater prominence in this mode of language learning.

Notes

1. From this point on we shall use the generic term 'fault' to refer to unacceptable deviations from the expected norm. We prefer this term to 'mistake', 'error', etc. because these have been used by different authors to denote specific types of deviations.
2. For instance, the criteria for Level 2 courses are Content ([1] Development and originality of ideas/understanding of stimulus materials; [2] Structure, organization and presentation of material) and Language; ([3] Accuracy of vocabulary and linguistic structures; [4] Range of vocabulary and linguistic structures).
3. Respondents were asked to select one of four possible answers ('excellent', 'good', 'satisfactory' or 'poor') to each question.
4. 2002: overall figures for the three weeks of residential schools; 2003: interim figures for the first week only.
5. The calculation of the ratings involves dividing the number of 'mistakes' or 'errors' either together or separately into the total word count for the piece of work. The process is explained in more detail in Bishop, 2001.

References

Anson, C.M. (2000) Response and the social construction of error. *Assessing Writing* 7, 5–21.

Bailey, K.M. (1998) *Learning about Language Assessment: Dilemmas, Decisions and Directions*. Cambridge, MA: Heinle & Heinle.

Berings, M. and Van der Meijden, H. (2001) Influence of teacher-feedback on students' activities during computer supported collaborative learning. Paper presented at the 9th Earli Conference, Fribourg, Switzerland, 28 August–1 September 2001.

Bisaillon, J. (1992) La révision de textes: Un processus à enseigner pour l'amélioration des productions écrites. *The Canadian Modern Language Review* 48 (2), 276–91.

Bishop, G. (2001) Using quality and accuracy ratings to quantify the value added of a dictionary skills training course. *Language Learning Journal* 24, 62–69.

Brooks, J.G. and Brooks, M. (1993) *In Search of Understanding: The Case for Constructivist Classrooms*. Alexandria, VA: ASCD.

Chaudron, C. (1983) A descriptive model of discourse in the corrective treatment of learners' errors. _Language Learning_ 27 (1), 29–46.

Corder, S.P. (1967) The significance of learner's errors. _IRAL_ 5 (4), 161–70.

Corder, S.P. (1971) Describing the language learner's language: Interdisciplinary approaches to language. _Reports and Papers 6._ London: CILT.

Fernández-Toro, M. and Jones, F.R. (2001) _DIY Techniques for Language Learners._ London: CILT.

Gardner, D. and Miller, L. (1999) Assessment in self-access learning. In D. Gardner and L. Miller (eds). _Establishing Self-Access: From Theory to Practice._ Cambridge: CUP.

Hamp-Lyons, L. (1990) Second language writing: Assessment issues. In B. Kroll (ed.) _Second Language Writing._ Cambridge: CUP.

Hunt, M. (2001) Checking on progress: developing approaches to giving formal and informal feedback. In L. Arthur and S. Hurd (eds) _Supporting Lifelong Language Learning: Theoretical and Practical Approaches._ London: CILT / The Open University.

Hurd, S., Beaven, T. and Ortega, A. (2001) Developing autonomy in distance language learning context: issues and dilemmas for course writers. _System_ 29, 341–55.

Hyland, F. (2001) Providing effective support: Investigating feedback to distance language learners. _Open Learning_ 16 (3), 233–47.

James, C. (1998) _Errors in Language Learning and Use: Exploring Error Analysis._ Harlow: Addison Wesley Longman.

Jarvis, P. (1978) Students' learning and teachers' marking. _Teaching at a Distance_ 13, 13–17.

Jonassen, D.H. (1991) Evaluating constructivist learning. _Educational Technology_ 31 (9), 28–33.

Kubota, M. (2001) Error correction strategies used by learners of Japanese when revising a writing task. _System_ 29, 467–80.

Leki, I. (1990) Coaching from the margins: Issues in written response. In B. Kroll (ed.) _Second Language Writing: Research Insights for the Classroom._ Cambridge: CUP.

Macdonald, J. (2001) Exploiting online interactivity to enhance assignment development and feedback in distance education. _Open Learning_ 16 (2), 179–89.

Murphy, S. (2000) A socio-cultural perspective on teacher response: Is there a student in the room? _Assessing Writing_ 7, 70–90.

Powell, B. (2001) Understanding errors and mistakes. In L. Arthur and S. Hurd (eds) _Supporting Lifelong Language Learning: Theoretical and Practical Approaches._ London: CILT / The Open University.

Ros i Solé, C. and Truman, M. (2000a) What does it take to agree on a mark? Approaches to the correction of linguistic inaccuracy in supported distance learning programmes in languages. In M. Fay and D. Ferney (eds) _Current Trends in Modern Languages Provision for Non-Specialist Linguists_ (pp. 151–66). London: CILT / APU.

Ros i Solé, C. and Truman, M. (2000b) Approaches to marking: learners' and teachers' perceptions. Paper presented at the CILT / FDTL / SCHML / UCML / TLTP Conference ('The New Communicators'), Nottingham, UK, 3–5 July 2000.

Straub, R. (2000) The student, the text, and the classroom context: A case study of teacher response. _Assessing Writing_ 7, 23–55.

Thorpe, M. (1998) Assessment and 'third generation' distance education. *Distance Education* 19 (2), 265–86.

White, C. (1995) Autonomy and strategy use in distance foreign language learning: Research findings. *System* 23 (2), 207–21.

White, C. (1999) Expectations and emergent beliefs of self-instructed language learners. *System* 27, 443–57.

Chapter 6

A Framework for Supporting Students Studying English via a Mixed-mode Delivery System

CARISMA DREYER, NWABISA BANGENI and CHARL NEL

Introduction

Higher education institutions are confronting problems of enormous proportions as university administrators grapple with forces that are changing the shape of their institutions, including:

- the need to increase global competitiveness;
- ensuring students keep up with and make use of rapidly changing technology; and
- coping with major changes in the nature of the workforce and student populations which are older, more diverse and increasingly dependent on frequent skill updates to cope with the information overload and rapidly changing business needs (cf. Schrum, 2000; Slaughter, 1998).

Many higher education administrators are, therefore, being challenged to think very differently about how education and training are organised and delivered to meet the educational needs of an increasingly diverse student population and society as a whole in the 21st century. Many South African institutions are therefore embracing the idea of offering distance learning programmes by means of a mixed mode of delivery. This represents a substantial departure from previous practice when many 'traditional' universities offered only full-time on-campus programmes. As a result, these institutions have extended university access to unprecedented numbers of disadvantaged and non-traditional (age 25 and over) students who are often less academically prepared than their peers (cf. Gardiner, 1994; Phillippe, 1995).

Institutions are also being confronted with unacceptably high dropout and/or failure rates among distance learners. According to a report in the South African _Sunday Times_ newspaper (2000), at least 100,000 students drop out each year, and institutions have poor follow through (70% or below) and graduation rates (15% or below). Statistics from the English Department at Potchefstroom University indicated a dropout rate of 25% and a failure rate of 26% in 2000 in the first-year Academic English course offered via Telematic Learning Systems. Kember (1995) reports attrition data that range from 28% to 99.5% in distance education settings in the USA. Given the present realities, it does not seem as if institutions presenting distance education programmes can take comfort in current attrition rates.

A report submitted by the South African task team for the Council on Higher Education (Department of Education, 2000) states that institutions have to become accountable to taxpayers for the large amount of money that the Government has spent on higher education, and that they have to answer to parents who spend their hard-earned money on tuition fees, only to see their children fail, drop out or leave without those job qualifications that the economy demands. The problem of attrition and failure in distance education cannot be solved simply by addressing institutional responsibilities. Tinto (1987: 181) states: 'To single out the institution as being solely responsible for student departure, as do many critics, is to deny an essential principle of effective education, namely that students must themselves become responsible for their own learning.' However, the institution does need to initiate a process to prevent students becoming part of the 'revolving door syndrome' (i.e. the ease with which students are able to enrol for distance learning programmes and the equal ease with which they can drop out or fail).

One way of doing this is by profiling distance learners proactively to determine who they are, what their strengths and weaknesses are, and what they need. By pinpointing possible factors that can lead to dropout, failure and/or success, programme/course developers, faculty, administrators, and/or facilitators are given an opportunity to identify students who are at risk, and to provide the necessary learner support. According to Moore and Kearsley (1996), knowledge of such factors as well as learners' likes/needs or expectations should dictate not only how the course or programme is designed and implemented, but also the nature of the teaching involved and the learner support services provided.

According to researchers (e.g. Lowe, 1997; Moore & Kearsley, 1996; Simpson, 2002), learner support in distance learning is a pivotal element in ensuring learner success and completion. Many studies have demonstrated a relationship between the provision of appropriate support and a decrease in attrition rates, both in traditional and distance institutions (cf. Gibson, 1996; Tinto, 1987). According to Butcher (2001), the need for well-developed systems of learner support, designed as an integral part of overall courses, is underestimated. In today's climate of educational accountability, considerable attention should therefore be focused on students' academic achievement and the educational environment necessary to develop and support achievement.

The purpose of this chapter is to:

- indicate how the process of profiling can be used to provide an effective and comprehensive learner support structure for learners within language programmes;
- identify and categorise the support services that English Second Language (ESL) learners typically indicate they would like/need;
- provide a framework that can guide administrators, academic language departments, and faculties in the provision of effective and efficient learner support services.

The outcomes of this study are based on the experience gained at the Potchefstroom University in South Africa.

Profiling Distance Learners

Attrition, failure or success is usually a result of no one cause, but of an accumulation and mixture of causes. A review of the literature indicates the highly complex and multi-dimensional nature of this issue (Chacon-Duque, 1985; Galusha, 1997; Kennedy & Powell, 1976; Sherry, 1996; Sweet, 1986). The majority of research studies, including the profiles of at-risk/dropout students, have limited themselves to investigation of the relationship between a few selected factors and dropout, failure or success, while ignoring other factors. The combining of multiple factors and the interaction between and among factors as possible reasons for dropout, failure or success have generally been overlooked.

A framework, adapted from Powell et al. (1990), was developed to address the need for a comprehensive approach to identifying factors that can affect the dropout, failure or success of distance English Second Language learning students (cf. Figure 6.1). On the basis of a comprehensive review of previous studies, it is possible to classify the factors affecting dropout, failure or success in distance education into two general categories, namely personal and contextual factors (cf. Dille & Mezack, 1991; Powell et al., 1990; Pythian & Clements, 1982; Rekkedal, 1983; Robinson, 1995; Sweet, 1986; Tinto, 1987; Wallace, 1996).

Personal factors

The first category consists of those factors students bring to the distance teaching learning process. These *personal factors* are either fixed (e.g. gender, prior learning experience, socio-economic status, etc.) or change slowly over the duration of a student's involvement with a distance education programme or course (e.g. strategy use, motivation, anxiety, etc.) and, as such, the effect these factors have on the student's chances of success needs to be considered when developing learner support services.

Demographic and background variables

Research attempting to measure the relationship of particular demographic characteristics to student success as measured by levels of persistence and/or achievement has often resulted in contradictory conclusions. Some studies have reported no correlation between these outcomes and specific demographic variables such as gender or ethnic background (Dille & Mezack, 1991). It is possible certain demographic variables, perhaps not in and of themselves but rather as the markers of an accompanying set of generalised characteristics, are related to student success. For a more complete discussion of demographic and background variables see the following sources: Galusha, 1997; Gordon, 2001; Kirkup and Von Prummer, 1997; and Tait, 1995.

Affective variables

According to Brown (1994: 135), affect refers to emotion or feeling. The affective domain is the emotional side of human behaviour, and it may be juxtaposed to the cognitive side. The development of affective states or feelings involves a variety of personality factors, feelings both about ourselves and about others with whom we come into contact.

According to Oxford (1999: 59), anxiety 'ranks high among factors influencing language learning, regardless of whether the setting is informal or formal'. White (1995: 208) states that distance learners 'report initial feelings of lack of preparedness and lack of confidence and a sense of inadequacy'. Findings from studies indicate language anxiety is negatively related to achievement in the L2 and is associated with 'deficits in scores on standardized tests, low scores in language courses or a combination of these factors' (Gardner *et al.*, 1997: 345).

In a study conducted by Parker (1999), locus of control as a single, independent variable was able to predict dropout with an accuracy of 80% using discriminant analysis. This finding corresponds to research conducted by Rotter (1989) that found locus of control to have a direct bearing on students' completion of coursework. Dille and Mezack (1991) reported that internal locus of control was positively correlated with success in

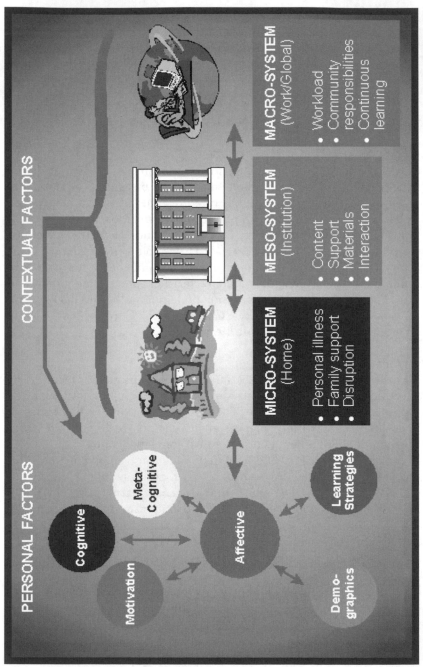

Figure 6.1 A framework for profiling distance learners

community college distance learning courses. Researchers hypothesised this to be the case as internals put in the necessary hours and hard work because they expect this effort to affect their success (Altmann & Arambasich, 1982; Rotter, 1989). Alternatively, external locus of control and a related construct, external attribution, have been reported to characterise at-risk distance education students (Dille & Mezack, 1991; Kember *et al.*, 1991). For a more complete discussion of a variety of affective variables see Dille and Mezack, 1991; Ellis, 1994; Pugliese, 1994; and Stirling, 1997.

Motivation

Motivation is a complex phenomenon. For this reason multiple factors may account for the motivational levels of students. Moreover, the influence of any one factor may differ from individual to individual and from situation to situation. Brophy (1988: 205–6) defines motivation to learn as ' . . . a student tendency to find academic activities meaningful and worthwhile and to try to derive the intended academic benefits from them'.

For distance language learners, the inherently demanding nature of self-instruction, together with the shift of locus of control from educator to learner, implies that only those who maintain their levels of motivation are likely to succeed (Hurd, 2000). Hurd (2000) reports that demotivation among language learners was caused by factors related to the distance learning situation, for example lack of opportunity to practise with others and share experiences, difficulty in assessing personal progress, and perceived inadequacy of feedback. For a more complete discussion of motivation see Abi-Samra, 2002; Caldwell and Ginther, 1996; Galusha, 1997; and Klesius *et al.*, 1997.

Cognitive variables

One learner variable that continues to attract much attention is learning style. Reid (1995a: viii) defines learning styles as a learner's 'natural, habitual, and preferred way(s) of absorbing, processing, and retaining new information and skills'. According to Keefe (1979: 4), learning styles are cognitive, affective and physiological traits that are relatively stable indicators of how learners perceive, interact with, and respond to the learning environment.

According to Wynd and Bozman (1996: 232), a prerequisite to higher education institutions becoming more productive is the identification of how students learn. Farrington (1999: 87) states that 'few, if any, classes are ever designed by first asking the question of how students might learn best'. Posing such a question can be beneficial, especially when deciding to use technology to support the course curriculum. Research indicates learning style is an important factor in the success of distance learners (cf.

Grasha & Yangarber-Hicks, 2000; Liu & Ginther, 1999; Ross, 1997). Therefore, the instructional adaptation and design of distance education programmes/courses to accommodate students' learning styles appear even more important than that in traditional classroom instruction. For a more complete discussion of cognitive variables see Grasha and Yangarber-Hicks (2000); Liu and Ginther (1999); and Vermunt (1996).

Learning strategies

According to Weinstein *et al.* (2000: 727), learning strategies include 'any thoughts, behaviors, beliefs, or emotions that facilitate the acquisition, understanding, or later transfer of new knowledge and skills'. Similarly, O'Malley and Chamot (1990) define learning strategies as 'the special thoughts or behaviours that individuals use to help them comprehend, learn, or retain new information'.

Research has clearly indicated that knowing about and using learning strategies is a major factor for discriminating between low achieving students and those who experience success (Alexander & Murphy, 1998; Dreyer, 1992). According to Shih and Gamon (1999), motivation and learning strategies accounted for more than one-third of student achievement in a web-based course. White (1995: 211) found that distance learners made greater use of metacognitive strategies than classroom learners, especially for self-management strategies. The distance learners also made 'proportionately greater use of the monitoring . . . and evaluation . . . dimensions of metacognition than did classroom learners' (White, 1995: 214). For a more complete discussion of learning strategies see Landbeck and Mugler, 2000; McKeachie *et al.*, 1986; and Vermunt, 1996.

Metacognitive variables

Self-regulation is a metacognitive process that governs many individual actions and is central to Social Cognitive Theory (Bandura, 1986). It is hypothesised that self-regulatory behaviour is critical when distance learning is the primary method of instruction. The student who self-regulates will be more successful at distance learning than the student who has problems in the area of self-regulation. Self-regulated learning is, therefore, important in distance learning because the student is dependent on his/her own resourcefulness to cope with learning.

Self-regulated learning implies a high level of cognitive engagement, making connections with existing knowledge, organising a specific approach to a learning task, and continuously monitoring progress (Corno & Mandinach, 1983). Bandura (1997: 175) states that 'A high sense of self-regulatory efficacy contributes to mastery of academic subject matter by building a sense of cognitive efficacy and raising academic aspiration in those domains.' For a more complete discussion of metacognitive variables see Bandura (1997); McLoughlin (1996); O'Malley and McCraw (1999); Pajares and Schunk (2001); and Zhang et al. (2001).

Contextual factors

The second category consists of *contextual factors*. Knox's (1977) developmental stage orientation of adult life stresses the importance of understanding an individual's contextual situation. We have divided this category into three components, namely the microsystem, the mesosystem and the macrosystem. This categorisation is based on a combination of an ecological perspective and a systems approach to learning (cf. Bronfenbrenner, 1979; Kaiser, 1993), and emphasises the importance of taking into account the total environment of the learner if we are to explain adequately how and why people learn.

Microsystem

At the innermost level there is the *microsystem*, which can be represented by the home and family. This component refers to those activities and interaction patterns in the learner's immediate surroundings that can disrupt or in some way alter the goals, expectations, and commitment of the learner (e.g. personal illness, disruption of family life, marital status, lack of family support and lack of time) (Bernt & Bugbee, 1994; Boston, 1992; Carney-Crompton & Tan, 2002; Kumar, 1999; Phillip, 1993; Schmeck & Nguyen, 1996; Wagner, 1993).

For the teaching-learning process to be most successful, educators of distance learners must be aware of the everyday realities adults face in the home environment that may affect their learning. Family responsibilities very often stem from a self-imposed commitment to family. Their significance in terms of impact depends on a learner's economic level, educational or financial level, and associated cultural or ethnic background.

Mesosystem

The next level is the *mesosystem* within which the distance learning institution and all its relevant teaching-learning features can be situated. Research indicates that quality and difficulty of course materials, amount and quality of feedback and interaction provided by lecturers/facilitators, access to a variety of support structures, and technological issues can affect learners studying via a mixed mode delivery system (Dreyer, 2001; Oaks, 1996; Rekkedal, 1983; Shaker, 2000; Sherry, 1996; Wood, 1996).

Macrosystem

The outermost level, the *macrosystem*, can include those factors within the individual's work, community (local, national and international) and country (e.g. workload, community responsibilities, continuous learning required within the technological era, etc.) (Gawe & De Kock, 2002; Kember *et al.*, 1991; Sherry, 1996; Wood, 1996).

Job requirements and expectations can also affect the learner's learning effort. Company owners and managers may emphasise the importance of education or training so that their companies can compete successfully in the marketplace. But this support often translates into 'You better get with it, because you may not have a job if the company goes under'. The learner then may perceive various kinds of pressures: 'If I don't keep up, I may lose my job; others are eager and pushing me from below.'

The contextual factors indicate that each learner is viewed as an inseparable part of a social system (e.g. a family, an institution, an organisation). To understand why some learners are more successful than others at learning, it is necessary to understand the kind of influence systemic factors have on different learners. The multi-directional interactive process both within and between systems is dynamic and multi-faceted (cf. Figure 1). Learning failure or success should, therefore, be seen in terms of a disparity between what the learner brings to the teaching–learning situation and the demands or expectations of the environment (Apter, 1978). The learning process must be viewed holistically (i.e. more than merely the sum of its parts) with as much emphasis on relationships and interactions as on the learner and the content of what is learned.

Learner Support

What is learner support? In our view it encompasses those learner-centred actions or interventions made by the institution to ensure a learner admitted to a programme of study will be able to fulfil the outcomes of the programme via an academically credible assessment system.

Research has shown that student support has a sizeable impact on student success and completion in a chain of equally important services and processes in distance education. According to Buchanan (2000), institutional support and services dictate the success or failure of a distance education programme. Academic institutions must remember that course content is only one element of the education they provide; support comparable to that received by on-campus students needs to be provided to distance learners (Spodick, 1995). In broad terms, this places the onus on the institution to provide clear and accurate information on admission routes and programmes (including – very important – pre-registration activities) to ensure the potential student achieves the best possible match between personal need and the programme of study they have undertaken. Once enrolled as a student, appropriate mechanisms need to be in place to support the learner. However, as Sewart (1993) has argued, the nature of the learner support system in any institution is unique in that it reflects the market aimed at, the package of teaching materials on offer, the delivery system, and the educational and social culture within which the institution operates. Closely aligned with those aspects is the issue of financial resources available to institutions. In this context, the institution has an element of control as, with any allocation of funds, it can prioritise between the four most important costs of a distance education system, namely the:

- extent and sophistication of the learner support system;
- range of courses offered and, in particular, the average annual enrolment per course;
- mature and complexity of the media mix used for delivering courses / programmes;
- acquisition of course materials – course development methods can fit on a continuum that extends from buying courses in from elsewhere, to using large in-house course teams within the institution itself (cf. Hancock, 2000).

Reid (1995b: 268) states that institutional perspectives of support fall within either a complementary or a compensatory position. A complementary position views student support as an essential integral component of the teaching/learning process, where the learner is the central focus; the compensatory position views students as having deficits in their learning that need to be fixed. So, the approach and attitude an institution adopts and communicates to students will also affect the reception of the services, and students' acceptance of them. Student support is a necessary and cost-effective way of retaining students as well as an essential humanising element of any distance learning system (cf. Simpson, 2002).

The Research Project

Background

The rapid political transformation in South Africa has led to transformation in various sectors, including that of higher education. The White Paper on Higher Education states: 'It must . . . generate new curricula and flexible models of learning and teaching, including modes of delivery, to accommodate a larger and more diverse student population' (Department of Education, 1997: 4).

In 1995, the Potchefstroom University took a strategic decision to change its traditional mode of delivery to that of mixed mode (Van Wyk, 2001). During the period 1995–1996 various programmes were identified as being part of the new mode of delivery. Consequently, various academic departments and specific lecturers were targeted with the development of the new courses. The Department of English was one of the first departments to become involved in this new venture. The first module to be delivered was the Business English module, which formed part of the Business Administration programme. In 1999, the academic English modules that formed part of the B.A. with Law subjects programme were developed and delivered via the Telematic Learning Systems unit of Potchefstroom University.

The high percentage of students who failed and/or dropped out of the first semester in various courses soon became a talking point among lecturers and a point of discussion at numerous telematic learning meetings. The failure rate in the Business English course ($N = 345$) was 18% in 1996 and the dropout rate was 29%, and the failure rate in 1997 and 1998 was 20% and the dropout rate was 30%. A similar trend occurred in the following years (1999–2002). On implementation of the B.A. with Law subjects course, the failure rate in the academic English module was 30% and the dropout rate was 15% after the first semester. Student failure and dropout became a significant concern for the Department of English. The researchers decided to initiate a research project with the hope of discovering the reasons for such high rates. Such a high percentage affects not only the individual, but also the academic department, the institution, the higher education system, business and industry, and society as a whole.

Aims of the research project

The Department of English felt the high failure and/or dropout rate in the English modules was unacceptable and every effort should be made to address the problem. As a result, the researchers initiated a small-scale study to address the following research questions:

- What factors can affect the failure/dropout or success of students taking the English modules via telematic learning systems?
- What support services do these students indicate they would like/ need?
- Can the most prominent factors affecting these students' failure/ dropout or success be addressed by means of the implementation of a comprehensive, well-structured and co-ordinated support system? If so, what support can be provided by the institution, and how can this be done?

Method of research

Design

A combination of qualitative and quantitative research methods was used. A case study approach was used to construct a detailed profile of unsuccessful (i.e. potentially at-risk) as well as successful English Second Language (ESL) learners studying via Telematic Learning Systems at the Potchefstroom University for CHE. Although a case study approach was used, the learners selected to participate in this study included all the learners ($N = 8$) taking English as a major within the B.A. with Law subjects programme.

Participants

The participants in this case study were eight adult learners (ENGL111, $n = 3$; ENF211, $n = 3$ ENF311, $n = 2$) enrolled in the B.A. with Law subjects course at the Potchefstroom University. These students were categorised into red (unsuccessful/at risk) and green (successful) profiles on the basis of their failure (1–45%) or success (65% and above) in the semester tests (mid-term test) and the end-of-semester examination in the English modules in their first semester of study. A correlation of $r = 0.92$ was found between the students' semester marks and their end-of-semester examination marks. The average of the semester mark and the examination mark was used to divide the students into the two groups.

Instrumentation

Five paper-and-pencil instruments were used in this study:

- The Style Analysis Survey (SAS) was used to determine the students' general approach to learning (i.e. it gives an indication of overall learning style preference) (Oxford, 1995).
- The Motivated Strategies for Learning Questionnaire (MSLQ) was used to assess the students' motivational orientations and their use of different learning strategies for university courses (Pintrich *et al.*, 1989).
- The Learning and Study Strategies Inventory (LASSI) was used to assess those student thought processes and behaviours that impact on their studying and learning. There are ten scales in the LASSI, five dealing with motivation and self-management and five with cognitive strategies (Weinstein *et al.*, 1987).
- The Strategy Inventory for Language Learning (SILL), a self-report survey of preferred language learning strategies (cf. Oxford, 1990).
- The TOEFL test was administered to determine the English profi-

ciency of the students. The test consists of three sections that are timed separately: Listening comprehension; Structure and Written expression; and Vocabulary and Reading comprehension (Educational Testing Service, 1989).

Biographical details about each student (e.g. age, gender, location, etc.) were acquired from the academic administration.

In addition to the questionnaires, the students participated in semi-structured telephone and e-mail interviews. The purpose of the interviews was twofold: first, to ask participants to indicate the type of support they currently received from TLS, as well as the support they thought they needed to complete their English studies successfully; and second, to indicate what contextual factors affected their ESL learning as well as the extent of the influence (e.g. support from the family; work responsibilities; difficulty of content; lack of interaction with lecturers, etc.).

Data collection procedure

The identified students agreed to participate in the study. They completed the questionnaires in a scheduled facilitation session. Students were telephoned and e-mailed using a personal information list obtained from Administration. The researchers explained the purpose of the interview and asked each student whether s/he would be willing to answer a number of questions related to his/her studying. The e-mail interview was used as a follow-up to clarify the correctness of responses, as well as to collect any additional information, and to provide students with the opportunity to comment on factors affecting their English studies and the support they needed/wanted from TLS.

Analysis

The quantitative data were analysed by means of descriptive statistics (e.g. means, standard deviations and percentages) and the qualitative data by means of qualitative narrative reporting.

Results

The results are presented under two headings: profiling and support. In this section only those results that have a bearing on the proposed framework for learner support are discussed.

Profiling

The aim of the framework presented in Figure 1 is to provide decision makers of all kinds with a reasonably comprehensive overview of the most important factors that need to be taken into account when profiling distance learners (i.e. to create an awareness of learner and contextual variability). The framework can, however, also be used for empirical analysis of the individual and or combined explanatory power of the various personal and contextual factors that can affect learning failure or success in a mixed mode delivery setting.

An analysis of the red (at-risk) student profiles revealed the following. With regard to demographic variables, the results indicated that four of the five at-risk students had had _no prior experience_ with distance learning. The requirements of self-study, self-regulation and structured time management might have been a problem for these students. In addition, the results indicated the English language proficiency of the at-risk students, specifically their _reading comprehension_, was equal only to that of Grade 8 to Grade 10 learners. These learners, therefore, enter distance learning underprepared for the reading demands that are placed on them within a distance learning programme.

When the affective variables are considered, the results indicated the at-risk students were _very anxious_. These learners' level of anxiety was above the norm set for first-year students in South Africa, namely $x = 26$ (cf. Van Aardt _et al._, 1994). The at-risk students also seemed to place more emphasis on an _external locus of control_. This finding is similar to that found in a study conducted by White (1999), where students who were struggling to recognise and accept the constraints of the distance learning context had an external locus of control, and tended to emphasise aspects such as the quality and amount of interaction with tutors and the quality of course material.

An analysis of their learning styles indicated that the at-risk learners had a decided _visual modality strength_. In specific situations they would also use a hands-on learning style. In addition to their visual and kinaesthetic perceptual learning style preferences, the at-risk learners were also more _concrete-sequential, closure-oriented, and analytic_. These results indicated these learners were concerned with concrete facts, which they preferred to be presented in a step-by-step organised fashion. They have a strong need for clarity and structure, and they want everything spelt out carefully and systematically. These findings seem to give a message to course developers to ensure materials give very clear explanations, help with self-monitoring, and provide ideas for practice and excellent feedback.

For the metacognitive variables (specifically _self-regulation_), the mean scores of the at-risk learners were fairly low. In terms of _cognitive and metacognitive learning strategy use_ the at-risk students' mean scores were also fairly low. The results of a study conducted by White (1995) indicate the importance of specifically metacognitive strategy use by distance learners. In addition, her results indicated the importance of the monitoring, evaluation and self-management aspects of metacognition for distance learners. The results of this study seem to indicate at-risk learners are not sufficiently equipped to handle the demands placed upon them by the distance learning environment. Now, possibly for the first time in their lives, they must take the initiative for their own learning, know how to structure their own learning organisation, plan their own schedule, pace themselves, and hold themselves accountable for whether or not an assignment is done today or tomorrow. Previously, all these learning tasks had been the responsibility of the lecturer or teacher, and the learner had simply to show up and follow directions. Suddenly, the traits of dependency that served this student so well in a traditional setting (also in school) now become a major barrier to learner progress in a distance learning environment.

An analysis of the contextual factors indicated at-risk learners rated the effect factors within the micro-, meso- and macrosystems had on their learning more highly than the successful learners; indicating perhaps that they were unable to reconcile the demands of everyday life with the demands of learning within a distance learning environment. Within the microsystem the following factors were emphasised by the learners: family illness, family disruption (mother studying), and lack of adequate studying facilities at home (by candle light). Within the mesosystem the following factors were emphasised by the learners: too much content (can't get through the work); administrative problems (e.g. registration chaos, materials received late); more contact with lecturers wanted; and assistance wanted with the writing of assignments. Within the macrosystem the following factors were emphasised by the learners: workload at work demanding; away from home because of work requirements; community responsibilities (e.g. church, sport).

An analysis of the green (successful) student profiles indicated the following. The results showed the successful students had some *prior experience* with distance learning (e.g. correspondence courses) and their language proficiency, specifically their *reading comprehension* ability, was better than that of the at-risk students.

These learners were *less anxious* and had a stronger *internal locus of control*. With regard to their learning styles the students had a *visual* modality strength. The successful learners were more *intuitive, open and global*. These learners like to take daring intellectual leaps and are comfortable if all information is not systematic. It is important to note, however, that the mean scores for the successful learners on the above-mentioned styles were close together, indicating successful learners are more likely to 'style flex' (i.e. they had the ability to vary their styles as the task or situation demands). It is also noticeable that their *self-regulatory abilities* were better than those of the at-risk learners. These learners used metacognitive, cognitive, compensation and affective strategies fairly frequently.

An analysis of the contextual factors indicated these learners coped better with the effect that external variables had on their learning. They seem to require less academic 'scaffolding' than the at-risk learners. With regard to the microsystem the learners emphasised that families had to take the back seat. As for the mesosystem, the following factors were emphasised by learners: more interaction with lecturers/facilitators and fellow students (e.g. for critical discussion); content overload; constructive feedback; and administrative aspects very time consuming. With regard to the macrosystem the following factor was emphasised: work responsibilities necessitate the 'leaving' of studies for up to two weeks.

Support

Three types of required support emerged from this case study: administrative, academic, and relational. Students indicated they often need assistance in dealing with the routine administrative aspects of a course or programme: registering, paying fees or getting tuition benefits, obtaining materials, obtaining a student card, talking to the most appropriate person for help with a problem, and acquiring information about assignment submission dates, information about exam dates and venues, etc. Academic support is defined in operational terms as including such elements as provision of competent lecturers/facilitators, quality materials, use of technology, library support, and other typical human and material resources. It also refers to the instructional design of courses, interaction with lecturers/facilitators and other students. Relational support describes the more affective dimension of the learning process wherein we encourage, motivate, and nurture learners at an emotional level in an attempt to strike a balance with the more intellectual/cognitive support typically provided by academic institutions of higher education.

To sum up, language learners with a *red profile* indicated that they needed the following support:

Administrative

- Procedure for the recognition of prior learning.
- Direct contact with people who could help them with registering and finding bursaries.
- Regular progress checks on administrative issues (e.g. obtaining a student card).
- Guidelines on the calculation of their participation marks (i.e. semester marks that give students access to the exams).

- Information on exam dates and exam centres.
- A 24-hour call centre for administrative issues.
- Timely delivery of study materials.
- University regulations (i.e. having access as well as understanding them).

Academic

- How to study a specific module (e.g. literature) (not the cryptic guidelines provided in the study guides).
- Learning assistance (e.g. tutorials as provided for on-campus students).
- Help with reading and studying in general.
- Quick feedback ('I don't know whether I am on the right track').
- How to deal with the immense volume of work (e.g. planning, organising and time management for literature and linguistic sections).
- Someone who could help them throughout the course (i.e. mentor or tutor).

Relational

- Someone who could listen to their problems and provide encouragement and motivational support.
- Guidance in terms of appropriate module choice within a specific programme.
- General counselling.

Language learners with a *green profile* indicated they needed the following support:

Administrative

- Specific people to assist with specific tasks (e.g. registering, recognition of prior learning).
- Timely delivery of materials.
- Bursary assistance.

Academic

- More interaction with lecturers/facilitators and fellow learners.
- More constructive feedback on assignments.
- Additional reading on aspects found personally interesting in the module.

- Greater use of technology to communicate and search for information.

Relational

- Someone to inspire them and keep them motivated when the going gets tough.

Support for distance learners should not be overlooked when planning distance programmes. It is clear that student support services should comprise a significant part of budgeted costs of the programme. Successful learner support strategies can thwart the 'revolving door syndrome' for many distance language learners and keep students enrolled long enough to accomplish what they set out to do.

A Framework for Learner Support Provision

What then, might an integrated support system look like for language learners and potential language learners in an ideal world? The purpose of the framework presented in Table 6.1 is to guide the design and delivery of learner support within a distance learning environment. The framework seeks to be prescriptive in that it suggests components that should be considered in order to ensure accountable learner support in various language courses and programmes.

The framework seeks to address the following questions, based on learner profiles and their self-identified learner support needs:

- What type of support should be provided?
- How can the support be described?
- When should the support be provided?
- What degree of support, and during what stage of study?
- Who will provide the support?
- How will the support be delivered?

The support needs of distance learners at the Potchefstroom University for CHE were divided into three categories: administrative, academic and relational support. The second component gives a description of the specific type of support that needs to be provided. The third component refers to when the support should be provided – at this institution three peak periods were identified, namely pre-registration, registration and post-registration. The fourth component of the framework refers to the degree of support – low, medium or high – as well as the stage when the support needs to be provided (e.g. first year, second year or third year of

Table 6.1 Framework for supporting distance learners

Support	Description of the support to be provided	When should support be provided?	Degree of support	Who will provide the support?	How will the support be delivered?
Administrative	Information on fees & financial support. Procedure for recognition of prior learning. Information on admission and registration. Information on administrative procedures and regulations.	Pre-registration	1st year: High 2nd year: Low 3rd year: Low	Administration section dedicated to distance education.	Booklet. University rules and regulations yearbook. In person. Letters. Telephone. E-mail. Fax.
	Control procedures to ensure all administrative issues are in order. Access to bookshop and library services. Delivery of learning materials.	Registration	1st year: High 2nd year: Medium 3rd year: Low	Administration section. Academic services. University library. Dispatch centre.	Letters. E-mails. Faxes.
	A 24-hour call service centre. Assistance with resources. Assignment and mark inquiries. Dispatch centre (postal issues). Contact details of specific lecturers responsible for modules in the programme. Where to go and who to contact when lost. Technology support and guidance.	Post-registration	1st year: High 2nd year: Medium 3rd year: Low	Administrative section of Academic services. Dedicated distance library personnel.	Telephone. E-mail. Fax. Booklet. Troubleshooting guide.
Academic	Induction into requirements and pressures of distance learning. Diagnostic and psychological testing. Language proficiency testing.	Pre-registration	1st year: Medium 2nd year: Medium 3rd year: Low	Academic services.	Print. Video/audio. Internet & WWW. Face-to-face.

Table 6.1 (*cont.*) Framework for supporting distance learners

Support	Description of the support to be provided	When should support be provided?	Degree of support	Who will provide the support?	How will the support be delivered?
Academic	Pre-course requirements and counselling. Assignment guidelines. Academic writing skills. Study skills and strategy training. Computer and internet training.	Registration	1st year: High 2nd year: Medium 3rd year: Medium	Academic services. Language centre. Dept. of Information Science	Print. Video/audio. Internet & WWW. Face-to-face.
	Learner support centres. Mentoring system. Feedback. Tutorials. Progress checks. Language support. Pre-examination training.	Post-registration	1st year: High 2nd year: High 3rd year: Medium	Academic services. Lecturers presenting module. Language centre. Academic services.	Print. Video/audio. Internet & WWW. Face-to-face.
Relational	Guidance and someone to talk to (asking general info questions). Encouragement.	Pre-registration	1st year: Low 2nd year: Medium 3rd year: Medium-High	Academic services.	Telephone. SMS. E-mail.
	Crisis hotline booklet with contact numbers and specific people who can be contacted. Encouragement and motivation to get started.	Registration	1st year: Medium 2nd year: Low 3rd year: Low	Academic services.	Booklet.
	Contact details of fellow students. Peer support/study groups. Psychological counselling. Crisis line. Religious counselling. Emotional progress checks. Course completion encouragement and motivation.	Post-registration	1st year: High 2nd year: High 3rd year: Medium-High	Administrative section of academic services. Academic services (specialists in the respective fields). University church ministers.	Letters. Telephone. SMS. E-mail. Internet & WWW.

study). The fifth component specifically states who should assume responsibility for providing the specified support, while the last component refers to how the support should be delivered.

The point of departure of the framework is that students at different stages of their study careers and studying different sorts of modules may have differing support needs. Care should therefore be taken not to assume that individual learning needs are stable, either over time or across different study programmes/course. This is not likely to be the case. The selection (or rejection) of particular support activities needs to be taken in the light of the knowledge that student dropout, failure or success is closely linked to the nature and level of support services.

Any institution can 'fill in the blanks' in the framework and identify specific support services that can be provided to match the level of student support needed. The outline enables institutions and even individual lecturers to organise the variety of strategies that may already be in place but which have no guiding or coherent master plan. By adopting such procedures, institutions increase their own student support services efficiency while enhancing the academic performance and learning outcomes of its students.

Conclusion

Learning failure or success should be seen in terms of the interaction among personal factors, the interaction among contextual factors, and the interaction between what the individual brings to the learning situation (i.e. personal factors) and the demands and expectations of the environment (i.e. contextual factors). The critical issue is to assist institutions, not just in improving dropout and failure rates, but in providing a high quality academic programme with specific support structures in a manner consonant with student needs.

Because of the dynamic nature of the individual learners and the continuously changing contextual factors, a 'generic' profile of distance learners does not exist. Continuous monitoring of personal and contextual factors will facilitate favourable learning outcomes. By profiling and supporting learners (both unsuccessful and successful) it is possible to highlight the factors that institutions and programme/course developers can change or do something about to improve future distance learning experiences for the diverse distance learner population, and to help them attain what we all seek – success.

Providing courses or programmes within a distance learning environment is a core educational strategy for many traditional universities. However, 'the potential for failure, or mediocre courses or programmes is high, unfortunately' (Buchanan, 2000). Developing proactive, strategic support plans requires the commitment of the entire institution, including faculty and students. Going that extra mile with student support will ensure that institutions get a competitive edge, just as some producers advertise not just the quality of their product but also the quality of the 'after-sales' service.

The purpose of the framework provided in this study is, therefore, to guide the administrative, academic and relational support services in a coherent and accountable fashion while at the same time helping all students, in particular the at-risk students and the students without prior distance learning experience, to become self-regulated lifelong learners.

References

Abi-Samra, N. (2002) Affect in language learning: Motivation – Online document: http://nadabs.tripod.com/motivation/#8 [2002, March 15].

Alexander, P.A. and Murphy, P.K. (1998) The research base for APA's learner-centered psychological principles. In N.M. Lambert. and B.L. McCombs. *How Students Learn: Reforming Schools through Learner-centered Education.* Washington, DC: American Psychological Association.

Altmann, H. and Arambasich, L. (1982) A study of locus of control with adult students. *Canadian Counselor* 16 (2), 97–101.

Apter, S.J. (1978) *Troubled Children: Troubled Systems.* Oxford: Pergamon.

Bandura, A. (1986) *Social Foundations of Thought and Action: A Social Cognitive Theory.* Englewood Cliffs, NJ: Prentice-Hall.

Bandura, A. (1997) *Self-efficacy: The Exercise of Control.* New York: Freeman.

Bernt, F.L. and Bugbee, A.C. (1994) Study practices and attitude related to academic success in a distance learning program. *Distance Education* 14 (1), 97–112.

Boston, R.L. (1992) Remote delivery of instruction via the PC and modem: What have we learned? *The American Journal of Distance Education* 6 (3), 45–60.

Bronfenbrenner, U. (1979) *The Ecology of Human Development.* Cambridge, MA: Harvard University Press.

Brophy, J.E. (1988) Synthesis of research on strategies for motivating students to learn. *Educational Leadership* 44, 40–8.

Brown, H.D. (1994) *Principles of Language Learning and Teaching.* Englewood Cliffs, NJ: Prentice Hall.

Buchanan, E.A. (2000) Going the extra mile: Serving distance education students -Online document: http://www.westga.edu/~distance/buchanan31.html [2002, March 27].

Butcher, N. (2001) Distance education in developing countries: Delivering on the promise. Paper presented at the E-Learning Conference, Caesars, Gauteng.

Caldwell, G.P. and Ginther, D.W. (1996) Differences in learning styles of low socio-economic status for low and high achievers. *Education* 117 (1), 141–47.

Carney-Crompton, S. and Tan, J. (2002) Support systems, psychological functioning, and academic performance of nontraditional female students. *Adult Education Quarterly* 52 (2), 140–54.

Chacon-Duque, F.J. (1985) *Building Academic Quality in Distance Higher Education.* Monograph in higher education evaluation and policy. Pennsylvania, PA.: Pennsylvania State University.

Corno, L. and Mandinach, E.B. (1983) The role of cognitive engagement in classroom learning and motivation. *Educational Psychologist* 18, 88–108.

Department of Education (1997) A programme for higher education transformation. *Education White Paper 3.* Pretoria: Department of Education.

Department of Education (2000) Meeting the equity, quality and social development imperatives of South Africa in the 21st century. Shape and size of Higher Education task team, Council on Higher Education – Online document: http:// www.education.pwv.gov.za/DoE_s . . . tion/CHE/CHE_Report30June2000. htm [2001, May 23].

Dille, B. and Mezack, M. (1991) Identifying predictors of high risk among community college telecourse students. *The American Journal of Distance Education* 5 (1), 24–35.

Dreyer, C. (1992) Learner variables as predictors of ESL proficiency. Unpublished PhD thesis. Potchefstroom: Potchefstroom University for CHE.

Dreyer, C. (2001) Profiling distance learning within the technological era. Paper presented at the 15th Open and Distance Learning Association of Australia's Biennial Forum, Sydney, Australia.

Educational Testing Service (1989) *TOEFL: The Institutional Testing Program.* Princeton, NY: Educational Testing Service.

Ellis, R. (1994) *The Study of Second Language Acquisition.* Oxford: Oxford University Press.

Farrington, G.C. (1999) The new technologies and the future of residential undergraduate education. In R.N. Katz (ed.) *Dancing with the Devil.* San Francisco, CA: Jossey-Bass.

Galusha, J.M. (1997) Barriers to learning in distance education – Online document: http://www.infrastruction.com/barriers.htm [2001, December 05].

Gardiner, L.F. (1994) *Redesigning Higher Education: Producing Dramatic Gains in Student Learning.* Washington, DC: George Washington University, Graduate School of Education and Human Development.

Gardner, R., Tremblay, P. and Masgoret, A-M. (1997) Towards a full model of second language learning: An empirical investigation. *The Modern Language Journal* 81 (3), 344–62.

Gawe, N. and De Kock, C. (2002) Higher education: Spectators or players in globalisation. *South African Journal of Higher Education* 16 (1), 36–40.

Gibson, C.C. (1996) Toward an understanding of academic self-concept in distance education. *The American Journal of Distance Education* 10 (1), 23–36.

Gordon, A. (2001) SAIDE's rural education research project: The Jozini case study. *Open Learning Through Distance Education*, March 10–12.

Grasha, A.F. and Yangarber-Hicks, N. (2000) Integrating teaching styles and learning styles with instructional technology. *College Teaching* 48 (1), 2–9.

Hancock, G.F. (2000) Delivering individual student support in a distance education system. Paper presented at the ICDE Asian Regional Conference. New Delhi, India.

Hurd, S. (2000) Distance language learners and learner support: Beliefs, difficulties and use of strategies. *Links and Letters 7: Autonomy in L2 Learning*, 61–80.

Kaiser, R. (1993) A change in focus . . . without losing sight of the child. *School Psychology International* 14 (1), 5–20.

Keefe, J.W. (1979) *Student Learning Styles: Diagnosing and Prescribing Programs.* Reston, VA: National Association of Secondary School Principals.

Kember, D. (1995) *Open Learning Courses for Adults: A Model of Student Progress.* Englewood Cliffs, NJ, Educational Technology Publications.

Kember, D., Murphy, D., Siaw, I. and Yuen, K.S. (1991) Toward a causal model of student progress in distance education: Research in Hong Kong. *The American Journal of Distance Education* 5 (2), 3–14.

Kennedy, D. and Powell, R. (1976) Student progress and withdrawal in the Open University. *Teaching at a Distance* 7, 61–75.

Kirkup, G. and Von Prummer, C. (1997) The threats and opportunities of new educational forms and media. *The European Journal of Women's Studies* 4, 39–62.

Klesius, J., Homan, S. and Thompson, T. (1997) Distance education compared to traditional instruction: The students' view. *International Journal of Instructional Media* 24 (3), 207–20.

Knox, A. (1977) *Adult Learning and Development.* San Francisco: Jossey-Bass.

Kumar, A. (1999) Learner characteristics and success in Indian distance education. *Open Learning* 14 (3), 52–8.

Landbeck, R. and Mugler, F. (2000) Distance learners of the South Pacific: Study strategies, learning conditions, and consequences for course design. *Journal of Distance Education* 15 (1) – Online document: http://cade.athabascau.ca/vol15.1/landbeck.html [2001, June 20].

Liu, Y. and Ginther, D. (1999) Cognitive styles and distance education. *Online Journal of Distance Learning Administration* 2 (3) – Online document: http://www.westga.edu/~distance/liu23.html [2001, March 06].

Lowe, S.D. (1997) The situational academic and relational support in distance education (SARSIDE) model – Online document: http://www.gospelcom.net/bakersguide/sarside.html [2001, April 12].

McKeachie, W.J., Pintrich, P.R., Lin, Y. and Smith, D. (1986) *Teaching and Learning in the College Classroom: A Review of the Research Literature.* Ann Arbor, MI: National Center for Research to Improve Postsecondary Teaching and Learning.

McLoughlin, C. (1996) Higher levels of agency for students: Participation, self-regulation and the learning process. In J. Abbot and L. Willcoxson (eds) *Teaching and Learning within and across Disciplines.* Proceedings of the 5th Annual Teaching Learning Forum, Murdoch University, Perth – Online document: http://cea.curtin.edu.au/tlf/tlf1996/mcloughlin.html [2002, March 06].

Moore, M.G. and Kearsley, G. (1996) *Distance Education. A Systems View.* New York: Wadsworth.

Oaks, M. (1996) *Western cooperative for educational telecommunications* – Online document: http://www.wiche.edu/telecom/techWASU.html [2000, September 16].

O'Malley, J.M. and Chamot, A.U. (1990) *Learning Strategies in Second Language Acquisition.* Cambridge: Cambridge University Press.

O'Malley, J.M. and McCraw, H. (1999) Students' perception of distance learning, online learning and the traditional classroom. *Online Journal of Distance Learning Administration,* 2 (4) – Online document: http://www/westga.edu/~distance/omalley24.html [2001, June 13].

Oxford, R.L. (1990) *Language Learning Strategies: What Every Teacher Should Know.* New York: Heinle & Heinle.

Oxford, R.L. (1995) Style analysis survey: Assessing your own learning and working styles. In J.M. Reid (ed.) *Learning Styles in the ESL/EFL Classroom*. Boston, MA: Heinle & Heinle.

Oxford, R.L. (1999) Anxiety and the language learner: New insights. In J. Arnold and H.D. Brown (eds) *Affect in Language Learning*. Cambridge: Cambridge University Press.

Pajares, F. and Schunk, D.H. (2001) Self-beliefs and school success: Self-efficacy, self-concept, and school achievement. In R. Riding and S. Rayner (eds) *Perception*. London: Ablex Publishing.

Parker, A. (1999) A study of variables that predict dropout from distance education. *International Journal of Educational Technology*, 1 (2) – Online document: http://www.outreach.uiuc.edu/ijet/v1n2/parker [2002, October 15]

Phillip, A. (1993) Problems for women in distance education at the University of Papua New Guinea. *Open Learning* 8 (1), 3–9.

Phillippe, K.A. (1995) *National Profile of Community Colleges: Trends and Statistics 1995–1996*. Washington, DC: Community College Press.

Pintrich, P.R., Smith, D.A.F. and McKeachie, W.J. (1989) *A Manual for the Use of the Motivated Strategies for Learning Questionnaires*. Ann Arbor, Michigan: School of Education.

Powell, R., Conway, C. and Ross, L. (1990) Effects of student predisposing characteristics on student success. *Journal of Distance Education*, 5 (1) – Online document: http://cade.athabascau.ca/vol5.1/8_powell_et_al.html [2003, May 13].

Pugliese, R.R. (1994) Telecourse persistence and psychological variables. *American Journal of Distance Education* 8 (3), 22–39.

Pythian, T. and Clements, M. (1982) Drop-out from third level math courses. *Teaching at a Distance* 21, 33–45.

Reid, J. (1995a) *Learning Styles in the ESL/EFL Classroom*. Boston, MA: Heinle & Heinle.

Reid, J. (1995b) Managing learner support. In F. Lockwood (ed.) *Open and Distance Learning Today*. New York: Routledge.

Rekkedal, T. (1983) Enhancing student progress in Norway. *Teaching at a Distance* 23, 19–24.

Robinson, B. (1995) Research and pragmatism in learner support. In F. Lockwood (ed.) *Open and Distance Learning Today*. London: Routledge.

Ross, J.L. (1997) The effect of cognitive learning styles on human-computer interaction: Implications for computer-aided learning. Masters thesis. University of Calgary.

Rotter, J.S. (1989) Internal vs. external control of reinforcement. *American Psychologist* 45 (5), 489–93.

Schmeck, R.R. and Nguyen, T. (1996) Factors affecting college students' learning styles: Family characteristics which contribute to college students attitudes toward education and preferences for learning strategies. *College Student Journal* 30 (4), 542–6.

Schrum, L.M. (2000) Online learning in the academy: The conundrum that may divide us – Online document: http://www.findarticles.com/cf_0/m)hkv/3_9/66408227/print.jhtml [2001, April 10].

Sewart, D. (1993) Student support systems in distance education. *Open Learning* 8 (3), 3.

Shaker, H.R. (2000) Distance education in Bahrain: Situation and needs. *Open Learning* 15 (1), 57–70.

Sherry, L. (1996) Issues in distance education. *International Journal of Educational Telecommunications* 1 (4), 337–65.

Shih, C-C. and Gamon, J. (1999) Student learning styles, motivation, learning strategies and achievement in web-based courses – Online document: http://iccel.wfu.edu/publications/journals/jcel/jcel990305/ccshih.htm [2002, April 3].

Simpson, O. (2002) *Supporting Students in Online, Open and Distance Learning*. London: Kogan Page.

Slaughter, S. (1998) Federal policy and supply-side institutional resource allocation at public research universities. *Review of Higher Education* 21 (3), 209–44.

Spodick, E.F. (1995) The evolution of distance learning – Online document: http://sqzm14.ust.hk/distance/evolution-distance-learning.htm [2001, February 02].

Stirling, D.L. (1997) *Learner control* – Online document: http://www.stirlinglaw.com/deborah/stir6.htm [2002, November 02].

Sunday Times (23 July 2000) – Online document: http://www.suntimes.co.za/2000/07/23/insight/in06.htm [2001, May 25].

Sweet, R. (1986) Student dropout in distance education: An application of Tinto's model. *Distance Education* 7 (1), 68–91.

Tait, A. (1995) Student support in open and distance learning. In F. Lockwood (ed.) *Open and Distance Learning Today*. New York: Routledge.

Tinto, V. (1987) *Leaving College*. Chicago: University of Chicago Press.

Van Aardt, A., Van Wyk, C.K. and Steyn, H.F. (1994) Assessment of student learning. *South African Journal of Higher Education* 8 (1), 226–32.

Van Wyk, L.A. (2001) The main contributors to the success rate in new learning models. Paper presented at the E-Learning Conference, Ceasars, Gauteng.

Vermunt, J.D. (1996) Metacognitive, cognitive and affective aspects of learning styles and strategies: A phenomenographic analysis. *Higher Education* 31 (1), 20–5.

Wagner, E. (1993) Variables affecting distance educational program success. *Educational Technology* 33 (4), 28–32.

Wallace, L. (1996) Changes in the demographics and motivations of distance education students. *Journal of Distance Education*, 11 (1) – Online document: http://cade.athabascau.ca/vol11.1/wallace.html [2002, July 07].

Weinstein, C.E., Palmer, D.R. and Schulte, A.C. (1987) *LASSI: Learning and Study Strategies Inventory*. Clearwater, Fl: H & H Publishing Company, Inc.

Weinstein, C.E., Husman, J. and Dierking, D.R. (2000) Self-regulation interventions with a focus on learning strategies. In M. Boekaerts, P.R. Pintrich and M. Zeidner (eds) *Handbook of Self-regulation*. New York: Academic Press.

White, C. (1995) Autonomy and strategy use in distance foreign language learning. *System* 23 (2), 207–21.

White, C. (1999) Expectations and emergent beliefs of self-instructed language learners. *System* 27, 443–57.

Wood, H. (1996) Designing study materials for distance students – Online document: http://www.csu.edu.au/division/oli/oli-rd/occpap17/design.html [2001, May 14].

Wynd, W.R. and Bozman, C.S. (1996) Student learning style: A segmentation strategy for higher education. *Journal of Education for Business* 71 (4), 232–5.

Zhang, J., Li, F., Duan, C. and Wu, G. (2001) Research on self-efficacy of distance learning and its influence on learners' attainments – Online document: http:// www/icce2001.org/cd/pdf/p13/CN100.pdf [2002, October 23].

Chapter 7

Assessing Intercultural Competence Gain in a German Distance Learning Course for Adults

MONICA SHELLEY and UWE BAUMANN

Introduction

The authors have carried out research with adult students studying German at a distance with the Open University which sought to investigate their motives in learning German, their experience of the language and the effects of the course on them. As a way of gauging what progress the students might have made in the acquisition of intercultural competence over the study of the course, we used a before-and-after questionnaire to assess their knowledge gain and to check whether the attitudes these students held towards Germans changed at all. We also examined their continuous and final assessment results to investigate how much their language skills had improved over the nine months' study of their course. Case studies of four students are included to demonstrate the inter-relationship of the three intercultural elements and to provide a qualitative demonstration of individual students' progress.

Auftakt: An Open University German course

This chapter reports on research carried out with adults studying German at a distance with the Open University in the United Kingdom. Founded in 1969, the University has extended and developed its curriculum over the past three decades, beginning the teaching of languages in 1995. There are currently (2003) several German courses available from the University, and students who complete enough of them to gain 120 credit points are awarded a Diploma in German. Credits accrued from the study of the German courses may also count towards the award of an undergraduate degree and, from 2003, towards a Modern Languages Degree. There are similar courses available in French and Spanish.

The research described here is based on students completing *Auftakt* in 1998 – at that time this was the lowest level German course available. Although there are no specific entry requirements, this is not a beginners', but rather an improvers' course: students progress from a level roughly equivalent to that reached by school pupils when they are examined at the end of Year 10 (usually at the age of 16) up to that needed to pass the Advanced Level examination (usually taken at the age of 18). In Open University terms, this is described as Level One. *Auftakt* is designed to be studied over nine months for approximately seven hours a week.

The Open University's improvers' course, *Auftakt* (Shelley, 1996) is a mixed-media course with course books, authentic video and audio documentaries, an audio drama which runs through the course and pre-recorded audio activities (Shelley, 1999). The core component of the course is the course book – designed on the basis of the principle established by Derek Rowntree (Rowntree, 1994) of the tutorial-in-print – integrating the various elements of the course and presenting them according to didactic principles which support the precepts of distance education (Baumann, 1999). The instructional design ensures that the student is guided through the course materials, is aware of what is expected of him/her and is fully involved in the teaching and learning process. The course is centred round contemporary themes, such as work, health and fitness, and features two German towns, Leipzig and Tübingen. Students are offered support through a well-established non-compulsory tutorial system. Assessment is both continuous and final, in the form of end-of-course written and spoken assignments. Students are thus offered a standard package of materials and support, with the result that their learning experience is comparable, wherever they live and whatever their circumstances.

Auftakt aims to help its students to develop intercultural competence. This chapter focuses on three teaching elements which have been defined (see below) as making up intercultural competence – skills, knowledge and attitudes. Having discussed the nature and purpose of intercultural competence in language teaching, this study then summarises research into the testing of languages and how this relates to the assessment of students learning languages at a distance and, in particular, the *Auftakt* students. It then examines the degree to which a particular cohort of students of *Auftakt* gained in knowledge of German culture, changed their attitudes towards Germany and the Germans over the course of their study and improved their language skills.

The development of intercultural competence

Three important and inter-connecting themes in the teaching of foreign languages today are _communicative competence, cultural awareness_ and _intercultural competence_. Intercultural competence has been described (Sercu, 2002) as building on the first two.

Communicative competence has most recently been defined and its implications spelt out within the Common European Framework for language learning, teaching and assessment, developed as part of the Council of Europe 'Language learning for European citizenship' project (Council of Europe, 2001; Trim, 2000).

Cultural awareness is described variously as cultural studies, _Landeskunde_ and civilisation in English, German and French, and has near-synonyms in other languages, with varying emphases on subjects, process and outcomes. As Risager points out, cultural awareness ' . . . is closely linked with the development of post-modern society with its interest in cultural difference and the relationship to "the Other", no matter whether the latter is different from a national, ethnic, social regional or institutional point of view. . . . Cultural awareness is a key concept which emphasises both cultural insight and attitude and identity awareness.' (Risager, 2000: 159)

Intercultural competence, defined as 'the ability to interact effectively with people from cultures that we recognise as being different from our own (Guilherme, 2000: 297), has been the subject of intensive research over the last three decades, notably by Byram (see particularly Byram, 1993, 1997; Byram & Zarate, 1997; Byram & Fleming, 1998) and Kramsch (Kramsch, 1993, 1995; Kramsch _et al.,_ 1996). Byram emphasises that intercultural competence is more complex than communicative competence, because it focuses on 'establishing and maintaining relationships' (Byram, 1997: 3) rather than just the exchange of information and sending of messages. Kramsch (1993) identifies the differences between cultural awareness and intercultural competence by highlighting the tendency in foreign language teaching to divide the teaching of culture from the teaching of language. ' . . . culture is often seen as mere information conveyed by the language, not as a feature of language itself; cultural awareness becomes an educational objective in itself, separate from language. If, however, language is seen as social practice, culture becomes the very core of language teaching' (Kramsch, 1993: 8). She also warns: 'Multiculturalism in education raises the sceptre of a moral relativism that teachers do not feel competent to deal with' (Kramsch _et al.,_ 1996: 100). So what are useful guidelines for teachers seeking to nurture the development of intercultural competence among their students? Sercu states that. . . . 'becoming an interculturally competent user of a foreign language not only involves the acquisition of communicative competence in that language, it also involves the acquisition of particular skills, attitudes, values, knowledge items and ways of looking upon the world' (Sercu, 2002: 63). So it is important to ensure that the elements Sercu has identified are present in any course which claims to offer the opportunity for intercultural competence development among its students.

Language Testing

There is a substantial body of research relating to the history and development of testing languages over the past 20 years, which reflects to a large extent different, evolving methods of language teaching (Bachman, 2000; Clapham & Corson, 1997; Clapham, 2000; McNamara, 1996, 2000 among others). Bachman has referred to 'the blossoming of language testing research that we have witnessed in this period [which] has provided us with a rich variety of research approaches and tools, while at the same time broadening the research questions that are being investigated.' (Bachman, 2000: 2). He summarised this 'broadening' under the headings of

- research methodology (new theories and approaches which have been employed, such as criterion-referenced measurement, generalisable theory);
- practical advances (this includes computer- or web-based assessment and testing languages for special purposes);
- research into factors that affect performance on language tests (such as the test-taking process or the characteristics of test takers);
- the nature of authentic, or performance assessment; and
- concerns with the ethics of language testing (ethics of test use, and the impact of tests on teaching – the so-called 'washback' implications).

While all these different aspects of language testing are relevant to the decisions made concerning the methods and nature of the assessment for *Auftakt*, research on performance assessment appears to provide important and relevant guidelines for a course like *Auftakt*. As Clapham (2000) emphasises, the move towards the communicative approach to teaching has encouraged testers to make their test items more integrated (less discrete) and the tasks more authentic in both content and purpose. This has been formalised as performance assessment, which McNamara describes as focusing on two issues: ' . . . (a) the *quality of the execution* of the performance . . . and (b) what the performance reveals about the *underlying state of language knowledge* in the individual being assessed' (McNamara, 1996: 6). He raises the important questions of *how* performances will be judged – and the use of performance criteria – and *how well* we can generalise from the test performance to subsequent performance – the question of predictive validity (McNamara, 1996). This raises the question of integrative and integrated test tasks: the difference between the two has been described as representing two ends of a continuum by Lewkowicz (1997: 121), who says 'To complete integrative tasks, test takers need simultaneously to employ more than one language skill. . . . As one moves along the continuum towards the integrated task, the test tasks increase in the degree of reality they attempt to replicate.' To achieve fully integrated tasks is the aim of performance testing.

Another body of research into achievement in second language learning which has relevance for the scope of the current study is that reported by Masgoret and Gardner (2003). This dealt with attitudes, motivation and second language learning and the use of the Attitude/Motivation Test Battery, mainly by Gardner and his associates. This work investigated the relationship of achievement in second language learning to five attitude/motivation variables from Gardner's socio-educational model:

- integrativeness (defined as attitudes towards the target language group, interest in foreign languages);
- attitudes towards the learning situation (including evaluation of the course and of the teacher);
- motivation (including attitudes towards learning the target language and desire to learn it);
- integrative orientation (desire for integration with the other language community and favourable attitudes towards the learning situation); and
- instrumental orientation (practical reasons for learning the language without any interest in getting closer socially to the language community); plus two additional variables: availability of the language in the community and age level of the students.

The outcomes of Gardner's research demonstrate clearly that the correlations between achievement and motivation are uniformly higher that those between achievement and integrativeness, attitudes and either integrative or instrumental orientation (which were considerably lower). Neither availability nor age had clear moderating effects. This raised the question of whether our students' motivation was echoed in their achievement (assessment outcomes) in their study of *Auftakt*.

The discussion so far has not, of course, related specifically to the distance teaching of languages but to face-to-face instruction in the classroom. While there are many transferable applications, the distance element makes particular demands on both course designers and the local tutors who provide the (optional) tuition and the feedback on the continuous assessments. Technology plays a more substantial role in teaching at a distance than in the classroom, and thus in the teaching of languages at a distance, where careful choices have to be made about the selection of appropriate systems. For a brief discussion of the development of teaching languages at a distance see Shelley (2000). There is a considerable body of published work on the assessment of distance taught material, notably Thorpe, who emphasised that 'In a distance teaching institution assessment has if anything an even sharper focus in the students' experience, given the physical difference between students and between students and the accrediting institution' (Thorpe, 1998: 268). Morgan and O'Reilly (1999) have usefully summarised the key qualities of open and distance assessments as a clear rationale and consistent pedagogical approach; explicit values, aims, criteria and standards; authentic and holistic tasks; a facilitative degree of structure; sufficient and timely formative assessment and awareness of the learning context and perceptions.

Relatively little published material is available which deals specifically with distance-taught languages, though Hyland (2001) has provided useful pointers about feedback, its importance and its delivery. Feedback has, moreover, been provided at a distance primarily for written work rather than spoken assignments: another challenge with *Auftakt* (as for the other Open University language courses) was the design, delivery and feedback of speaking tests. Some of the problems and challenges of testing the spoken language are identified by Rubin and Schramm (1997) and Fulcher (1997), who focus in particular on the need for spoken language which is being assessed to be interactive.

Particular features of the way in which *Auftakt* students were assessed reflect the current debates summarised above, and are outlined below. While the *Auftakt* assessment could not yet be described as fully integrated, it is well on the way along the continuum towards that goal, as can be seen from the details of one pair of TMAs described below. There is a large body of research relating to the theory of test design, but this chapter does not touch on that, since it is not the purpose of the current study.

Continuous assessment of *Auftakt* in 1998 was of two types: Computer Marked Assignments (CMAs), which were written in the form of answers to multiple-choice question and Tutor Marked Assignments (TMAs), both written and spoken (recorded on to tape). Based on the course content, teaching activities and media, the TMAs were integrated assessments, with carefully scaffolded non-assessed preparatory activities. Instructions were precise, almost prescriptive, so that students were left in no doubt as to exactly what was expected of them. TMAs 3 (written) and 4 (spoken), for example, were based on a radio programme about the problems tourists might face when visiting a city when a trade fair was being held (the trade fairs in Leipzig had been covered in the course materials). Students were invited to work through a number of preparatory activities which enabled them to identify important points from the programme before writing a letter to a friend giving information based on the programme, but also including his or her own opinion. The spoken assignment was based on more material from the same recording, concentrating on the forthcoming furniture fair. After completing preparatory activities, the students had to record a spoken message to a friend advising him on what he might find at the fair and what practical arrangements he could make. Full assessment criteria for both written and spoken TMAs were provided, covering content, structure, development of ideas, accuracy and range of expression used and for the spoken assessment – pronunciation and fluency. Feedback to the TMAs was provided by each student's tutor, and the feedback was monitored by a different member of the teaching team.

Students had to attend a test centre for the final assessment. The written examination was similar to the written TMAs, but the spoken examination was different again: students were sent preparatory materials in advance, where they were given four different scenarios for a particular situation, which they were advised to study. On arrival for the oral examination, they were told which of the scenarios they were to present, which they did for two minutes in a group of four students. They then took part in a group discussion relating to the situation for a further period of time. This discussion was recorded and monitored. Both written and spoken assessments correspond to McNamara's description of performance tests as ' . . . tests of speaking and writing, in which a more or less extended sample of speech or writing is elicited from the test-taker, and judged by one or more trained raters using an agreed rating procedure. These samples are elicited in the context of simulations of real-world tasks in realistic contexts' (McNamara, 2000: 6).

Research Aims and Methodology

Although the Open University carries out initial market research surveys before courses are presented for the first time, students on new courses are always – to some extent – an unknown quantity. This was especially the case for the courses in modern languages. The Open University also carries out extensive surveys of their current students, especially those on new courses: these large-scale surveys concentrate on the basic demographics, students' educational qualifications on entry, their credit standing and educational aims for study with the Open University and their impressions of the materials. Assessment data are also collected regularly, both for continuous and the final assessments.

As two of the designers of *Auftakt*, we wanted to look beyond these relatively easily measurable data to investigate the nature of the students and
their learning experience in greater depth. It was decided to look at a
number of aspects which could provide more detailed information about
these adult students, their interaction with the course materials and
important aspects of their learning experience. So while we wanted to
know more about how, when and where our students gained their
knowledge of German, their experience of German-speaking countries and
their cultures, how motivated they were and what they hoped to get from
studying the course, we concentrated in particular on three new and previously undeveloped areas of research. The first was to gauge how much
knowledge about Germany these distance students gained when studying,
the second was some investigation as to whether these (mature) students
had particular attitudes towards Germany and its people and whether
study of the course had any influence on these attitudes respectively, and
the third was to gauge what progress the students made with language-related skills, as reflected through continuous and final assessment.
For a further discussion of research concerning knowledge of distance
learners, see White, 2003.

Students on this presentation of *Auftakt* were sent a qualitatively
pre-tested questionnaire at the beginning of their study and then again at
the end of the academic year. The first part of the questionnaire dealt with
demographic information, the students' experience of learning German
and contacts with German-speaking countries. The second part contained
questions about their knowledge of Germany and the German way of life
and their attitudes towards Germans.

The questions about the students' knowledge covered general information about Germany, almost all of which was taught explicitly in the course,
Auftakt. The few points not specifically taught in the course were included
to give students the opportunity to show what other information about
Germany and the Germans they might have gathered, either from their
prior experience or from additional study. We were also aware, and wished
to acknowledge, that adult students are not empty vessels embarking on
their course with little knowledge of Germany: we felt sure (but wanted to
verify this) that they bring a wide range of experience, concepts and
knowledge to their study. The questions of knowledge covered a number
of areas: geography, the political organisation of Germany, recent German
history, work and business, everyday life, and who they considered to be
famous Germans. The questions to do with these distance students'
assumptions about Germans were designed to investigate the nature of the
stereotypical images as to what Germans were like as held by these adults.
The students were asked to assess their attitudes towards Germans by

responding to a series of 25 bi-polar 5-point adjective scales covering a wide range of potential attributes.

Outcomes

Demographics

This research project has supplied a considerable amount of information about these adult learners of German at a distance. We know now that more than half of these *Auftakt* students have already learned German, either at school or in evening classes, or both, and more than half have already tried independent study of one form or another.

When asked to assess their level of German, more students assessed their receptive skills as good or excellent (reading: 43%, listening: 29%) than their productive skills (writing: 20%, speaking: 19%). Nearly a quarter (23%) considered their level of spoken German and written German (25%) to be less than adequate (see Table 7.1).

Table 7.1 Self-assessment of linguistic skills among respondents

	Slight	*Adequate*	*Good*	*Excellent*
Speaking	23%	58%	17%	2%
Writing	25%	54%	19%	1%
Listening	17%	54%	25%	4%
Reading	12%	45%	42%	1%

Few wanted to learn German for work-related reasons – the majority were motivated by the pleasure of study and the challenge presented by the course. One-third had chosen to study with the Open University because of its flexibility and convenience. A substantial number (one-third) had lived in Germany for varying amounts of time and two-thirds had friends or relatives there (see Baumann & Shelley, 2003).

Knowledge Gain

The students surveyed demonstrated a reasonably extensive knowledge of towns and cities in western Germany; but towns in the east of Germany (except for Leipzig) were more or less unknown to them. The focus on Leipzig and Tübingen in the course materials certainly impacted on them, since they mentioned both these towns much more frequently at the end of the course than at the beginning. Their knowledge about the names of German federal states improved substantially over the study of the course – they knew much more about east German states at the end than at the beginning.

In their suggestions of top German politicians, Willy Brandt featured both at the beginning and the end and students were obviously aware of the coming-to-power of Gerhard Schröder, since 60% of them mentioned him the second time around, even though he was not described in the course materials at all. Their knowledge of the main German political parties and structures also improved.

Their knowledge of the cataclysmic events of 1989–90 and the re-unification of the two Germanies had increased, since they were better able to give correct dates by the end. One aspect of everyday life where there was a marked knowledge gain were details of the health service and spa visits. Students also remembered the festivals to which they had been introduced in the materials (see Baumann & Shelley, 2003).

Finally, the video and print materials about hiking had left their mark – students mentioned walking or rambling as a favourite German hobby much more frequently at the end of the course. *Auftakt* students nominated a wide variety of Famous Germans – but with a relatively strong emphasis on men from the world of literature and music, though sports people were also mentioned.

Overall, the adult learners demonstrated a wide and relatively sophisticated knowledge of Germany, which showed that these adult students who opted for distance study possessed a wide range of knowledge to serve as a basis for their language learning.

Attitudes towards Germans

Analysis of the students' response to the adjectival scales describing typical Germans revealed that, overall, they were generally reluctant to commit themselves to either very positive or very negative views by choosing the ends of the 5-point adjectival scales. In the comments that some of them made, they were very careful to differentiate between what they perceived to be crude stereotypes and their own views. Their perceptions of Germans overall were generally positive, with some few exceptions. These included the attributes 'arrogant' and 'aggressive'. At the start and the end of the course over half the OU students found the Germans 'fairly arrogant' and at the beginning of the course nearly half the students rated the Germans as 'fairly aggressive', though this reduced slightly by the end. We set out to investigate whether study of this course might have some effect on students' attitudes towards Germans, but in the event there was very little change in their perceptions of what a typical German is like, and what did change did occur was not clear-cut. By the end of the course, students appeared to find Germans more conservative, slightly more racist and less tidy than they did at the beginning (see Baumann & Shelley, 2003).

On the basis of this sample, adult learners of a language know a reasonably large amount about the country where that language is spoken, have formulated their (stereotypical) perceptions of that country and are unlikely to change them, even in the light of a distance course of study in higher education. Attitudes towards Germany were generally positive, but study of *Auftakt* did very little to modify them in any way. Our experience was that the study of a standard package of course materials had very little discernible effect on our adult students' attitudes towards Germany and the Germans.

Assessment and Achievement

The following figures illustrate various results of the assessment process for the students surveyed for this study. Figure 7.1 compares their continuous assessment results with those for the whole cohort of students that studied this course. Figure 7.2 gives all the results, for both continuous and final assessment, for the sample of students surveyed. Figure 7.3 focuses in on the continuous assessment results and Figure 7.4 on the final exami-

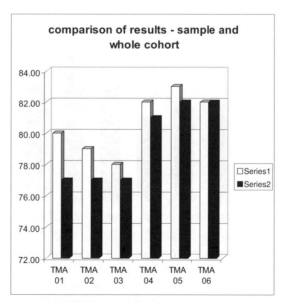

Figure 7.1 Comparison of TMA results

Series 1 – sample of students surveyed (*n* = 158)
Series 2 – whole cohort of students studying the course (*n* = 807 for TMA1; *n* = 640 for TMA6)

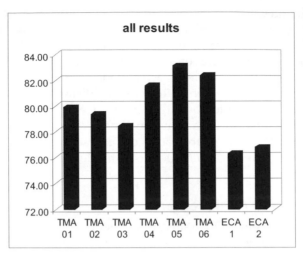

Figure 7.2 Results for continuous and final assessment (ECA) for the sample of students surveyed (*n* = 158)

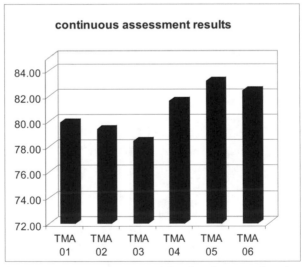

Figure 7.3 Continuous assessment results for the sample of students surveyed (*n* = 158)

nation results for the sample. Figures 7.5 and 7.6 concentrate on the spoken and written continuous assessment results. The numbers on the left-hand side of the figures relate to student scores.

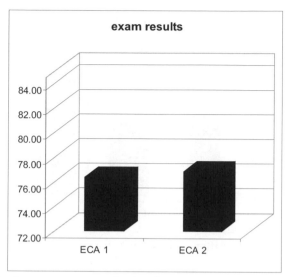

Figure 7.4 Final assessment results for the sample of students surveyed (*n* = 158)

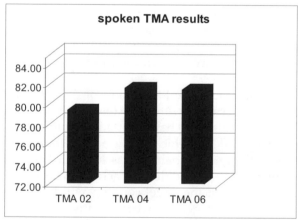

Figure 7.5 Results of spoken assessments for the sample of students surveyed (*n* = 158)

Outcomes

From these figures it can be seen that the sample of students surveyed did better on average than the whole cohort of *Auftakt* in the year under investigation. They scored higher marks in each of the TMAs (with the exception of TMA 6, where the marks were virtually the same). It should

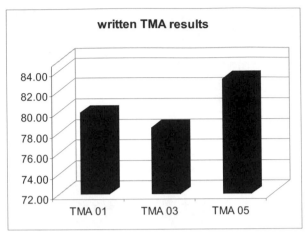

Figure 7.6 Results of written assessments for the sample of students surveyed (n = 158)

be acknowledged that this sample was a self-selected group of students – and one of these reasons they might have felt confident in taking part in this study was because they achieved high scores in the assessments. As happens frequently with distance students, the students scored lower on average in the final examination than in the continuous assessment.

Students in this sample of the 1998 cohort of *Auftakt* learners did relatively well in their assessment, with some few exceptions. On the basis of the research surveyed, this could be attributed to a number of factors. First, the motivation of the students, which, on the basis of the demographics and their responses to the questionnaires, was high. In line with Gardner's research, their motivation helped them to achieve reasonably high scores, and their attitudes towards the target country (which also scored high in Gardner's evaluations) were generally very positive. Second, the tests were thematically linked, with input provided which formed the basis for the responses to be generated by test takers, so thus met the definition of performance testing, and provided a context which, as far as possible, approximated real-life language use (Lewkowicz, 1997). And third, the design of the assessment ensured that students knew what was expected of them, both from the point of view of each assignment, but also how they should measure up to the assessment criteria.

Students did – predictably – get different results in their assessments, determined by their background, motivation and language skills when starting the course. The following case studies spell out progress and results in detail for four very different students.

Four *Auftakt* Students

Each case study contains some information about each student relating to their background and motivation to learn German and charts changes and progress, if any, between their filling in the first and second questionnaires marking the beginning and end of their study of *Auftakt*. Their continuous and final assessment scores are given.

Student A

In the 50–59 age group, and female, she did not take German at school, but had studied it for 12 months 25 years before at a technical college. She had then made 'very intermittent' attempts to study German using the BBC course tapes, and also worked through the OU preparatory pack, *Café Einklang*. She claimed to be unable to speak or write German when she started the *Auftakt* course, with only slight knowledge of listening and reading. She wanted to learn German so as to communicate with friends in German-speaking countries. She was accustomed to the OU mode of distance study, since she already had an OU degree.

When she completed the second questionnaire she named two East German towns not previously mentioned and was more accurate about the number of German *Bundesländer* (country states). She named three German political parties the first time, but only one the second. She displayed a reasonably accurate knowledge of recent history on both questionnaires, but could name only four German companies the second time (previously five). She improved her knowledge of the German health system and of specifically German festivals, both of which were covered in the course. She had no problem nominating ten Famous Germans on either occasion.

Student A's professed attitudes towards Germans as marked on the 5-point scales underwent little change over the course. She made some adjustments, from Neither boring nor amusing to Fairly boring, from Neither conservative nor progressive to Conservative (both changes recorded by other students) and shifted to Reliable (from Fairly reliable), to Efficient (from Fairly efficient) and to Serious (from Fairly serious). When asked whether she felt her attitudes to Germans had changed over the study of the course, she said no, since she had had a reasonable amount of contact with Germans in the past.

This student scored consistently in the 60s and 70s for her continuous assessment, with very little variation. She dropped to 58 for the written and 50 for the spoken exam.

Summary

Although Student A claimed to have very low levels of German at the beginning of her study, she gained some knowledge over the course, and got relatively good, consistent marks, considering her starting level. Her prior experience of distance learning might have stood her in good stead here. Typically, she dropped some marks on the final exam, which often occurs with students learning at a distance. Her small degree of attitudinal change was, again, typical of *Auftakt* students.

Student B

This student was male, in the same age group as Student A (50–59). While he had not taken German at school in England, he had lived and worked in Germany for 15 years where he had taken a number of adult education courses. Asked to assess his skills when he started *Auftakt*, he described Speaking, Listening and Reading all as Good, and Writing as Slight. He was studying German for the pleasure of study and intellectual stimulation. He chose the OU because of convenience, no entrance exams and the low cost.

Student B had no problems naming German towns, and got the full number of *Bundesländer* right, though he could name only ten of them out of 16. He named three less well known German politicians, but got one fewer political party the second than the first time. His knowledge of recent history was reasonably good (apart from assigning Bismarck's first unification of Germany to 1911 the first time and 1908 the second, over 40 years too late in each case). He was familiar with the names of German companies and the German health system on both questionnaires. He could name typical German hobbies – and used the German words for them the second time. When nominating his ten Famous Germans he mentioned two the second time who had been described in the course materials. His opinions of Germans were mainly positive and unequivocal; he felt that they had not changed over the course.

This student's results varied quite considerably, from 49% to 80% for continuous assessment, and 48 and 55% for the exam. They were, however, consistently higher for spoken than for written German.

Summary

Having lived in Germany for some considerable time, it is not surprising that this student began the course with a good general knowledge of Germany – but his knowledge did increase over the course and he had obviously gained from it. His assessment marks showed considerable fluctuation and, overall, he scored less well than Student A, who had rated her language skills so low when she started. His spoken German was, however, more fluent.

Student C

This student was older (in the 60–69 age group), female, and born in Vienna. She left Austria as a refugee in 1938 and attended school in England, where she was the only student to take examinations in German, but learnt little grammar. She has maintained reading and writing in German and described all her skills (speaking, listening, reading and writing) as Excellent. She said that she wanted to continue learning German for the challenge and sense of achievement.

Student C had no problem naming German cities – and included an East German one the second time. While she got the total of *Bundesländer* wrong the first time, and didn't list them, she named 13 correctly the second time. She demonstrated her awareness of political events in Germany by including the new (at that time) German chancellor, Schröder, on the second occasion. She named one more political party the second time, but was unsure of the dates of recent historical events ('Sorry! No head for dates!'). She knew of many German companies, including some obscure ones, named all the different types of school in Germany and was familiar with the names of German festivals. Curiously, she didn't pick up on the favourite German hobby described in the course in some detail, but named others. She included an Austrian playwright among the Famous Germans.

She changed her assessment of her attitude towards Germans on almost every count between filling in the first and second questionnaires, sometimes quite dramatically. She commented, however: ' . . . I am not judgmental about people as a whole and do not think *Auftakt* has changed my attitudes. I ask – Are the individual people pleasant? Then I react accordingly.'

This student scored the highest marks of all students in this sample of the *Auftakt* cohort – well over 90% for all assignments and 100% for both the written and the spoken exam.

Summary

Since she was – at least originally – a native speaker, it is not surprising that this student scored so well and consistently in her assessments. Her knowledge of Germany and Austria was obviously good, but improved over the life of the course. Her attitudinal ratings varied quite considerably between start and finish – but this was not an important issue for her.

Student D

Student D was again an older student (60–69). He had not studied German at school, nor as an adult, but he had worked through the OU preparatory pack, *Café Einklang*. He assessed his speaking, listening and writing skills as slight, reading as adequate for basic needs. In common with the majority of other students, he was studying for the pleasure of study and intellectual stimulation. He had lived in Germany for 18 months, but had no friends or relatives there.

Student D was the only one of these four students to get all the names of the 16 German *Bundesländer* right, both at the beginning and end of his study. Like Student C, he picked up on Schröder the second time around. He had a reasonable grasp of recent German history and was familiar with the names of German companies. The second time round he named all the different types of German school and improved his knowledge of the German health system. He picked up on a couple of German hobbies which had been described in the course materials, and added a Famous German to his list who had been mentioned in the course.

There were some modifications to Student D's attitudes towards Germans over the course. He changed from Fairly progressive to Fairly conservative, from Fairly direct to Direct and from Fairly tidy to Tidy. He did not feel that he had changed his attitudes over the study of the course.

Student D's continuous assessment showed a fairly steady progression over the course, starting with marks in the sixties for the first couple of assignments and working up to marks in the eighties. He scored 67% for the written and 80% for the spoken exams.

Summary

Motivated, as so many of these students were, by the pleasure of study and intellectual stimulation, Student D made steady progress, improving his scores consistently and reaching a good level by the end of the course, despite his low ratings of his language skills originally and lack of language learning experience. His spoken examination score was a particularly good achievement. His knowledge gain was considerable and reflected the course teaching. Once more, in common with the other *Auftakt* students, he did not feel that his attitudes had changed much.

Conclusions

- Typically, students of German at the Open University are extremely interested in German life and culture and bring a considerable amount of knowledge with them to their study; besides using the course materials they are aware of current events in Germany and are able to retain and build on their knowledge. The ability to build on this knowledge would indicate that these students were able to exercise a fair degree of intercultural competence.

- Open University students have already formulated their attitudes towards Germany and the Germans when they start their study. Though such stereotypical attitudes may change a little and be modified over the life of the course, basically there will be little change. The results of the project indicate that study of a language and culture cannot be assumed to have a profound effect on adults' viewpoints and attitudes. So in this case we cannot claim that the attitudinal change which would be associated with the gain of intercultural competence took place when adult students studied *Auftakt*.

- Both continuous and final assessment in *Auftakt* may be described as a form of integrated, performance testing which reflects the multi-media course materials as well as real-life German situations. Using this form of assessment, students in this sample scored reasonably well and demonstrated a clear increase in intercultural competence.

- For a variety of reasons, these students of *Auftakt* were generally well-motivated to learn, and this was reflected in their relatively high assessment scores.

As far as future research in this area is concerned, the outcomes from this study would suggest the following directions:

- An important objective for course development, teaching and research is to track more closely the kinds of progress students make in different aspects of the language.

- Future research with students of German at the Open University will be carried out with different, more advanced cohorts of students, to investigate whether they react to a standard pack of teaching materials in the same way as the students studied here.

- Further work needs to be undertaken to develop more accurate ways of measuring the gain of intercultural competence in adults studying foreign languages at a distance.

References

Bachman, L.F. (1990) *Fundamental Considerations in Language Testing*. Oxford: OUP

Bachman, L.F. (2000) Modern language testing at the turn of the century: Assuring that what we count counts. *Language Testing* 17 (1), 1–42.

Baumann, U. (1999) Deutsch im Fernstudium an der Open University. In G. Kischel and E. Gothsch (eds) *Wege zur Mehrsprachigkeit im Fernstudium*, Dokumentation des Hagener Workshop 13–14 November 1998 (pp. 209–20). Hagen: Fern-Universität.

Baumann, U. and Shelley, M. (2003) Adult learners of German at the Open University: their knowledge of, and attitudes towards Germany. *Open Learning* 18 (1), 61–74

Byram, M. (1993) Foreign language teaching and multicultural education. In A.S. King and M.J. Reiss (eds) *The Multicultural Dimension of the National Curriculum* (pp. 173–86). London: Falmer Press.

Byram, M. (1997) *Teaching and Assessing Intercultural Communicative Competence.* Clevedon: Multilingual Matters.

Byram, M. and Zarate, G. (eds) (1997) *The Sociocultural and Intercultural Dimension of Language Learning and Teaching.* Strasbourg: Council of Europe.

Byram, M. and Fleming, M. (eds) (1998) *Language Learning in Intercultural Perspective.* Cambridge: CUP.

Clapham, C. (2000) Assessment and testing. In M. Byram (ed.) *Routledge Encyclopedia of Language Teaching and Learning* (pp. 48–53). London: Routledge.

Clapham, C.and Corson, D. (eds) (1997) *Language Testing and Assessment*, Volume 7 Encyclopedia of Language and Education. Dordrecht/Boston/London: Kluwer Academic Publishers.

Council of Europe (2001) *A Common European Framework for Language Learning, Teaching and Assessment.* Cambridge: CUP.

Fulcher, G. (1997) The testing of speaking in a second language. In C. Clapham and D. Corson (eds) *Language Testing and Assessment*, Volume 7 Encyclopedia of Language and Education (pp. 75–85). Dordrecht/Boston/London: Kluwer Academic Publishers.

Guillerme, M. (2000) Intercultural competence. In M. Byram (ed.) *Routledge Encyclopedia of Language Teaching and Learning* (pp. 297–300). London and New York: Routledge

Hyland, F. (2001) Providing effective support: Investigating feedback to distance language learners. *Open Learning* 16 (3), 233–47.

Kramsch, C. (1993) *Context and Culture in Language Teaching.* Oxford: OUP.

Kramsch, C. (1995) The cultural component of language teaching. *Language, Culture and Curriculum* 8 (2), 83–92.

Kramsch, C., Cain, A. and Murphy-Lejeune, E. (1996) Why should language teachers teach culture? *Language, Culture and Curriculum* 8 (1), 99–107.

Lewkowicz, J. (1997) The integrated testing of a second language. In C. Clapham and D. Corson (eds) *Language Testing and Assessment*. Volume 7 Encyclopedia of Language and Education (pp. 121–30). Dordrecht/Boston/London: Kluwer Academic Publishers.

McNamara, T. (1996) *Measuring Second Language Performance.* London and New York: Longman.

McNamara, T. (2000) *Language Testing.* Oxford: OUP.

Masgoret, A.-M. and Gardner, R.C. (2003) Attitudes, motivation, and second language learning: a meta-analysis of studies conducted by Gardner and Associates. *Language Learning* 53 (1), 123–63.

Morgan, C. and O'Reilly, M. (1999) *Assessing Open and Distance Learners.* London: Kogan Page.

Risager, K. (2000) Cultural awareness. In M. Byram (ed.) *Routledge Encyclopedia of Language Learning and Teaching* (pp. 159–62). London and New York: Routledge.

Rowntree, D. (1994) *Preparing Materials for Open, Distance and Flexible Learning.* London: Kogan Page.

Rubin, D.L. and Schramm, G. (1997) The testing of L1 speaking. In C. Clapham and D. Corson (eds) *Language Testing and Assessment.* Volume 7 Encyclopedia of Language and Education (pp. 29–37). Dordrecht/Boston/London: Kluwer Academic Publishers.

Sercu, L. (2002) Autonomous learning and the acquisition of intercultural competence: some implications for course development. *Language, Culture and Curriculum* 15 (1), 61–74.

Shelley, M.A. (ed.) (1996) *Auftakt: Get Ahead in German.* Milton Keynes: The Open University/Hodder and Stoughton).

Shelley, M.A. (1999) Entwicklung der Fremdsprachen an der Open University. In G.Kischel and E. Gothsch (eds) *Wege zur Mehrsprachigkeit im Fernstudium,* Dokumentation des Hagener Workshop 13–14 November 1998. (pp. 203–08) Hagen: FernUniversität.

Shelley, M.A. (2000) Distance learning. In M. Byram (ed) *Routledge Encyclopedia of Language Teaching and Learning* (pp. 183–85). London: Routledge.

Thorpe, M. (1998) Assessment and 'third generation' distance education. *Distance Education* 19 (2), 265–86.

Trim, J.L.M. (2000) Common European framework. In M. Byram (ed.) *Routledge Encyclopedia of Language Learning and Teaching* (pp. 122–4). London and New York: Routledge.

White, C.J. (2003) *Language Learning in Distance Education.* Cambridge: CUP.

Chapter 8

Developing Professional Intercultural Communicative Competence: Reflections on Distance Learning Programmes for Language Educators and Translators/ Interpreters in Bulgaria

RICHARD FAY and LEAH DAVCHEVA

Introduction

This chapter discusses two distance learning programmes with similar origins and curricular objectives. In broad terms, these projects are located in the distance education provision emerging in Bulgaria since 1989. More specifically, the programmes are the outcomes of British Council projects involving collaboration between local curriculum teams in Bulgaria and distance learning practitioners at the University of Manchester. The local teams have been brought together especially for these projects. They consist of colleagues with limited experience of distance education and course design but who are experienced practitioners in the areas concerned and have prior experience of British Council projects in Bulgaria.

As their titles indicate (see below), the two programmes are also products of what can be termed the 'intercultural turn' in Bulgarian language teacher education dating from the early 1990s. They share a concern with the professional development of experienced language specialists; specifically their intercultural communicative competence (ICC) and the ways in which this should inform their professional practice.

The *Intercultural Studies for Language Teachers* (ISLT) programme was developed in 1999–2001 and is being presented for the fourth time as we write in 2003. The participants are experienced English language teachers based mostly in Bulgaria. A few teachers come from neighbouring countries (Romania and Greece), a welcome cultural and contextual broadening of the programme's participant base. The second programme, *Intercultural Communication for Translators and Interpreters* (ICTI), is still being written. It is aimed at experienced translators and interpreters working with the English language in Bulgaria but participation by a broader range of translators and interpreters will also be encouraged.

In the following discussion, we first consider three aspects of the developmental context for the programmes before exploring the area of intercultural communicative competence that informs their content and objectives. Our discussion then turns to the evaluation of the first programme. This has identified the need for further conceptualisation work on what was, we now realise, only an implicit programme objective, namely the development of the participants' professional intercultural communicative competence (PICC). To this end, we are creating a model for PICC to be used in the design and content of the new programme. We hope it will also inform the revision of the first programme. We conclude the chapter reflectively, with some insights drawn from these projects in terms of distance education and the professional intercultural aspects of the in-service education of language specialists.

The Development Contexts

The two projects can be contextualised in terms of the emergence of distance learning in Bulgaria, the increasingly intercultural orientation of professional education for language specialists there, and the collaborative bases of the projects themselves. We now discuss these areas in turn.

Distance learning in Bulgaria

Distance learning in Bulgaria began soon after 1989 (Totkov *et al.*, 2000) when the New Bulgarian University established two distance education units. The School of Management works in collaboration with the British Open University regarding materials adaptation, evaluation and certification. The Centre of Distance Learning designs and delivers its own programmes in areas such as Ecology and Environmental Studies, Economics, Tourism and Marketing. The two units have an annual intake of about 2500 students. In addition to the New Bulgarian University, distance learning programmes are also offered by local institutions, such as The University of World Economy and the universities of Plovdiv and Russe, and by foreign universities, for example City University (USA). Current distance learning provision in Bulgaria is characterised by its combination of print-based study guides and face-to-face contact sessions.

However, elearning is being developed (see Galabov *et al.*, 2003) and technology-based provision is in preparation at the New Bulgarian University, The Bulgarian Academy of Sciences and the University of Sofia.

These distance education providers are innovators who have overcome a number of obstacles. Before 1989, there was little motivation to adopt distance learning because Bulgaria, as a small country with well-distributed universities, did not appear to need it, and the impetus provided by new technologies was still to come. In general, Bulgarian education was isolated from international developments, with few opportunities for collaboration and know-how exchange. Traditional Bulgarian educational practices – which we typify as centralised with institutional rather than individual responsibility for learning, and as teacher-centred with little scope for learner autonomy – went largely unchallenged, and the fields of adult education and life-long learning were poorly conceptualised, ideologically unacceptable, and consequently underdeveloped.

In contrast, the socio-political and economic changes that took place after 1989 have encouraged the development of a small but significant distance learning sector. Enabling factors include:

- the establishment of the National Centre for Distance Education that *inter alia* promotes broadened access, active involvement, collaborative learning, learning by doing, and independent and critical thinking;
- the substantial progress made in telecommunications since 1997 (Galabov *et al.*, 2003);
- the energies of, particularly younger, academics within the established universities;
- the availability of some distance learning development funding from the Know-How Fund, the World Bank, and the TEMPUS and PHARE projects;
- the emergence of social groups able and willing to pay for their education, for example personnel in small and medium enterprises (see Dochev *et al.*, 2003);
- changing social attitudes towards time and its uses, changes that have produced a demand for concurrent study and work possibilities; and
- the desire of politicians and educationalists to bring Bulgarian education in line with European norms and standards.

Initially, the *Intercultural Studies for Language Teachers* programme development was not integrated into this accumulating distance education practice. Instead, its origins lay in a British Council project involving training in distance learning methodology from the University of Manchester. The programme was trialled within the British Council project before it was subsequently presented as a fully-fledged component within the distance provision of the New Bulgarian University. A similar development pattern is now in progress for the second programme.

Intercultural professional development for language specialists

The two programmes focus on the intercultural communicative competence of language professionals. The motivation for, and understandings of, this focus developed through a series of home-grown projects during the 1990s that also included consultancy support from colleagues based in the UK.

In 1993, English language teachers in Bulgaria started a Cultural Studies Network (CSN) to develop new approaches to language-and-culture education (Davcheva, 2000). Over the next three years, they recorded and shared their classroom experiences. This enabled their concerns about the existing information-oriented, culture-specific and teacher-centred approaches to language teaching to be articulated clearly for the first time. To begin addressing these concerns, they then developed and disseminated a pool of new culture teaching materials (e.g. Dobreva, 1998; Georgieva, 2001; Madjarova *et al.*, 1998; Metodieva Genova, 2001; Mondachka, 1998; Reid-Thomas *et al.*, 1998; Topuzova, 1998).

A dedicated group of 60 CSN teachers, supported by a bespoke teacher-education programme from the University of Strathclyde, initiated a bottom-up process of curriculum innovation. The aim was to develop and promote new ways of integrating language- and culture-focused teaching. The CSN group wanted to challenge the teacher-centred, knowledge-based, target-language-and-target-culture focus of much of the existing language teaching. To this end, they developed ideas, and designed and trialled lessons, for an approach that was learner-centred, skills-based, and intercultural in orientation. The outcome of their activities was the publication of the 'Branching Out: Cultural Studies Syllabus' (British Council, 1998) in which the objective of language education was reformulated as follows: 'The goal of teaching Cultural Studies today is to enable students to develop, alongside their linguistic competence, the kind of intercultural competence which will provide them with the means to interpret cultures and communicate more successfully in an intercultural context' (British Council, 1998: 10).

Having already experienced the process of professional discovery and innovation (Davcheva *et al.*, 1999), the CSN members wanted to create a larger circle of language teachers who could implement the Branching Out syllabus ideas and develop their own culture teaching skills. So, during the Dissemination Project (1998–2000), the CSN group of teachers introduced

600+ foreign language teachers to experimental and innovative teaching for intercultural communicative competence (Davcheva & Fay, 2000; Georgieva, 2001). This teacher development programme involved over 40 face-to-face seminars, each of them initiating small-scale classroom research projects in which teachers applied ideas and used materials from the Branching Out syllabus.

At this point, it became clear that to sustain the initial enthusiasm and creative drive, and to ensure language teachers and other language special-ists were offered longer term and more rigorous development opportuni-ties, the mode of providing professional education had to be re-shaped. This is where the distance learning part of the story begins.

Transnational collaboration

Transnational collaboration involving local curriculum teams and con-sultants from the UK was a feature of the above intercultural projects. The distance education projects follow a similar pattern, although the involve-ment of a Manchester-based consultant resulted from a chance set of circumstances. A Bulgaria-based EFL teacher focused his Manchester Masters dissertation (Kelly, 2000) on the Dissemination Project. As a result, the Project Manager (Leah Davcheva) invited the Dissertation Supervisor (Richard Fay) to visit the project. The main outcome of this visit was a jointly conceived plan to extend the Dissemination Project (see above) using distance learning.

This plan was based on the local realisation that sustainable professional education could not be achieved through continued use of face-to-face seminars because of the costs involved in so frequently taking teachers away from their classrooms. The plan also involved two areas of Manches-ter's distance learning experience. First, since the late-1980s Manchester had been developing distance learning mode language teacher education programmes in institutional contexts where distance learning was not the norm. Second, Manchester had substantial experience of working collabor-atively with other institutions in the UK and overseas (e.g. Fay *et al.*, 2000) to develop context-sensitive models of language teacher education delivered through distance learning mode. These areas of experience informed the input from the Manchester side of the collaboration.

The plan coalesced into the *Intercultural Studies for Language Teachers* project that involved a local Manager (Leah Davcheva), a development team drawn from the Dissemination Project trainers, a distance learning and course design consultant (Richard Fay), and support from the Bulgarian Ministry of Education and Teacher Training Institute. In profile, the development team were:

- experienced language teachers with some language teacher education experience;
- participants in the previous intercultural projects in Bulgaria;
- knowledgeable about the local language teaching and teacher training context;
- largely inexperienced regarding distance learning; and
- largely inexperienced in developing language teacher education
  programmes.

This ambitious project was divided into two year-long phases. Year 1 consisted of programme specification and courseware development with the resulting English-medium ISLT programme being trialled in Year 2. Four three-day workshops were used to train and support the team in their specification of the programme and development of the courseware for it. The Manchester-designed training covered the philosophy and methodology of distance learning, and the course design process. Additionally, considerable workshop time was spent specifying the programme and beginning to draft the courseware. In between these workshops, writers worked on their drafts with support from each other and from the Manchester consultant regarding distance learning methodology and content coherence. The final drafts were then edited by the Project Manager to ensure presentational consistency and accuracy.

In keeping with the imported know-how from Manchester, the programme mixes the more traditional distance learning practices of print-based courseware supported by contact sessions with practices innovative in the local context, including asynchronous computer-mediated communications. When this use of technology was first mooted, it was feared that some of the potential participants – because they worked in poorly resourced state schools – would be excluded because of access difficulties. In practice, this has not been problematic. Although for many of the teachers participation in the electronic discussion group has been a new experience, they have valued it as a lively site where they can discuss the programme's content and procedures and interact with each other more frequently. In doing so, we believe they have also developed some of the interactional skills vital in creating the intended learning environment. Thus, they have had opportunities to negotiate and make meanings, to identify and manage risky topics, to recognise and accept difference, to offer and receive constructive criticism. In short, they have had on-line opportunities to engage in facework (Cupach & Metts, 1994) in an emerging context, opportunities simulating the intercultural contexts in which they are professionally involved.

Reflections on our transnational collaboration

There are three main areas where our reflections on the collaboration, and its processes and outcomes, are influencing the continuing collaboration for the second programme. First, all transnational collaborations involve cross-cultural communication and the concomitant risk of inexactitude in the 'shared' understandings of the collaborators. In our case, we can now see that there was such inexactitude in the Project Manager's and the distance learning Consultant's understanding of the project team and their needs. In fact, these needs included the deepening of their intercultural understandings as well as the development of their distance education competences. The former need was understood by the Manager but not by the Consultant. As a consequence, a training approach was adopted inappropriately, focusing more on distance learning understandings and skills than on needs concerning intercultural conceptualisations.

Relatedly, as the project developed, we realised that the operational model was overly complex. The size of the team (12 writers) made it difficult to ensure everyone was fully and effectively supported as they developed their distance learning skills. Equally, the programme itself was perhaps too large to be accommodated in the relatively condensed course specification and development timeframe we had allowed.

The plan for the project to develop the *Intercultural Communication for Translators and Interpreters* (ICTI) programme takes these learnings into account. It involves a smaller team (six writers instead of 12), a smaller programme, a longer timeline for programme and courseware specification and development (two years), and an emphasis on developing programme content for conversion into distance learning format rather than on distance learning practice *per se*.

Finally, an important reflection concerns the issue of appropriate methodology (re culturally appropriate distance learning methodology, see Fay & Hill, 2003) that the collaboration has brought with it. Whereas the intercultural objectives of the programme were largely home-grown, the distance learning methodology of the programmes was based on the imported Manchester model of distance learning (West, 1995, 1996; West & Walsh, 1995). This is task-based, interactive, and learner- and learning-centred in keeping with the language teaching background of its architects. The ease with which this model took root in the ISLT programme is probably due to the language teaching background shared by the ISLT development team and their Manchester colleagues. It remains to be seen whether the translators and interpreters developing and taking part in the new programme will take to this style of course presentation as well as the language teachers did.

Understandings of Intercultural Communicative Competence

The intercultural orientation arising through the projects described above has been enriched by ideas drawn from the consultants and the literature. Important in this regard is the concept of intercultural communicative competence. Our thinking has been influenced by the different discourses on intercultural communicative competence in the fields of Intercultural Communication Training, English Language Teaching, and Foreign Language Education.

Intercultural Communication Training perspectives

The most established discussion about intercultural communicative competence is to be found in the Intercultural Communication Training literature. This field of training practice developed after 1945 due to the post-war situation of overseas military placements, extensive refugee and resettlement programmes, and a delicate political situation. The field continued to develop in response to increasingly international possibilities of trade, education, and tourism. It was called upon to help people cope with the cultural challenges of long-established political conflicts and culturally diverse societies, and the impact of globalisation and the technological possibilities of recent decades have added renewed impetus to intercultural communication training efforts. Dinges (1983) details the early discussions. Since then, there have been many more contributions (e.g. Dinges & Baldwin, 1996; Philipsen, 2002; Spitzberg, 1994).

Much of this discussion assumes the interactions take place overseas rather than in the home context (as a host or a member of a multicultural society) or through education (e.g. language learning). It also tends to concentrate on face-to-face rather than virtual or mediated interaction. Illustrative of this discussion is Brislin (1981), in which intercultural communicative competence is seen to consist of attitudes such as non-ethnocentrism and non-prejudicial judgements, personal traits such as tolerance, personality resilience, empathy and social role flexibility, and skills including language, communication, and task-completion skills. Each of these areas can be expanded. For example, O'Sullivan (1994: 97–137) discusses the communication skills necessary for managing intercultural interactions.

Discussions of Intercultural Communication Training also include discussions of the possible training approaches (e.g. Brislin *et al.*, 1983; Gudykunst *et al.*, 1996; Gudykunst & Hammer, 1983). Typically, approaches based mainly on information transmission are criticised, while experiential learning is advocated and Intercultural Communication

Training course design favours the inclusion of affective and behavioural dimensions as well as the traditional cognitive dimension.

English language teaching perspectives

This narrower area of discussion about intercultural communicative competence (e.g. Alptekin, 2002; Andrews & Fay, 2000; Baxter, 1983; Fay & Hyde, 1999; Hyde, 1998) provides a bridge between the other two areas. Where Intercultural Communication Training focuses on the cultural aspects of communication in general, the English Language Teaching discussions of intercultural communicative competence focus specifically on the language skills necessary in intercultural interactions. Where Foreign Language Education focuses on communication involving at least one native-speaker of a language, the English Language Teaching field increasingly focuses on lingua franca communication because of its frequency and global spread.

Foreign language education perspectives

Discussions of intercultural communicative competence began to appear regularly in the foreign language education literature from the 1990s onwards (e.g. Alred *et al.*, 2003; Byram, 1997; Byram & Fleming, 1998; Byram *et al.*, 2001; Guilherme, 2002; Jensen, 1995). These discussions built upon the 'cultural revolution' in the 1970s (Lafayette, 1975, 1978; Seelye, 1974) and the Cultural Studies focus of the 1980s (e.g. Byram, 1989). In the 1980s, a noticeable difference in emphasis emerged between Foreign Language Education discussions in Europe and the USA. The former focused more on Cultural Studies (e.g. Byram, 1989), the latter inclined towards Intercultural Communication (e.g. Damen, 1987). Such differences in emphasis persist to this day (Tumposky, 2002). As a result, terminology can be quite confusing. Our understanding of this territory follows.

Intercultural communication possibilities in language education

In Figure 8.1, the large shaded box represents the fields of English Language Teaching and Foreign Language Education in relation to intercultural communication. The activities and approaches within this territory can be understood in terms of two axes.

The vertical axis represents the culture-specific versus culture-general spectrum of possibilities. These terms can be applied to both the assumed target and the assumed home culture. Thus, a cross-cultural Foreign Language Education classroom makes culture-specific assumptions about both cultures; for example, French children learning British English and vice versa. In comparison, an English for Intercultural Communication

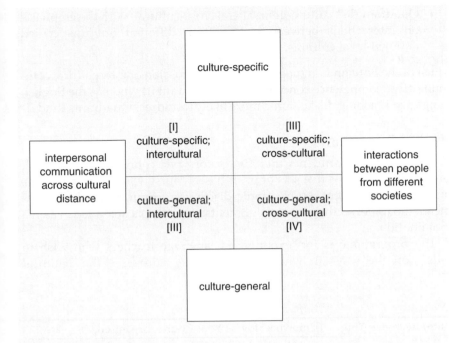

Figure 8.1 Understandings of intercultural communication in language education

classroom might make culture-general assumptions about both cultures; it might accept the cultural complexity of the students in it and try and prepare them to use English as a lingua franca in unspecified contexts.

The horizontal axis represents a spectrum of possibilities in relation to the assumptions made about the interactants. They might be seen as culturally unique and culturally complex individuals who cannot usefully be understood in terms of a nationality or region, or they might be seen as individuals communicating in ways influenced by the cultural background of the (national) group with which they are associated. The two axes create four possibilities:

- Quadrant (I) culture-specific and intercultural, with the emphasis on interpersonal communication across known cultural distance;
- Quadrant (II) culture-general and intercultural, with the emphasis on interpersonal communication across unknown cultural distance;
- Quadrant (III) culture-specific and cross-cultural, with the emphasis on interactions between people from different and specified national-level cultures; and

- Quadrant (IV) culture-general and cross-cultural, with the emphasis on interactions between people from different but unspecified national-level cultures.

Much of the Foreign Language Education discussion of intercultural communicative competence concentrates on Quadrant III whereas the English Language Teaching discussion is more likely to address Quadrants I and II.

The ISLT Programme

With about 20 students and five tutors per cohort, this 12-month programme involves five sets of print-based courseware (see Figure 8.2), one face-to-face event, an electronic discussion group, tutorials, recommended parallel reading, two assignments, and a thesis defended in a viva examination.

The programme is for 'experienced language teachers who wish to reflect on the ways in which their teaching addresses the "cultural

Modules	*Units*
Introduction to Your Course	Unit One: How Is Your Course Organised?
	Unit Two: Studying Culture – Views and Choices
	Unit Three: Distance Learning Study Skills
Module One: Conceptual Perspectives: Culture and Intercultural Communication	Unit One: Culture
	Unit Two: Intercultural Communication
	Unit Three: Cultural Learning
	Unit Four: Intercultural Communicative Competence
Module Two: Disciplinary Perspectives: Ways of Experiencing Culture	Unit One: Intercultural Communication Training
	Unit Two: Ethnography in Language Education
	Unit Three: Media Studies
	Unit Four: Literature and Intercultural Studies
Module Three: Language Education Perspectives: Syllabus Innovation	Unit One: Cultural Studies for Language Teachers – a Bulgarian Case Study
	Unit Two: The Cultural Studies Syllabus
	Unit Three: The Skills–Based Approach to Intercultural Studies – a Wider Perspective
Action Research Pack	Unit One: Action Research
	Unit Two: Carrying Out Your Action Research Project

Figure 8.2 The structure of the ISLT programme (adapted from British Council, 2001: 15)

dimension" of language education' (British Council, 2001: v–ix). It is closely linked to the *Branching Out: Cultural Studies Syllabus* (British Council, 1998) whose model of intercultural language teaching and learning we locate mainly in Quadrant III above. It also includes aspects which are in keeping with the characteristics common in intercultural language education, where the emphasis is on:

- 'learners becoming aware of analysing the cultural phenomena of their own society as much as those of other societies';
- 'the development of skills of analysis and interpretation of unfamiliar social and cultural data from a foreign society';
- 'the opportunities to collect data oneself, either by stepping outside the classroom into the society in which the learners live, or at a distance with the help of old and new technology . . . '; and
- 'the use of literary texts to stimulate affective as well as cognitive understanding of otherness and the use of the students' literary imagination' (Byram *et al.*, 2001: 3).

The programme's interculturality is thus rooted in the understandings developed in the preceding intercultural projects, as discussed above. It is also resonant with the UNESCO-derived wider educational objective of 'learning to live together' as well as simply 'learning to know' (cf. Guilherme, 2002: vii). During the content specification, this interculturality was enriched to include this tri-partite understanding of culture:

- culture-as-content (linked to the field of Cultural Studies and skills of analysis interpretation of cultural phenomena);
- culture-as-communication (linked to the field of Intercultural Communication and skills for managing interactions across cultural distance); and
- culture-as-context (linked to issues of appropriate, or context-sensitive, methodology).

Furthermore, given the increasing scale and diversity of English usage, the programme makes certain assumptions about English language (teacher) education. In contrast to more traditional target-language/culture perspectives in foreign language education, it embraces heterogeneity in language (i.e. Englishes) and culture (i.e. understood in relation to increasingly multicultural societies comprising of culturally unique and complex individuals, cf. Singer, 1998). Culture is not something to be studied only cognitively; it is also an emerging process (Holliday, 1999; Street, 1993) to be studied experientially. The study of culture is not just about otherness but also about our own cultural identities. As a result,

(English) language teachers need to be concerned less with students' knowledge and competence in the target language-culture and more with their developing skills in communicating across cultural distance and in dealing with cultural phenomena, from whatever source.

We have recently reviewed the intercultural dimension of the programme in terms of content and modus operandi. Regarding intercultural content, the aims and learning outcomes (see Figure 8.3) involve a movement from cognitive study (Module One), to experiential learning (Module Two), to applied practice (Module Three). However, the aims are largely content-focused and do not fulfil the experiential expectations raised. The learning outcomes mix study content and experiences with intended exit competencies (academic and professional). These tend to be specified mainly in cognitive and behavioural terms.

We saw the programme at first as 'monocultural' since it was developed in Bulgaria, largely by Bulgarians, with Bulgarian participants, tutors, and examiners, and with experiences based largely in Bulgaria and focused on Bulgarian language classrooms. When we looked more closely, we realised that participating teachers were involved in three overlapping 'learning contexts' (Figure 8.4), all of which were involved in some way in the programme itself.

This realisation led us to reject the dichotomy between educational context and real world experience, since both the language classroom and the distance learning programme are real and contribute to the teachers' actual experience. However, LC1 and LC2 are in some ways safer environments for learning to be intercultural, for trying out new identities and roles, for practising new skills than are the more random and often ethnocentric environments in which we all live (LC3). It is thus useful to consider the participants' development as *in vitro* (LC1) and *in vivo* (LC3), or as a mixture of the two (LC2).

It is also worth emphasising that the distance learning programme is an educational culture in its own right, which, because of its novelty for participants, provides an intercultural educational encounter of sorts. Traditionally in Bulgaria, language teachers were not expected to take responsibility for their own learning, to learn how to learn, to interrogate sources, to live with and tolerate ambiguity, or to self-appraise. However, the increasing interculturality of their professional roles now requires them to do so. The distance learning course provides them with the experience of moving from the traditional teacher education environment with which they are familiar to a professional development context that is emergent and therefore unfamiliar. This kind of transition is not dissimilar to that involved in being part of the interculture that emerges when people from differing backgrounds interact.

Aims Your course aims to . . .		Learning Outcomes By the end of the course you will . . .
1	. . . introduce conceptual understandings of culture, intercultural communication, cultural learning, and intercultural communicative competence [Module One]	[1.1] . . . have been introduced in a helpful manner to key terms, concepts and theories about culture, intercultural communication, cultural learning, and intercultural communicative competence
		[1.2] . . . be able to engage critically with theories of culture, intercultural communication, cultural learning, and intercultural communicative competence
2	. . . provide you with experiences of different disciplinary approaches to cultural phenomena [Module Two]	[2.1] . . . have experienced different ways of responding to and interpreting cultural phenomena
		[2.2] . . . be able to outline in broad terms selected ways of interpreting a variety of cultural phenomena and to demonstrate developing skills in one or more of these ways
3	. . . introduce, through the Bulgarian case study, language education perspectives on intercultural studies [Module Three]	[3.1] . . . have been provided with a chronological and developmental case study of the Cultural Studies syllabus innovation in Bulgaria
		[3.2] . . . have been provided with a description and analysis of the Cultural Studies syllabus
		[3.3] . . . as a result of having been to some alternative models to the Cultural Studies syllabus, be able to evaluate skills-based approaches to Intercultural Studies in language education and the potential skills these approaches might involve
4	. . . introduce Action Research as a means of developing reflective classroom practice and provide you with a structure with which to become an Action Researcher and undertake an Action Research project culminating in your Thesis [Action Research Pack]	[4.1] . . . have been introduced to Action Research within an understanding of research in general and to some key Action Research concepts, approaches, and techniques
		[4.2] . . . have developed Action Research skills as exemplified in the area of Intercultural Studies
		[4.3] . . . be able to demonstrate an ability to execute and write up your Action research project in the area of Intercultural Studies

Figure 8.3 The aims and learning outcomes of the ISLT programme (adapted from British Council, 2001: 13–14)

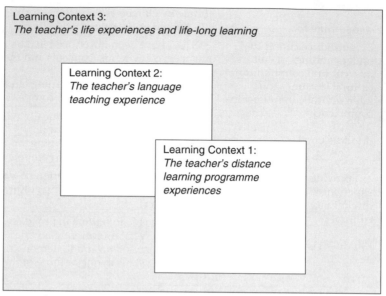

Figure 8.4 The three learning contexts in the ISLT programme

Further, the participants experience and engage with 'the cultural' through a variety of modes (mediated, virtual, vicarious, and face-to-face) and we therefore see the three LCs as small cultures (cf. Holliday, 1999) involving individuals mediating, in part through facework (Cupach & Metts, 1994), their emerging identities in relation to the groups to which they (are beginning to) belong.

Professional Intercultural Communicative Competence (PICC)

Our review of the ISLT programme has identified areas where the emerging practice has outstripped the planning. For example, when we looked at tutor feedback on assignments, it was apparent that tutors were looking to assess assignment-evidenced attitudes and skills, many of which were from LC3, from the participants' lives outside school and outside the course context. Tutors were intuitively looking for the 'whole person change'. However, this criterion was not encapsulated in any of the learning outcomes or specified assessment criteria. The tutors found themselves, in the absence of anything more formal and explicit, having to formulate PICC-type assessment criteria. Reflecting on this outcome, and noting that the term PICC does not appear anywhere in the programme specification, we realised the need to tease out such implicit understandings to revise the programme as well as inform the new programme development.

Insights into professional intercultural communicative competence

We are now in the enviable position of being almost overwhelmed by ideas about professional practice and the intercultural educational agenda. To date, our thinking has been influenced by the language education and by the ICT literatures from which we have taken insights about learning experiences, the rationale for intercultural courses, the transformative nature of the undertaking, and the characteristics of those involved with it.

First, the literature outlines the cognitive, affective, and behavioural dimensions of intercultural learning (e.g. Morgan, 1998; Paige, 1993) and emphasises the affective domain (e.g. Rios *et al.*, 1998). We now realise that the ISLT, like many training programmes before it, has focused on the cognitive and behavioural at the expense of the affective. But, through the tutor feedback endeavours described above, we can detect a home-grown understanding of the value of this kind of learning experience is emerging.

Second, the literatures provide a political and philosophical rationale for professional intercultural communicative competence. For example, Sercu (1998) demonstrates how teachers might be helped to develop the skills and professional identity allowing them to contribute to international understanding and peacemaking at home and abroad, and Guilherme (2002) focuses on the need to educate foreign language and culture teachers about human rights and democratic citizenship, critical pedagogy, cultural studies, and intercultural communication. The ISLT course, although not as explicit as these examples, does have a similar objective. When it is revised, this objective will be made more explicit.

Third, the literature devotes considerable space to the individuals involved in intercultural courses. Here we note that the development of PICC is particularly appropriate for language specialists. Byram and Risager (1994) emphasise the importance of the language teacher's professional identity, which they believe incorporates both the linguistic and cultural dimensions. Similarly, for Fantini (1997), the intercultural language teacher's competencies include:

- awareness of, and attention to, the sociolinguistic variables and uses of appropriate target language in social interactional activities;
- sensitivity towards, and respect for, student cultural differences;
- ability to organise activities comparing and contrasting target and native cultures;
- ability to respond to intercultural conflicts if they arise; and

- awareness of, and sensitivity and responsiveness to the intercultural challenges of the teaching situation (in the classroom, institution, community, and target culture).

We believe these areas are well covered on the ISLT course.

Fourth, there is a need for face validity on the part of professionals concerned with interculturality. For example, Levy (1995) argues that if trainers seek to develop cultural self-awareness, tolerance and culturally appropriate behavioural responses in trainees, they should possess these skills and attributes themselves, and this presupposes personal cross-cultural experience. The trainers involved in intercultural courses have a responsibility to develop their own capacities continuously and to link intellectual capacities with the heart and the spirit (Ramsey, 1996). Further, interculturally oriented professionals – both trainers on the course and the language teachers who are their students – need to enhance their own cultural awareness and intercultural competence and to consider a shift in their professional identity from being a teacher of language to being a teacher of intercultural communication (Byram & Risager, 1994). As interculturalists, they need to be adept at learning in new ways in unfamiliar contexts and at helping their trainees and students do likewise. The ISLT course, through the 'strangeness' of its distance learning mode can play a part in this competence.

A tentative model of Professional Intercultural Communicative Competence

Putting the above insights together with those from our ISLT review, we have begun to model what the acquisition of PICC might involve for our distance education programmes (see Figure 8.5). Overall, this must be informed by the intercultural orientation developed through these projects in Bulgaria as well as the literature discussed above. This requirement is signalled on the figure by the detail of the model being contained within the two larger shaded boxes representing these informing influences.

The inner detail of the model represents a matrix with two axes: one focusing on the cognitive, affective, and behavioural dimensions of (intercultural) learning, the other carrying the three learning contexts discussed above. The arrows suggest the three dimensions should be present in the three learning contexts, and vice versa. The matrix offers nine possible types of learning plus the points where they might combine. We can use these possibilities to evaluate what range of learning types the ISLT programme offers and also as a planning tool to monitor the learning types within the emerging ICTI programme.

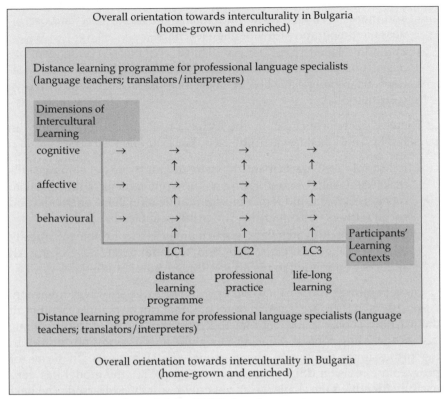

Figure 8.5 An initial model for PICC development

Using the PICC Model with the Two Programmes

Revisiting the ISLT programme

It is not surprising, given the professional-academic slant of the programme, that there is ample coverage in the cognitive dimension, and this tends to fall in the LC2 professional context and the LC1 distance learning academic context. For example:

- in Module One, participants will have 'an increased understanding of theories of culture, IC, cultural learning, and ICC', and more specifically, 'a broad understanding of the term "culture" with an appreciation of various and varied theoretical slants to it (as demonstrated through critical engagement with theory)';
- in Module Two, participants will have 'an increased understanding of the selected ways of interpreting a variety of cultural phenomena',

and more specifically, will 'understand the importance and usefulness of ethnography for language teachers'; and
- in Module Three, participants will have 'an increased understanding
  of skills-based approaches to intercultural studies in language education' and, more specifically, 'be aware of models of ICC which involve
  cultural skills'.

There is some coverage in the behavioural dimension, largely in
personal LC3 and distance learning LC1. For example:

- in Module Two, participants have to 'demonstrate developing skills
  in selected ways of interpreting cultural phenomena' and 'be able to
  recognise, avoid, and repair miscommunication in interpersonal and
  social settings which may be due to cultural factors'; and
- in the Action Research Pack, participants have to 'be able to critically
  analyse a range of literary texts' and 'to demonstrate developing AR
  skills as exemplified in the area of Intercultural Studies'.

Disappointingly, no learning outcomes relate to the affective dimension.
Also, although there are learning outcomes that can be mapped against all
the learning contexts, we feel that the concentration is in the academic
distance learning context (LC1), with significant missed opportunities in
the professional (LC2) and the personal (LC3) contexts. In terms of
programme revision (ISLT) and specification (ICTI), the model has very
usefully identified the challenge as yet only partially addressed. The next
stage is doing something about it. For example, in the ICTI course currently
in development there are four units, one of which constructs its objectives
and learning outcomes completely in terms of experiential learning experiences (such as a simulation and several viewings of filmic clips) designed to
maximise learnings in the affective domain.

Specifying PICC in the ICTI programme

The 6-month ICTI programme targets experienced translators and interpreters, but is not linked to any academic-professional body. The proposed
programme elements are the same as for the ISLT programme. Because of
the ISLT development experience – where team members were inexperienced in distance learning methodology and became bogged down in presentational and design issues, failing to take full advantage of their
substantial professional experience – the ICTI programme content is being
planned in face-to-face terms and then converted into distance learning
mode. Given the teacher-centred educational traditions in Bulgaria, there is
a tendency for print-based materials to be written very much in the style of
textbooks rather than instructional materials. Because the materials devel-

opers have not actually taught this course before, we have worked on the basis of first creating a face-to-face course (specified in contact hours, for example) and then thought about how this on-site set of learning experiences, resources, activities, input, and relationships might be best converted into distance education mode.

The structure and content are now being specified by means of pro formas such as that presented in Figure 8.6.

The objectives and learning outcomes are being specified more systematically than in the ISLT programme. Thus, the objectives are linked to the programme structure and articulated in terms of content and learning experiences. The learning outcomes are to be explicitly linked to assessment and are framed consistently according to the following developmental process: 'the course will take the participants from awareness (i.e. knowledge in principle) to analysis (i.e. interpretation of phenomena, consideration of implications, etc.) to action (i.e. practice, skills, strategies)' (taken from PF1, Section 5). In this way, the three dimensions of intercultural learning are represented. This intention is made explicit: '[the programme uses an approach which is] sufficiently academic for face validity in Bulgaria and to usefully suit the participants' accustomed learning styles . . . *but* . . . as practical as possible so as to maximise relevance for participants' practice and to include a behavioural dimension . . . *and* . . . as experiential as possible so as to include an affective dimension' (ibid.).

The point we have now reached involves specifying the programme at unit and session level and planning the contact sessions and structure for the virtual community. In these documents, the LCs of the model will be included as well as the learning dimensions. The intention is to create a programme that does not neglect any of the matrix possibilities, thus avoiding the missed opportunities of the ISLT programme. The final product will be finished and trialled by 2004.

Concluding Comments

In a sense, our discussion in this chapter represents a course design and evaluation case study with diverse elements. Our own development experience has demonstrated that it is very difficult to keep a firm eye on all these elements at the same time within the constraints and opportunities of real projects. In the ISLT programme, our attention focused mainly on the developing distance learning competence of the team and the retention of the home-grown intercultural orientation of the earlier projects. As a result, there was a much reduced focus on appropriate distance learning methodology and the PICC aspects of language specialists' continuing professional development. However, through evaluation of what that

Macro-Level Specification – Course Level		
No	Item	Details
		YOUR COURSE . . .
4a	Objective 1 addressed in Units 1 & 5	. . . introduces conceptual understandings of the roles of the translator and interpreter as determined by different historical and cultural contexts.
		This involves reflection on your own practice as well as an introduction to some of the literature and scholarship in this area.
	Learning Outcomes assessed in [add details]	By the end of this course you will: • be aware of the different perceptions and self-perceptions of the translator/interpreter as a cultural being; • have critically thought about the role of the translator/interpreter as an intercultural mediator; and • be able to develop pro-active models of professional behaviour.
4b	Objective 2 addressed in Unit 2	. . . introduces key ideas from the disciplines of Intercultural Communication and Translation Studies.
		This involves an introduction to some of the literature and scholarship in these two disciplinary areas and an opportunity to synthesise them and so gain an understanding enriched by both areas.
	Learning Outcomes assessed in [add details]	By the end of the course you will: • be aware of these key ideas from the disciplines of Intercultural Communication and Translation Studies; • have critically engaged with such ideas resulting in a synthesis of them as evaluated in terms of their usefulness for your professional practice; and • be able to apply such ideas in the interpretation of general and more professional intercultural communication contexts.
4c	Objective 3 addressed in Unit 3	. . . provides you with experiences of activities designed to investigate the complexities of intercultural communication.
		This involves a number of communicative experiences (some simulated, others related to your course, and others occurring outside the course in both personal and professional domains of your life) and reflection in light of some key complexities of intercultural communication as presented in the course materials.
	Learning Outcomes assessed in [add details]	By the end of the course you will: • be aware of the complexities of intercultural communication; • have reflected on your own culturally-influenced communication practices; and • be able to evaluate your professional and more general intercultural performances in terms of these complexities.

Figure 8.6 Extract from ICTI Programme Specification (PF1, Section 4)

Macro-Level Specification – Course Level		
No	Item	Details
		YOUR COURSE . . .
4d	Objective 4 addressed in Unit 4	. . . introduces the skills required in the effective and appropriate management and mediation of intercultural communication.
		This involves the identification of some of the key skills as discussed in the literature in the field of Intercultural Communication and . . .
	Learning Outcomes assessed in [add details]	By the end of the course you will:
		• be aware of the skills set associated with the effective and appropriate management and mediation of intercultural communication;
		• have critically evaluated your own skills for managing and mediating professional and more general intercultural communication contexts; and
		• be more confident in your competence in managing and mediating professional and more general intercultural communication contexts because of your enhanced skills.

Figure 8.6 (*cont.*) Extract from ICTI Programme Specification (PF1, Section 4)

programme achieved and of its emerging practices, we have been able to refocus our attentions for the new parallel programme.

Acknowledgements

This chapter owes a great debt to the hard work and boundless energy of the development teams for the ISLT and ICTI programmes. For further information about these programmes, please contact: Dr Leah Davcheva, The British Council, 7 Krakra Street, Sofia 1504, Bulgaria (leah.davcheva@ britishcouncil.bg).

References

Alptekin, C. (2002) Towards intercultural communicative competence in ELT. *English Language Teaching Journal* 56 (1), 57–64.

Alred, G., Byram, M. and Fleming, M. (2003) (eds) *Intercultural Experience and Education*. Clevedon: Multilingual Matters.

Andrews, J. and Fay, R. (2000) Researching communication norms in language testing: Interculturality and examiner perspectives. In M. Beaumont and T. O'Brien (eds) *Collaborative Research in Second Language Education* (pp. 165–80). Stoke: Trentham Books.

Baxter, J. (1983) English for intercultural competence: An approach to intercultural communication training. In D. Landis and R.W. Brislin (eds) *The Handbook of Intercultural Communication Training* (Volume II) (pp. 290–324). Oxford: Pergamon.

Brislin, R.W. (1981) *Cross-cultural Encounters: Face-to-face Interaction*. New York: Pergamon.

Brislin, R.W., Landis, D. and Brandt, M.E. (1983) Conceptualizations of intercultural behavior and training. In D. Landis and R.W. Brislin (eds) *The Handbook of Intercultural Communication Training* (Volume I) (pp. 1–35). Oxford: Pergamon.

British Council (1998) *Branching Out: A Cultural Studies Syllabus*. Sofia: The British Council Bulgaria.

British Council (2001) How is your course organised? Unit 1 of *Introduction to Your Course* (Intercultural Studies for Language Teachers). Sofia: The British Council Bulgaria and the Teacher Training Institute.

Byram, M. (1989) *Cultural Studies in Foreign Language Education*. Clevedon: Multilingual Matters.

Byram, M. (1997) *Teaching and Assessing Intercultural Communicative Competence*. Clevedon: Multilingual Matters.

Byram, M. and K. Risager (1994) *Language Teachers, Politics and Cultures*. Clevedon: Multilingual Matters.

Byram, M. and Fleming, M. (1998) (eds) *Language Learning in Intercultural Perspective: Approaches through Drama and Ethnography*. Cambridge: Cambridge University Press.

Byram, M., Nichols, A. and Stevens, D. (2001) (eds) *Developing Intercultural Competence in Practice*. Clevedon: Multilingual Matters.

Cupach, W. and Metts, S. (1994) *Facework*. London: Sage.

Damen, L. (1987) *Culture Learning: The Fifth Dimension in the Language Classroom*. Reading, Addison Wesley.

Davcheva L. (2000) Establishing a teachers' network in English-medium secondary schools in Bulgaria. In A. Mountford and N. Wadham-Smith (eds) *British Studies: Intercultural Perspectives* (pp. 116–29). Harlow: Longman.

Davcheva, L. and Fay, R. (2000) A cultural studies syllabus for the language classroom in Bulgaria: Teacher collaboration as a dissemination tool. In M. Beaumont and T. O'Brien (eds) *Collaborative Research in Second Language Education* (pp. 95–108). Stoke: Trentham Books.

Davcheva, L., Reid-Thomas H. and Pulverness, A. (1999) Cultural Studies Syllabus and materials: A writing partnership. In C. Kennedy (ed.) *Innovation and Best Practice* (pp. 59–68). Harlow: Longman.

Dinges, N.G. (1983) Intercultural competence. In D. Landis and R.W. Brislin (eds) *The Handbook of Intercultural Communication Training* (Volume I) (pp. 176–202). Oxford: Pergamon.

Dinges, N.G. and Baldwin, K.D. (1996) Intercultural competence: A research perspective. In D. Landis and R.S. Bhagat (eds) *The Handbook of Intercultural Communication Training* (2nd edn) (pp. 106–23). London: Sage.

Dobreva, M. (1998) Cultural Studies off the sheets of the 'PREP' class textbook 'A world of English'. In R. Cherrington and L. Davcheva (eds) *Teaching Towards Intercultural Competence – IATEFL Conference Proceedings* (pp. 251–59). Sofia: Tilia.

Dochev, D., Pavlov, R. and Monova-Zheleva, M. (2003) Principles, quality requirements and solutions for on-the-job e-yraining in SME. Paper given at the European Distance Education Network Annual Conference and published in the Proceedings, A. Szucs, E. Wagner and C. Tsolakidis (eds) *The Quality Dialogue: Integrating Quality Cultures in Flexible, Distance and eLearning* (pp. 518–23). Budapest: EDEN Secretariat.

Fantini, A. (1997) Checking teacher culture / intercultural competencies: The YOGA form. In A. Fantini (ed.) *New Ways in Teaching Culture Teachers of English to Speakers of Other Languages* (pp. 36–9). Alexandria: TESOL Inc.

Fay, R. and Hill, M. (2003) Educating language teachers through distance learning: The need for culturally-appropriate DL methodology. *Open Learning* 18 (1), 9–27.

Fay, R. and Hyde, M. (1999) Language norms and intercultural competence: Target norms and effective negotiation. Paper given at the SIETAR Europa Congress, Trieste, Italy and subsequently published in A. Cuk and F. Del Campo (eds) *One Community and Many Languages: On the Crossroads of a New Europe* (SIETAR Europa Proceedings 1999) (pp. 266–75). Trieste: Batello Stampatore.

Fay, R., Spinthourakis, J-A. and Anastassiadi, M-C. (2000) Teacher education for teachers of English and French: Developing parallel distance learning programmes in Greece. In M. Beaumont and T. O'Brien (eds) *Collaborative Research in Second Language Education* (pp. 109–22). Stoke: Trentham Books.

Galabov, B., Kovachev, V., Shishiniova, M., Nedialkov, R., Petkov, I., Stefanov, K. and Koutzarov, S. (2003) Introduction of E-Learning for students in natural sciences at the Sofia University 'St. Kliment Ohridski', Bulgaria. Paper given at the European Distance Education Network Annual Conference and published in A. Szucs, E. Wagner and C. Tsolakidis (eds) *The Quality Dialogue: Integrating Quality Cultures in Flexible, Distance and eLearning* (pp. 414–19). Budapest: EDEN Secretariat.

Georgieva, I. (2001) An approach to implementing a Cultural Studies Syllabus. In M. Byram, A. Nichols, and D. Stevens (eds) *Developing Intercultural Competence in Practice* (pp. 77–92). Clevedon: Multilingual Matters.

Gudykunst, W.B. and Hammer, M.R. (1983) Basic training design: Approaches to intercultural training. In D. Landis and R.W. Brislin (eds) *The Handbook of Intercultural Communication Training* (Volume I) (pp. 118–54). Oxford: Pergamon.

Gudykunst, W.B., Guzley, R.M. and Hammer, M.R. (1996) Designing intercultural training. In D. Landis and R.S. Bhagat (eds) *The Handbook of Intercultural Communication Training* (2nd edn) (pp. 61–80). London: Sage.

Guilherme, M. (2002) *Critical Citizens for an Intercultural World: Foreign Language Education as Cultural Politics*. Clevedon: Multilingual Matters.

Holliday, A.R. (1999) Small cultures. *Applied Linguistics* 20 (2), 237–64.

Hyde, M. (1998) Intercultural competence in English language education. In *Modern English Teacher* 7 (2), 7–11.

Jensen, A.A. (1995) Defining intercultural competence: A discussion of its essential components and pre-requisites. In L. Sercu (ed.) *Intercultural Competence: A New Challenge for Language Teachers and Trainers in Europe* (Volume 1: The Secondary School) (pp. 41–52). Aarlborg, Denmark: University of Aarlborg Press.

Kelly, K. (2000) A Bulgarian teacher education project: The influence of action research on culture teaching. Unpublished masters dissertation, Faculty of Education, University of Manchester.

Lafeyette, R.C. (1975) *The Cultural Revolution in Foreign Language Teaching*. Skokie: National Textbook Company.

Lafeyette, R.C. (1978) *Teaching Culture: Strategies and Techniques* (Language in Education Series, No. 11). Arlington: Center for Applied Linguistics.

Levy, J. (1995) Intercultural training design. In S. Fowler and M. Mumford (eds) *Intercultural Sourcebook: Cross-Cultural Training Methods* (Volume 1) (pp. 1–15). Yarmouth: Intercultural Press.

Madjarova, T., Botsmanova, M., and Stamatova, T. (1998) 'I thought my teacher fancied me'. In R. Cherrington and L. Davcheva (eds) *Teaching Towards Intercultural Competence – IATEFL Conference Proceedings* (pp. 243–50). Sofia: Tilia.

Metodieva Genova, M. (2001) Visual codes and modes of presentation of television. In M. Byram, A. Nichols, and D. Stevens (eds) *Developing Intercultural Competence in Practice* (pp. 60–76). Clevedon: Multilingual Matters.

Mondachka V. (1998) Cross cultural comparison of tourist material. In R. Cherrington and L. Davcheva (eds) *Teaching Towards Intercultural Competence – IATEFL Conference Proceedings* (pp. 280–85). Sofia: Tilia.

Morgan, C. (1998) Cross-cultural encounters. In M. Byram and M. Fleming (eds) *Language Learning in Intercultural Perspective* (pp. 224–41). Cambridge University Press.

O'Sullivan, K. (1994) *Understanding Ways: Communicating Between Cultures.* Sydney: Hale and Iremonger.

Paige, M.R. (1993) Trainer competencies for international and intercultural programs. In M.R. Paige (ed.) *Education for the Intercultural Experience* (pp. 169–200). Yarmouth: Intercultural Press.

Philipsen, G. (2002) Cultural competence. In W.B. Gudykunst and B. Mody (eds) *The Handbook of International and Intercultural Communication* (2nd edn) (pp. 51–67). London: Sage.

Ramsey, S. (1996) Creating a context: Methodologies in intercultural teaching and training. In H.N. Seelye (ed.) *Experiential Activities for Intercultural Learning* (Volume 1) (pp. 7–24). Yarmouth: Intercultural Press.

Reid-Thomas, H., Ivanova, K., Davcheva L. and Pulverness, A. (1998) Working towards a syllabus for Cultural Studies. In R. Cherrington and L. Davcheva (eds) *Teaching Towards Intercultural Competence – IATEFL Conference Proceedings* (pp. 123–36). Sofia: Tilia.

Rios, F., McDaniel, J. and Stowell, L. (1998) Pursuing the possibilities of passion: The affective domain of multicultural education. In M. Dilworth (ed.) *Being Responsive to Cultural Differences* (pp. 160–81). Thousand Oaks: Corwin Press Inc.

Seelye, H.N. (1974) *Teaching Culture: Strategies for Intercultural Communication* (1st edn). Skokie: National Textbook Company.

Sercu, L. (1998) In-service teacher training and the acquisition of intercultural competence. In M. Byram and M. Fleming (eds) *Language Learning in Intercultural Perspective: Approaches through Drama and Ethnography* (pp. 255–89). Cambridge University Press.

Singer, M.R. (1998) *Perception and Identity in Intercultural Communication.* Yarmouth: Intercultural Press.

Spitzberg, B.H. (1994) A model of intercultural communication competence. In L.A. Samovar and R.E. Porter (eds) *Intercultural Communication: A Reader* (7th edn) (pp. 347–59). Belmont: Wadsworth.

Street, B. (1993) Culture is a verb: Anthropological aspects of language and cultural process. In D. Graddol, L. Thompson and M. Byram (eds) *Language and Culture* (pp. 23–43). Clevedon: Multilingual Matters in association with BAAL.

Topuzova, K. (1998) A students' research project. In R. Cherrington and L. Davcheva (eds) *Teaching Towards Intercultural Competence – IATEFL Conference Proceedings* (pp. 237–42). Sofia: Tilia.

Totkov, G., Somova, G. and Doneva, R. (2000) Distance education in Bulgaria and its development. In G. Totkev (ed.) *Collection of Scientific Research* (pp. 266–71). Plovdiv, University of Plovdiv.

Tumposky, N. (2002) Intercultural communicative competence in European teacher education. In *Intercultural Communication Newsletter* 5 (2), 5–7. (Newsletter of the Intercultural Communication Interest Section of TESOL).

West, R. (1995) *Print-based Materials* (Unit 5 of MD462 Distance Learning and Distance Teaching). Manchester: School of Education, University of Manchester.

West, R. (1996) Concepts of text in distance education. In G. Motteram, G. Walsh and R. West (eds) *Proceedings of the Distance Education for Language Teachers 2nd Symposium, June 1996, Victoria University of Manchester* (pp. 62–72). Manchester: School of Education, Victoria University of Manchester.

West, R. and Walsh, G. (1994/95) Inputs and outputs of distance education. Paper given at *The Distance Education for Language Teachers Symposium, University of Edinburgh 1994*. In R. Howard and I. McGrath (1995) (eds) *Distance Education for Language Teachers* (pp. 133–41). Clevedon: Multilingual Matters.

Chapter 9

Teaching Foreign Language Skills by Distance Education Methods: Some Basic Considerations

BÖRGE HOLMBERG

This chapter, much of which closely follows the first part of a research report (Holmberg, 1989), will discuss some theoretical aspects of foreign language teaching at a distance on the one hand, and the methods and media applied on the other. To avoid misunderstandings the concepts to be discussed are defined at the outset.

Concepts

In this chapter what is regarded as a *foreign language* is a language that is spoken and written today, but is not native to the learner. Latin and Classical Greek are therefore not included.

Distance education is seen as a form of teaching and learning which is not under the supervision of teachers present with their students in lecture rooms or generally on the same premises, but which benefits from the support of a tutorial organisation.[1] It has two constituent elements: the mediated presentation of learning materials (print, recordings, etc.), and interaction between students and tutors (in writing, by e-mail, on the telephone etc) and now also peer-group interaction in online or tele confer-ences (on which see Holmberg, 2003: 60–1.) Teaching and learning a modern foreign language by distance education methods, that is, without teacher and learner meeting face-to-face, has been practised since the end of the 19th century (cf. Gaddén, 1973: 24–33, 40, 60–6). Correspondence courses, supplemented in some cases almost from the beginning by audio recordings (on Hermods' phonograph cylinders made of wax from the first decade of the 20th century, see Gaddén, 1973: 61) have been used to teach a great number of languages, among them English, French, German, Italian, Russian and Spanish. There is no tenable reason why any language should be considered unsuitable for distance teaching and learning; rather, there is much evidence of the effectiveness of distance teaching of foreign languages (Abrioux, 1982; Boyesen, 1964; Gaddén, 1973; Stringer, 1982). Nevertheless, more information about today's practice is called for.

Applicable Educational and Linguistic Theory

Behind all attempts to teach and otherwise facilitate the learning of a modern language there are inevitably theoretical considerations. They concern language theory, the attempted study goals (communication skills or capacity to read and appreciate literary texts, for example), the view of the learner (a thinking person or a mechanistic executor of skills) and of the teaching organisation (as a guide and supporter or as a stand-in for a drill sergeant), epistemological principles (preference for inductive or deductive approaches) and so on.

Languages are taught and learned for different purposes. While in some cases the capacity to read texts of an academic or professional type is the chief aim of the study, the overall goal in other cases is the capacity to speak with some fluency, to write correctly, or to read and appreciate literary texts, poetry and drama etc. In general education the order of priority is usually

- reading and understanding;
- listening and understanding;
- speaking; and
- writing.

The majority of 167 distance teaching organisations answering a questionnaire regarded *reading and understanding* the foreign language as the most important study aim (Holmberg, 1989: 2). *Listening and understanding* comes third among the aims listed, while *skills in writing* is mentioned as an important aim by a majority of the respondents. Developing *skills in speaking* is also mentioned as an important aim by a majority of the respondents. The prominence given to reading and understanding nevertheless seems to indicate that the written language is regarded as the most important study objective. Modern everyday usage is seen as more important than narrative, descriptive and argumentative prose, poetry and drama (Holmberg, 1989: Part II 6).

These goals are very general. To be useful as practical guides for content selection and methodology they must be analysed so that more specific objectives can be catered for. For instance, does the capacity to write French imply translation into French or free writing of, say, essays, reports, letters? How to decide on and implement broad goals and detailed objectives of teaching and learning have also been discussed extensively from the point of view of distance education. Some educators of the behaviourist school, influenced particularly by Magers's methods for 'preparing instructional objectives' and the taxonomies of Bloom and Kratwohl (Bloom *et al.*, 1956, 1964; Mager, 1962), have insisted that objectives expressed in behavioural terms should guide all course development. This means that the objectives must specify what a student should be able to do after study. Definitions of learning objectives are expected to avoid verbs such as *know, understand, realise, grasp, master,* as these are ambiguous. Verbal expressions of action like *recognise the symptoms of, explain by means of synonyms or a sentence, translate, conduct an experiment, demonstrate, do, enumerate, calculate, quote arguments for and against, prove, write an account of, report orally on* are examples of expressions found more acceptable in definitions of objectives.

While this technique can be useful in many contexts, its value is limited. For a discussion of this in relation to distance education in general see Holmberg, 1995: 38–44, for example.

Behavioural thinking is based on the stimulus-response theory. This implies that in teaching and learning certain stimuli cause foreseeable reactions or responses. These responses, rather than what the student thinks or feels, are considered important as indicators of learning. Feedback, reinforcing correct replies is used to consolidate learning. Reinforcement correlated with the response, not with the stimulus, was stressed by Skinner, perhaps the most influential behaviourist (cf. Bower & Hilgard, 1981: 171).

Pure behaviourism seems to have few proponents in the educational debates of today. Cognitivism and constructivism, which do not preclude the consideration of objectives which cannot be expressed in behavioural terms, are more typical of current educational trends. 'The stimulus response theorist and the cognitive theorist come up with different answers to the question: What is learned? The answer of the former is 'habits', the answer of the latter is 'cognitive structures' or "factual knowledge"' (Bower & Hilgard, 1981:15). A basic question is whether those teaching foreign languages should act as educators or as drill sergeants.

The observation that each learner constructs his or her own knowledge by interaction with the subject matter and that, therefore, students learn different things from the same course (cf. Jonassen, 1991) applies also to language learning.

A problem which has concerned many linguists over the last couple of decades is whether our cognitive structure is receptive right from the beginning to a kind of general grammar that can be considered a common human inheritance. An indication this could be so is that normal children pick up highly complex grammars very quickly. Our ability to generalise information and make hypotheses is related to (includes) this skill. Chomsky based his generative transformational grammar on this assumption, submitting that the differing systems of individual languages are surface reflexes of one and the same deep structure. Chomsky assumed that:

> ... knowledge of language – a grammar – can be acquired only by an organism that is 'preset' with a severe restriction on the form of grammar. This innate restriction is a precondition, in the Kantian sense, for linguistic experience, and it appears to be the critical factor in determining the course and result of language learning. (Chomsky, 1972: 91)

> According to Chomsky's conception, the child formulates hypotheses about the rules of the linguistic description of the language whose sentences he is hearing, derives predictions from such hypotheses about the linguistic structure of sentences he will hear in the future, checks these predictions against the new sentences he encounters, eliminates those hypotheses that are contrary to the evidence, and evaluates those that are not eliminated by a simplicity principle which selects the simplest as the best hypothesis concerning the rules underlying the sentences he has heard and will hear. (Katz, 1966: 275)

This discussion should be related to the induction-deduction problem. [2]

Methods and Media

What has been said so far illuminates some important aspects of educational and linguistic theory influencing the way foreign languages are taught and learnt at a distance.

Pattern exercises

Behavioural thinking has some important methodological implications for language teaching. It gives rise to rather mechanistic exercises which reproduce the foreign language, so-called pattern drill, with no explanation of contrast between the student's mother tongue and the foreign language, or any applied principle. Thus, instead of explicitly telling students that the French object forms of the personal pronouns *me, te, se, nous, vous* precede *le, la* and *les*, which in their turn precede *lui* and *leur*, a doctrinaire behaviourist would merely expose the student consistently to the correct usage, and make him or her imitate and repeat:

Il m'a donné le livre. Il me l'a donné.
Je vais lui donner le livre. Je vais le lui donner.

Students may then be asked to answer questions such as

A-t-il leur parlé?   (Oui, il leur a parlé.
                            Non, il ne leur a pas parlé.)

or to change a positive sentence into a negative one:

Ils leur ont parlé. (Ils ne leur ont pas parlé.)
Prêtez lui le livre. (Ne le lui prêtez pas.)

In the same way, students of German can be exposed to sentences such as the following without being made to consider the principles that govern the use of *haben* and *sein* as auxiliaries:

Ich habe gut geschlafen   Ich bin schnell eingeschlafen
Ich habe ein Buch gelesen   Ich bin krank geworden
Ich habe die Vase auf den Tisch   Ich bin sofort zurückgafahren.
gestellt

The theory is that after a sufficient number of reading and listening, speaking and writing exercises the student will automatically express him or herself correctly within the limits of the patterns thus practised. Paradoxically, Chomsky's argument, which entirely rejects behaviourism, could also be referred to in support of pattern drill, if each step in language learning is considered to be a hypothesis, an interim grammar. This is, of course, what happens when children learn their mother tongue. They produce increasingly correct sentences as they reject the implicit hypotheses on which they have based earlier ungrammatical sentences. If educators believe that a second language can be learnt in the same way – and in the case of most distance education, if they believe adults can learn a language in the same way and that it is a practical method – they will refrain from references to logics, grammar, the mother tongue and discussion generally. However, no such method for adult learning or for the study of foreign languages in general has been found useful in organised teaching and learning.

A method for teaching foreign languages that could justifiably claim to be based on first language acquisition would have to meet the following requirements at the very least:

(1) It would allow the learner to progress by forming a series of increasingly complete hypotheses about the language.
(2) In consequence, it would permit and indeed encourage the learner to produce sentences that are ungrammatical interims of full native competence, in order to test these hypotheses.

(3) It would emphasise the perception of patterns rather than the intensity of practice.
(4) Its teaching techniques would include partial repetition of sentences, verbal play and situationally appropriate expansions of the learner's sentences.

No method can at present claim to fulfil these requirements. It remains to be seen whether they can in principle be fulfilled, whether in fact, the analogy between first and second language learning is sound. (Cook, 1969: 215–16)

This does not mean, however, that pattern drill should be avoided in adult language learning. Pattern drill lends itself easily to applications in distance education, both in writing and on audio-tape. In the latter case (cf. the latter part of the French example given above) the question or instruction is recorded and after a pause the correct reply is given, thus providing 'feedback'. The student is expected to use the pause for recording his or her reply.

It is evident that exercises of this kind are useful. But they might be more helpful if the underlying principles were explained before the activities actually begin, thus making them more of an intellectual endeavour than a mechanistic skill activity. Doing this would indicate the use of what is called a cognitivist approach rather than the behaviourist one. Empirical studies have shown that this cognitive approach is superior to one which is merely behaviourist (Lindell, 1970; Smith & Berger, 1965) in that the students achieve more and their attitudes to study are more favourable than those resulting from pattern drill.

In any study of the distance teaching of modern languages it is therefore of interest to find out if and how pattern drill is practised. Are the exercises carried out on the basis of explanations and understanding, or merely as training of mechanistic skills?

Whether students should be helped to develop linguistic proficiency via the study of grammar and principles, or by imitation exercises has long been a bone of contention among educators. Attempts to combine the two approaches seem to be common everywhere. Ambivalence over this debate can also be found in the replies given to the questionnaire mentioned above. Pattern drill is practised by most respondents, but in the majority of cases such drills are preceded by explanations of the principles governing the language usage being taught. There can thus be no question of the respondents preferring a wholly imitative method. A combination of the learning of principles (grammar, etc.) and imitative practice is evidently preferred (Holmberg, 1989: Part II, 9).

As an example, the following frequently practised way of teaching grammatical structures in German can be mentioned:

(1) A presentation of typical sentences selected from texts read from which the student infers what principles govern the usage (like 'Ich gab ihnen die Bücher. Gab er euch die Bücher? Er gab ihr einen Ring. Ich sah sie auf der Strasse. Sie bat ihn um Hilfe. Schickte er Ihnen keine Blumen?)

(2) A discussion of the findings made which specify the principles illustrated, explaining, for example., why the dative form is used after the verb in five of the sentences and the accusative form in the other two. This is done in a Socratic way referring to students' observations.

(3) Exercises of a self-checking character.

(4) A discussion of the exercises, relating the individual examples to the general principles discovered according to 1 and 2.

Pronunciation

A similar controversy concerns the way in which the pronunciation of a foreign language is taught. Imitation here is a *sine qua non*, but is it enough? The way many languages are pronounced by non-natives even after many years of practice indicates it is not. The 'ear' and imitative capacity of most people are simply not good enough. In Closset's *Didactique des Langues Vivantes* this is stressed as follows:

> L'opinion courante, suivant laquelle l'assimilation des sons étrangers pourrait se faire par l'imitation pure, repose sur une méconnaissance totale de la tâche difficile de l'enseignement des langues vivantes et de ses exigences les plus urgentes. Apprend-on à jouer du violin en regardant jouer un violiniste? Or le jeu des organes phonateurs est bien plus rapide, bien plus complexe. Remarquons en outre que le nombre des élèves de type auditif est, dans une classe, fort peu élevé. (quoted from Thorén, 1957: 92)

The truth of this can be confirmed by any teacher of English. Many students who have listened to, and consciously tried to imitate British English for years do not distinguish between *walk* and *work* in their speech, pronounce *camp* as though it rhymed with *hemp*, and are still heard to pronounce an [r] of some kind in words such as *more* and *forty*, which although good Scottish and American English is definitely not RP.[3] The inability to distinguish between [-eit] and [-it] in words such as *moderate* also supports Closset's conclusions. In the last mentioned example lack of insight into the relationships between spelling and pronunciation (-ate = [it] at the end of nouns and adjectives, [eit] at the end of verbs) is to be blamed, whereas in other cases it is acoustic perception and articulation that are deficient. Exact descriptions of sounds and phonetic transcription combined with recorded speech (students listening to audio-cassettes, imitating and comparing) would seem to be the answer. How is a French student to learn how to pronounce the English [i] in *him, sit*, etc. if he or she is not made aware of the difference between this sound and its equivalent in French, which by English standards is very tense indeed? Without explicit explanations many students mispronounce words like occurred ['ə kə:d] and entered ['entəd].[4]. For clarity here, phonetic transcription seems indispensable, which is not necessarily the case in the teaching and learning of all other languages.

Most distance educators are aware of these difficulties and apply solutions of various kinds in their pre-produced courses and in the ensuing non-contiguous communication. Apart from phonetic transcription, the use of audio recordings both for listening and interaction (i.e. communication between students and tutors) contributes to good results; this is also true for stress and intonation, particularly when combined with, or based on explanations giving students insights into the rules behind the usage. The telephone is useful for interaction generally, but is inadequate for some pronunciation exercises. It may, for example, be difficult to distinguish between [s] and [z] on the telephone.

The majority of the distance teaching institutions answering the questionnaire referred to above use recordings (audiotape-cassette) to teach pronunciation, stress and intonation, and a great number use the recordings in combination with other media, such as phonetic transcriptions (see Holmberg, 1989: Part II, 8).

The use of the mother tongue

When communicative rather than reading skills are the most important learning objectives, the use of the mother tongue in the teaching–learning situation is usually limited in favour of the foreign language that is being studied. While this makes sense in everyday use of the language, this is really not the case when grammatical or phonetic subjects are being discussed. The educator must ask him or herself if the vocabulary required for this sort of discussion is really important to the student, or if terminology of little interest to the non-linguist is required. If not, the obvious choice as the teaching medium is the mother tongue.

Most situations and contexts and many words can be explained easily in the foreign language. In such cases translations are not necessary, though many students feel more secure if such translations are available. There are some cases, however, in which translations are required because explanations can be misleading or not sufficiently exact. It makes little sense to avoid translations of names of animals or plants, as demonstrated in some examples actually occurring in textbooks (and quoted by Lindell): *lily* described simply as 'white flower' (Lindell adds: 'from daisy to orchid!') and 'A shark is a very big fish. A herring is a small fish; a cod is rather big' (Lindell, 1970: 76). It is certainly doubtful whether students realised from these descriptions which flowers and fishes were meant. It would be worthwhile finding out what common practice is nowadays in distance education in this respect given that there is little current belief in behaviourism.

Contrastive and 'direct' methods

Germane to the problem areas discussed so far is the question of contrastive analyses of the foreign language in relation to the mother tongue. Extreme protagonists of the so-called direct method find all references to the mother tongue objectionable as obstacles to learning the foreign language; others insist that explanation of language mechanisms are necessary for exactitude and student security and for such explanations comparisons with the mother tongue are necessary. Cf. James (1969), who illustrates the need for contrastive analysis with these examples of the indicative and the subjunctive in Spanish.

> Ha coleccionado mariposas que tienen alas rojas.
> He's collected butterflies which have red wings.

> Busca mariposas que tengan alas rojas.
> He's looking for butterflies which have red wings. (quoted from Malmberg, 1971: 120)

Most educators probably find contrastive discussion is required in a number of cases, for instance when English speaking students have to learn German expressions such as 'Er hätte es tun sollen' (= He should have done it).

Speech

It is difficult to see how the ability to converse in a foreign language can be learnt without practice in conversation. Telephone conversations seem to offer the best solution here if nothing but non-contiguous communication is possible. Speech in the sense of speech making, giving lectures, etc. can, of course, be practised and commented on audio-tape. Nevertheless, most speech training is difficult to do without face-to-face practice. This does not, however, need to be part of a course, but can be provided in other ways (private meetings, on the job, etc.) even though there is then usually little feedback on the correctness of the learner's speech.

Conclusion

The concerns described above play an important part in most attempts to develop language teaching at a distance. A number of further problems could well have been added. Nevertheless, those discussed briefly here seem to be of particular importance. They concern basic issues relating to language, general education and distance learning and teaching.

Detailed studies of distance education practice in the areas discussed are called for. The questionnaire study repeatedly referred to above (Holmberg, 1989) may be regarded as a beginning. We have reason to believe much can be done to improve the teaching of foreign languages at a distance. Reliable information about actual practice today would seem to be a useful starting point.

A general methodological conclusion from experience and the thinking referred to above seems to be that explicit explanations are required in the distance teaching of modern languages. Examples quoted above are the need for lucid rules for the placing of French personal pronouns, the pluperfect subjunctive of German *sollen* and *können* in expressions like *Er hätte es tun können/sollen.* (He could / should have done it) and the principles of English pronunciation of the ending -ed in *talked* (= t), *sobbed* (= d) and *parted* (= id) (4). A great number of other cases where such explanations are of vital importance could be added, for instance the use of English adverbs ending in -*ly*, the word order in German subordinate clauses, the use of French *être* and the German *sein* to create the perfect and pluperfect tenses (*Il est tombé; nous nous sommes trompés; er ist gestorben; sie sind nach Frankreich gefahren*) and the practical rule that in English pronunciation the vowel in the third syllable from the end of the word, i.e. the antepenult, is usually stressed and short competitor/kəm'petit?) but compete/kəm'pi:t/). Directing students' attention to matters like these is not futile theorising, but a real help in distance learning.

Notes

1. The concept of distance education has been fully analysed by Keegan, 1990: 3–47.
2. Leading linguists have paid much attention to this dichotomy. To Saussure *la langue* – the general system – is of prime interest rather than *la parole*, which is his designation for the language in a particular situation. Louis Hjelmslev follows up the Saussure approach. He insists on 'a deductive method, not an inductive one, and thus derives the linguistic structure from a number of a-priori theoretical premises'. Hjelmslev's approach, 'glossematics', is generative in the sense that the rules defined make it possible to create any length and any number of statements ('texts') in the language in question. They thus constitute a calculation leading to prediction . . . (Malmberg, 1971: 21). On generative grammar cf. Chomsky (1965): A generative grammar of English 'is one that contains a list of

symbols . . . and a list of rules for combining these symbols in various ways to produce every English sentence' (Thomas, 1965: 8).

3. RP = Received Pronunciation, a kind of English propagated by upper and upper-middle class tradition in England (cf. Gimson, 1962: 83).

4. The simple rule is that the verb ending -ed is pronounced [d] after voiced sounds except [d] where it is pronounced [id]; [t] after voiceless sounds except [t] where it is [id]. Thus *played* [pleid], *filled* [fild], *stopped* [stpt], but *handed* ['hændid], *limited* ['limitid]. As *occur* and *enter* are pronounced [əkə:] and ['entə], the ending -ed follows a vowel (a voiced sound) in these words, thus [d].

References

Abrioux, D. (1982) Teaching university French from a distance: The student population examined. In J. Daniel, M. Stroud and J. Thomsen (eds) *Learning at a Distance. A World Perspective* (pp. 232–35). Edmonton: Athabasca University/International Council for Correspondence Education.

Bloom, B.S. *et al.* (1956 and 1964) *Taxonomy of Educational Objectives I–II*. New York: McKay.

Bower, G.H. and Hilgard, E.R. (1981) (5th ed.) *Theories of Learning*. Englewood Cliffs: Prentice Hall.

Boyesen, E. (1964) *Norsk Korrespondansekole Giennon 50 år 1914–1964*. Oslo: NKS.

Chomsky, N. (1965) *Syntactic Structures*. The Hague: Mouton.

Chomsky, N. (1972) *Language and Mind*. New York: Harcourt Brace Jovanovich.

Cook, V.J. (1969) *The Analogy Between First and Second Language Learning*. IRAL VII).

Gaddén, G. (1973) *Hermods 1898–1973*. Malmö: Hermods.

Gimson, A.C. (1962) *An Introduction to the Pronunciation of English*. London:Arnold.

Holmberg, B. (1989) *Distance Teaching of Modern Languages (with a summary of questionnaire data in co-operation with R. Scheumer and D. Klintz)*. Hagen: Fernuniversität ZIFF.

Holmberg, B. (1995) *Theory and Practice of Distance Education*. London and New York: Routledge.

Holmberg, B. (2003) *Distance Education in Essence*. Oldenburg: Bibliotheks- und informationssystem der Universität Oldenburg.

Jonassen, D.H. (1991) Objectivism versus constructivism: Do we need a new philosophical paradigm? *Educational Technology Research and Development* 39 (3): 5–14.

Katz, J.J. (1966) *The Philosophy of Language*. New York and London: Harper & Row.

Keegan, D. (1990) *Foundations of Distance Education*. London and New York: Routledge.

Lindell, E. (1970) Behovet av kriterier in A.Ellegård and E.Lindell (eds) *Direkt eller insikt?* Lund: Gleerup.

Mager, R.F. (1962) *Preparing Instructional Objectives*. Palo Alto:P Cal: Fearon.

Malmberg, B. (1971) *Språkinlärning. En orientering och ett debattinlägg*. Stockholm: Aldus/Bonniers.

Smith, P. and Berger, E. (1965) *An Assessment of Three Foreign Language Teaching Strategies Utilizing Three Language Laboratory Systems*. Washington DC: US Department of Health, Education and Welfare.

Stringer, M. (1982) Learning French at a distance: The student's perspective. In J. Daniel, M. Stroud and J. Thomsen (eds) *Learning at a Distance: A World Perspective* (pp. 236–39). Edmonton: Athabasca University/International Council for Correspondence Education.

Thomas, D. (1965) *Transformational Grammar and the Teacher of English.* New York: Rinehart and Winston.

Thorén, B. (1957) *Mål, medel och metoder vid skolans språkundeervisning.* Lund: Gleerup.

Chapter 10

Course Design for the Distance Learner of Spanish: More Challenges than Meet the Eye

CECILIA GARRIDO

Introduction

Course design in any discipline is the outcome of decisions dependent on a number of interacting factors that include learning theories, teaching methods and the various stakeholders involved in the teaching and learning process. In language teaching, decisions about a course syllabus take account of, among other things, the ethos of the institution, the students' needs and the path that will take learners to expected levels of language competence at the end of a given programme of studies. These challenges are especially difficult to tackle when teaching and learning languages at a distance.

In addition to helping students develop their linguistic skills, distance learning course designers have to bear in mind other factors such as the implications of integrating culture in the foreign language curriculum and the role of ICT in developing linguistic and intercultural competence. These factors raise challenges that are much easier to deal with in a face-to-face environment. The physical separation of teacher and learner presents difficulties for the development of interactive skills. The interaction between tutors and students or between students and their peers is very important in language learning since it provides practice opportunities for performance in real life.

This study reflects on the experience of the Spanish team at the UK Open University (OU), which began the development of its current distance learning language programme in 1996. It will revisit the initial assumptions that led the team to the chosen course design and will also discuss the thinking that evolved as the courses were developed and the challenges that have arisen since.

The Challenges of Teaching and Learning Languages at a Distance

Breaking new ground

Over time course design for language teaching purposes has run parallel to research into second language acquisition. It is therefore not difficult to find abundant information on syllabus design for language teaching. Krahnke (1987), Nunan (1988), Widdowson (1990), Wilkins (1976), Yalden (1987), and more recently Richards (2001), among others, provide sound advice on the various alternatives available in syllabus design and the pedagogic and cognitive principles behind each approach. Richards in particular provides guidance not only on the types of syllabus available, but also – more importantly – on the factors that should inform the decision-making process. He also discusses the stages in course planning and development, as well as the role of appropriate materials, the frameworks needed to provide quality teaching and the evaluation of teaching programmes. This matches to a great extent the approach to curriculum and course design followed by the OU Spanish team, although Richards' publication was not available at the time.

Most of the sources listed above assume the physical proximity of teachers and learners, e.g. a non-distance-learning environment. Similarly, advice on materials development for the distance learner is often available generically as in Lockwood (1994) and Rowntree (1992), but does not often relate to foreign language learning in particular.

The Open University's philosophy, as reflected in its name, is based on principles of openness: Open as to people, open as to places, open as to methods, and open as to ideas. The university therefore attracts and accepts students from all walks of life and all levels of ability. Given this wide student background, the Spanish courses needed to be motivating and capable of guiding students along a route that would help them reach a specific level of language competence leading to a Diploma in Spanish. The course team needed to focus not only on obvious aspects such as realistic objectives, type of syllabus, strategies for the recruitment and retention of students and quality control standards, but also on how best to support students to achieve their language objectives at a distance. At this juncture it is important to note that in the Open University organisation, course teams operating from the university's headquarters in Milton Keynes are tasked with the design of courses and the development of materials, and the tutors (officially called Associate Lecturers) in regions in the UK and in many parts of the world, represent the interface with the students, providing opportunities for direct contact, be it face-to-face, over the telephone, by e-mail or by post.

In any educational environment, students have a set of expectations of the instruction they will receive and the goals they want to achieve. Given the wide variety of backgrounds of potential Spanish students at the OU, and based on their assumed personal goals and previous language learning experiences, it would be only natural that some might expect a structural approach, others a functional one, while yet others might expect a mainly communicative experience. Whatever the approach, there had to be a high degree of flexibility built into the courses to meet wide-ranging expectations. Such a level of flexibility requires the design of materials that allow for individual engagement, according to individual goals and needs. It would include, for instance, grammar for the analytical learner, interactivity for those who prefer a communicative approach, and enough guidance and feedback to all to instil confidence without being patronising.

Needs analysis and student profile

To address students' expectations with a reasonable degree of confidence, the likely profile of the potential Spanish students was established. Our approach to the needs analysis roughly reflects the Munby model described by Schutz and Derwing in Figure 10.1.

The Spanish team drew on the experience of the OU French and German programmes developed in advance of Spanish and, like them, began with a

1. Personal	Culturally significant information about the individual, such as language background
2. Purpose	Occupational or educational objective for which the target language is required
3. Setting	Physical and psychological setting in which the target language is required
4. Interactional variables	Such as the role relationships to be involved in the target language use
5. Medium, mode, and channel	Communicative means
6. Dialects	Information on dialects to be utilised
7. Target level	Level of competence required in the target language
8. Anticipated communicative events	Micro- and macro-activities
9. Key	The specific manner in which communication is actually carried out

Figure 10.1 Profile of communicative needs
Source: Schutz & Derwing, 1981: 32

first course aimed at students with a lower intermediate level of language competence. It also consulted with colleagues at other institutions delivering courses to similar types of students (mainly adults with a vocational interest in learning Spanish, but also others looking to achieve university qualifications) and did some research on the level of language competence that could be expected of students, based on the time they could devote to studying the courses. This analysis set the level of competence, the type of syllabus and the thematic and linguistic contents for each course.

Because Spanish is a language spoken in many different parts of the world, deliberations also took place concerning the type of Spanish students would be expected to learn. Traditionally, Spanish courses in the UK focus on the Castilian variety, and feedback from colleagues in other institutions suggested we should continue with this traditional approach. The team was, however, very aware of the importance of the courses' cultural content and the need for them to be truly representative of Spanish speaking cultures. This was considered essential to ensure our students would become interculturally competent Spanish speakers.

Defining the standards

The need for increased mobility beyond national boundaries in Europe has made it necessary to develop language competence standards that are transparent and portable across countries. At the time the Spanish programme was being developed (1996), opinions differed at the OU about the appropriateness of the official UK foreign language standards for adult learners at a distance. The Spanish team decided to research on the suitability of the Common European Framework of Reference for Languages (CEF) and found the principles on which it is based (flexibility, openness, multipurposeness, dynamism and non-dogmatism) fitted well with the team's approach (Council of Europe, 1998: 5). The CEF not only provided a solution to the practical problem of specifying the standards to measure our students' linguistic competence, but also opened up new ways of thinking around issues of syllabus and course design, especially in reference to the development of intercultural competence (Council of Europe, 1998: 19–62). This decision made the team more aware of the importance of these issues in the distance-learning context.

Assessment and feedback

Feedback is an essential ingredient in any learning situation, more so in the distance-learning environment. In the case of OU students there are two main sources of advice: the course materials and the comments students receive from their tutors. Although OU students are assigned to a tutor and have the opportunity to attend a number of face-to-face tutorials, such tutorials are not compulsory, and students should be able to meet the course objectives without attending them. As a consequence, issues of interaction, the acquisition of language skills and self-evaluation, and thus the development of autonomous learning are to a great extent determined by the materials provided. Besides providing guidance to support students in the acquisition of such useful skills, the feedback embedded in the text is geared to maintaining a dialogue with the learner throughout the course.

Tutor feedback also plays a crucial role and poses several challenges in the distance-learning environment. Besides giving students a perspective of their success, feedback is an important learning tool in the development of student confidence and autonomy. Separately, for those students aspiring to a qualification, feedback on their assignments is essential to progress and meeting the required standards. Tutor feedback varies according to individual teaching styles and the tutor's perceptions of students' needs. Students also have their own views as to the feedback they need and how it can be useful to them (Hyland, 2001). In addition, feedback can be misinterpreted, and unless there is an opportunity for dialogue between students and tutors, there is a danger of a mismatch between what the students want and need, and what the tutor provides. It is therefore essential to provide tutors with training and support that engenders useful and encouraging feedback.

In the context of the OU Spanish courses, tutor training turned out to be one of the main challenges. The team soon realised that the tutors – in the majority Spanish nationals – didn't feel confident enough to provide feedback on aspects of Spanish as a language of global communication. This applied not only in relation to linguistic issues, but also to cultural and intercultural matters, where students needed to be encouraged to reflect and analyse the attitudes and meanings behind the course materials. Although this situation is not unique to the distance learning environment, the circumstances under which tutors operate – working mostly on their own – do not foster sharing good practice or learning from each other's expertise. Some research carried out among students and tutors confirmed the weaknesses in providing adequate feedback that had been suspected, and it was necessary to make provision for additional guidance to tutors via briefings and the marking notes that accompany the various assignments.

The decision-making process

On the basis of the potential student profile, the analysis of their needs, their learning expectations and the mode of learning, the team therefore decided the OU Spanish courses needed to:

(1) meet students' requirements in terms of thematic and linguistic content through a wide spectrum of cultural experiences conducive to the achievement of the course objectives and learning outcomes;

(2) provide opportunities for the development of communicative strategies to enable students to perform competently and confidently in the foreign language in situations relevant to their needs;

(3) encourage students' autonomy to make them feel in charge of their own learning;

(4) allow students to reflect on their learning and to revisit grammatical, semantic, situational and communicative structures and strategies at various levels of complexity;

(5) provide fertile ground for the consolidation and expansion of linguistic knowledge and communicative competence by the use of authentic language and useful and relevant feedback.

All the above was to be achieved by means of an integrated syllabus that would reflect a set of teaching priorities rather than absolute choices. The courses were to expose students to language that was representative of the cultures that speak it and help them engage in communicative experiences likely to be encountered when interacting with other Spanish speakers. Against the prevailing consensus, the team also decided to approach Spanish as a global language of communication with no bias towards a particular dialectal variety. This decision gave rise to further questions in the design and development of the courses.

Approaching Spanish as a global language brought up two aspects that have been the subject of extensive debate in foreign language teaching for some time: the role of culture in language learning and the types of skill students should develop in relation to the target culture(s). These aspects in turn engender debates about cultural diversity, attitudes to cultural identity and to linguistic norm and standards, which will be discussed later in this study. Admittedly, such challenges apply to language learning in general, but dealing with them successfully is more difficult when teaching the language at a distance. The role teachers play in a face-to-face situation helping students to discover links between cultures and interpret their differences has to be fulfilled in distance learning by the language materials and resources, the activities and tasks students are encouraged to do, the guidance available within the materials, and the type of evaluation and feedback provided.

The development of oral skills

Any discussion about communicative language interaction implies the development of productive and receptive skills. In distance language learning, however, it is oral proficiency that presents the main challenge. Consequently, the course materials and the methodological approach adopted must offer students ample opportunities to develop oral accuracy and fluency, as well as the ability to use linguistic skills interactively. Accuracy and fluency relate to pronunciation, an area often neglected in foreign language teaching. Interactivity refers to the ability to communicate and negotiate meaning with other speakers.

Pronunciation is considered by many to be 'a kind of "frill" – something which may or may not be "added on" later and so pronunciation is often taught incidentally, if at all'. Pronunciation is an important language skill, which if poor, 'interferes with the accurate transmission of linguistic messages' (Conrick, 1999: 180–1). In the distance-learning environment it is therefore essential to set up a framework that guarantees students have opportunities and support to progress in this vital area of speech. The OU language courses encourage oral practice through activities embedded in the teaching materials, the tasks students have to record on tape and the feedback they receive from their tutors. In the specific case of Spanish, the team felt that in the absence of compulsory face-to-face interaction, students should have resources that would encourage pronunciation practice, either independently or linked to specific tasks. Students are able to improve their pronunciation through activities that elicit spoken responses or through pronunciation practices (available on CD), focused on specific sounds, rhythm and intonation patterns.

Developing interactive skills is not an easy goal to achieve at a distance, especially if students are unable to attend face-to-face tutorials or are reluctant to contact their tutor. This is an area in which the integration of ICT has much to offer, as discussed below.

Until now the development of interactive skills among OU Spanish students has been achieved through activities that promote a degree of interaction with the audio-visual stimuli available within the course, the optional contact with tutors and compulsory attendance to a residential school. Students are also encouraged to organise self-help groups. Such activities provide useful opportunities for both linguistic and socio-cultural learning.

A framework to support the distance language learner

Apart from clear and measurable objectives, and interesting and realistic content, distance learners need a teaching and learning framework that engenders a high level of motivation to help them stay on track during the learning process. Leo van Lier's 'triple A' approach to curriculum design (1996) offers such a framework, which coincides to a great extent with the approach adopted by the Spanish team. Although van Lier's approach refers to general language learning contexts, it is particularly relevant to distance language learning because the principles he establishes – *Awareness, Autonomy* and *Authenticity* – are, in my view, basic to the success of the distance learner. *Awareness* relates to being able to perceive the need to learn something, focus on it and subsequently apply previous knowledge and experience to acquire new knowledge. *Autonomy* has to do with choice and responsibility. Learners can only succeed if they have control, ownership, choice, competence to do the work and the ability to assess their progress. *Authenticity* refers not only to the language input to which students are exposed, but also to the realism of the situations in which they are expected to perform as part of the learning process (van Lier, 1996: 5–13).

These three principles are closely interrelated, and they provide the framework that will nurture the motivation required to succeed when learning on one's own: once students become aware of learning strategies and processes, and of their own learning style, they will gain confidence in their learning capabilities. The authenticity and relevance of the language and situations they engage with will help focus their attention, and as a result a high level of motivation is likely to be maintained. In the context of the OU Spanish courses relevant activities and authentic language resources created opportunities for students to develop knowledge based on new and prior experience and encouraged them to reflect and verify their progress.

Van Lier's approach adds a fourth A, *Achievement* (part of a second triad that also includes *Assessment* and *Accountability*). *Achievement* relates to accomplishment through autonomy and motivation. As mentioned above, it is important that distance learners gain knowledge and awareness of their progress. At the OU this is normally accomplished through feedback from tutors and in activities within the courses. As is to be expected, the highest sense of achievement for OU students comes from the interaction with other speakers, whether native or non-native, tutors or peers. This becomes evident when students participate in self-help groups outside the formal teaching and learning context, and interact with their tutors or their peers during tutorials or the compulsory residential school. Research has proved that in the case of Spanish, students not only value highly the linguistic skills they have developed, but, given the global nature of the language, also appreciate the possibility of being able to interact with Spanish speakers of various cultural backgrounds (Beaven & Garrido, 2000: 181–90).

Evolving Challenges

From the previous sections it should be clear that as the initial challenges were tackled new ones arose. They evolved mainly from the implications of teaching language and culture in an integrated manner, and the opportunities and threats of the information age. Both raise a number of questions about the role and the degree of responsibility of teachers and students in the teaching and learning process.

Culture and the language syllabus

Although the importance of culture in language teaching and learning has long been recognised, until fairly recently most of the canonical literature on course and syllabus design gave little or no importance to the integration of culture in language teaching, even though it is difficult to see how real communicative language competence can be accomplished in a cultural vacuum. It is widely accepted that full communicative competence cannot be achieved without intercultural understanding. According to Saville-Troike:

> Clear cross-cultural differences can and do produce conflicts and inhibit communication [. . .] even such matters as voice level differ cross-culturally, and speaker intent may be misconstrued because of different expectation patterns for interpretation [. . .] The concept of communicative competence must be embedded in the notion of cultural competence or the total set of knowledge and skills which speakers bring into a situation. (Saville-Troike, 1989: 21–2)

Approaches to developing intercultural understanding have historically evolved from the transmission of cultural information in an attempt to impart knowledge, to give students the tools to help them interpret phenomena in the target culture. More recent approaches encourage learners to engage in the interpretation of their own meanings as well as those of the culture they are learning about (Kramsch, 1993). In the distance learning environment the learning materials and activities need to give students opportunities to engage actively in acquiring knowledge, interpreting cultural events and inferring meaning from cultural phenomena. This strategy fits closely with Byram's model for success in intercultural communicative competence (ICC), which in his view requires the development of culture-related knowledge, skills to discover, interpret and relate the target culture to one's own, and the development of attitudes that will be conducive to mutual cultural understanding (Byram, 1997).

This strategy also fits with general models of intercultural communication (Brislin & Yoshida, 1994), which promote the need for the development of awareness, knowledge, attitudes and skills to communicate successfully with other cultures. Such models give considerable emphasis to the need to reflect on others' and one's own values and biases and their effects, and to be comfortable with the differences without feeling that one necessarily has to adopt or behave according to the value system of others.

As discussed in a previous study, a teaching model to develop ICC requires:

(1) the formulation of cultural aims and outcomes during the curriculum planning process;
(2) the design of a syllabus showing quantifiable and achievable cultural objectives with corresponding assessment criteria;
(3) the selection of varied authentic materials portraying crucial aspects of the foreign cultures;
(4) the development of teaching methods that explicitly deal with and invite reflection upon cultural issues, as well as the development of learning strategies that enable learners to become multiculturally competent;
(5) the evaluation of the achievement of cultural objectives. (Álvarez & Garrido, 2001: 155)

Although the importance of ICC has been acknowledged, language teachers are still struggling to find out how to promote its development. At the OU, the Spanish team's success in implementing the five principles above varied considerably. Principles 3 and 4 were not particularly difficult to implement, although considerable financial commitment was required to gather audio-visual and other resource materials at several Spanish-speaking locations around the world. On the other hand, the team had to go through a fairly steep learning curve in the formulation of cultural objectives. The curve eased as more courses were developed. The main hurdles encountered related to the formulation of evaluation and assessment criteria (principles 2 and 5 above). This was so not because courses were being taught at a distance, but rather due to the lack of experience in evaluating ICC. Also, even when the specific criteria were identified by the course team, some tutors did not feel confident enough to give students feedback, especially on personal attitudes and interpretations of the target culture(s).

Developing and assessing ICC is a complex process because, on the one hand, as it implies 'personality development', it is difficult to define levels of intercultural proficiency that match existing levels of linguistic competence. On the other hand, it seems that the tendency among language teachers is still to set out language tasks that do not require deep engagement and reflection on intercultural issues (Sercu, 2002). In the distance-learning environment, these issues are exacerbated by the limited opportunities available for immediate interaction between tutors and learners, and the difficulty in carrying out group activities and collaborative construction of intercultural knowledge.

Additionally, it appears that standard assessment practices do not fit the evaluation of those aspects of learning that are not easily quantifiable, as in the case of ICC. The assessment of shift in cultural attitudes is hardly suitable for quantitative and summative evaluation, and the qualitative evaluation of such skills requires 'complex tools which are perhaps not easy to design and which have not yet been sufficiently studied and produced' (Artal *et al.*, 1997).

Provided it is clearly understood that evaluation cannot always equate to a grade on a set assessment scale, the compilation of language portfolios is likely to be a much better tool for the evaluation of ICC. Besides giving the distance learner an opportunity to document his or her intercultural experiences, portfolios can be learning tools that bridge the teaching–assessment divide and provide a continuum to the teaching and learning process. Although portfolio assessment is becoming more popular these days, it is still regarded as a tool not easy to evaluate, and language teachers are not automatically attracted to it. At the OU, where over 7000 students are learning French, German and Spanish at any one time, the evaluation of such a large number of portfolios presents considerable logistic and financial challenges. Also, traditional assessment via tests and examinations prevents the development of more innovative means of evaluation that can really measure the competences acquired by language students today. The OU Spanish team would certainly like to develop assessment strategies that include portfolio evaluation.

The challenges of cultural diversity

Besides the difficulties of evaluation mentioned above, the development of ICC also raises a number of issues regarding the diversity of the culture(s) being taught, the authenticity of the materials and the values and attitudes that such resources will encourage.

The development of intercultural competence should encourage students to formulate their own interpretation of cultural meanings in their own culture as well as the target culture(s). Therefore, students also need to have the tools to demystify and decode discourse and strip it of the prejudices it may conceal. This can be supported effectively if the materials provided to the students are varied and diverse, and students are made aware of their cultural significance. Variety and diversity imply not only a wealth of contexts within one culture, but also the representation of the various cultures of the target language, which is an imperative in the case of Spanish, given its wide spread around the globe. This cultural diversity is essential for learners to interpret and discover meaning. The absence of diversity will only work to the detriment of the students' linguistic and cultural experience.

The concept of diversity also raises new challenges _vis-à-vis_ language standards and attitudes to linguistic norms. The idea of a language standard is based on parameters that in most cases have little to do with logical or linguistic rules. The so-called 'standard varieties' of language often have their origin in historical accidents or, more often, value judgements completely unrelated to language use (Bourdieau, 1991: 220–3). This in turn applies to the concepts of the norm of correctness, associated with the dominant classes from which the standard variety originates (the Castilian variety in the case of Spanish). Although there is currently more interest in the importance of dialectal varieties, many people still believe that the final objective in language learning is the mastery of a language standard. In reference to the teaching of English as a foreign language, Searle finds such a goal highly objectionable, as mastering a so-called standard language variety has strong echoes of an imperialistic history that oppressed native cultures over which the (English) language imposed its power (cited by Pennycook, 1997: 50).

A language standard is also often associated with a particular national identity. Apart from the fact that it is impossible to talk about one standard in relation to languages of global communication such as English or Spanish – or indeed other languages spoken in more than one country – it is difficult to accept the association of a single language standard to a particular national identity. What is perhaps worse, in my view, is that the concept of an accepted standard suggests other language varieties are 'non-standard', an idea that is in itself discriminatory and not conducive to the objective knowledge and understanding of other cultures.

It could be argued that learning a specific language standard may be easier for students and this would avoid confusion. However, the reality of the Spanish-speaking world is that there are several standard varieties and therefore, depriving students from exposure to such diversity is likely to result in communication difficulties when encountering other dialectal variants. This deprivation would also deny students the opportunity to equip themselves with coping strategies that will ease communication when interacting with speakers of unfamiliar dialectal varieties.

As mentioned before, the limited interaction between learners and tutors in the distance learning environment, and the difficulties of exploring cultural diversity collaboratively, put distance learners at a disadvantage because in isolation personal views cannot be shared or challenged. For this reason, the course materials need to offer opportunities for reflection, engagement and dialogue. They need to represent the varying values, attitudes and world-views of the target culture(s), which are essential to provide an accurate picture of the target language culture(s). Access to plentiful authentic resources was a challenge until some years ago, but this is no longer the case thanks to information technology and modern communications. The challenge today is how to manage the implications and opportunities offered by the information age.

Being able to tackle all the aspects above is possible but requires the careful integration of the intercultural element from course inception to delivery and evaluation. The Spanish team has been quite successful in integrating culture in the OU Spanish courses by:

(1) developing materials that present the Spanish language as it is, as students are likely to encounter it in its cultural setting;
(2) highlighting cultural and linguistic characteristics to raise awareness of differences as well as similarities;
(3) presenting the Spanish speaking cultures as dynamic entities that reflect the world they live in;
(4) giving students opportunities to reflect on their own culture in relation to the culture of others;
(5) ensuring the graded development of intercultural understanding.

The assessment of ICC is still a matter to be addressed. Although the OU Spanish materials do allow for self-assessment of intercultural skills, the current assessment strategy, common also to French and German, is not very conducive to the evaluation of ICC, and until it is reviewed at departmental level the Spanish team will not be in a position to set up a different evaluation approach.

Another difficulty mentioned above is the need for teacher training so that tutors feel confident to engage with their students in debates of intercultural nature even if they raise political and ethical questions.

The role of the new technologies in foreign language learning

The arrival of the information age and computer-mediated learning has opened opportunities that can be particularly beneficial in the distance learning environment, where learners can work at their own pace and without constraints of time and geography. When the first Spanish courses were being developed opportunities to take advantage of these openings were limited, but the experience of teaching languages at a distance, and the increased accessibility of ICT have generated debate and new developments within the OU language teaching programme. The beginners' Spanish course launched in 2003 provides students with online tuition.

Computer-mediated learning facilitates multiple ways of accessing and transmitting knowledge. At their best the new technologies provide ways of learning that challenge traditional educational frameworks. They allow non-linear learning that encourages relational thinking and structuring of the phenomena observed in a non-conventional manner, without following prescribed orders. Learning is context-bound, and authentic materials or 'real life materials', as Kramsch (1993) calls them, offer global domains of cultural knowledge that need to be accessed through a variety of contexts.

Developing knowledge does not result necessarily from a gradual, linear, cumulative learning experience. More often the learner requires skills to re-interpret and re-organise previously acquired knowledge. Access to computer-based materials facilitates students' construction of knowledge within the social reality they represent (Felix, 2002). In turn, students no longer depend on their teachers to provide the limited content for their learning experience or to transmit set knowledge to them (Fitzpatrick, 2002; McConnell, 2000). Students can find both content and knowledge independently. The challenges for language educators, and especially for the distance learning course designer, is therefore three-fold: first, they must assume responsibility for finding out the pedagogical advantages of the use of the new technologies; second, they must ascertain what their students might be able to learn through these media to meet their objectives; and third, they must learn to convince themselves of the value of the new educational processes, to participate fully in the creation of knowledge in their role as facilitators.

The immediacy of access to current information about all sorts of cultural contexts provides tools for intercultural understanding, but it does not automatically lead to it. ICT does undoubtedly create opportunities for the development of a cross-cultural process that is interactive and not simply the result of passive reception of information. For instance, OU students have access to ROUTES, a library service that provides quick and easy access to quality-assessed internet sites. In the case of Spanish such sites provide students and tutors with a gateway to cultural experiences that could not be provided through the standard course materials.

However, it is important to remember that although computers open new channels of communication and that the Internet is having a major impact on language and language use, it is also true that research on the effects of this impact has not been easy to carry out (Crystal, 2001). In addition, research on CALL although abundant is still finding ways of bringing coherence and direction to the field (Levy, 2002). Among language practitioners there is still a feeling of uncertainty as to where ICT is taking us in terms of the pedagogy for language teaching and learning. There is also the perception that for various reasons, and necessarily because of resistance to the use of computer technology, ICT has not yet gained the favour of all language teachers (Gillespie & Barr, 2002).

According to Chapelle, 'the majority of those who teach language and contribute to teacher education appear not to be engaged in discovering how best to use technology in language teaching' (cited by Fitzpatrick, 2002: 52).

In distance learning, the new technologies can provide much-needed interaction, and can help diminish the feeling of isolation typically associated with working on one's own. ICT can also provide the distance learner with a framework for collaborative learning and construction of knowledge. For the past few years the OU has been piloting the use of *Lyceum*, an audiographic application that allows oral, synchronous communication at a distance. This development gives students who normally cannot attend face-to-face tutorials the opportunity to practise their oral skills and carry out collaborative work online.

It is important to recognise that managing and implementing new learning systems is not always easy and that as yet the technologies themselves do not offer cheap, easy and trouble-free access to all. While this becomes a reality, teachers need to acquaint themselves with what the technologies offer for best pedagogical advantage so that new teaching contexts are developed around learning objectives and not around the availability of specific technologies. In distance learning, educators need to resist the idea of adopting new technologies just because they might solve logistical difficulties. Without clarity of purpose and outcomes, technology may present learners with retrograde approaches to learning instead of innovative ways forward.

Conclusions

There is no doubt that curriculum and course design are processes as dynamic as language itself and therefore open to continuous challenges and transformation. The OU Spanish courses have overcome many of them but there are many more here and in the horizon. Those issues, as always, have to do with our ability to meet students' expectations, our responsibility as facilitators in the language teaching process, and the students' responsibilities in the learning process as the main stake-holders.

The emergence of ICT and the role it plays in education raises all sorts of questions for language learners and teachers alike. This environment seems to have the potential to fill in some of the gaps that distance education could not bridge until now, but there is a risk that governments, institutions and to a lesser extent teachers may want to make use of distance learning and ICT to provide cheap, ready-made solutions that will work to the detriment of good education. As teaching and learning methodologies evolve, so do students' expectations. The new OU Spanish course will give us an opportunity to find out how online communication will impact on language use and interaction at a beginner level, and how the new approach meets or does not meet our students' expectations. It will also inform research into the pedagogy that should guide the use of ICT in distance language learning.

Nowadays, we expect students, among other things, to be reflective where their learning is concerned; skilful at interpreting cultural events and active players in the achievement of intercultural understanding. To accomplish these objectives distance language learners will continue to require useful and encouraging feedback from their tutors. Currently teacher education falls short when it comes to preparing language educators to guide their students through new challenges such as the development of high-level skills of intercultural understanding. The goal should be to develop teachers who are able to engage in debates that look critically at traditional pedagogical concepts; teachers who are aware of, and happy with their new role as counsellors and facilitators.

In the distance learning environment course designers, materials writers and tutors need to provide students with tools to interpret the meanings behind language discourse and make a difference to the cultural experiences in which they take part. Being able to accept the role of educator as an agent for change is a challenge in itself. To do this to any degree teachers have to engage in detailed observation of their students' learning behaviour and in critical reflection of their own teaching practices. Only by putting the two together can we expect changes in course design that are the result of an objective appreciation of the challenges in hand.

References

Álvarez, I. and Garrido, C. (2001) Strategies for the development of multicultural competence in language learning. In J.A. Coleman, D. Ferney, D. Head and R. Rix (eds) *Language Learning Futures*. London: Centre for Information on Language Teaching and Research (CILT).

Artal, A., Carrión, M. J. and Monrós G. (1997) Can a cultural syllabus be integrated in a general language syllabus? In M. Byram and G. Zarate (eds) *The Sociocultural and Intercultural Dimension of Language Learning and Teaching*. Strasbourg: Council of Europe Publishing.

Beaven, T. and Garrido, C. (2000) El español tuyo, el mío, el de aquél . . . ¿Cuál para nuestros estudiantes? Zaragoza: Proceedings of the 11th ASELE Congress.

Bourdieau, P. (1991) *Language and Symbolic Power*. Cambridge: Polity Press.

Brislin, R. and Yoshida T. (1994) *Intercultural Communication Training: An Introduction*. London: Sage Publications.

Byram, M. (1997) *Teaching and Assessing Intercultural Communicative Competence*. Clevedon: Multilingual Matters.

Conrick, M. (1999) Norm and standard as models in second language acquisition. In A. Chambers and D.P. Ó Baoill (eds) *Intercultural Communication and Language Learning* (pp. 175–85). Dublin: The Irish Association for Applied Linguistics (IRAAL).

Council of Europe (1998) *Modern Languages: Learning, Teaching, Assessment. A Common European Framework of Reference.* Strasbourg: Council for Cultural Co-operation.

Crystal, D. (2001*) Language and the Internet.* Cambridge: Cambridge University Press.

Felix, U. (2002) The web as a vehicle for constructivist approaches in language teaching in *ReCALL* 14 (1), 2–15.

Fitzpatrick, A. (2002) *The Impact of New Information Technologies and the Internet on the Teaching of Foreign Languages and on the role of Teachers of a Foreign Language.* Strasbourg: Directorate General of Education and Culture, The European Commission.

Gillespie, J.H. and Barr, D. (2002) Resistance, reluctance and radicalism: A study of staff reaction to the adoption of CALL/C&IT in modern language departments. *ReCALL* 14 (1), 120–32.

Hyland, F. (2001) Providing effective support: Investigating feedback to distance language learners. *Open Learning* 16 (3), 233–47.

Krahnke, K. (1987) *Approaches to Syllabus Design for Foreign Language Teaching.* Englewood Cliffs: Prentice Hall.

Kramsch, C. (1993) *Context and Culture in Language Teaching.* Oxford: Oxford University Press.

Levy, M. (2000) Scope, goals and methods in CALL research: Questions of coherence and autonomy. *ReCALL* 12 (2), 170–95.

Lockwood, F. (1994*) Materials Production in Open and Distance Learning.* London: Paul Chapman Publishing Ltd.

McConnell, D. (2000) *Implementing Computer Supported Cooperative* Learning. London: Kogan Page.

Nunan, D. (1988) *Syllabus Design.* Oxford: Oxford University Press.

Pennycook, A. (1997) Cultural alternatives in autonomy. In P. Benson and P. Voller (eds) *Autonomy and Independence in Language Learning.* London: Longman.

Richards, J.C. (2001) *Curriculum Development in Language Teaching.* Cambridge: Cambridge University Press.

Rowntree, D. (1992) *Exploring Open and Distance Learning.* London: Kogan Page.

Saville-Troike, M. (1989) *The Ethnography of Communication.* Oxford: Blackwell.

Schutz, N. and B. Derwing (1981) The problem of needs assessment in English for specific purposes: Some theoretical and practical considerations. In R. Mackay and J. Palmer (eds) *Languages for Specific Purposes: Program Design and Evaluation.* Rowley, MA: Newbury House.

Sercu, L. (2002) Autonomous learning and the acquisition of intercultural communicative competence: Some implications for course development. *Language, Culture and Curriculum* 15 (1), 61–74.

van Lier, L. (1996) *Interaction in the Language Curriculum.* London: Longman.

Widdowson, H.G. (1990) *Aspects of Language Teaching.* Oxford: Oxford University Press.

Wilkins, D.A. (1976) *Notional Syllabus.* Oxford: Oxford University Press

Yalden, J. (1987) *Principles of Course Design for Language Teaching.* Cambridge: Cambridge University Press.

Chapter 11

Learner Autonomy and Course Management Software

DONALD WEASENFORTH, CHRISTINE F. MELONI and
SIGRUN BIESENBACH-LUCAS

Introduction

Distance learning and learner autonomy

Distance education has provided significant opportunities for the promotion of learner autonomy (Garland, 1995; Jung, 2001; Moore & Kearsley, 1996; Spector & Anderson, 2000; White, 2003). It poses new demands and opportunities for students to direct their own learning environment and their own learning. As a consequence, distance education has given rise to a reconceptualisation of learner autonomy entailing not only student independence and control but also counterbalancing support of various types that promote the cognitive autonomy of learners (cf. White, 2003).

Learning opportunities related to distance education are especially *efficient* in promoting autonomy for large numbers of learners (Moore, 1986). We argue in this chapter that the technologies available to distance instructors can be similarly *effective* in fostering learner autonomy (Bonk & King, 1998; Fernandez, 2000; Weasenforth *et al.*, 2002), an issue which has received insufficient attention in the literature.

However, the realisation of pedagogical objectives – including learner autonomy – in distance courses must take place primarily through curriculum design, appropriate applications of technology and support of different kinds offered via materials and student resources (Sherry, 1996; Weasenforth *et al.*, 2002; White, 2003). As with any instructional technology, instructional success hinges on the pedagogical uses of the technology rather than on the technology itself. In this chapter, we accept learner autonomy as a primary pedagogical objective and focus on the technological support that can be used in distance learning courses to reach this objective.

Learner autonomy

Language teaching has undergone revolutionary changes since the days of the grammar-translation and audio-visual methods. Fundamental changes have occurred in the roles of the teacher and the learner. Educators today generally disapprove of the teacher who acts as 'the sage on the stage' and who provides passive learners with endless rules and monotonous drills. The needs and interests of the learners are the central focus, and learner autonomy is one of the ultimate goals of the learning process as well as a crucial pedagogical consideration. Autonomy was 'the buzzword of the 90s' (Little, 1991). It continues to be an essential concept in the 21st century and, with the increase in opportunities for distance learning, has become even more important.

Holec (1981) defines autonomy as 'the ability to take charge of one's learning'. Little and Dam (1998) point out that there is 'broad agreement in the theoretical literature that learner autonomy grows out of the individual learner's acceptance of responsibility for his or her own learning'. Autonomous learners are consciously aware of what they want to learn and why; they are able to monitor and evaluate their progress toward their goals. Some students develop learning strategies on their own and are, therefore, more successful learners than other students. Wenden (1991: 15) explains that:

> . . . [autonomous] learners have learned how to learn. They have acquired the learning strategies, the knowledge about learning, and the attitudes that enable them to use these skills and knowledge confidently, flexibly, appropriately and independently of a teacher.

Benson and Voller (1997: 30) suggest 'learners could benefit greatly in the long run if a substantial proportion of the formal learning time available were given over to training students in ways of learning for themselves' (also see Chan, 2001). In light of the erroneous assumption that autonomy is fostered by simply carrying out computer tasks, Benson and Voller (1997: 11) warn, 'The new technologies of language learning have tended to latch onto autonomy as one justification for their existence'. While the new technologies *can* promote autonomy, it is necessary to provide explicit learning strategies instruction.[1] If distance education courses offer such instruction and are well designed so that they promote learner autonomy, students will receive invaluable experience in developing and furthering their autonomy as learners.

Autonomy is not synonymous with individualisation. Svensson (1998) states that, while both have the independence of the learner as their goal, the terms must be distinguished. Individualisation is related to the use of pedagogical tools, while autonomy is related to the process by which individuals take their way of learning into their own hands.

Autonomous students are independent but, with the use of course management software, they develop the ability to engage with, participate in, and learn from different learning environments. Students are encouraged to take responsibility for their learning while at the same time gain support from within a learning community (Andersen & Garrison, 1998; Breen & Littlejohn, 2000; Garrison & Archer, 2000; White, 2003).

Numerous characteristics of autonomous learners can be found in the literature (cf. Holec, 1981; Wenden, 1991; White, 2003). Four characteristics appear to be particularly promoted by course management software and have been chosen for the current discussion. These are the ability to: (1) work without supervision, (2) become teachers and researchers, (3) exercise choice, and (4) benefit from feedback other than the 'right answer'.

This chapter discusses how two university instructors in the United States used course management software (CMS) in courses to improve the English language proficiency of international students, particularly in the areas of reading and writing, and to make them more autonomous learners. The students had traditional face-to-face sessions with their instructor and fellow students, and they also spent several hours a week in cyberspace within the Prometheus framework, communicating primarily with their fellow students but also with their instructor.

A total of 100 students were involved over a period of four semesters, with an average instructor–student ratio of 1:12 for each class. While the majority of students were at an advanced level of English language proficiency, some were at an intermediate level. All were in a regular instructional setting taking a 15-week semester-long course. With the exception of two students, none of the students had had experience with CMS. The instructors, on the other hand, had been working within this kind of learning environment for six years.

Course management software

In brief, CMS is a web-based software package that allows instructors to organise and manage course materials and student records and to provide students with opportunities for communication and collaboration. Of the over 30 currently available CMS packages, all offer essentially the same features (for a comparison, see EduTools, 2002), but only a handful are used at the majority of institutions of higher learning in the United States, most notably Blackboard (also known as CourseInfo), WebCT, and TopClass.

The focus of the current discussion is to investigate how three features of CMS can be used to develop autonomy in language learners. These features are _Discussions_ (Web board), _Files_, and _Testing_ and are defined as follows:

Discussions: This feature is a Web board or an electronic bulletin board that participants can use to communicate asynchronously. The students are free to participate in discussions started by the instructor or by fellow students (unless participation is limited to a specific group of students).

Files: This feature allows instructors to post, edit, and delete files that can be word-processed documents that may contain graphics and sound. Students can also use this feature to share files with their classmates without the intervention of the instructor.

Testing: In Prometheus instructors may use this feature to create online quizzes in a variety of formats – true / false, multiple choice, short answer, and long answer. The first two formats are graded automatically without instructor intervention. (In Blackboard several additional formats are available including matching, fill in the blanks, and multiple answers.) Instructors may also create surveys using a variety of the question formats.

Prometheus is the software used by the authors, but the discussion that follows is relevant as well for the two leading CMS systems, Blackboard and WebCT, or other types of course management software (see EduTools for a summary of the features of most CMS systems). Also, while the courses that the authors taught were dual mode (partly face-to-face and partly distance), the discussion applies equally well to courses taught completely at a distance.

Using Technology to Promote Autonomy

The following discussion of the usefulness of the three CMS features in promoting learner autonomy is organised according to the four selected characteristics of autonomous learners: (1) work without supervision, (2) become teachers and researchers, (3) exercise choice, and (4) benefit from feedback other than the 'right answer'.

Work without direct supervision

Autonomous language learners work without supervision. They are able to initiate, plan, organise, and carry out an assignment or an activity independently.

Discussions

Discussion board forums provide learners with unique opportunities to complete a course task independently without direct supervision. While the instructor may determine the parameters of discussion board postings – length, frequency of postings, prompts – students can decide when to complete the postings and how to approach the prompt/topic. If students are assigned to groups, they also need to establish among themselves how the group will manage the discussion – who will begin, who will respond when to whom, how the task is to be continued, or whether it needs to be interrupted (Ying, 2002). These decisions need to be made without intervention from the instructor.

Since discussion board postings are typically made on a weekly basis (of course, more or fewer postings can be made by students) and occur with greater frequency than most other class assignments, learners are required to read their classmates' postings. Thus, they read more material in English on their own than they might otherwise expose themselves to during the course of their English studies. Classmates' postings not only become formal models of how to structure a response, they also represent a forum of ideas against which students can compare their own contributions to tasks.

Students must take the initiative for a posting, plan their thoughts, organise their arguments, and negotiate meaning in response to their classmates' postings. Without instructor intervention, students make individual contributions, but also interact and reflect critically on course content and classmates' postings. Learners thus get regular practice in working without supervision on tasks, they get more practice using English for written communication, and they learn to rely less on the instructor and more on their own abilities (Ying, 2002).

Files

The Files feature was used for student peer review of writing assignments and for joint writing projects. The process of peer review and of writing joint essays was carried out with instructor supervision to manage the learning activities. However, direct intervention by the instructor was minimised throughout the semester to allow students to share their own resources and develop decision-making abilities.

Both peer reviews and joint writing projects are, of course, common practices in ESL writing classes. Traditionally, however, students either work in class – workshop style – and the instructor decides when and how much time they spend on this activity or need to meet physically outside class, which is difficult, especially for university students who frequently live far from their classmates and have different schedules. With the Files feature, students can collaborate independently in cyberspace when it is convenient. Here are two examples of the use of the Files feature that demonstrate students working on their own with minimal supervision.

For a major research paper assignment, students in advanced writing classes were divided into small research groups of four or five students each. After completing the first draft of each part of the research paper (the outline, the thesis statement, the body, introduction and conclusion, the bibliography, and the abstract), the students posted their drafts to the specific Files section reserved for their group. The other students checked the site, downloaded the draft (or read it on the screen), and carried out peer reviews. They then reposted the writing along with their comments. Students revised their papers in line with their classmates' comments and submitted the final draft of the paper to the instructor.

In the second example, one of the authors of this study used Files for a joint writing project called 'Culture Capsules' in an intermediate-level course. She divided the class into pairs in which no student had a partner from the same country. Each pair was asked to write an essay in which they compared an aspect of their cultures. One pair, for example, chose dance: the student from Argentina wrote about the tango, and the Italian student the tarantella. Much of the work was completed using the Files function. The students posted their drafts to the Files Manager and then exchanged feedback. When they were satisfied, they submitted their essays to the instructor for final evaluation. The pairs were given class time to discuss topic choice and to collaborate on their outlines. The rest of the work was completed outside class without direct instructor intervention.[2]

Testing

Use of testing software provides students with the opportunity to complete tests online, offering a measure of independence. This opportunity provides students with some choice as to when they complete the test. If, for example, a student would like additional time to study for the test, he or she may decide to complete the test later in the instructor-designated time period. Although the design and administration of the test may still be supervised by the instructor, students have some autonomy in deciding when they take tests and possibly the amount of time spent taking them. This eliminates the need for instructor supervision of test completion and allays testing anxiety for some students.[3]

Self-correcting test items likewise cut down on the need for instructor supervision and thus provide students with some autonomy. CMS can automatically correct discrete-item questions – multiple choice, true-false and matching questions – and display the results instantly along with correct answers. This immediate feedback promotes learning since it prompts students to reconsider their answers at a time when they are probably most receptive to feedback. Learning is reinforced through the confirmation of a correct response as well as through the correction of incorrect responses. Our students were eager to explain incorrect responses to these types of tests, partly because of their heightened attention prompted by the immediacy of corrections.

Discrete-item tests can be used as independent, non-assessed reviews of course material. This allows students to review their understanding of course material in an unsupervised manner. Students can complete these reviews in groups on one or multiple computers, thus enhancing the collaborative nature of the self-assessment. Most students referenced in this chapter were engaged by this type of review, and collaboratively discussed the nature of the test items, evaluated the possible responses and explained their group's choice of incorrect responses without the direct supervision of the instructors.

CMS automatically archives tests, providing students with immediate access to tests and test results. Instructors can also archive tests used in previous semesters and make the tests available to current students, thus facilitating students' unsupervised review of course material so they can reinforce their knowledge, fill gaps in their learning and prepare for subsequent tests without the direct control of their instructor. Many of our students took advantage of this opportunity, partly because of the potential it offered for better scores on the actual tests. Many worked together in groups to test themselves, asking for the instructor's help only when group consensus could not be found.

Become teachers and researchers

Students become teachers by examining critically their own work and that of their fellow students. They also become researchers as they are inspired to go beyond the work in class to increase their knowledge on topics of particular interest to them (Jung, 2001).

Discussions

Since discussion board postings are posted in a public forum accessible to any student enrolled in the course, learners take over a role that is typically relegated to the instructor, namely that of commenting on their classmates' writing. While this review may not take the form of overt peer assessment, learners nevertheless read each other's postings and may respond to other learners by agreeing or disagreeing with their points of view in an objective and non-confrontational manner. This is a role that – in writing – is typically relegated to the teacher, who assesses and comments on students' work through evaluation. The public nature of discussion board postings thus encourages language learners to inform each other about their points of view. Ying (2002) argues that the more frequently students are assigned to respond to classmates' postings, the more they improve their language proficiency, and the more opportunities they obtain for finessing relevant social and linguistic skills, hence becoming more autonomous in terms of becoming teachers and researchers (Kahmi-Stein, 2000; Lamy & Goodfellow, 1999). Learners need to assess the relevance of a classmate's argument, and the soundness of that argument, as well as how the classmate's ideas contribute to their own learning. Discussion board postings provide this teaching-learning opportunity for language learners in an effective manner.

A number of studies have found students who are reticent in the classroom have much to share with their classmates in a discussion board forum (Collins & Berge, 1996; Drake *et al.*, 2000). In postings, learners have the opportunity to tell their classmates about themselves, their cultural background, or their specific fields of study, and to discuss course content with reference to applications from their own experiences (Kahmi-Stein, 2000). The classroom tends to provide many fewer opportunities for such sharing as instructional objectives need to be met. Students can also become teachers when they rephrase and explain concepts and ideas from course readings and discussions in their postings: students with stronger English language abilities model language for students with weaker skills.

Discussion board postings also encourage learners to become researchers as they need to make sure the information they provide is credible and supported, and this may take more than relying on their own experiences; students may consult textbooks, reference works, and the Internet, and integrate these in their postings, providing an authentic purpose and opportunities for language learners to practise these skills (Rossman, 1999; Wegerif, 1998). As Garrison and Archer (2000) point out, this type of activity develops a student's cognitive autonomy through collaboration with other students and other types of external support.

Similar to the use of Files discussed earlier, research projects can become topics for discussion board postings. Students can examine one or several classmates' project ideas critically and provide critical comments and/or provide suggestions, and this is what instructors may want to encourage. Teachers are rarely willing or able to devote frequent class time to such peer support activities because of the time required to complete them. However, collaborating on research via a discussion board forum presents an enriched writing situation for students as they can address a broader audience than just their instructor. Such online collaboration also presents valuable preparation for the real-life online collaboration with peers many students will experience after they complete their English courses (Rossman, 1999). Since discussion board postings appear in a public forum accessible to and read by everyone in the course, each learner's ideas can contribute in a unique way to the entire class's broadened horizon and learning. The students in our advanced-level writing classes, for example, collaborated on the selection and shaping of their research topics at the beginning of the semester. With some instructor supervision, students critically evaluated aspects – scope, clarity and audience appropriateness – of each other's research topics. In the process, some decided to continue collaborating by choosing the same topic and working together on the actual research as well.

As students begin to see how their postings contribute to class learning, they tend to generate standards for such postings, especially for length, format, and acceptable content, and may or may not mention these standards explicitly within the discussion board forum. They thus take on a role usually associated with the professor, the role of establishing criteria for students' work so as to enhance their learning (Breen & Littlejohn, 2000; White, 2003).

Files

Student writers must eventually learn to edit their own work because they will not always have access to their English teacher to help them with their writing assignments. In effect, they must take on the role of being their own teacher. Editing the writings of classmates, essentially taking on the role of instructor, is useful for developing one's own editing and revising skills. Many students do not become familiar with the editing process until they are required to edit the work of others. The Files feature makes it easy for students to share their writings for their classmates to edit.

In addition to the role of teacher, students may also be stimulated to take on the role of researchers. As they become involved with the writing of their peers, they might become interested in a topic that is new to them and do some research of their own on this topic. For example, in a class of one of the authors, a student became interested in Prague after reading a classmate's essay on this city. His interest might, of course, have been attracted in the regular classroom as well; however, while he was online reading the classmate's essay in the Files section, it was an easy step to access a search engine and carry out an online search of Prague.

While reading a classmate's draft, students might want to offer more explanation to make a point to help the writer. For example, one student became very interested in his classmate's research paper on global warming and did a Web search on his own government's position on this topic. Using the Files feature, he was able to follow his spontaneous desire to research the topic on his own because of the community that had developed in the CMS space. His classmate was pleased both with the additional information that he obtained on his topic and with the demonstration of sincere interest in his writing. The software facilitates this kind of work and motivates the students by providing a comfortable 'space' in which they can work.

Testing

In addition to test creation, the testing feature of CMS provides the opportunity for students to design surveys that can be used to collect data for their research. Online access to surveys allows for remote collaborative development in which students can examine each other's work on the survey. The process of jointly constructing surveys provides opportunities for students to learn from each other about survey design and the topics that serve as the focus of the surveys. These opportunities, in turn, improve the research and language skills of the students. Some CMS also include facilities for automatic computation of descriptive statistical analyses of survey results, which can be presented in graphic and/or numerical formats.

The collection and analysis of data present numerous opportunities for students to learn with each other. The automatic generation of simple descriptive statistics makes it possible for students with little or no statistical knowledge to carry out some quantitative research. Since the results are generated automatically by the software, students can focus on the more significant aspects of the research and articulation of their discussions in English rather than on the tedious counting of responses and calculation of statistics.

Exercise choice

Autonomous students exercise choice. They can, for example, modify and adapt tasks to their own needs or interests, and to their own learning style, rhythm and speed. They can also create their own tasks, even though this may in fact take time to develop.

Discussions

Discussion board postings can be an optional element graded as part of a student's participation grade. It is thus the student's choice to participate in a discussion board forum and to determine the frequency of that participation. Discussion board forums also allow students to make a posting when it is convenient to their schedules (Ying, 2002). They allow students to start a new discussion thread or to respond to an existing one; and within an existing thread, students can further decide which particular prior posting – or postings – from a classmate they might want to respond to.

Instructors can allow learners to exercise even more choice by determining the parameters of postings in flexible ways. Rather than requiring a pre-determined number of postings per semester or per week, students can be given options, thus increasing the responsibility learners take for their own learning and development of autonomy (Ying, 2002). For example, rather than requiring a posting once a week to accumulate a certain number of postings by the end of the semester, instructors can ask students to post 'x' times during the first and second half of the semester. If the instructor provides posting prompts, learners can be given a choice in selecting 'x' number of prompts to respond to. Students then have to make decisions about when and about what to post, perhaps based on convenience of scheduling, but also likely based on posting topics that appeal to their needs or interests.

Since learners engage in discussion board forums outside the classroom and away from the intervention of the instructor, they are able to adapt posting tasks to their own needs and interests, not only in terms of content, but also in terms of their learning preferences. So it is not uncommon for students to volunteer to become moderators of the developing online discussion by, for example, soliciting contributions from their classmates, summarising postings at certain intervals, or encouraging the discussion to move in a certain direction (Weasenforth *et al.*, 2002).

Discussion board postings also allow more reflective learners to take time to draft and revise contributions before submitting them to the forum (Collins & Berge, 1996); in contrast, more impulsive learners, or learners with stronger English skills, can compose online and submit their postings instantaneously. The software thus allows learners to adapt the task to the way they learn best.

Files

As students share their individual work or collaborate on a joint project by using Files, they will necessarily develop strategies that reflect their own needs, interests, and learning styles. For example, the authors found that some students preferred to receive peer feedback at the beginning of the writing process, after they had written an outline. On the other hand, other students preferred to wait until they had prepared a final draft before sharing their work. Some students wanted to give immediate feedback, as opposed to those who preferred to take more time to re-read a classmate's file before making carefully crafted comments. While critiquing classmates' writings, some students felt the need to consult reference tools such as dictionaries, grammar books, or textbooks. Students can also choose how they will organise their group work. They are free to decide the timing, the procedures, and the individual role of each group member.

As noted by Fernandez (2000), students can share easily in this online environment and they are thus less dependent on materials provided by the instructor. They can, for example, select relevant materials that they themselves find on the Web and attach them to their Files documents.

Testing

Students can exercise choice by writing test and exercise questions, which the instructor may incorporate in class tests and exercises. While the instructor is ultimately responsible for the content and design of tests, students have the opportunity to design tests that reflect their own needs, interests and learning styles. The students in our classes completed this activity as a means of test preparation. Many found it very useful to evaluate course materials carefully enough to write questions about them, and especially helpful when they worked with classmates in a joint analysis of materials and questions. With the use of CMS, students can create test items that can then be easily revised and incorporated into the final draft of the test by the instructor. The software greatly facilitates this process in distance courses by allowing students to add/revise test items within the same online test template. The draft can be viewed at any time by students and the instructor, and revisions and comments for revision are instantly viewable.[4]

As noted earlier, instructors can make available online 'practice' tests for review of course material. Students may choose to take the optional review tests if they feel that they would benefit.

With the use of CMS technology, not all students in a class have to listen to audio-visual materials – commonly used for oral communication course tests – at the same times or for the same number of times. Students are able to determine – within constraints set by the instructor – the rate and number of repetitions of the presentation of these materials so as to meet their own needs. This makes it more likely that students will use this experience and combine it with other learning experiences.

Benefit from feedback other than the 'right answer'

Autonomous learning involves an understanding of the complexities of issues and the ability to address those complexities in various ways (Fernandez, 2000). Student autonomy is promoted by feedback (from instructors and other students) that challenges students' own views by raising issues they might not otherwise have considered.

Discussions

Most class assignments are read and evaluated by the instructor, who provides a grade. Such evaluation suggests there is a quantifiable right answer students should provide. However, discussion board postings that are primarily composed for, and read by, classmates are not assessed on the right answer basis. Rather, as indicated above, the feedback classmates provide on posted thoughts and opinions is of a much more qualitative nature. Students react to a classmate's posting – perhaps by pointing out something they do not understand – a likely reaction among learners of English, who will then need to negotiate meaning to ensure mutual comprehension (Lamy & Goodfellow, 1999). Students may react by showing agreement with their classmate's opinion, or by expressing surprise or disagreement. Learners' mutual feedback to discussion board postings should centre primarily on content and how ideas are understood through a process of ongoing negotiation of meaning, for which students themselves can take the initiative. In this way, learners are freed from concerns with product and view their ideas as evolving and dynamic rather than static expressions of opinions.

Files

In the CMS environment students can share writings in Files easily and by this means they are exposed to more sources of feedback. They receive a variety of comments and opinions and do not hear only one 'correct' answer. They may receive feedback from a partner, group members, or the entire class. They no longer depend exclusively on the instructor's feedback. They learn to evaluate feedback from others, and they accept and reject this feedback based on the criteria they construct themselves.

Frequently, students also benefit from more instructor feedback – valuable feedback before a final grade. An instructor may allow or even encourage students to post drafts of writing assignments in Files, for example. By this means students will have more control over the writing process, since they can seek feedback whenever they need it and will be able to reshape their paper more frequently before turning in the final product for the final evaluation that will reflect the 'right' answer.

Testing

CMS testing software is not limited to discrete types of testing where there is only one right answer. Many test formats are available as optional CMS test templates. Moreover, files of any type (e.g. text, html, jpeg, multimedia) can be attached to test items, greatly expanding possible test formats. A test for oral conversation comprehension, for instance, may incorporate discrete test items, open-ended critical evaluation items and a linked video clip in which a conversation is recorded. The discrete items might target basic comprehension while the open-ended items might ask students to discuss the social appropriateness of visual cues or comments made in the conversation. As an example from our writing courses, students were typically asked to read a text – sometimes linked to the online test – then answer multiple choice and/or true-false items that assessed basic comprehension. These were followed by essay questions of a more critical nature to assess more global aspects of reading comprehension through extended writing.

Testing software also offers the instructor the option of attaching notes to a student's test answers during the grading process. This option is useful in providing helpful, critical feedback to students well beyond the simple indication of whether the student's answer was correct. Any type of information can be included in the attached notes students see when they review their evaluated test answers.

Conclusion

Distance education provides a number of opportunities for students to participate in a wide range of online learning experiences supported by the combined resources of the learning group, thereby fostering learner autonomy. To develop such learner autonomy, students should be provided with appropriate feedback that is accessible while reflecting the complexity of issues. Students must also be allowed to work at times without instructor supervision and to exercise their own choice so that they become independent learners as well as teachers and researchers. Students must be given some measure of independence to manage their learning environment and learning. At the same time, this independence should be balanced with appropriate measures of support from technology, instructors, materials and other students.

In the process of promoting learner autonomy, there are a number of key issues to consider, including possible resistance of students to becoming autonomous. Resistance may be the result of personal or socio-cultural preferences for more dependent learning styles as noted by Chan (2001) or other factors, such as age and experience with computers and the online environment as Huang found (2002). It is thus important to find an appropriate balance between provision of support and granting learner independence as students develop (Chan, 2001). It is also helpful to explain to students why it is in their own best interest to become autonomous learners, to discuss their responsibilities in the process and to describe how the process will be carried out.

Knowledge of how instructional technologies can promote student autonomy is also a key issue, as pointed out in this chapter. Familiarity with the capabilities of various CMS technologies is necessary to understanding how the technologies can be useful in developing learner autonomy, a characteristic found to be crucial to the academic success of all – and perhaps especially – distance learners.

There remains a need to identify the usefulness of various technologies in promoting autonomy, that is, how various aspects of individual technologies can be combined with other types of support to meet pedagogical objectives (Bonk & King, 1998; White, 2003). With language learning specifically in mind, we need to determine how technologies might promote autonomy in improving language skills such as conversation and pronunciation that are thought to be difficult to acquire without continuous and direct supervision of instructors. This concern is intricately related to the first concern since the technologies needed for such language skills are not yet available or not widely accessible to learners. As a consequence, it may be that learner autonomy in these cases may be limited by technological development and more instructor support may be needed until such technologies become accessible.

Notes
1. Guidelines abound. See O'Malley and Chamot (1990) and Oxford (1994).
2. The instructor did, however, check the students' progress periodically and in a few cases had to respond to complaints from students that their partners were not doing their share of the work.
3. Similar tests can be found online, and links can be created to these sites from within course management software. The use of the testing facilities in course management software, however, allows an instructor to tailor the tests to specific needs of the class. It also provides some test security.
4. The use of the testing software allows the instructor to avoid copying/pasting and the reformatting that is often necessary when copying from different documents. A separate course account should be created so that students can create their own test items. Creating a separate account is necessary to protect testing information in the main account.

References

Andersen, T.D. and Garrison, D.R. (1998) Learning in a networked world: New roles and responsibilities. In C.C. Gibson (ed.) *Distance Learners in Higher Education: Institutional Responses for Quality Outcomes* (pp. 97–112). Madison, Wisconsin: Atwood Publishing.

Benson, P. and Voller, P. (eds) (1997) *Autonomy and Independence in Language Learning*. London: Longman.

Bonk, C. and King, K. (eds) (1998) *Electronic Collaborators*. Mahwah, NJ: Lawrence Erlbaum.

Breen, M.P. and Littlejohn, A. (eds) (2000) *The Process Syllabus: Negotiation in the Language Classroom*. Cambridge: Cambridge University Press.

Chan, V. (2001) Readiness for learner autonomy: What do our learners tell us? *Teaching in Higher Education* 6 (4), 504–18.

Collins, M. and Berge, Z. (1996) Facilitating interaction in computer mediated online courses. Paper presented at the *FSU/AECT Distance Education Conference*, Tallahassee, FL, June 1996.

Drake, B., Yuthas, K. and Dillard, J.F. (2000) It's only words: Impacts of information technology on moral dialogue. *Journal of Business Ethics* 23 (1), 41–59.

EduTools (2002) Compare all products by all features – Online document: http://edutools.info/course/compare/all.jsp

Fernandez, J.M. (2000) Learner autonomy and ICT: A web-based course of English for Psychology. _Education Media International_ 37 (4), 257–261.

Garland, M.R. (1995) Helping students achieve epistemological autonomy. In D. Sewart (ed.) _Selected Papers from the 17th World Conference of the International Council for Distance Education: Vol. 2. One World, Many Voices: Quality in Open and Distance Learning_ (pp. 77–80). Birmingham, UK: International Council for Distance Education.

Garrison, D.R. and Archer, W. (2000) _A Transactional Perspective on Teaching and Learning: A Framework for Adult and Higher Education_. Oxford, UK: Pergamon.

Holec, H. (1981) _Autonomy in Foreign Language Learning_. Oxford, UK: Pergamon.

Huang, H.M. (2002) Student perceptions in an online mediated environment. _International Journal of Instructional Media_ 29 (4), 405–22.

Jung, I. (2001) Building a theoretical framework of web-based instruction in the context of distance education. _British Journal of Educational Technology_ 32 (5), 525–34.

Kahmi-Stein, L. (2000) Looking to the future of TESOL teacher education: Web-based bulletin board discussions in a methods course. _TESOL Quarterly_ 34 (3), 423–55.

Lamy, M-N. and Goodfellow, R. (1999) Reflective conversation in the virtual classroom. _Language Learning & Technology_ 2 (2), 43–61.

Little, D. (1991) _Learner Autonomy 1: Definitions, Issues and Problems_. Dublin: Authenik.

Little, D. and Dam, L. (1998) Learner autonomy: What and why? Plenary talk at JALT98. _The Language Teacher Online_ 22 (11) – Online document: http://langue.hyper.chubu.ac.jp/jalt/pub/tlt/98/oct/littledam.html

Moore, M.G. (1986) Self-directed learning and distance education. _Journal of Distance Education_ – Online document: http://cade.athabascau.ca/vol1.1/moore.html

Moore, M.G. and Kearsley, G. (1996) _Distance Education: A Systems View_. New York: Wadsworth.

O'Malley, J. and Chamot, A.U. (1990) _Learning Strategies in Second Language Acquisition_. New York: Longman.

Oxford, R. (1994) Language learning strategies: An update. _ERIC Digest_ – Online document: http://www.cal.org/ericcll/digest/oxford01.html.

Prometheus 3.0–4.7. (1998–2001). http://company.blackboard.com/prometheus/ [Online courses server software].

Rossman, M.H. (1999) Successful online teaching using an asynchronous learner discussion forum. _Journal of Asynchronous Learning Networks_ 3 (2), 18.

Sherry, L. (1996) Issues in distance learning. _International Journal of Educational Telecommunications_ 1 (4), 337–65.

Spector, J.M. and Anderson, T.M. (eds) (2000) _Integrated and Holistic Perspectives on Learning, Instruction and Technology_. Boston: Kluwer Academic Press.

Svensson, M. (1998) _L'Adaptation des Outils Multimédia dans un Contexte d'Auto-apprentissage_. Lyon: Institut National des Sciences Appliquées – Online document: http://www.insa-lyon.fr/Departements/CDRL/adaptation.html

Weasenforth, D., Biesenbach-Lucas, S. and Meloni, C. (2002) Realizing constructivist objectives through collaborative technologies: Threaded discussions. _Language Learning and Technology_ 6 (3), 58–86.

Wegerif, R. (1998) The social dimension of asynchronous learning networks. *Journal of Asynchronous Learning Networks* 2 (1), 34–49.

Wenden, A. (1991) *Learner Strategies for Learner Autonomy*. London: Prentice Hall International.

White, C.J. (2003) *Language Learning in Distance Education*. Cambridge: Cambridge University Press.

Ying, F. (2002) Promoting learner autonomy through CALL projects in China's EFL context. *Teaching English with Technology* 2 (5) – Online document: http://www.iatefl.org.pl/j_article11.html.

Chapter 12

Chatlines for Beginners: Negotiating Conversation at a Distance

VINCENZA TUDINI

Introduction

SLA research indicates negotiation promotes interlanguage development and learners are most likely to negotiate if opportunities for oral
interaction are available. Campus-based learners' progress in speaking the
target language is supported and monitored mainly through classroom
interactions. If students do not attend classes on campus, how do they gain
the reported benefits of oral interaction? Recent studies indicate chatting
online provides opportunities for the negotiation of meaning, as occurs in
oral interaction. Furthermore, this occurs on an equal playing field, with
fewer opportunities for the domination of discussions by the teacher and
confident students. This study presents an analysis of negotiations by a
group of beginner (*ab initio*) learners of Italian interacting on a university
chatline without teacher supervision and discusses its implications for
distance language learning. While the need for vocabulary is the main
trigger for negotiation, there is evidence in this study that as beginner
learners improve their linguistic knowledge, they begin to concern themselves with pragmatic skills such as sequencing and turn-taking.
Self-repairs recur as often as collaborative negotiations, which indicates
that chatting may promote 'noticing' of errors and linguistic modifications.

Background

It is essential that distance language courses provide learners with
opportunities for oral interaction, since it is within this context that negotiation of meaning and interlanguage development are most likely to occur.
According to the findings of Second Language Acquisition (SLA) research:

> *Negotiation for meaning* is the process in which, in an effort to communi-
> cate, learners and competent speakers provide and interpret signals of

their own and their interlocutor's perceived comprehension, thus provoking adjustments to linguistic form, conversational structure, message content, or all three, until an acceptable level of understanding is achieved. (Long, 1996: 418)

In campus-based courses, classroom interactions provide opportunities for speaking practice while at the same time allowing the language teacher to support and monitor learner progress. Even though distance language courses are becoming more and more popular, many potential students believe such courses lack the same levels of interactivity and teacher support as campus-based courses. In particular, anecdotal evidence suggests many would-be distance language learners do not comprehend how they can learn to speak the language through distance study. This is despite the increased integration of Computer Mediated Communication (CMC) tools into language courses being delivered in combined distance/online mode (Goodfellow *et al.*, 1999; Kötter, 2001; Shield & Hewer, 1999). As part of the Cassamarca Foundation project *Italian Online* at the University of South Australia, the potential of online chatting as a bridge to oral interaction that promotes negotiation in Italian is being explored. In particular, this chapter aims to discuss the value of chatlines and contribute to the debate in this area by ascertaining whether learner chatlines can really offer optimal environmental conditions for SLA by providing opportunities to notice errors and negotiate meaning, particularly in the case of beginners. This study also aims to draw conclusions about the usefulness of chatlines as pedagogical tools for learners who are starting language study and who are new to the distance education context.

Previous research on synchronous CMC

Research studies relating to Computer Mediated Communication (CMC) have uncovered similarities between text-based interactions via computer and face-to-face interactions. These studies have been carried out mainly with campus-based learners working under teacher supervision in computer laboratories, but have important implications for distance language study. In particular, two aspects of chatting have been reported as especially effective in promoting language learning: chatting provides a bridge to face-to-face oral interaction, and an optimal environment for SLA.

On the issue of oral interaction, Sotillo (2000) finds that chatline discourse resembles spoken language closely: the types of interactional modifications in CMC are similar to those found in face-to-face conversation. Smith suggests learners use communication strategies during chat sessions that are similar in many ways to those found in face-to-face interaction (2003: 41). Negretti (1999) finds that chatting displays conversational features that, according to conversation analysis research, assist the acquisition of oral proficiency, despite the restrictions of the chat medium. Tudini (2002) also finds that the discourse of chatting, even among learners, is closer to the oral than the written medium. Gastaldi (2002) refers to Italian NS (native speaker) chat discourse as 'italiano parlato digitato' (typed, spoken Italian).

Chatlines can offer an optimal environment for SLA as occurs in conversation, in that they provide opportunities for negotiation of meaning, thus promoting language acquisition according to Long's Interaction Hypothesis (1998: 22) as summarised by Hegelheimer and Chapelle:

> The most useful interactions are those which help learners comprehend the semantics and syntax of input and which help learners to improve the comprehensibility of their own output . . . In face-to-face conversation, comprehension can be achieved through negotiation of meaning . . . one reason that negotiation of meaning is valuable is that it can result in modified input-input which is better tuned to the learner's level of ability. (2000: 42)

Several studies on synchronous CMC have in fact found that comprehensible input and modified output can arise from negotiation of meaning (Blake, 2000; Pellettieri, 2000; Toyoda & Harrison, 2002; Warschauer, 1998). Pellettieri's study focuses on grammatical competence and finds that both implicit and explicit feedback leads to repair of errors and incorporation of 'target' forms. In Blake's study, most negotiations were 'incidental lexical' (2000: 1), while there were few syntactic negotiations. Toyoda and Harrison's (2002) study, based on discourse analysis methods, sorted negotiations between Japanese NS (native speakers) and NNS (non-native speakers) into categories according to the cause of difficulty in communication. Many of these communication difficulties led to modified output by both NS and NNS.

It has also been claimed that chatline environments may present some advantages over face-to-face interactions, which are conducive to SLA. For example, learners are more likely to monitor and edit their language production, since they can view their language while they produce it and after the chat sessions by examining chat logs (Kern, 1995; Pellettieri, 2000). This aspect of chatting may promote 'noticing', an important principle of SLA research, described by Swain and Lapkin:

> In producing the L2, a learner will on occasion become aware of (i.e. notice) a linguistic problem (brought to his/her attention either by external feedback (e.g. clarification requests) or internal feedback).

Noticing a problem 'pushes' the learner to modify his/her output. In doing so, the learner may sometimes be forced into a more syntactic processing mode than might occur in comprehension. (1995: 373)

Chatline interactions also have an equalising effect. Chun (1994), Kern (1995) and Warschauer (1996) noted the decentralisation of the instructor and the increased role of learners in managing the discourse. These studies indicate that domination of discussions by confident students and the teacher is dramatically reduced since even shy students can take the floor easily when chatting.

However, most of the synchronous CMC studies referred to above are based on interactions taking place between intermediate to advanced language learners, while none explored interactions between beginners. If chatting is to be considered as a negotiation/speaking tool for distance language learners, research into the impact of chatting on the largest group of language learners – beginners – is required since this has particular implications for task design and assessment, as well as contributing to research on SLA.

Also, most research on text chat communication tools has been carried out with learners chatting under supervised conditions. To test the suitability of chat tasks for distance language learners, participants in this study carried out simple, easy-to-follow chat tasks in their own time.

Drawing on findings of SLA research, one objective of this study is to provide a qualitative assessment of whether chatlines can really offer optimal environmental conditions for SLA by providing opportunities for the negotiation of meaning, in unsupervised conditions. In particular, this study focuses on instances of noticing, negotiation of meaning and modification of output. This study also aims to draw conclusions about the usefulness of chatlines as pedagogical tools for beginners studying at a distance, where oral activities or simulations that can be monitored are most urgently required.

The following section describes current strategies used in online distance education Italian courses at the University of South Australia and the possible role of chatlines in providing beginner learners with additional supported opportunities for simulated oral interactions.

Opportunities for oral interaction at a distance

In the case of campus-based students, learners' progress in speaking the target language is supported and monitored mainly in the classroom. As far as external students at the University of South Australia are concerned, metropolitan area (city-based) students are encouraged to attend the language and small group classes that focus on oral interaction. Atten-

Table 12.1 Tasks and technological tools for the development of speaking skills by students of Italian enrolled at a distance

Tasks/technological tools	Degree of monitoring & assessability	Level of interactivity
Conversations with lecturer (by phone or in person)	High	High
Teleconferences (phone)	Average	High
Multimedia resources (audiotapes, videotapes, CDs)	High	Low
Italian community radio	Low	Low
Italian government funded conversation classes	Average	High
Italian national TV via cable/satellite	Low	Low
Italian films and news broadcasts via the state funded SBS (Special Broadcasting Service)	Low	Low
Projects requiring interviews with the local Italian community	Average	High
Conversations with Italian neighbours, friends or relatives	Low	High
Chatline conversations (students only)	High	High
Chatline conversations with native speakers	High	Average-High
Voice (audio) emails and forums	Low	Average

Source: Adapted from Tudini (2003)

dance is not feasible for non-metropolitan students who are dispersed all over Australia or abroad. Both conventional and new technologies can be used to deliver distance language programmes that seek to address the issue of competence in oral interaction.

Table 12.1 lists some strategies for the development of speaking skills within Italian distance education programmes at the University of South Australia for students who cannot attend intensive courses or regular conversation classes. It should be noted that the presence of a substantial Italian community in Australia and other countries provides some additional opportunities for language practice for the distance learner of Italian, which are not necessarily available for other languages. A rating from low to high has been provided to assess the degree of monitoring and assessment the language lecturer can realistically provide for each of the cited activities.[1] The level of interactivity or potential for negotiation has also been rated.

The strategies listed in Table 12.1 have both advantages and disadvantages for teacher and learner that will not be spelt out here. Suffice to say that, despite the various listening comprehension activities, instructions, tasks and assessment procedures in place to promote oral interaction, the weighting of this skill in assessment is very low (20–30%) and reflects the degree of monitoring that can realistically be provided to external students, especially since some of the most interactive and monitorable activities require lecturers to spend time one to one with students. For this reason, the use of chatlines was introduced as an assessed component (5–10%) of both internal (campus-based) and external (distance) courses.

Methodological Overview

Participants

This study was conducted over one semester at the University of South Australia, with a group of 91 beginner learners of Italian. This group includes false beginners who may have been previously exposed to Italian, either formally or informally. Students with a high school certificate in Italian are excluded from the beginners' group where possible. Seventy-seven of these students were enrolled as internal students who attended regular classes. Fourteen students were enrolled externally at the commencement of the academic year (March in Australia). External students were based mainly in Adelaide, although one student was based in Clare (South Australia), another in Tasmania, and a third in Switzerland.

External students follow the same language programme as internals but they generally do not attend class and follow a different assessment programme from internal students. Some city-based external students did, however, attend classes when possible. The online chatline exercise was common to both internal and external programmes, and permitted members of the two groups to meet online.

Some enrolled students did not take part in chat sessions for various reasons. This was due partly to student dropout but might also be attributed to the instability of the chatline because of the upgrade of the university online teaching and learning environment. This made it particularly difficult for students who left all chatline assessment requirements until the end of semester rather than spacing them out over the whole semester, as had been recommended. The low assessment value (5%) of the chatline tasks may also have contributed to some students' lack of interest in this resource.

Procedure

As part of their assessment in Semester 1, carried out over 13 weeks, students were requested to use a learner-only password-protected chatline available on the university's online learning environment http://www.unisanet.unisa.edu.au/unisanet/. They were encouraged to use the chatline as preparation for oral language tests and as a venue for practising oral tasks taken from the set text *Prego! An Invitation to Italian* (2000) by Lazzarino *et al.* Use of set text activities allowed students to carry out tasks that were well integrated in the curriculum and that provided adequate preparation and support both for the chatline and oral tasks. This was considered particularly important for those students who had started the course as complete beginners and needed support to maintain 'conversation' flow during chat sessions. The use of structured conversational tasks therefore set up conditions to investigate the suitability of beginner chatline discourse as preparation for oral interaction in Italian, a venue for negotiation and enhanced noticing of errors, as described by Swain and Lapkin (1995), cited earlier.

The researcher introduced the chatline to internal students during class time at the start of the semester. Two academic staff members were involved in teaching internal students, while the researcher was responsible for supporting external students. At the end of the course, students were surveyed using course evaluation questionnaires, which included questions on chatlines as language learning tools.

The data

The corpus of data analysed for this study consists of chat sessions between 56 learners, recorded between 2 March and 24 June 2002.These chat sessions are made up mainly of one-to-one interactions although small group sessions (3–4 students) were also carried out. A total of 2012 turns were recorded.

Criteria for linguistic analysis

To verify whether chatlines offer optimal environmental conditions for SLA by providing opportunities for negotiation, the linguistic analysis used identifies sequences that show evidence of negotiation of meaning and modified output. Identification of negotiations is based on Long's definition:

> ... denser than usual frequencies of semantically contingent speech of various kinds (i.e. utterances by a competent speaker, such as repetitions, extensions, reformulations, rephrasings, expansions and recasts)

which immediately follow learner utterances and maintain reference to their meaning. (1996: 452)

Sequences of turns that include instances of both implicit and explicit feedback by interlocutors are included as examples of negotiation, since research indicates both types of feedback promote the incorporation of target language forms by learners (Gass & Varonis, 1989). Comprehension checks and clarification requests initiated by learners are also included as signals of negotiation sequences, since these indicate difficulties in communication and subsequent attention to form that encourage the modification of learner discourse.

Instances of self-repair have been included as examples of negotiation because they signal learners' attempts to achieve successful communication with an interlocutor via the noticing of errors. Self-repairs are distinguished from other negotiations, which are referred to as 'collaborative' negotiations as they involve the input of an interlocutor. The self-correction of errors that are clearly not typographical are included in this category. This type of error and modification of output is very common to the chat discourse of both learners and native speakers, given the need to type quickly. However, it is not always clear whether learners are correcting a typing, spelling or pronunciation error. Obviously typographical errors have been excluded.

Outline of tasks and conditions

Chatline tasks were based mainly on the *Prego!* set text and resources, and included the same tasks that had been chosen for oral language tests. The following summary of tasks provided learners with a basis for chatline interactions, with some degree of choice. Learner chatline topics and tasks for Semester 1 2002 were described in the student handout as follows:

Topics and questions suggested above for oral tests are excellent conversation starters in chatline sessions. These are also excellent practice for your oral tests. You may wish to commence by introducing yourself to your chatline partners and talking about yourself, your family, pets and home. Other interesting chat sessions could be based on the 'Attività' exercise which concludes the 'Videoteca' section at the end of each chapter of the *Prego!* textbook.

One particularly interesting chatline task to carry out by week 7 can be based on the 'Identikit' exercise (F) on page 25 of your *Prego! Laboratory manual*. Imagine that you haven't met your partner before and arrange a meeting with him/her. You will of course need to provide a physical description so that you can recognise one another.

The only contact with the researcher regarding these online tasks concerned submission dates or technical issues (e.g. how to print the sessions), indicating task descriptions were sufficiently clear for external students to follow.

Analysis

While negotiations were a feature of beginner chat sessions, with 36 negotiation sequences evident in a total 2012 turns, 18 of these consisted of self-repairs after noticing an error. Excerpt 1 is representative of this type of negotiation2:

Excerpt 1 Self-repair

K.   *Vado ad abitare con gli amici*
          I'm going to live with friends

. . . . . .

C.   *Quanti amici?*
          How many friends?

K.   *Uno amica, suo chiamo e'Eve*
          One friend, her call is Eve

K.   *Ignoro last response*

K.   *Uno amica, si chiama Eve*
          One friend, her name is Eve.
          (p. 36, turns 562, 567–570)

The self-repairs were triggered mainly by morphosyntactic (8), spelling (7) and lexical difficulties (3). The remaining 18 negotiations were collaborative in nature, given that two or more interlocutors were involved. Fifteen of these were triggered mainly by gaps in learners' vocabulary, although two of these could also be attributed to a lack of knowledge of structural aspects of the language as in Excerpt 2:

Excerpt 2

J.   *Vai a molte feste?*
          Do you go to lots of parties?

A.   What does this question mean?

F.   Do you go to lots of parties?

A.   *Grazie!*
          Thank you

F.   *Prego! No non molte, ma vado spesso a cinema. E tu?*
          You're welcome! No not many, but I often go to the cinema. What
          about you?
          (p. 51, turns 894–898)

An example of the main type of collaborative negotiation triggered by lack of vocabulary is provided in Excerpt 3. In this instance, the 'new word' is incorporated in the learner's discourse:

Excerpt 3

F.   *Come stai stasera, J?*
         How are you tonight, J.?

T.   *Cosa vuol dire 'stasera' in inglese?*
         What does 'stasera' mean in English?

J.   *F. meet my partner T non ce male grazie, e tu?*
         F meet my partner T. not bad thanks, and you?

F.   *Stasera e' 'tonight'. Piacere T. Sone bene stasera, grazie. fa freddo stasera, NO?*
         Stasera is 'tonight'. Pleased to meet you T. I'm well tonight, thanks. it's cold tonight, ISNT IT?

T.   *Piacere F. Si, freddo stasera.*
         Pleased to meet you F. Yes, cold tonight.
         (pp. 42–43, turns 684–688)

Students generally did not correct one another unless asked. Feedback was only provided when requested as in the example of Excerpt 4.

Excerpt 4

A.   *J, dov'e musica ti piaci?* (F. did I ask this question right?)

J.   where is music do you like yourself?

F.   *Quale musica ti piaci (perhaps) Dov' = where is*
         Which music do you like yourself (perhaps) . . .

A.   *Si, grazie, F.*
         Yes thanks, F.
         (p.33, turns 502–504)

There was, however, one case of possible implicit feedback regarding gender agreement of possessive adjectives and nouns. This was the only collaborative negotiation, which was clearly related to morphosyntactic issues as opposed to the predominantly lexical negotiations. The corrected learner did not appear to register the correction:

Excerpt 5

D.   *Qual?? il tuo cibo preferito?*
         Which is your favourite food?

F.   *Mi pieace il cibo italiana, particolarmente la pasta al sugo di pomodoro (mia preferito) e alla carbornara. Anch'io mi piace il risotto. Tutti tipi! E qual'e'il touo bevanda preferito?*
         I like Italian food, especially pasta with tomato sauce (my favour-

ite) and carbonara sauce. I also like risotto. All sorts! And what is
your favourite drink?

F.   *Scusi . . . Qual'e' il tuo bevanda preferito? (spelling corrected but not*
        agreement of possessive adjective:' la tua' and adjective 'preferita')
        Sorry what is your favourite drink?

D.   *La mia bevanda favorita?(correct agreement) il champagne e la birra. Mi*
        piace anche il vino.
        My favourite drink? champagne and beer. I also like wine.
        (p. 95, turns 1780–1783)

The remaining two collaborative negotiations were concerned with
pragmatic issues, in particular with sequencing and turn taking organization. This is evident in Excerpt 6 where the learners prefer to log off and log
on again when restarting a conversation they believe is not proceeding in
the correct order:

Excerpt 6

P.   *Quanto templ studia la lingua italiana?*
        How long have you been studying the Italian language?

P.   *Solo un mese?*
        Only one month?

P.   *E' sposata e sola forse divorzianta?*
        Are you married and alone maybe divorced?

M.   P log out and log back in because what you have written does not
        sound correct as I should have asked you quanto temp studia . . .
        and you should had answered solo yn mese and then I say si anche
        io. Let's start again means we need to log out for a second.

P HAS LEFT THE ROOM

M HAS LEFT THE ROOM

P HAS JOINED THE ROOM

P.   *Ciao come si chiama?*
        Hi what is your name?
        M HAS JOINED THE ROOM

M.   *Mi chiamo M E' lui?* (meaning 'e lei':and you: polite 'you';è = is, e =
        and)
        My name is M is he?

CHATTERS LOG IN AND OUT AGAIN

P.   *Ciao come si chiama?*
        Hi what is your name?

M.   *Mi chiamo M E' lui?*
        My name is M is he?

P.   *Mi chiamo P*
           My name is P
M.   *Quanto temp studia la lingua italiana?*
           How long have you been studying the Italian language?
P.   *Solo un mese*
           Only one month
M.   *Si, anche io*
           Yes, me too
           (p. 80, turns 1482–1493)

In the following excerpt, beginners' concern for turn-taking organisation is evident when a learner goes so far as to provide his/her interlocutors with a turn-taking tool 'e tu' to provide a signal that it is the interlocutor's turn to 'take the floor'. When communication breaks down, however, learners tend to revert to English.

Excerpt 7
A.   *Che cosa hai fatto il weekend scorso?*
           What did you do last weekend?
S.   Sorry A was that about you getting a dog? Maybe I should write something down so I don't hold you up all night
A.   Yeah it was, but my next question was about what you did last weekend.
A.   If you want we can start again and I'll ask the same questions. After the weekend question that will probably be enough because then you can add e tu at the end of your response and I'll answer.
S.   *Bene grazie*
           OK thanks
A.   *OK*
S.   *ciao A, come stai?*
           hi A, how are you?
A.   *Ciao S, Come Stai?*
           Hi S, How Are You?
S.   *Non c'e male, Grazie, e tu?*
           Not bad thanks, and you?
A.   *STo bene grazie. S, che cosa hai fatto ogi?*
           I'm well thanks. S, what did you do today?
           (pp. 105–106, turns 1988–1997),

It is interesting to note that learners regularly prefer to start the 'conversation' again when one of their computers disconnects, apparently in an attempt to sequence the conversation. In summary, of the 18 collaborative negotiations, seven lead to modified output, if the two pragmatic negotiations are included. Of the 36 negotiations, there were therefore a total of 25 instances of modified output – if the self-repairs are included. A total of 18 negotiations (including three self-repairs) were related to lexical issues, while the remaining 18 negotiations were concerned with morphosyntax (9), spelling (7) and pragmatic issues (2).

The negotiations described above do not include instances of meta-linguistic talk; a type of thinking aloud that consisted mainly of asking questions about vocabulary, sometimes in Italian, sometimes in English. Questions were often left unanswered, possibly to keep up conversation flow, as in the following excerpt.

Excerpt 8

> *Ho lavorato a venerdi sera. Sono uscita con mia amici e abbiamo guardato il film nel cinema a Marion. Poi sono tornata a casa per . . . (come si dice bonfire in italiano?) A domenica ho studiato l'italiano per l'esame.*
>
> I worked on Friday evening. I went out with my friends and we watched a movie at the cinema at Marion. Then I returned home for . . . (how do you say bonfire in Italian?) Sunday I studied Italian for the exam.
>
> (p. 75, turn 1396)

Initially, learners were very dependent on the prescribed textbook exercises. At the beginning of the chat period, they would switch to English, particularly when arranging their next chat appointment or giving instructions on how to manage the chatline. While dependence on the textbook indicates the text was a useful support for the chatline tasks, it was encouraging to see students became more spontaneous in their use of Italian as the semester progressed. This is evident in Excerpt 9 where a student is able to make a spontaneous request for instructions on how to get to the library in Italian.

Excerpt 9

T.	*Io preferito la musica perche e' molto divertente. E' tu?*
	Io prefer music because it is good fun. Is you? (meaning 'and you')
L.	*Mi piace italiano ma e' molto difficile*
	I like Italian but it's very difficult
T.	*bene, ho un domande*
	well, I have a question (s)
L.	*si*
	yes
T.	*Dove la biblioteca*
	Where's the library

L.   *La bibliotecca e' vicino i computers*
        The library is near the computers.
T.   *Grazie. Io ho andare alla bibliotecca.*
        Thanks. I have to go to the library.
L.   *Bene, tanti baci*
        OK, lots of kisses
T.   *ciao*
        (pp. 99–100, turns 1873–1891)

It is also worth noting that the learner uses the conversational strategy of framing her request with the premise '*bene ho un domande*' before changing the subject with her key question.

Discussion

Although a larger sample of chatline interactions is required to assess long-term learning outcomes, this study has demonstrated that it is worth including chatlines as a learning tool when setting up language pro-grammes for complete beginners learning at a distance. The learner chatline is particularly useful for distance learners since it provides an opportunity to establish connections with each other and internal students, in a colloquial, non-threatening context.

According to the samples of learner chat discourse quoted in this study, negotiations appear to be mainly of two kinds: self-repairs and collabora-tive negotiations. Lack of vocabulary appears to be the main trigger for negotiations and any adjustments learners make to their linguistic produc-tion. This is not surprising, given that beginner language courses require learners to acquire a vast amount of new vocabulary in very little time. It also confirms previous research on chatting (Blake, 2000) although this research was based on interactions by intermediate level learners of Spanish.

It is, however, interesting to consider the two instances of learners' concern for pragmatic skills at this early stage of learning. This has implica-tions for language textbook design and the need to include pragmatic aspects of conversation. For example, in Excerpt 9, there is no evidence that framing is specifically taught in the textbook and in this case is likely to be self-taught, based on L1 knowledge (see Kasper & Rose, 2001: 6–7). The same is true of the cited examples of sequencing and turn-taking organisa-tion (Excerpts 7 & 8) where textbook-based routines are followed, but the turn-taking tool *e tu* (and you) is likely to be transferred from L1. The con-nection between tasks, conversational strategies and L1 transfer require further investigation in the CMC context.

The analysis also indicates that chatlines are a valuable resource to promote noticing of errors that may or may not lead to collaborative negoti-ation. Fifty per cent of linguistic modifications were made to learners' own production, without the assistance of interlocutors. The fact that learners can read their real-time linguistic production on the screen may be a con-tributing factor.

Interaction with peers on chatlines seems to promote a type of thinking aloud, or self-monitoring, evident in the self-repairs or in the meta-linguistic talk cited in Excerpt 8. The openness that characterised these sessions may be due to the fact that the chatline fostered a collaborative learning environment that brought together both internal and external students, some of whom were communicating at a significant distance from each other. This type of discussion has been reported previously as typical of talk between learners working in the same laboratory within close proximity of each other (Mrowa-Hopkins, 2000). Chatting at a distance may thus require learners to compensate for the metalinguistic talk that normally occurs in a shared space where face-to-face interaction is possible.

From an assessment point of view, the potential for printing out the logs of learners' interactions is a useful monitoring and assessment tool for language students studying at a distance. Unlike tape recordings or contri-butions to voice forums, where students can write responses before recording them, the immediacy of real-time interactions via computer provides a snapshot of learners' interlanguage as it might occur in an oral setting. It is also more difficult for students to submit work that is not their own when chatting for assessment points, since their password-protected chat sessions are recorded in real time and can be accessed by the lecturer and other students enrolled in their course.

Assessment criteria are, however, an issue when dealing with this new medium, especially when lecturers are not involved in the research and may not understand the benefits of negotiation. Criteria need to be spelt out clearly both to lecturers and students, and need to emphasise negotiation and evidence of improvement of learner language rather than accuracy. Also, to encourage the participation of all students, the chatline interac-tions need to be worth at least 10% of the assessment. If possible, the due date for submission also needs to be as early as possible in the semester to enable students to overcome possible technical problems without stress. While an early submission date is difficult for beginners, the final week of semester is too late for some learners who leave their work until the last minute. Although this issue did not arise during this particular study, it is important that slow typists are not disadvantaged by the chat resource as typing speed may impact on fluency. An alternative form of assessment, such as an email task, needs to be available when students have such difficulties.

Conclusion

While chatting cannot replace the physical aspects of oral discourse such as pronunciation and other non-verbal features, on the basis of this preliminary enquiry learner chatlines promise to offer an optimal learning environment because they encourage noticing of errors, negotiations and modified output. The opportunity to negotiate is of particular use to the external student aiming to become a competent speaker of the target language. On the basis of the benefits reported in this study, however, this opportunity should not be restricted to external students only. According to chat logs, internal students appreciated the opportunity to converse with students who were studying outside their own city. Interaction with other learners is also of value in building distance language learners' support networks and confidence in interactive conversational language. This study suggests chatline interactions offer learners a type of informal conversational practice that includes a central component, namely, negotiation of meaning. Such conversation practice can occur in an unthreatening forum where learners can without embarrassment engage in metalinguistic discussions and rehearse conversational strategies such as the organisation of turn taking. Further research is required to consider the impact of task type in promoting beginner negotiations and conversational strategies. In particular, the usefulness of chatlines as a venue for building language learners' pragmatic competence requires further exploration.

Notes
1. Teleconferencing via computer is worth considering in future as a conversation option for distance language learners but is currently limited by bandwidth and low take-up issues. Email exchanges and written discussion forums have not been included in this list of conversational activities, despite their use in distance language programmes and potentially high level of interactivity, as described by Mondada (1999).
2. To protect chat participants, initials are used in place of full nicknames in any excerpts presented. Excerpts cited here exclude turns that are not relevant to the main conversation thread, though their presence is indicated by dots. Where possible, errors are reflected in English translation.

References
Blake, R. (2000) Computer mediated communication: A window on L2 Spanish interlanguage. *Language Learning and Technology* 4 (1), 120–36.
Chun, D. (1994) Using computer networking to facilitate the acquisition of interactive competence. *System* 22 (1), 17–31.

Gass, S. and Varonis, E. (1989) Incorporated repairs in nonnative discourse. In M. Eisenstein (ed.) *The Dynamic Interlanguage: Empirical Studies in Second Language Variation* (pp. 71–86). New York: Plenum Press.

Gastaldi, E. (2002) Italiano digitato. *Italiano e Oltre* 3, 134–7.

Goodfellow, R., Manning, P. and Lamy, M. (1999) Building an online open and distance language learning environment. In R. Debski and M. Levy (eds) *WORLDCALL: Global Perspectives on Computer-assisted Language Learning* (pp. 267–85). Lisse: Swets & Zeitlinger.

Hegelheimer, V. and Chapelle, C. (2000) Methodological issues in research on learner-computer interactions in CALL. *Language Learning and Technology* 4 (1), 41–59.

Kasper, G. and Rose, K.R. (2001) Pragmatics in language teaching. In K.R. Rose and G. Kasper (eds) *Pragmatics in Language Teaching* (pp. 1–9). Cambridge: Cambridge University Press.

Kern, R. (1995) Restructuring classroom interaction with networked computers: Effects on quantity and characteristics of language production. *The Modern Language Journal* 79, 457–76.

Kötter, M. (2001) Developing distance language learners' interactive competence – can synchronous audio do the trick? *International Journal of Educational Telecommunications* 7 (4), 327–53.

Lazzarino, G., Aski, J.M., Dini, A. and Peccianti, M. (2000) *Prego! An Invitation to Italian*, 5th ed. New York: McGraw-Hill.

Long, M.H. (1996) The role of linguistic environment in second language acquisition. In W.C. Ritchie and T.K. Bhatia (eds) *Handbook of Research on Language Acquisition, Vol. 2: Second Language Acquisition* (pp. 413–68). New York: Academic Press.

Mondada, L. (1999) Formes de séquentialité dans les courriels et les forums de discussion: une approche conversationnelle de l'interaction sur Internet. *Apprentissage des Langues et des Systèmes d'Information et de Communication* 2 (1), 3–25.

Mowra-Hopkins, C. (2000) Une réalisation de l'apprentissage partagé dans un environment multimédia. *Apprentissage des Langues et des Systèmes d'Information et de Communication*, 3 (2), 207–23.

Negretti, R. (1999) Web-based activities and SLA: A conversation analysis research approach. *Language Learning and Technology* 3 (1), 75–87.

Pellettieri, J. (2000) Negotiation in cyberspace: The role of chatting in the development of grammatical competence. In M. Warschauer and R. Kern (eds) *Network-based Language Teaching: Concepts and Practice* (pp. 59–86). Cambridge: Cambridge University Press.

Shield, L. and Hewer, S. (1999) A synchronous learning environment to support distance language learners. In K. Cameron (ed.) *CALL and the Learning Community* (pp. 379–90). Exeter: Elm Bank.

Smith, B. (2003) The use of communication strategies in computer-mediated communication. *System* 31 (1), 29–53.

Sotillo, S. (2000) Discourse functions and syntactic complexity in synchronous and asynchronous communication. *Language Learning and Technology* 4 (1), 82–119.

Swain, M., and Lapkin, S. (1995) Problems in output and the cognitive processes they generate: A step towards second language learning. *Applied Linguistics* 16, 371–91.

Toyoda, E. and Harrison, R. (2002) Categorization of text chat communication between learners and native speakers of Japanese. *Language Learning and Technology* 6 (1), 82–99.

Tudini, V. (2002) The role of online chatting in the development of competence in oral interaction. In the *Proceedings of the Innovations in Italian Workshop, November 2000*, Griffith University – Online document: http://www.gu.edu.au/centre/italian/

Tudini, V. (2003) Using native speakers in chat. *Language Learning and Technology*, 7 (3), 141–59 http://llt.msu.edu.

Tudini, V. (2004) Conversational elements of online chatting: speaking practice for distance language learners? *Apprentissage des Langues et Systèmes d'Information et de Communications*, January – Online document: http://www.alsic.org/.

Warschauer, M. (1996) Comparing face-to-face and electronic communication in the second language classroom. *CALICO Journal* 13, 7–26.

Warschauer, M. (1998) Interaction, negotiation, and computer-mediated learning. In M. Clay (ed.) *Practical Applications of Educational Technology in Language Learning*. Lyon, France: National Institute of Applied Sciences. Retrieved June 6, 2001 – Online document: http://www.insa-lyon.fr/Departements/CDRL/interaction.html

Chapter 13

Making Online Students Connect: Ethnographic Strategies for Developing Online Learning Experiences

ANDREAS SCHRAMM

Introduction

There is much debate in the literature about the relationship between online and face-to-face courses (e.g. Brumfit *et al.*, 1985; Mason & Kaye, 1989; Warschauer, 1999). Obviously, there are some major differences between these two types of courses: type of access, language medium, amount of interaction, learner control, or interactivity to name but a few (Herring, 1996; Warschauer, 1995a, 1995b; Warschauer *et al.*, 2000). To conduct their learning online students require as a minimum a modem and a computer but do not have to congregate physically in real-time. Traditional students have to be able to transport themselves to a place of learning at a given time. Students in face-to-face courses conduct much of their interaction with each other orally while online courses are often text-based but with many more potential multi-media options than most face-to-face courses can offer. Online students have 24/7 access to course materials and tools. Traditional students' access is limited to class time. There are almost unlimited resources at the online learners' disposal on the World Wide Web that afford much more control to that learner. And interactivity is much higher because tools permit every learner to connect with all the others, thus providing much greater access in online course.

At the same time, there are also clear parallels between traditional and online courses (e.g. Brumfit *et al.*, 1985; Herring, 1996; Mason & Kaye 1989). Participants are motivated to learn, the setting is designed for learning, learners communicate through language, visuals, and other channels and codes. Class topics can be the same, but don't have to be, and familiar learning activities may be employed. Students will develop social relationships as they interact with each other. Given these similarities and differences, online learners can fall back on some of their old skills and competencies, but clearly have to develop a new set of skills and learn new online competencies as well.

In this chapter, I have chosen to focus on a number of the similarities between the two educational settings. This is not to say that the differences are less important. Yet I believe it will be very helpful to anyone interested in working towards a course in an online format to become aware of these parallels, since my experiences have been that for many Web-course developers the differences tend to dwarf the similarities. Once the similarities become apparent, the major shifts required to accomplish teaching and learning in an online format become easier.

Background

This study offers an explanation of the principles used to move several courses of an on-campus ESL teacher education programme to an interactive online format. The guiding principles behind the design of our courses are explained, and examples demonstrating the implementation of these principles are given. The courses are entirely online, Web-based courses taught at Hamline University, a small, private university in St Paul, Minnesota, USA. Minnesota has experienced a large influx of immigrants from Laos, Cambodia, Thailand, Somalia, and Latin America in the past 15 years, generating a great need for ESL teachers in the public school system. Students who finish our programme may obtain a state license to teach ESL to children from kindergarten through grade 12. Other students will obtain a certificate to teach English as a foreign language abroad or may continue to a Master's degree in ESL. Our students already have Bachelors' degrees. Many of them have been practicing teachers for many years and are now adding the ESL teaching license as a second license to their area of specialization. They take their courses during the evenings and weekends when they are not at their regular jobs. Some of our students take their coursework from outside the American Upper Midwest or even the United States and may live all over the world. They tend to work in schools where they teach English to children or adults. The majority are native speakers of English, but not all, and they range in age from early 20s to over 60.

The courses taught online are Linguistics for Language Teachers, Basics of Modern English (grammar), Language and Society, Second Language Acquisition, History of English, Development of Literacy Skills, and Testing and Evaluation of ESL Students. All Web courses are offered twice a year. As a course quality assessment measure, online students are given the same course evaluation as on-campus students. This consists of two sections, a course evaluation and an instructor evaluation. On a 5-point scale, students give their ratings on ten questions about course quality and four questions about instructor quality.

In a recent study, we compared student satisfaction for two courses taught online and face-to-face respectively as reflected in these course evaluations and other feedback. For one of these pairs of courses, one question out of 14 showed significantly different results. For the other course pair, four questions showed a significant difference. We also looked at the comparison of student performance as demonstrated by assignment and test scores. Statistical analysis showed no significant difference between the two classes in this respect. Course quality thus did not differ much with regard to the measures compared.

Development Standards

Re-creating traditional courses in a Web-based setting naturally requires other standards than just student satisfaction and performance for the assessment of course quality before and after the re-creation of the course to ensure the development was successful. Generally, such assessment is not straightforward. Ample evidence has been cited to demonstrate both that there are significant differences in quality between Web-based and traditional courses and that such differences do not exist (Tele-Education, 2002a, 2002b). Furthermore, while more studies citing significant differences between traditional and Web-based courses report advantages of Web-based learning over traditional learning, there are some reports that students in traditional settings performed better than their Web colleagues. These inconsistencies in relation to evaluation of the quality of Web-based courses can be traced back to the lack of an agreed-on set of standards for Web-based courses (Frydenberg, 2002). As with all courses, Web-based courses are complex entities embedded in complex contexts, so there are many variables to consider and control when assessing course quality. Among the variables that may make a difference in course quality assessment are learner population, subject matter, ability level, or amount and type of technology used. Without a consistent set of standards, assessment of successful online course experiences will not be meaningful.

Traditionally, such standards in the USA have been provided by (1) professional faculty associations, (2) regional accrediting agencies, and (3) university faculty and administrators (Frydenberg, 2002). The following nine domains of quality have evolved as the basis for setting course standards: executive commitment; technological infrastructure; student services; design and development; instruction and instructor services; programme delivery; financial health; legal and regulatory requirements; and programme evaluation. Even though they are of significance for the e-learning experience overall, most of these domains fall outside the immediate scope of the current endeavor because they are determined by extraneous circumstances rather than the faculty implementing Web-based courses.

This chapter concentrates on the two remaining quality domains: instructional design/course development and instruction/instructors. The first domain features two requirements: (1) the design must be guided by the objectives, and (2) it must enable interactivity. While interactivity can take many forms, the main focus for the current purposes will be on course interactivity that occurs through discourse. The second domain has to address one core concern in Web-based courses, namely, that the distributed learner tends to study in isolation. This way of learning can only be counterbalanced when the instructor emphasizes and reinforces overtly that Web-based course members form a group of learners. For this reason, interactivity from the design domain and group-orientation from the instruction domain are intimately linked. A group learning experience, Web-based or not, cannot be achieved without student interactivity.

Process of Development

In our traditional programme, interactiveness/interaction is central to the teaching. We espouse a student-centered constructivist education philosophy (Mezirow, 2000). The challenge in moving our courses to the Web was to transfer and implement this philosophy to our Web-based, entirely online courses. So the question for online course design and instruction became: How can an interactive, student-centered classroom experience be moved to the Web?

We adopted the position that communication is central to this experience (Hymes, 1972; Urmston Philips, 1983). Courses can be viewed as communicative situations taking place in a physical setting. Yet ultimately, this setting is secondary to the communication itself. As with all communicative situations, an ethnographic analysis of the situation can be conducted to identify its communicative components (Hymes, 1964; Bauman & Sherzer, 1975). These components can then be reproduced in a Web-based setting. Thus the outcome of the ethnographic analysis provides a communicative template that applies, independent of the teaching setting.

The design of our Web courses is based on the assumption that most of the components of communication in the traditional course can be reproduced on the Internet. With an ethnographic focus on the setting and its participants, three major *modes of interaction* can be identified: public/ private; student/instructor; student/student. A focus on classroom events yields *types of interaction*, such as group exercises, discussions, informal exchanges, etc. And finally, a focus on the forms and topics of course communication provides not only the *means of interaction* through language, topics, humor, visuals, but also study resources such as course readers and library materials.

Creating Courses

As mentioned earlier, the first step in the course development approach described here is to analyze the main communication components in the traditional courses to be moved to the Web. The next step is to identify the tools by which those components can be re-created on the Internet. We opt for simple, off-the-shelf tools to ensure technology does not get in the way of communication. They are Web pages, bulletin boards, and electronic mail. For the course development to be successful, each of the communication components must be matched with an appropriate tool that ensures the components' functionality is preserved.

Modes of interaction

Communal interaction

Starting with the focus on the setting and participants in course communication, the communal or public mode of interaction can be identified as prominent in an ethnography of instructional communication as it is very common. This mode includes such settings as the lecture hall, the classroom as a meeting place for whole-class interactions, and the classroom as a meeting place for group exercises. In all three settings all participants can, theoretically, interact with one another.

The lecture hall, as the name suggests, is characterized by the instructor's delivery of information in a lecture-like format. The instructor holds the floor. The majority of instructors spend some, if not a substantial, portion of class time delivering content in the lecture format. To reproduce this communicative component, Web pages are appropriate because they allow instructor-focused content delivery. They contain a write-up of the materials that would traditionally have been delivered as a lecture. A description of the lecture event itself is given below in the section 'Types of interaction', which has a focus on course events.

Another frequently used public mode of interaction in courses is 'plenary meetings'. Such meetings typically take place in the classroom and are characterized by the fact that potentially all course members may interact with one another and the instructor. There may be questions about course contents, discussion contributions, inquiries, information exchanges, etc. There is equal access to the floor for students and for the instructor. This interaction mode was reproduced by choosing an electronic bulletin board as a tool. Bulletin boards allow equal access to the 'floor'.

Plenary online meetings are implemented by creating a single bulletin board discussion item with instructions to students as to its purpose and use. All online students are encouraged to post messages about this discussion item and to discuss one another's messages. Likewise, the instructor drops in on these discussions to maintain a presence and to provide direction to the whole-class discussion if needed. Here, group discussion feedback is provided through regular postings to the whole class as well.

The final public interaction mode to be discussed here is that of group meetings to conduct exercises. Again, such meetings normally occur in the classroom, but such groups are mostly subsets of course members who may interact with each other and the instructor. Communication in small groups will be about group-based tasks, activities, or questions given to each group by the instructor to be handled in the group setting. There is equal access to the floor by students and also by the instructor when s/he is present. The reproduction of this communicative component is accomplished using the bulletin board as well. In contrast to plenary meetings, however, several bulletin board discussion items are created – one for each group. Students are assigned to a group and instructed as to the group's objectives. As before, students are instructed to post and discuss each other's messages; they are also asked to post a minimum of three messages per week to ensure participation and interactivity. Just as in traditional courses, the instructor stops by groups and provides feedback to the whole class several times per week on the basis of individual group discussion postings.

Private interaction

The settings that can be identified ethnographically to be of this mode in a traditional classroom are private exchanges 'off to the side' during class breaks or during office hours. Meetings held, for example, in the library or at students' homes, not in the official classroom, are also included here.

One-on-one interactions are an important communicative component of every course. Many students have a strong need for privacy when discussing grades, asking questions about materials unclear to them, or informing the instructor of personal concerns. To reproduce this communicative component, electronic mail was used. E-mail provides an individualized channel for private point-to-point exchanges between student and instructor that resemble the off-to-the-side or office hour settings of the traditional course. In addition, e-mail is more flexible and accessible than talking to an instructor in the traditional setting; anecdotally, students appreciate the promptness of instructor replies.

Groups of students in traditional courses often meet to work on research projects. Such meetings take place in settings away from the classroom, and for this reason can also be viewed as private. As in the other group settings described above, electronic bulletin board discussion items can be set up to accommodate such private research group meetings. Unlike the public discussion groups, which are created automatically and where participation is not optional, such bulletin board discussions are set up on request from students.

Types of interaction

When the ethnographic focus is shifted from settings and participants in instructional communication to course events, the following prominent events emerge: group exercises, lectures, chatting/mingling, discussions, questions, announcements, or work on research projects. The events mostly take place in the settings discussed above, but instead of concentrating on the implementation of the setting, the focus will be on the Web implementation of the events themselves.

Given the student-centered approach that is central to our teaching, group exercises are a very important communicative event in our classroom instruction. As discussed earlier, the actual group meetings take place linked to electronic bulletin board items with group members posting discussion contributions. The event itself, however, starts earlier. It is set up inside the lecture, i.e. on a Web page with the written-up lesson contents. Students are given detailed, clear instructions for a content task or question that was developed in the lesson and is to be explored in a group setting. Students are then assigned to a group.

Typically, groups number five to seven members. This number of students strikes a good balance between a group being too small or too large. With fewer students, the discussion doesn't always get started promptly since it is conducted asynchronously over a week, with some students coming in earlier in the week than others. With more students the discussion logistics become unwieldy.

Students are also given explicit instructions to decide first on an initial answer to the question or a solution to the task and only then to visit the bulletin board for this exercise. They post this initial answer or solution at the bulletin board. They must then visit the bulletin board a minimum of two more times for a discussion of other initial postings and other students' comments. This participation requirement ensures that students do not feel lost or isolated but rather interact with each other.

Each of the three postings corresponds to a conversational turn in a group in the traditional course discussion event. Online group discussions therefore happen asynchronously over a week with turns being taken as participants sign on to the bulletin board. The Web exchanges are not as immediate but often exhibit greater depth and thoughtfulness, since students have more time to prepare them and may be less tired compared with the typical on-campus evening class student.

Web group discussion events – whether in a small discussion group or a full-class setting – thus start with a Web page lecture and end a week or more later at the bulletin board. Such larger events may also subsume smaller question or announcement events initiated by students or the instructor. Research or study groups operate in the same way. Students are given a task or topic in a Web page lesson, subsequently form their study groups, and proceed with their group work by taking virtual turns at the bulletin board.

Informal chatting or mingling events that are an important social aspect of traditional classes can be reproduced in this manner as well. Rather than receiving instructions in a lesson, students are informed at the beginning of the course by means of a letter or at an on-campus orientation meeting that there is a bulletin board for informal social student-to-student interactions. They are assured that the instructor will not enter this bulletin board as it is available for student use only. Students have the opportunity to chat together without the presence of the instructor.

Finally, there is the lecture event. Online students receive weekly written 'lectures' delivered to them via the Web in lieu of the typical oral lecture on campus. Lectures are structured such that they contain an initial overview document. This overview consists of a short lesson summary, lesson goals, key concepts, housekeeping information, and assignments (see Figure 13.1). These are all communicative sub-events of a traditional lecture as well, just presented online instead.

The rest of the lecture contains discussion and demonstration of textbook content as well as instructions for group discussions, elaborations on assignments, rationale for course projects, etc. Lecture events start at the beginning of a week, typically Saturday afternoon, and officially end the following Sunday after the next lesson has gone up the day before. The Saturday / Sunday overlap is provided because weekends are prime study time for our non-traditional students, who are at work during the week. The lecture stays available for the rest of the course and can be revisited at any time. The next section groups course components according to the final communicative concern of *means of interaction*.

Lesson Summary

We will finally deal with meaning explicitly in this lesson, after we have touched on meaning issues several times before in this course. The *subfield of linguistics studying meaning* is called *semantics*. Semantics targets understanding *the meaning of words, sentences, and texts*. After discussing some common approaches to describing meaning, we will look at *semantic feature analysis* as one practical method for dealing with meaning. Specifically, we will explore *meaning relationships* on the *word level* of language. Semantic analysis on the *sentence level* will address understanding the important semantic domain of aspect. This last topic prepares us for our discussion of *text level semantics, pragmatics,* and *psycholinguistics* in the last lesson next week. We will also talk about an outline and the rubric for the final paper.

Main Goals

- After completing this lesson, you will:
- know four common approaches to meaning
- understand the concept of semantic features
- be able to use semantic features to analyze meaning
- understand the basic meaning relationships in language
- have a basic knowledge of the semantic domain of aspect
- know one possible outline for the final paper

Main Ideas

- semantic features
- synonymy, antonymy, and hyponymy meaning relationships
- aspect
- 0-state, 1-state, 2-state situation aspect
- perfective, imperfective viewpoint aspect

Housekeeping

1. A reminder on the paper: please include a *literature review* and *reference section*. Since we were able to provide library services online to you, I expect you to conduct a library search.
2. Please check *General Classroom Discussion* in the discussion area for my feedback on project statements. I will continue to check if anyone else has posted a statement. Thanks!
3. I gave an outline of the final paper in Lesson 4 as part of the guidelines for the Language Lesson Proposal. The last step, Step 6, contains a possible outline. Please consult it! Thanks!

Homework Assignments

1. Read File 7 *Semantics*
2. Read and answer the questions about the stories in Lesson 11.4; please follow the instructions at the beginning of the stories. Post your answers in the discussion topic *StoryAnswers*.
3. By drawing on the paper outline given in Step 6 of Lesson 4.5, work on final drafts of your Language Feature Research Papers.

Now you can go to the next section of this lesson, *Lesson 11.1: Approaches to Meaning*, by clicking here.

Updated last: 05.09.03 © Andreas Schramm and Hamline University

Figure 13.1 Sample lecture overview section

Means of interaction

This section has an ethnographic focus on forms and topics of classroom communication. The communicative concerns investigated here will be the topics discussed, the non-verbal visual elements employed for communicating course content, and study resources such as the course reader or library materials, which students access for communication of additional course content. The form of the language used could also be considered here, such as, informality and humor, but this aspect of communication has been well documented elsewhere in the literature. As before, the course components discussed here are identified generically as the means of communication in a course; their reproduction in a Web course is then explained.

Topics and visuals

Some topics are presented more easily in a traditional setting (and vice versa on the Web), but it is desirable to keep topics intact as much as possible when a course is reproduced on the Web. A case in point is the topic of speech sounds in a linguistics course. To communicate certain concepts connected with this topic, it is necessary for the instructor to demonstrate sounds. To keep this online topic as close to its campus counterpart as possible, an audiocassette with sound samples can be created. These sound samples are numbered and will be referred to during the lesson at the appropriate time. Other media now available for transmitting sound would be CD-ROMs or audio streaming, but we have not yet used them. It is therefore relatively easy to transfer the audio components of a lesson to the Web while retaining its similarity to its counterpart in a traditional course.

The related linguistic topic of sound systems deals with somewhat abstract concepts; it is very helpful to use concrete objects to support their presentation and promote learning. On campus, these concepts are demonstrated with K'Nex toys (a set of multi-color struts and connectors that snap together) and an organic chemistry model set. To keep things technologically simple, digital photos of the toys are presented to online students, and the movements of the physical demonstration are described verbally. This Web solution is not ideal, but enough students usually recognize the parallels between the concepts and the visual aids as evidenced by discussion contributions. They in turn help other students who struggle with grasping the concepts. Improvements to the visual representation of course concepts are necessary and are being sought at this time. Since visualization is one of the strengths of the Web, good options should be forthcoming soon.

Resources

Finally, course content may be located in articles in a reader or through resources obtained via a library. Traditionally, articles for a reader are photocopied and handed out to students. Online students are not present physically, however, and an alternative must be found. Mailing is an option if good mail services are available. Sometimes online students may be abroad in remote areas with less reliable and expedient mail services. In addition, mail may be censored in some parts of the world depending on content. Furthermore, changes to the course reader are hard to implement.

There are, however, electronic alternatives to a physical reader. Documents can be digitized by scanning, which is more involved, or with a fax module, which is quick and easy. Online reader documents can be accessed and printed by students at a secure, password-protected Web site. Changes to the reader articles can be made within minutes. An online reader allows the reproduction of this means of communication in the online setting.

Students may also access course content by means of library research. Many instructors specify the submission of a research project that involves library research. In such instances, course content is provided not by the instructor or other students, but by the authors of articles or book chapters. Looking up library resources is not a problem nowadays, since such resources are typically available on the Web, regardless of whether a student is in a traditional or Web-based course. Acquiring the actual reading materials, however, is more difficult.

Students in the traditional courses have to go to the library and physically pick up their books and articles. This is not an option for many online students, who are too far from campus. Instead, an online solution must be provided for students working at a distance when one reproduces this communicative component of a course. There are electronic interlibrary loan and document delivery software systems available. Documents can be requested online. They will also be delivered electronically via the Web after the student receives a URL and password for picking up the documents. Copyright laws are protected, since a document is deleted automatically after printing. Providing library services online is somewhat time-consuming for the institution, but it is feasible.

Conclusion

By viewing interactive, student-centered teaching in a course as a communicative situation and by conducting an ethnographic analysis of the communicative components in a course it was possible to describe the reproduction of traditional courses on the Web. By focusing on the course setting and its participants, several communicative components, such as public versus private, student-to-student, and student-to-instructor inter-action, could be grouped under *modes of interaction*. An ethnographic focus on course events provided *types of interaction* such as group exercises, dis-cussions, chats, etc. Finally, a concentration on forms and topics led to communicative components dealing with the formality of language, humor, topics, audio-visuals, and study resources such as a reader and library articles. The implementation online of each course component was also described. Adopting an ethnographic approach demonstrated the principles that underlie the successful transformation of traditional courses to an interactive online format.

References

Bauman, R. and Sherzer, J. (1975) The ethnography of speaking. *Annual Review of Anthropology* 4, 95–119.

Brumfit, C., Phillips, M., and Skehan, P. (eds) (1985) *Computers in English Language Teaching*. Oxford: Pergamon Press.

Frydenberg, J. (2002) Qualitative standards in eLearning: A matrix of analysis. *International Review of Research in Open and Distance Learning* 3 (2) – Online document: Retrieved February 21, 2003, from http://www.irrodl.org/content/v3.2/frydenberg.html

Herring, S. (ed.) (1996) *Computer-mediated Communication: Linguistic, Social and Cross-cultural Perspectives*. Amsterdam: John Benjamins Publishing Company.

Hymes, D. (1964) Introduction: Toward ethnographies of communication. *American Anthropologist* 66 (6), 12–25.

Hymes, D. (1972) Introduction. In C. Cazden, V. John and D. Hymes (eds) *Functions of Language in the Classroom* (pp. xi–lvii). New York: Teachers College Press.

Mason, R. and Kaye, A. (eds) (1989) *Mindweave: Communication, Computers and Distance Education*. Oxford: Pergamon Press.

Mezirow, J. (2000) Learning to think like an adult: Core concepts of transformation theory. In J. Mezirow (ed.) *Learning as Transformation* (pp. 3–33). San Francisco: Jossey-Bass.

TeleEducation (2002a) The 'No significant difference phenomenon' – Online document: http://teleeducation.nb.ca/nosignificantdifference/

TeleEducation (2002b) The 'Significant difference phenomenon' – Online document: http://teleeducation.nb.ca/significantdifference/

Urmston Philips, S. (1983) *The Invisible Culture: Communication in Classroom and Community on the Warm Springs Indian Reservation*. New York: Longman.

Warschauer, M. (1995a) *E-Mail for English teaching: Bringing the Internet and Computer Learning Networks into the Language Classroom*. Alexandria, Virginia: TESOL.

Warschauer, M. (ed.) (1995b) *Virtual Connections: Online Activities & Projects for Net-working Language Learners*. Manoa, Hawai'i: University of Hawai'i.

Warschauer, M. (1999) *Electronic Literacies: Language, Culture, and Power in Online Education*. Mahwah, New Jersey: Lawrence Erlbaum Associates.

Warschauer, M., Shetzer, H. and Meloni, C. (2000) *Internet for English Teaching*. Alexandria, Virginia: TESOL, Inc.

Chapter 14

From Parrots to Puppet Masters: Fostering Creative and Authentic Language Use with Online Tools

JOHN MILTON

Problems in Foreign Language Education

The teaching and learning of English as an international – albeit foreign – language in SE Asia are beleaguered by a number of problems, which in a general sense are faced in the teaching and learning of other types of knowledge and skills as well. One of the most frequently discussed is the force-fed pedagogy in which many teachers and students find themselves trapped (Zeng, 1999). Many educators believe that 'teaching to the exam', which is common in public and private institutions in SE Asia, encourages imitative practices by dampening students' desire and ability to learn (e.g. Paris, 1995). This problem is related to the often-observed tendency toward an imitative rather than a creative approach to learning in SE Asian classrooms (Cheng, 1999).

Narrowly focused teaching practices dominate the curriculum from primary to tertiary and are rationalized by the face validity that norm-referenced standardized assessment promises. An unhappy outcome is that many students spend the bulk of their education memorizing formulae easily parroted in examinations, but inadequate for life outside the classroom. In the case of foreign language learning, stock phrases are often made to substitute for grammatical and communicative competence in the target language. The foreign language (L2) that students acquire is often a constrained and unnatural version of the language they need for academic, professional, business or social communication (see Milton, 2001). This situation is further exaggerated in English as a Foreign Language (EFL) teaching by a dearth of proficient teachers, insufficient time and resources to develop effective learning opportunities, and lack of coordination of the substantial efforts made by dedicated teachers.

A Distributed Model for Teaching and Learning EFL

Where Internet (especially broadband) access and computer ownership are common, making resources available online would seem to be one way of partially addressing these problems. In principle it is possible to coordinate best practices through a distributed model of delivery while allowing considerable choice and flexibility on the part of students and teachers. It has long been realized that a curriculum incorporating online elements can provide greatly enhanced directed instruction as well as more opportunities for autonomous exploration and discovery (Barnett, 1993). The need to meet local standards can also be addressed more efficiently, while wasted time and resources can be reduced, and teachers and students can be freed to engage in collaborative as well as individualized creative activities. Implementing these possibilities so that technology helps reform instruction and learning, rather than simply amplifying bad pedagogy, is both a design and social challenge. In this chapter I will briefly illustrate high interest interactive activities that can be aimed at the specific interlanguage problems of L1 speakers; useful pedagogical tools that can be made widely accessible; and technically enhanced opportunities for communication among students and between teachers and students.

I will first outline the rationale for Web-based EFL resources and then describe four tools that lend themselves to progressive approaches to broader learning opportunities. I have incorporated these tools into an online course development system that supports several online EFL courses aimed at various groups of learners. These include full-time secondary school students, undergraduates, post-graduate students enrolling in MBA courses, and continuing education students. They are mainly Chinese (Cantonese and Putonghua) speakers at a wide range of English proficiency levels, needing to acquire a broad array of receptive and productive English skills.

Parameters for an Online EFL Course System

Before attempting to design anything new, I set about looking for an online content development and management system to assist materials developers and teachers to create engaging and meaningful learning activities. My criteria were that this system should support learning that follows generally agreed educational principles and that meet pressing logistic needs by:

- appealing to a wide range of learner proficiencies and interests by providing quality, individualized instruction;

- motivating low-proficiency students to find intrinsic uses for the language;
- ensuring a coherent, planned and progressive curriculum based on SLA theory, while also providing opportunities for self-discovery, participation, creativity and the pursuit of individual learning paths (i.e. the type of quality assurance guidelines outlined by Alley & Jansak, 2001);
- enabling and encouraging teachers to act more often as mentors, and less often as pedagogues;
- enabling a transparent system of student and teacher accountability by integrating intrinsic, criterion-referenced and performance-oriented formative assessment into the learning process, thereby minimizing the need for extrinsic, norm-referenced summative assessment;
- providing timely and reliable reporting to the teacher, allowing for reliable, consistent grading, and timely and effective feedback to learners; and
- permitting ongoing evaluation of the content and methodologies by the students and teachers.

The commercial course delivery systems I evaluated give reasonably good support for the management of students and materials and allow basic information delivery, assessment and text-based communication. However, none seemed fully to exploit the possibilities suggested above. The systems do not incorporate tools or resources that accommodate individual learners by making the L2 more readily available than it is possible through print resources, nor do they explicitly include techniques for encouraging the creative or authentic use of language. Although new forms of Internet communication and interaction continue to be developed, these new technologies often take considerable time to be integrated into commercial course delivery systems, and new technologies cannot be easily incorporated into most learning platforms on an *ad hoc* basis. Also, most systems leave much to be desired in the ease with which content can be authored (see Jensen, 2003, for a detailed critique on course management systems). I was disappointed to find that, despite the promise of Internet technology, no ready-made content delivery system seemed to offer the range of activity types and tools that meet the Web's potential to create and deliver courses for dynamic language learning.

However, database-driven Internet technologies have matured to the extent that it is technically and economically feasible to develop original, customizable systems that can be used to create, deliver and manage appropriate online tools and content directed at a specific discipline such as language learning. I decided to take this route, and with a small team of students, developed a course delivery and student management system specifically to manage language learning. The chief advantage of this custom-built system is that it incorporates a number of tools and activity types designed for language learning, and new technologies can easily be integrated into the central management architecture as they are needed or become available. To date over 300 activities that take advantage of the language learning tools described below have been written for this system. These include objective, automatically graded tasks (such as multiple choice, gap fill, drag-and-drop, matching, etc.) and productive, subjectively evaluated activities for which computer-enhanced feedback can be provided by the teacher. In the remainder of this chapter I will describe four tools aimed at providing practice in speaking the L2, making L2 lexis, structures and texts more accessible, improving teacher feedback and promoting creative use of the L2.

Targeting Oral Fluency: Asynchronous Voice Messaging

Graduates from SE Asian classrooms are often observed to have low spoken English fluency. This is not surprising since most students in these contexts have little perceived opportunity to use the target language in their daily lives: in many cases little communication takes place in English outside (and often inside) traditional classrooms. Although the communicative approach, with its emphasis on spoken language, is enshrined in teacher training courses, there is often little interaction in spoken English among students or between students and their teachers, and spoken English is rarely assessed. One of the tools incorporated into the online course system introduced above facilitates and motivates L2 speech by enabling students to hold conversations via the Web and by making it easy for teachers to promote and monitor these conversations.[1]

Teachers can leave recorded messages to encourage discussions and they can elicit responses that focus on specific skills (e.g. pronunciation and intonation), or that model various spoken business, academic and social situations. Full-time students are required, in groups of two or three, to schedule regular times to hold and record conversations. Continuing education students have the option to log on at any time over the course of a week to comment on weekly themes. Messages are posted to Web pages reserved for each pair or group of students and their teacher, and are archived so they can be accessed as a threaded oral discussion forum. A similar procedure has been successfully practised in Japan for a number of years using tape recorders (Schneider, 1997). Despite the obvious limitations in having students of the same L1 carry on a conversation in an L2, those using the technique in Japan have reported considerable evidence of learners encouraging and teaching one another (Kluge & Taylor, 2000). I have found that students take to this activity more eagerly than they do more conventional academic tasks, that interaction among learners tends more often to rely on the L2 than in classroom situations, and that particular skills (such as telephone language) can be easily modeled. Many of the technical and procedural difficulties of using tape recorders are overcome by this Web-based conversation practice. Although detailed monitoring and interaction by the teacher is time-intensive and not always possible, occasional teacher participation and feedback appears effective in encouraging fluency practice. Most learners report increased confidence after a few weeks of conversation practice, and their increased ease with the language has led many of my students to report a newly discovered relevance for English.

Depending on their goals and needs, teachers and learners can concentrate on this type of fluency practice. They can also access online references and activities directed at lexical acquisition and improved accuracy, as described below.

Online Data-driven Language Learning

Among the references available to learners in this system is a discovery-based lexical lookup tool (*Word Neighbors*). I designed this tool based loosely on the linguistic principles described by Sinclair (1991) and on the concordancing techniques outlined by Johns and King (1991). It allows the lookup (including the use of wild cards[2]) of immediate contexts of any selected word or phrase in various large corpora from a right-mouse button context menu. This method provides a way of enabling learners to become self-reliant in discovering the collocational properties of the language. Students are encouraged to use this tool in a number of ways, such as in the completion of autonomous logged activities which assist with proofreading skills and vocabulary acquisition. Some of these activities are illustrated in Figure 14.1. Students are also encouraged to use it when they write, as I illustrate in the next section. This tool remains available to students as a writer's aid after they have completed their course and can be called directly from their word processor.

Providing Feedback on Student Writing

Although the oral approach is emphasized in current theories of language pedagogy, EFL curricula and examinations in schools and universities tend to concentrate on written accuracy (often at the sentence level), and 'error-free' writing is a common preoccupation at school and on the job. However, there is little agreement on what form teacher feedback to student writing should take or at what level of written expression (sentence or text) it should be aimed. In fact, possibly no issue is more contentious in language teaching than the debate over how to respond to students' written work. Even when process-writing methods are adopted, the procedure for making comments is often frustrating, and the usefulness of our remarks is often questionable. Teachers usually have few, if any, objective empirical criteria for commenting on students' interlanguage, or by which to check progress and arrive at justifiable grades. The most conscientious teachers often find that detailed and copious comments seem not to result in measurable difference in students' writing. There is also the danger that when our comments are attended to, they run the risk of forcing students into conservative strategies of error avoidance, since they usually focus on errors of commission rather than errors of omission (Perkins, 1983). Nevertheless, detailed response to students' written work is viewed as a critical part of our job, and students say that they value and expect it (Ferris, 1995). This leaves many teachers overwhelmed by the volume of correction that students appear to need, or that the curriculum mandates. Yet, this demand continues relentlessly, despite the lack of consistency and accuracy in our feedback (Biggs & Telfer, 1987), and regardless of its less than entirely desirable consequences.

Students rarely have access to the didactic or procedural resources they need to correct the errors we are able to identify, or to choose alternative L2 structures and lexis that are authentic and textually relevant. They are often not held accountable for proofreading or correcting their work, or for demonstrating improvement from one assignment, semester or course to another. Instructors of mainstream courses frequently consider commenting on the language of written assignments a waste of time or none of their concern, with the result that students can spend three or four years at university without receiving much useful feedback on their writing or any evidence of the relevance of effective writing skills. They may in fact not write very much at all, since assessment in many subjects at university is largely by multiple-choice responses.

My approach to this situation has been, first, to collect a large corpus (several million words) of the writing of my students (Cantonese speakers), and to compare this with the writing of native speakers of the same age and educational level so as to identify misuse, as well as 'overuse' and 'underuse' of selected structural, lexical and discourse features (Milton, 2001). Based on this analysis, I maintain an extensive online grammar/ writing guide (currently about 1000 pages). This guide contrasts standard and nonstandard forms and includes quizzes so that students can focus on and practise problems specific to the writing of speakers of Chinese.

Word Neighbors

Show [0 ▼] words before |play a role| Show [1 ▼] words after
* = any characters in a word;
? = 1 character

Search in [Newspaper Articles (3,000,000 words) ▼]   Sort by [Frequency ▼]

☐ Link to [Learners Dictionary ▼]   Find it!

Contexts for your search word(s):	Frequency
play a role in	6
play a role as	1
play a role similar	1

Total Expressions: 8 (maximum number of hits = 1000)
Select and right-click to hear or look up any words.

Scientists can [play a role] at improving energy efficiency.

They should operate to a   What preposition follows

This year HP should benef   "play a role"? Look it up in

An experience for my own past confirms this.   Word Neighbors.

I should have more confidence to myself.

a) proofreading activity in which learners look up how, which and whether prepositions combine with various verbs and help form verbal idioms.

Show [0 ▼] words before |likely| Show [0 ▼] words after
* = any characters in a word;
? = 1 character

Search in [Newspaper Articles (3,000,000 words) ▼]   Sort by [Frequency ▼]

☐ Link to [Learners Dictionary ▼]   Find it!

Contexts for your search word(s):	Frequency
likely	534
unlikely	210

dis- / mis- / in- / im- / un- / re-

1. The package arrived [____] *registered.
2. He was [____] *able to go.
3. [____] *afraid, she accepted the challenge.
4. It was an [*likely] [____] turn of events.

b) a gap fill activity in which learners retrieve possible morphemes.

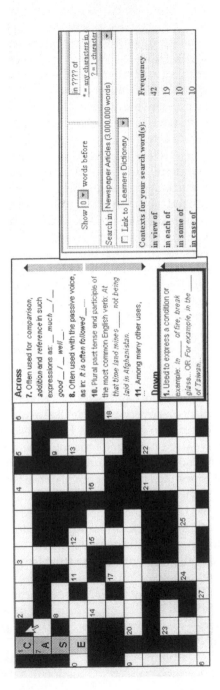

Across

7. Often used for *comparison, addition and reference in such* expressions as: ___ *much* ___ / ___ *good* ___ / ___ *well* ___.

8. Often used with the passive voice, as in: *It is often followed* ___.

10. Plural past tense and participle of the most common English verb: *At that time land mines* ___ *not being laid in Afghanistan.*

11. Among many other uses, ___

Down

1. Used to express a condition or example: *In* ___ *of fire, break glass... OR For example, in the* ___ *of Taiwan.*

Show [0 ▾] words before

Search in | Newspaper Articles (3.000.000 words) |

☐ Link to | Learners Dictionary ▾ |

In ???? of
* = any characters in
? = 1 character

Contexts for your search word(s):	Frequency
in view of	42
in each of	19
in some of	10
in case of	10

c) a crossword activity in which learners look up the components of common, but unknown or frequently avoided, phrases.

Figure 14.1 various activities requiring learners (a) to look up how, which and whether prepositions combine with various verbs and verbal idioms, (b) to retrieve inflections, and (c) to complete frequently avoided, misunderstood or unknown common phrases. The learners must make a conscious choice among the lexical options made available by the text retrieval program *Word Neighbors*. They also have access to online dictionaries, encyclopedias, etc., from the context menu to assist in choosing the appropriate expression.

Next, I designed a marking tool (*Mark My Words*) which teachers can use to insert comments in students' electronic documents. This marking tool can be used to point to the online guide and to other references (such as *Word Neighbors*, described above). Students (who have access to these online references when they write) submit their documents to a Web page 'drop box'. Teachers then retrieve the documents, insert pre-defined and individualized comments based on what the students are expected to have mastered, and post the documents back to the Web (often within the same day assignments are submitted). Students can be requested to resubmit their work if substantial changes are needed, based on these comments. Comprehensive pre-defined comments can be inserted in written work in about 20% of the time it takes to mark up paper submissions. Tedious individualized correction is minimized since most of the errors made by students of the same L1 are recurrent, and the students are held responsible for using deductive processes, such as the *Word Neighbors* text retrieval program, to correct their errors. Figure 14.2 illustrates a pre-defined comment inserted in a student document and some of the online resources this procedure makes available. Teachers can also use the normal commenting and tracking features of their word processor to make individualized remarks if necessary (these remarks can then be archived or incorporated into the online guide).

Online Role Plays

I have so far demonstrated online tools and activities that can provide learners with oral fluency practice, discovery-based lexical acquisition and enhanced feedback on their writing. In this section I will describe a tool aimed at motivating the creative use of language through the scripting of spoken English. This tool can also be used as a means to promote both fluency and accuracy. Since it is perhaps the most novel of the techniques I describe in this paper, I will first dwell in some detail on the rationale for its use as a language acquisition device.

Oscar Wilde observed that 'Education is an admirable thing. But it is well to remember from time to time that nothing that is worth knowing can be taught' (1913: 104). How to make known the unteachable may in some sense be answered by Muriel Rukeyser's 1960 remark that 'The universe is made of stories, not of atoms'. Encouraging the language learner to adopt the role of narrator seems particularly relevant as a means of acquiring language skills. Teachers across disciplines often encourage protected immersion in the L2 through role-playing activities, usually face-to-face, but more recently at a distance (e.g. using 'virtual worlds' such as MUDs). The benefits of role-playing for generalized educational settings are

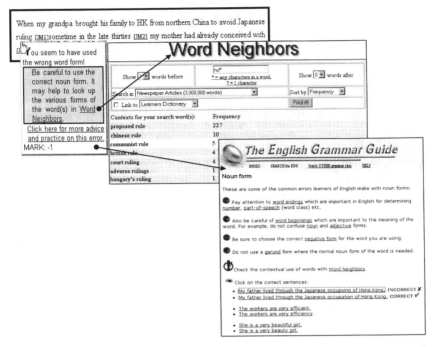

Figure 14.2 A student submits a written assignment to the Web site; the teacher then opens the document and inserts comments using the marking tool. The student sees relevant popup comments, from which *Word Neighbors* and other references, including the *English Grammar Guide* can be accessed.

detailed in Jones (1985), and specifically for language learning in Ladousse (1987), Crookall and Oxford (1990) and Bambrough (1994).

Several theorists recommend the use of dramatization, 'actualization' and narrative techniques for effective learning, regardless of the age of the learners (e.g. Oller, 1993). Scarcella and Crookall (1990) also review research to show how simulation facilitates second language acquisition by giving students the opportunity to try out new language in a safe environment. The learning theories they discuss claim that learners acquire language when:

- they are exposed to large quantities of comprehensible input through being engaged in genuine communication as part of the roles assigned to characters;

- they are actively involved in worthwhile, absorbing interaction that tends to make students forget they are learning a new language; and
- they experience positive feelings and attitudes.

More recent studies have investigated the effects of students' participation in multimedia narratives on language learning and have also found positive results (e.g. in lexical gains – Duquette *et al.*, 1998; Nikolova, 2002 – and in a greater variety of rhetorical structures and increased audience awareness – Warschauer, 1999). These studies claim that the dramatization of 'real life' problems helps students develop both their critical thinking and language-related problem solving skills. Role-playing appears to be a useful language acquisition activity in that it raises the L2 from mere examination fodder to the status of a vehicle for the realization of social transactions.

This 'scripting tool' which I designed and incorporated into the course delivery system allows students to create animated role plays online. Students manipulate characters on screen, assign them movements and gestures and write dialogue that is synthesized and 'spoken' by the characters, whose mouths move to match the dialogue. This tool uses technology ('MS Agent') that was originally developed to give a social dimension to the computer interface (Ryokai *et al.*, 2003).[3] Figure 14.3 illustrates the scripting tool and an example of an animated play, with feedback using the marking tool described above. Of course, teachers can dispense with detailed lexical or structural feedback, and concentrate instead on the pragmatics of the learners' discourse.

The text-to-speech capability of this technology allows students to listen to their dialogues (or any other text on a Web page) rendered with standard American or British synthesized pronunciation. The current state of development in freely available text-to-speech engines is such that the synthesized suprasegmentals (e.g. stress, rhythm and intonation) are not entirely human, but the students who have taken the courses (almost 1000 to date) rarely complain about the quality of the synthetic voices. Indeed, they report finding the relatively high accuracy in pronunciation useful (the voice synthesis can be replaced by a recording of a human voice if the student or teacher wishes, e.g. where prosodic modeling is crucial).

The scripting tool based on this technology gives teachers and students the opportunity to script and edit conversational dialogue, thereby bringing another dimension to the presentation of, practice with and feedback on oral language. Since teachers have access to the written script, they can supply feedback on the accuracy, fluency and effectiveness of the students' dialogues, using the marking tool described in the previous section of this paper. This makes it possible to provide more detailed and

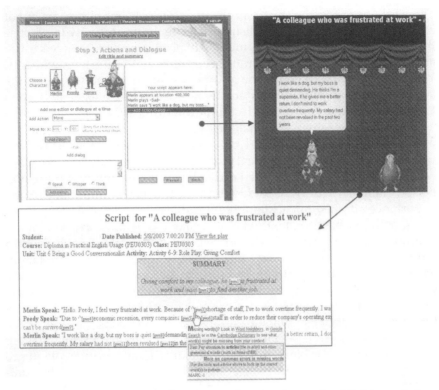

Figure 14.3 A scripting tool that allows the creation and publishing of plays on the Web: the resulting play uses animated agents and synthesized speech. Teachers and students assign behaviors and dialogue to the animations according to the focus of a unit (e.g. language points, social themes, etc.). The *Mark My Words* marking tool can be used to comment on the script, and the student has several references available to correct the script.

non-intrusive comments on the structure, lexis and pragmatics of the students' spoken language than is normally possible.

As well as being a useful vehicle for practice in conversational language devices, this tool gives learners the chance to demonstrate 'higher order' linguistic skills such as the pragmatic devices necessary for developing a narration, resolving a conflict, conducting a negotiation, etc. Before creating a play, the students' attention is focused through preparatory activities on commonly avoided, misused or overused language devices. The role-playing activity gives students the opportunity to be creative, to learn how to express the values of another culture, and to develop practical language strategies for handling business and social communication.

Those who are normally shy to speak spontaneously in a classroom out of concern for their imperfect English appreciate the opportunity to practise the language in this context. This method of producing scripted speech also appears less prone to plagiarism than conventional writing assignments. The dialogues tend to be unique and personalized possibly because the activity is not associated with academic assessment and right/wrong answers, as is often the case with standard writing activities.

This role-play activity (normally assigned several times throughout a course) enables students to work collaboratively at a distance. However, while role-playing may be an ideal participatory exercise, this ideal cannot be fully realized if students find it difficult to schedule meetings (either in person or online) in order to co-design plays. It is interesting, in light of the importance attached to collaborative activities by various learning theories, that the working students who have taken the courses in a continuing education context usually choose not to collaborate with other students in writing their role-plays. They do, however, often work with family members in designing and scripting the plays. Even when they write their plays alone, they socialize through the public production of the scenarios, by giving and receiving classmates' feedback, and through the virtual relationships they establish among the animated characters. Several of the 'higher-order' outcomes that are claimed for team-based role-playing activities are also possible in the creation of individually written role-plays, such as increased confidence in language production, heightened discriminatory skills, and the sheer fun that comes from the act of personal expression and creation. Collaborative elements can be retained even when students choose not to produce the plays collaboratively. In addition to commenting on and grading each other's plays (by assigning 'stars'), students often spontaneously continue narrative lines from their classmate's plays in their own scenarios.

Fellow students as well as the teacher supply feedback to each play, and students can re-write their scripts. Care is taken to make the purpose and structure of the role-plays clear, since many students are more accustomed to conventional essay assignments than they are to communicative methods of evaluation (see Li (1999) for a discussion of the mismatch between student expectations for teacher-led instruction and the participatory methods often preferred by Western-educated teachers).

Using this technique the course developer and teachers can also present the learners with a wide range of language features in communicative contexts, including problematic or unknown grammatical structures and lexis. Scripts written by learners often make use of surprisingly authentic dialogue. Students more easily adopt opposing points of view than when they write in essay form, and they seem to make more efforts at modeling challenging encounters and problematic language, which they normally avoid in formal writing. The language difficulties they naturally meet provide relevant teaching opportunities, and are evidence of involvement in genuine communicative acts, rather than the mere completion of academic exercises in error avoidance. This role-playing exercise is one of the most popular of the activities made available by the online course system: almost all students find this activity 'very interesting', and most mention it as one of their favorite activities.

Conclusion

The system outlined in this chapter allows language teachers and course writers to take advantage of ongoing advances in Internet technology to deliver principled language instruction. It makes possible and encourages independence and life-long learning skills supported by access to tools that provide oral fluency practice, that expose and explain the characteristics of authentic English texts, that enable the teacher to provide timely and relevant feedback, and that encourage the creative use of the L2. The components of this system seek to address cognitive, affective and social learning needs and to allow students to pursue their own language learning goals free of many of the logistic limitations of the classroom. However, all students have the option of attending face-to-face tutorials as well. These online activities are not meant to replace the classroom experience, but they can extend and enhance it.

The specific modalities highlighted in this chapter combine Internet delivery with online voice chat, free-text retrieval, computer animation and speech technology to enable language learners to experiment with the second language in simulated and supported contexts and to enable teachers to track the students' success. Various functional thematic contexts (telephone skills, encouraging and criticizing, the language of negotiation, etc.) are addressed in the courses developed on this system. Relevant grammar, lexis and discourse features, along with the prosodic features of spoken language (e.g. stress, rhythm, intonation and pronunciation), are presented to and practised by students through a variety of high-interest interactive activities. Spoken and written input and feedback are based on extensive research (Milton, 2001) into the student's interlanguage, and the resources made available are more accessible, authentic and copious than is normally possible in the confines of a classroom. Approaches such as those outlined in this chapter may help liberate learners from some of the wooden limitations of traditional pedagogy, and may help free teachers from having to pull the strings.[4]

Acknowledges

The author wishes to acknowledge the support of the *HKUST College of Lifelong Learning* (http://www.cl3.ust.hk/), and the *HKUST Language Centre* (http://lc.ust.hk/), who provided assistance in administrating and teaching the courses described in this chapter.

Notes

1. This program was developed in collaboration with a colleague at my university and is freely available at http://www.cs.ust.hk/gong/. A commercial program that has many of the same features is available at http://www.wimba.com.
2. These wild cards consist of an asterisk to represent any number of characters in one word and a question mark to represent one character (e.g. 'in???? of' = in view of, in each of, in some of, in case of . . . ; 'match*' = match, matches, matched, matching, matchmaking, matchless).
3. The technology I used to develop the scripting tool is described at http://www.microsoft.com/msagent/default.asp.
4. Some measure of improvement in language acquisition can be claimed for students who have taken courses on this system. The approximately 1000 students who have taken these courses so far have shown an average increase of 35% in listening comprehension, 24% in grammatical accuracy and 10% in vocabulary acquisition over an average period of 10 weeks, based on standardized pre- and post-tests.

References

Alley, L. and Jansak, K. (2001) Ten keys to quality assurance and assessment in online learning – Online document: http://www.worldclassstrategies.com/papers/keys.htm.

Bambrough, P. (1994) *Simulations in English Teaching*. Buckingham: Open University Press.

Barnett, L. (1993) Teacher off: Computer technology, guidance and self-access. *System* 21 (3), 295–304.

Biggs, J. and Telfer, R. (1987) *The Process of Learning*. Sydney: Prentice Hall Australia.

Cheng, J (1999, Oct 1) Opening the window of opportunity. *South China Morning Post*, A22–A23.

Crookall, D. and R.L. Oxford (eds) (1990) *Simulation, Gaming, and Language Learning*. New York: Newbury House.

Duquette, L., Renie, D. and Laurier, M. (1998) The evaluation of vocabulary acquisition when learning French as a second language in a multimedia environment. *Computer Assisted Language Learning* 11 (1), 3–34.

Ferris, D. (1995) Student reactions to teacher response in multiple-draft composition classrooms. *TESOL Quarterly* 29 (1), 33–53.

Jensen, B. (2003) The history and future of course authoring technologies – Online document: http://www.trinity.edu/rjensen/290wp/290wp.htm.

Johns, T. and King, P. (eds) (1991) *Classroom Concordancing*. Birmingham: Birmingham University.

Jones, K. (1985) *Designing Your Own Simulations*. London: Methuen & Co. Ltd.

Kluge D. and Taylor, M. (2000) Boosting speaking fluency through partner taping. *The Internet TESL Journal*, VI (2) – Online document: http://iteslj.org/Techniques/Kluge-PartnerTaping.html.

Ladousse, G.P. (1987) *Role Play*. Hong Kong: Oxford University Press.

Li, M-S. (1999) Perceptions of the place of expatriate English language teachers in China. PhD thesis, La Trobe University – Online document: http://my.glasscity.net/~xiong/tic/li.html.

Milton, J. (2001) *Elements of a Written Interlanguage: Institutional Influences on the Acquisition of English by Hong Kong Chinese Students*. Hong Kong: The Hong Kong University of Science and Technology.

Nikolova, O. (2002) Effects of students' participation in authoring of multimedia materials on student acquisition of vocabulary. 6 (1), 100–22.

Oller, J.W. Jr. (1993) Reasons why some methods work. In J.W. Oller, Jr (ed.). *Methods that Work* (pp. 374–85). Boston, MA: Heinle and Heinle.

Paris, S.G. (1995) Why learner-centered assessment is better than high-stakes testing. In N.M. Lambert and B.L. McComb (eds) *How Students Learn: Reforming Schools through Learner-centered Education* (pp. 189–209). Washington, DC: American Psychological Association.

Perkins, K. (1983) On the use of composition scoring techniques, objective measures, and objective tests to evaluate ESL writing ability. *TESOL Quarterly* 17 (4), 651–71.

Ryokai, K., Vaucelle, C. and Cassell, J. (2003) Virtual peers as partners in storytelling and literacy learning. *Journal of Computer-Assisted Learning* 19 (2), 195–208.

Rukeyser, M. (1960) *The Speed of Darkness*. New York: Random House.

Scarcella, R. and Crookall, D. (1990) Simulation/gaming and language acquisition. In D. Crookall and R.L. Oxford (eds) *Simulation, Gaming, and Language Learning* (pp. 223–30). New York: Newbury House.

Schneider, P. (1997) Using Pair Taping. *The Internet TESL Journal*, III (2) – Online document: http://iteslj.org/.

Sinclair, J. (1991) *Corpus, Concordance and Collocation*. Oxford: Oxford University Press.

Warschauer, M. (1999) *Electronic Literacies: Language, Culture, and Power in Online Education*. Mahwah, NJ: Lawrence Erlbaum Associates.

Wilde, O. (1890) Reprinted in R. Ellmann (ed.) (1998) *The Artist as Critic: Critical Writings of Oscar Wilde* (p. 349). New York: Random House.

Zeng, K. (1999) *Dragon Gate: Competitive Examinations and their Consequences*. London: Cassell.

Chapter 15

The Challenges of Implementing Online Tuition in Distance Language Courses: Task Design and Tutor Role

MIRJAM HAUCK and REGINE HAMPEL

Introduction

The Department of Languages (DoL) of the Faculty of Education and Language Studies at the Open University is the UK's largest modern foreign language learning provider with a current (2004) enrolment of approximately 6500 students of French, German and Spanish, all of whom study on their own at home, at a distance both from each other and from their tutors. For the last ten years, these learners have been using traditional Open University methods of course delivery such as print materials and video and audio cassettes as well as attending up to 21 hours of face-to-face tutorials per academic year. More recently, however, real-time audio and audio-graphic conferencing tools were trialled in a number of pilot projects to provide students with more flexible opportunities to practise their speaking skills.

In 2002 then, DoL began – in line with the university's Learning and Teaching Strategy – a progressive move towards offering online tutorials for all language courses, using Lyceum, an Internet-based audio-graphic conferencing system developed by the Open University. The findings presented in this chapter are based on our experience from the pilot projects with Lyceum as well as the first year of presenting a mainstream Open University language course (Level 2 German) with tutorials 'online only'. Apart from using the conferencing system, tutors and students on this course draw on a website with general course-related information. The site also supports the tutorials by offering an activity bank with tasks designed to foster communicative interaction and collaborative learning. The presentation of the course was accompanied by a study on student and tutor perception of the benefits and challenges of online learning and teaching (see Hampel, 2003).

The data for the research were collected through logbooks and questionnaires from a number of volunteer participants.

In contrast with the face-to-face classes, networked environments such as Lyceum are available 24 hours per day and seven days per week, thus allowing for greater flexibility when arranging tutorials or having to change arrangements at short notice. Moreover, students can 'meet' online outside the scheduled sessions to communicate with each other synchronously via voice at any time convenient to them. By using an online environment for the delivery of tutorials, DoL also sought to address the problem of non- or irregular attendance at face-to-face tutorials. As with other institutions of higher education offering campus-based language courses, Open University language courses suffer from problems of occasional absenteeism. In addition, many Open University students – especially those who come from the Scottish mainland, or from the islands, as well as those living in Continental Western Europe – find themselves unable to travel to tutorials.

It is of course not sufficient to provide tutors with an online platform and expect that they use it like a conventional classroom. Instead, issues such as task development and the impact on tutor role need to be taken into account when implementing online tuition using collaborative virtual learning environments (CVLEs) such as Lyceum. This chapter will summarise our findings, highlight challenges arising from online as compared with face-to-face tuition, and show potential solutions.

Developing Online Language Learning at the Open University

One of the main aims of all DoL courses is to develop the ability to communicate in the spoken language at a level appropriate to the year of study. However, providing opportunities for the development of interactive oral and aural skills has presented a major challenge for the course developers. Until recently, practice in these skills and engagement in peer group oral interaction could only be offered every four to six weeks in face-to-face tutorials at the university's 13 regional centres. Apart from one week of total immersion in the target language at Residential Schools in Caen (France), Jena (Germany) and Santiago (Spain), these face-to-face tutorials provided the only opportunity for Open University language students to practise oral skills in authentic communicative settings. But as participation in Open University tutorials is voluntary, many learners – for a variety of reasons – either chose not to, or were simply unable to attend the sessions. This meant that for many students developing oral fluency – as opposed to accuracy – was limited to practising with listening exercises that required students to speak, and to record their own contributions on audio tape, which they then sent to their tutor for feedback. As a result students concentrated primarily on the development of accuracy of form, not only in written assignments, but also in their oral contributions to the continuous assessment (see Hewer, 2000a). In cognitive terms, this was not very satisfactory.

Since 1995 DoL (previously Centre for Modern Languages) has been investigating other media in order to create opportunities for students to improve their oral fluency, media that are accessible from their home and/or workplace or even when travelling. These investigations began with telephone conferencing, moved to telephone conferencing plus e-mail (see Stevens & Hewer, 1998), and, more recently, as Internet technologies have become increasingly robust, have involved learning environments that use voice-over-Internet audio-conferencing and audio-graphic conferencing tools (see Hauck & Haezewindt, 1999; Kötter *et al.*, 1999; Shield *et al.*, 2000, 2001).

Initially, learners who were enrolled on a French (Open University Level 1) course participated in tutorials delivered via a telephone conference. The pedagogical approach for the telephone tutorials replicated that used in face-to-face tutorials. These typically involved both full class activities designed to improve accuracy and build vocabulary, and limited role plays to help students to improve fluency. However, due to the limitations of the learning environment:

> [e]xercises focusing on either vocabulary building, practice in the use of structures and accuracy of form predominated and activities ostensibly designed to encourage fluency were often over-prepared, with students reading their input from previously prepared 'scripts'. (Shield *et al.*, 2001: no page)

At this time Chun's work (1994) on improving oral interaction among students using computer-based text chat facilities suggested a way ahead combining the use of e-mail and telephone conferencing. Thus, in the next phase of the telephone conferencing tutorials, e-mail was included in the learning environment, and the researchers decided to move away from the exercise-based approach of the earlier pilot studies to one that was task-based. Students and tutors from all French and German courses of the three-year diploma programmes in presentation at the time took part in scheduled telephone conferences at the beginning and the end of a learning activity. In between the scheduled sessions they communicated via e-mail. Hewer (2000a: 4) reports that encouraging learners to collaborate with each other via e-mail between scheduled events led to an increase in the spontaneous use of language and in student confidence to be able to interact orally. Students were more prepared to take risks, which contributed to the development of fluency.

At the same time, students reported a decrease in their feeling of isolation and welcomed the opportunity to work with other students towards a common end, thus highlighting the potential impact of affective and social factors such as confidence and camaraderie on linguistic performance.

In view of this experience, the next series of pilot studies using an Internet-based learning environment also took a task-based approach to the online learning activities. VoxChat, the audio-conferencing tool adopted for these pilot studies, allowed students to create several virtual 'breakout' rooms and thus supported small group work more effectively than the telephone conferences. In addition, the software offered an 'invite' facility, which made it possible for students to call the tutor into their 'room' when help was needed. Students were made aware of the possibilities of meeting online at times of their own choosing in between scheduled group sessions.

In the study involving German (Open University Level 1) learners, the activities were collaborative and required students to work together – to devise questionnaires, for example. Plenary sessions included problem-solving and information-gap activities such as '20 questions' or 'Who am I?' where learners worked in teams to find the answer to some problem. For the French (Open University Level 2) learners, activities followed the conflict/collaboration model and learners were provided with a topic for debate as well as a role.

Encouraged by further positive results, it was decided to pursue the possibilities of oral interaction offered by the Internet further. It was also decided to integrate a graphics facility into the learning environment 'not least to focus the attention of students, to introduce a visually dynamic dimension into the group sessions and to enable students to have something to talk about as a support to their actual words' (Hewer 2000a: 4), and Lyceum was introduced. Technical difficulties – mainly due to the fact that earlier versions of the software required what was then perceived to be a high spec PC (64k RAM) – were outweighed by the opportunities offered by the new learning environment, and the majority of student feedback was, again, positive. The findings indicated in particular that the use of previously unseen images for which students know the relevant vocabulary and structures helps promote fluency for the distance language learner (see Hewer, 2000a).

Finally, in 2002, DoL began a progressive move towards offering online tutorials for all language courses using Lyceum. The course where – for the first time – tutorials were delivered 'online only', was a Level 2 German course. The students' participation in the tutorials was – as is the case for all Open University tutorials – optional. In line with the Open University equal opportunities policy, telephone tutorials were organised as a fallback option for those learners without access to a PC.

The Online Learning Environment

The learning environment as it is used today has three main components:

- Lyceum, the audio-graphic conferencing client;
- a website;
- e-mail.

Lyceum

In Lyceum, students and tutors use headsets and microphones to work together in real-time over a single modem line that transmits both their audio data and the information generated on the screen. The conferencing system thus enables them to hear each other simultaneously and talk to each other, but not to see each other.

Apart from the voice facilities, the software offers a range of tools, such as an on-screen *whiteboard*, a so-called *concept map* and a *document*. By using (shared) text and images, these tools introduce an additional visually dynamic dimension into the online group sessions.

The *whiteboard* (Figure 15.2) offers the possibility to present students electronically with previously unseen images and pictures, thus stimulating the cognitive processes necessary to interact orally in the target

Figure 15.1 Audio/voice facility and virtual rooms

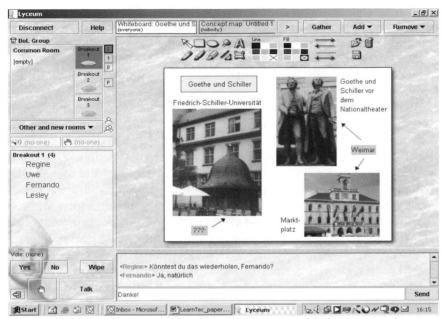

Figure 15.2 Audio/voice facility, virtual rooms, whiteboard and text chat

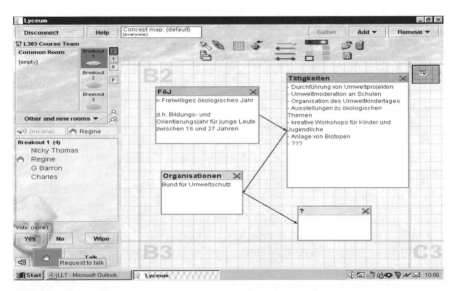

Figure 15.3 Audio/voice facility, virtual rooms and concept map

language. The *concept map* (Figure 15.3) is suitable for brainstorming exercises and word associations as well as any other vocabulary-building activities, and the *document* can be used for collaborative writing activities. A text-chat box (Figure 15.2) providing limited space for additional written input can be opened to supplement the voice facility and the tools. Furthermore, the software allows learners to create their own sub-conferences (virtual 'rooms') where they meet in pairs or small groups to engage in real-time interaction (for a more detailed technical description see Hampel & Baber, 2003).

Because of the synchronous, two-way interaction, students are provided with the opportunity to work in collaboration with others and to make the transition from learning in isolation to communicating with their peers. Since there are no restrictions on the use of the tools provided and the learners have open and unlimited access to the learning environment, they have individual as well as joint control over their input. As learner interaction is one-to-one or one-to-many, depending on how many people are logged on at a given time, they can modify and edit their input.

Benson (2001), building on Holec's (1981) and Little's (1991) definitions of autonomy, sees the capacity to take such control of one's own learning as one of the determining factors of learner autonomy. This is a view also shared by van Lier (1996:12–13), for whom autonomy is about the learner being 'able to make significant decisions about what is to be learned, as well as how and when to do it'.

Lyceum also provides opportunities for frequent and instant feedback by fellow students as well as tutors, which – apart from providing opportunities for communication and thus the development of fluency – is probably another important justification for the use of networked environments in distance language learning.

Website

Lyceum is complemented by a course website updated on a regular basis by the course administrator. The site offers learners course-related information, an activity bank and associated resources such as links to other websites relevant for the online activities. These links are accessible via ROUTES, the Open University library service offering selected quality-assessed Internet resources for Open University courses. Providing students with the latest news about their course, with task specifications for the tutorials including the outcomes for each individual activity as well as an outline of the scheduled sessions, can help to maintain learner motivation and to manage learner expectations regarding content and structure of the tutorials. In trying to combine features of central sites for 'web-focused' courses (such as the tutorial materials) with those of more peripheral sites for 'web-enhanced courses' (such as general course-related information), the course team opted for a hybrid version in terms of course website.

It was hoped this approach would also contribute to a reduction of the disruptions caused to the flow of scheduled sessions by the irregular attendance of some learners observed during the online pilot studies. However, the most recent experience with online course delivery confirms that those students who tend to participate irregularly in scheduled as well as more spontaneous student-initiated sessions are also less likely to consult a course website on a regular basis.

A cross-faculty team is currently looking at ways in which Open University course teams can be helped to develop their understanding of the usability of course-related websites. Acknowledging that '[i]n the fast-moving climate both within and outside the Open University, it has not been possible to develop a definitive, rigid set of guidelines' (Kukulska-Hulme *et al.*, 2003: 11), they have come up with '10 Challenges for Course Website Usability' representing the range of technical and pedagogical issues likely to be encountered in the development and application of course-related websites.

E-mail

E-mail not only enables tutors to communicate with their groups and with individual learners but it also allows learners to correspond and to collaborate with each other. Thus tutors use this asynchronous tool mainly to give written feedback and also, occasionally, to send out additional information related to the tutorial tasks; students exchange information and work together in small groups on tasks in between official tutorials before meeting online. They also use it for peer support.

The components of this learning environment, that is, Lyceum, the website and e-mail, seem to be particularly well suited to respond to the growing demand for language practice in more authentic communicative settings (see Chapelle, 1999; Felix, 1999) and provide tutors and course writers with a wealth of possibilities in terms of task design for distance language learning. The approach taken by the course designers in DoL will be described in more detail in the following section.

Task Design

Pedagogical rationale

The challenge faced by the course team members in developing the tasks for the online tutorials was twofold. On the one hand they wanted to make optimal use of the environment as a whole, and on the other they decided on the basis of the findings in the pilot studies that the activities should be designed in a way that would allow learners to familiarise themselves gradually with the various tools of the main component of the environment, i.e. Lyceum. The findings of the pilot projects had also indicated that Lyceum's various features (i.e. voice conferencing, plenary and sub-grouping facilities, graphic and writing tools) not only allow students to create, modify and edit their own input, but also actually encourage them to do so. Hewer (2000b) found the new technologies, which offer varying types and levels of interaction, have an impact on students' contributions as, very often, these have a more 'preliminary' and 'provisional' character than more traditional course materials. According to her, this '[. . .] results in changes in the student's cognitive processes during production tasks by encouraging reflection and self-evaluation, both of which are likely to lead to deep learning' (Hewer, 2000b: 8).

This confirms Kearsley and Shneiderman's (1998: 20) claim that 'technology can facilitate engagement [with learning activities] in ways which are difficult to achieve otherwise', an aspect of online language learning which seems to be particularly relevant for language students in distance education who depend on conferencing systems such as Lyceum to meet and engage in learning activities. At the same time, the findings of the pilot studies confirm Shneiderman's (1994: no page) observation that '[. . .] students are not strongly motivated by the goals of acquiring facts, accessing information, drill & practice [. . .]', but 'rather [. . .] prefer to create, communicate, plan, explore, build, discover, participate, initiate, and collaborate'.

Task features

In designing the activities then, the course team members tried to make best possible use of the notion of 'provisionality' for potential learner input as well as the varying types and levels of learner interaction and engagement referred to above. The main aim was to foster the development of oral fluency and to provide opportunities for language use in the target language that – at least for distance language learners – are not possible without online technology. Given that one of the requirements for the development of fluency is an ability to take risks and 'have a go' despite not being confident of producing accurate language, the task design was guided by the following principles:

- The content of the online activities is complementary to existing course materials.
- The activities build on structures and vocabulary presented in the corresponding units of the course.
- Each major task is broken down into sub-tasks.

- Each major task is intended for use over a two-week period, which covers two tutor-supported online sessions.

Moreover, Shield and Hewer's (1999) typology of characteristics of fluency-orientated online tasks was taken into account:

- There should be no prior specification of the linguistic code by teacher or student.
- There should be no attempt on the part of the task designer to 'drill' specific structures or vocabulary except as required by the student to convey meaning.
- The carrying out of the task should be student-dominated.
- The task should be meaning-based.
- Tutor expectations should match those implied in the task design.
- The objectives of the task should always be distinct from the formation of accurate language.
- The intervention of the tutor should always be as interlocutor within the context of the task, rather than as manager / assessor.
- The potential for unpredictability in the task is essential as the context develops so that participants have a reason to read and / or listen, as well as to create their own spoken and / or written output.
- Tasks should always include genuine information and / or opinion gaps to provide real reasons for listening, reading, speaking and writing.
- Procedures to deal with error correction should be non-intrusive and should never be allowed to inhibit the student while the task is in progress. The procedure(s) and the reasons for them should be explained carefully to students.

This typology is based on their analysis of the factors related to fluency, as described primarily by Brumfit (1984), and on their assumption that the purpose of a learning activity determines whether its focus lies in the development of accuracy – when a learner is demonstrating or developing knowledge of the language – or fluency – when the learner is trying to convey meaning (see Shield & Hewer, 1999).

Thus the tasks require the students to participate in role plays or other pre-arranged learning activities based on collaborative interaction. As a result, learners are engaged in project work and problem-solving activities designed so that additional online meetings outside the scheduled tutorials need to be arranged to exchange ideas, negotiate solutions, and prepare joint presentations of their work.

Scheduled online sessions

During the fortnightly scheduled sessions the students engage in tutor-led plenary meetings followed by break-out meetings in virtual 'rooms' created either beforehand by the tutor or during the tutorial by the students themselves. The tutors can 'visit' the learners on their own initiative or wait in the plenary space until they are called upon for assistance.

As mentioned earlier, there are usually two tutor-supported sessions per task as well as student interaction without the tutor in between these sessions. The tutor acts as chair of the two plenary sessions. The first session is typically a kick-off audio conference to set up the task and – in the case of a simulation – to allocate roles, discuss methods of working, and sort out any practical issues such as who would like to meet with whom, when and where in Lyceum during the following two weeks, as well as exchange of e-mail addresses. The activities involve collaboration with a sub-group followed by discussion with at least one other sub-group. Student interaction between scheduled tutorials takes place during sub-group meetings that the learners set up themselves. In addition to this synchronous work, some asynchronous work is undertaken via e-mail and attached files if students decide to exchange written notes or if some written input such as the design of a brochure is part of the task. The final debate, discussion or presentation is the outcome for which the students have to prepare themselves. The second tutor-supported session takes the form of a round-up audio-conference in which students debate the issues involved in the task and take relevant decisions.

Findings

Student feedback suggests that participating in intense interactions with fellow learners as well as carrying out collaborative tasks is the most exciting aspect of learning and practising a language in a CVLE such as Lyceum. As the following quotes from learners show, the gains from using this conferencing system have proven to be cognitive as well as affective.

> I particularly enjoyed the opportunity to prepare for a discussion with another student over a period of time rather than in a hurried 15 minutes before the discussion starts.

> The contact with a group was very good for me as I mostly worked completely alone – being based in Germany.

> The informal sessions [. . .] made the whole thing more relaxed and enjoyable i.e. making friends, knowing people and their interests.

Feedback from tutors, however, confirms Dymock and Hobson's (1998: no page) observations that there is '[. . .] a considerable degree of variation in student preparation of tasks between individual groups'. The pilot studies as well as the first year of presentation of the German course offering tutorials 'online only' have also shown that it is not necessarily any easier to get together for online as for face-to-face meetings, or, as Hurd *et al.* (2001: 342) put it: 'Motivation is essential, as with it comes persistence when the going gets tough, and energy to keep studying when other commitments encroach on your time.' When motivation is flagging, voluntary tutorials are often not a priority for students.

This has led the course team to review the methodology to minimise the disruptions of scheduled tutorials caused by the absence of some students at particular times during course delivery. In addition to the tasks described above, the activity bank on the website now features single, self-contained units for each scheduled tutorial based on the same content, structures and vocabulary as those activities which are spread over two weeks. This approach takes into account that participation in tutorials is voluntary and it offers both tutors and students greater flexibility. Moreover, it allows for varying degrees of learner commitment at different times during course delivery and encourages students to plan ahead. Two years of course presentation based on this new approach have shown that the situation has improved. The great majority of tutors confirm that the stand-alone units are easier to work with.

Our findings also suggest that smaller, autonomous groups – the current tutor/student ratio is 1:15 – are more likely to succeed and that students who are less skilled at managing their own learning might need additional support to be able to participate in a satisfactory way in sessions without a tutor present. In her keynote address at EUROCALL 2002, Felix stressed that we cannot assume a 'metaskill base' in students. In addition the technology can – at times – constitute an insurmountable challenge for online learners. We therefore maintain that helping learners to enhance their meta-cognitive knowledge and thus improve their control and flexibility in learning strategy use should become one of the determining aspects in future task design for language learning in CVLEs such as Lyceum. Such support can, at least to a certain degree, also be offered by the tutor. The impact of the learning environment and the described approach to task design on the role of the tutor are discussed in the next section.

Tutor Role

The virtual environment and the way in which the tasks for this medium were designed, has had an impact on the role that tutors and students play in tutorials. It has been observed (e.g. Warschauer, 1997) that written computer-mediated-communication using a learner-centred approach can boost student participation and communication and improve the quality of the students' discourse. Studies found that students play a greater role in managing the discourse than in a face-to-face situation (e.g. Chun, 1994; Engler, 2001; Kelm, 1998; Kern, 1995; Ortega, 1997), taking over some of the tutor's authority and becoming more autonomous.

Feedback from tutors involved in our pilot studies as well as from tutors describing their experience with Lyceum in 2002 endorses this. Students became more autonomous, gaining more control over their learning situation and as a result one tutor described her approach as generally having been 'more hands-off'.

The tutor as facilitator and organiser

The role of the tutor is no longer that of an instructor and a transmitter of knowledge. Instead, as well as facilitating the communication between the learners, the tutor guides the learners through the tasks, moderates and, in addition, acts as a participant in the learning process. This corresponds to the role of the teacher as facilitator, which Richards and Rodgers (2001: 199) describe in the context of cooperative language learning and which they see as similar to the tutor role in task-based language learning or communicative language teaching: 'In his or her role as facilitator, the teacher must move around the class helping students and groups as needs arise'. They explain this using a quote from McDonell (1992: 169):

> During this time the teacher interacts, teaches, refocuses, questions, clarifies, supports, expands, celebrates, empathizes. Depending on what problems arise, the following supportive behaviors are utilized. Facilitators are giving feedback, redirecting the group with questions, encouraging the group to solve its own problems, extending activity, encouraging thinking, managing conflict, observing students, and supplying resources.

CVLEs such as Lyceum allow tutors to move around the virtual classrooms, supporting students in the manifold ways McDonell describes. In a virtual learning context, the affective aspects of the tutor's role are especially important because the lack of body language makes the environment much more anonymous than a face-to-face session. The tasks for Lyceum were designed in a way that would allow the tutor to take on this role of the facilitator, and our pilot studies as well as the experience with Lyceum in 2002 have confirmed that this is what happens in practice. Thus Hauck and Haezewindt (1999: 50) observed that the tutor 'turned gradually into a manager of learning resources and an organiser of learning events'.

Social tutor versus cognitive tutor

Another useful way of describing the role of the online tutor is that of the 'social tutor' vs. the 'cognitive tutor'. Reporting on their work with asynchronous text conferencing, Lamy and Goodfellow (1999: 467) identified these two major tutoring styles that seem to occur in this learning environment. In contrast to the 'cognitive tutor', who is 'subject-knowledge oriented', the 'social tutor' encourages socialisation. In terms of the outcomes of the conferences analysed by Lamy and Goodfellow, where students produced significantly more messages when their tutor acted as social tutor than when he or she was in the role of the cognitive tutor, these tutoring styles appear to be somewhat analogous to the fluency/accuracy division; the cognitive tutor concentrates on construction of knowledge about the language (accuracy-focused), while the social tutor allows social exchanges between group members (fluency-focused). This finding supports Brumfit's claim: that '[a]ccuracy will tend to be closely related to the syllabus, will tend to be teacher-dominated, and will tend to be form-based' whereas '[f]luency must be student-dominated, meaning-based and relatively unpredictable towards the syllabus' (Brumfit, 1984: 161).

It is important to remember these different styles when considering tutor roles since we found that they have a direct impact on tutor–learner interaction in synchronous as well as asynchronous online learning environments. Reflection on this distinction is therefore part of the induction programme offered to Open University tutors by central academics and experienced colleagues each year during the month before the official courses start.

The tutor as teacher and administrator

Findings from our pilot studies as well as from our experience with Lyceum in 2002, suggest that audio-graphic conferencing also requires tutors to take on the 'teacher' role, at times providing content for the course website and answering student e-mail. They take on duties such as convenor of plenary sessions and time keeper. In these roles, they are neither 'cognitive' nor 'social' tutors, but what Shield *et al.* (2001) refer to as the 'administrative tutor' or 'manager of learning events'. These administrative aspects of tutoring are particularly relevant in new learning environments such as Lyceum, and on the basis of our experience we would argue that they are as important for online learning events as are the social and the cognitive styles since, without them, an activity can founder or lose its way, arriving at no final outcome.

Findings

Open University tutors experienced a range of roles during their work with learners in synchronous online audio-conferencing. Based on Dias' (1998) typology of teacher roles identified in the context of an e-mail project, Shield *et al.* (2001) have proposed the following preliminary model for the types of tutor role that occur in different types of online learning activities at different levels (see Table 15.1).

A tutor may, of course, fill more than one of these roles at the same time. For example, while taking the role of 'co-learner/student' in a role-play, he or she also acts as 'observer', a role that leads logically into that of 'teacher' when he or she provides learners with feedback and error correction. These findings substantiate White's claim (2003) that flexibility and a shift in mindset are essential for online tutors to succeed in developing new kinds of awareness and skills, and to make the required adjustments to new language learning settings, such as Lyceum.

> The ability to develop understanding of a new language learning context, the use of new mediums (e.g. course delivery tools), and new ways of learning and teaching is crucial. (White 2003: 69)

Error correction

According to the characteristics of a fluency-orientated task as identified earlier, error correction should be non-intrusive and should not inhibit the students. Moreover, the learners should be made aware of the chosen procedures considering that their expectations regarding the tutor's role are often quite different from those identified above. Our findings indicate that in-task correction should be avoided as it is a known deterrent to the development of fluency. But error correction should not be abandoned and is therefore another main feature in the initial training sessions for tutors where we suggest:

- that it takes place either at the end of a plenary session (in the form of anonymous correction); or
- that tutors use e-mail.

If they choose to use e-mail, they can either send out anonymous round robin messages alerting all students to recurring errors, or personal messages for the correction of individual errors. However, if communication is felt to be breaking down during a scheduled session, it seems advisable tutors should intervene, in role, summarising, for example, what was probably intended, or requesting clarification with some suggestion as to what might be said.

Table 15.1 A preliminary typology of online tutor roles according to activity-type, tutoring style and OU [Open University] learner level (level 1 = pre-undergraduate; level 2 = first/second year undergraduate; level 3 = second/final year undergraduate)

Tutor role	Activity/Material	Tutoring style	Learner level (OU)
• Teacher • Content expert	Course website content	• Cognitive • Cognitive	All
• Trouble-shooter • Teacher • Human being	Answering e-mail	• Administrative • Cognitive • Social	All
• Convenor • Time keeper • Trouble-shooter • Observer • Teacher • Compere • Human being	Problem solving	• Administrative • Administrative • Administrative • Cognitive • Cognitive • Social • Social	All
• Convenor • Time keeper • Trouble-shooter • Observer • Teacher • Nervous parent • Co-learner • Human being	Devising questionnaires	• Administrative • Administrative • Administrative • Cognitive • Cognitive • Social/admin. • Cognitive/social • Social	1
• Convenor • Time keeper • Trouble-shooter • Observer • Teacher • Nervous parent • Co-learner • Human being	Debating	• Administrative • Administrative • Administrative • Cognitive • Cognitive • Social/admin. • Cognitive/social • Social	2/3
• Convenor • Time keeper • Trouble-shooter • Observer • Teacher • Co-learner • Human being	Presentation	• Administrative • Administrative • Administrative • Cognitive • Cognitive • Cognitive/social • Social	2/3
• Trouble-shooter • Observer • Teacher • Co-learner • Human being	Simulation/role-playing	• Administrative • Cognitive • Cognitive • Cognitive/social • Social	2/3

Next Steps

The prime purpose for using CVLEs such as Lyceum in distance language learning is to provide students with opportunities to communicate in the target language. It has proved to be the only way that clearly plugs a gap in existing DoL course provision, namely the provision of frequent opportunities for oral interaction in the target language and the development of interactive oral fluency. Using audio-graphic conferencing for communication in both tutor-led as well as autonomous groups enables learners to retrieve as required appropriate vocabulary and structures previously learned independently and in isolation from each other.

The integration of CVLEs such as Lyceum into mainstream course delivery has shown that using the medium as a vehicle for collaborative work also has an impact on the learners' meta-cognitive skills, especially in terms of self-management. This seems to be particularly evident in the context of the described task-based approach as students have to plan their work more carefully and adhere to their plans when working with each other, rather than on their own. However, as indicated above, not all learners seem to possess the meta-cognitive knowledge required to draw on learning strategies appropriate for such learning environments.

We are therefore currently exploring how task design based on Strategies Based Instruction (SBI) as defined by Cohen (1998) in the context of Second Language Acquisition can be used in virtual language learning contexts to raise second language students' awareness of their most effective ways of learning. Cohen (1998: 266) sees instruction in language learning strategies as the most efficient way to heighten learner awareness and to impact on their performance in the second language:

> This approach is considered by a growing number of experts to be the most natural, most functional, in some ways the least intrusive, and potentially the most supportive means of getting the message to learners that how they mobilize their own strategy repertoire will have significant consequences for their language learning and use.

SBI also contributes to the shift of responsibility for learning from tutors to students and thus promotes an increase in learner autonomy. In her study, White (1995) has explored the relationship between learner autonomy, the instructional context and strategy choice in distance learning. She defines learner autonomy as 'an attitude on the part of the learner towards taking control of the language learning process and assuming responsibility for the process' (White 1995: 209). To become autonomous, learners have to develop an understanding of the language-learning process and their role in it. In her view, autonomy is something internal to the learners and therefore not necessarily linked to any particular mode of study (face-to-face or distance). However, she claims the demands and opportunities of a distance learning context make it necessary for students to re-evaluate their role and responsibilities as language learners. Their need for self-direction requires them to develop a comparatively higher degree of self-knowledge as a basis for devising their own means of learning and of managing their learning. White's findings reveal that distance language learners make greater use of meta-cognitive strategies than classroom learners do, self-management being their most frequently used meta-cognitive strategy. According to O'Malley and Chamot (1990: 137), self-management involves 'understanding the conditions that help one successfully accomplish language tasks and arranging for the presence of those conditions'. We therefore want to find out how instructed meta-cognitive strategies have the potential to support the learners' understanding of those conditions and facilitate their access to them and how this will impact on the tutor role. Furthermore, we should like to investigate whether this new approach to more efficient strategy use through increased self-awareness can lead to more efficient language learning and contribute to an increase in learner autonomy in CVLEs such as Lyceum.

References

Benson, P. (2001) *Teaching and Researching Autonomy in Language Learning*. Harlow: Pearson's Education Ltd.

Brumfit, C. (1984) *Communicative Methodology in Language Teaching: The Roles of Fluency and Accuracy*. Cambridge: Cambridge University Press.

Chapelle, C. (1999) Theory and research: Investigation of 'authentic' language learning tasks. In J. Egbert and E. Hanson-Smith (eds) *CALL Environments: Research, Practice, and Critical Issues* (pp. 101–15). Alexandria: TESOL.

Chun, D.M. (1994) Using computer networking to facilitate the acquisition of interactive competence. *System* 22 (1), 17–31.

Cohen, A.D. (1998) *Strategies in Learning and Using a Second Language*. Harlow: Addison Wesley Longman Ltd.

Dias, J. (1998) The teacher as chameleon: Computer-mediated communication and cole transformation. In P. Lewis (ed.) *Teachers, Learners and Computers: Exploring Relationships in CALL* (pp. 17–26). Nagoya: JALT Comp-Sig.

Dymock, D. and Hobson, P. (1998) Collaborative learning through audio-conferencing and voicemail – A case study. *Distance Education* 19 (1), 157–71. Online document: http://fehps.une.edu.au/f/s/pHobson/collaborative_learn.rtf

Engler, L. (2001) Deutsch lernen über das Internet: Die Möglichkeiten eines didaktischen Chats. *Linguistik online* 9 (2/01) – Online document: http://www.linguistik-online.de/9_01/Engler.html

Felix, U. (1999) Web-based language learning: A window to the authentic world. In R. Debski and M. Levy (eds) *WORLDCALL: Global Perspectives on Computer-assisted Language Learning* (pp. 85–98). Lisse: Swets & Zeitlinger.

Hampel, R. (2003) Theoretical perspectives and new practices in audio-graphic conferencing for language learning. *ReCALL* 15 (1), 21–36.

Hampel, R. and Baber, E. (2003) Using internet-based audio-graphic and video conferencing for language teaching and learning. In U. Felix (ed.) *Language Learning Online: Towards Best Practice* (pp. 171–91). Lisse: Swets & Zeitlinger.

Hauck, M. and Haezewindt, B. (1999) Adding a new perspective to distance (language) learning and teaching: the tutor's perspective. *ReCALL* 11 (2), 39–46. Online document: http://www.hull.ac.uk/cti/eurocall/recall/rvol11no2.pdf

Hauck, M., Hewer, S. and Shield, L. (1999) Online media for language learning. *CILT CALL Report 1998*. UK: CILT.

Hewer, S. (2000a) OL3–3 Lyceum Pilot Study with L221 CML students: October–December 1999. Unpublished report, The Open University UK.

Hewer, S. (2000b) Criteria for the selection of ICT media to be employed in ab initio foreign language courses, with particular reference to Lyceum. Unpublished report, The Open University UK.

Holec, H. (1981) *Autonomy and Foreign Language Learning*. Oxford: Pergamon Press for the Council of Europe.

Hurd, S., Beaven, T. and Ortega, A. (2001) Developing autonomy in a distance language learning context: issues and dilemmas for course writers. *System* 29, 341–55.

Kearsley, G. and Shneiderman, B. (1998) Engagement theory: A framework for technology-based teaching and learning. *Educational Technology*, September–October 1998, 20–3.

Kelm, O.R. (1998) The use of electronic mail in foreign language classes. In J. Swaffar, S. Romano, P. Markley and K. Arens (eds) *Language Learning Online: Theory and Practice in the ESL and L2 Computer Classroom* (pp. 141–53). Austin, TX: Labyrinth Publications.

Kern, R.G. (1995) Restructuring classroom interaction with networked computers: Effects on quantity and characteristics of language production. *The Modern Language Journal 79* (4), 457–76.

Kötter, M., Shield, L. and Stevens, A (1999) Real-time audio and email for fluency: promoting distance language learners' oral and aural skills via the Internet. *ReCALL* 11 (2), 47–54. Online document: http://www.cti.hull.ac.uk/eurocall/recall/rvol11no2.pdf

Kukulska-Hulme, A., Shield, L. and Muir, A.F.G. (2003) 10 challenges for course website usability. Unpublished report, The Open University UK.

Lamy, M-N. and Goodfellow, R. (1999) Supporting language students' interactions in web-based conferencing. *CALL Journal* 12 (5), 457–77.

Little, D. (1991) *Learner Autonomy 1: Definitions, Issues and Problems*. Dublin: Authentik.

McDonell, W. (1992) The role of the teacher in the cooperative learning classroom. In C. Kessler (ed.) *Cooperative Language Learning: A Teacher's Resource Book* (pp. 163–74). Englewood Cliffs, NJ: Prentice Hall Regents.

O'Malley, J.M. and Chamot, A.U. (1990) *Learning Strategies in Second Language Acquisition*. Cambridge: Cambridge University Press.

Ortega, L. (1997) Processes and outcomes in networked classroom interaction: Defining the research agenda for L2 computer-assisted classroom discussion. *Language Learning & Technology* 1 (1), 82–93. Online document: http://llt.msu.edu/vol1num1/default.html

Richards, J.C. and Rodgers, T.S. (2001) *Approaches and Methods in Language Teaching*. Cambridge: Cambridge University Press.

Shield, L. and Hewer, S. (1999) A synchronous learning environment to support distance language learners. In K. Cameron (ed.) *CALL & the Learning Community, Proceedings of Exeter CALL 99* (pp. 379–391). Exeter: Elm Bank Publications.

Shield, L., Hauck, M. and Kötter, M. (2000). In P. Howarth and R. Herrington (eds) *EAP Learning Technologies* (pp. 16–27). Leeds: University Press.

Shield, L., Hauck, M. and Hewer, S. (2001) Talking to strangers – the role of the tutor in developing target language speaking skills at a distance. *Proceedings of UNTELE 2000*, Volume II – Online document: http://www.utc.fr/~untele/

Shneiderman, B. (1994) Education by engagement and construction: Can distance learning be better than face-to-face? Online document: http://www.hitl.washington.edu/scivw/EVE/distance.html

Stevens, A. and Hewer, S. (1998) From policy to practice and back. In *Proceedings of LEVERAGE Conference Cambridge 1998*. Online document: http://greco.dit.upm.es/~leverage/conf1/hewer.htm

van Lier, L. (1996) *Interaction in the Language Curriculum: Awareness, Autonomy and Authenticity*. London and New York: Longman.

Warschauer, M. (1997) Computer-mediated collaborative learning: Theory and practice. *The Modern Language Journal* 81 (4), 470–81.

White, C.J. (1995) Autonomy and strategy use in distance foreign language learning: Research findings. *System* 23 (2), 207–21.

White, C.J. (2003) *Language Learning in Distance Education*. Cambridge: Cambridge University Press

Chapter 16

Closing the Distance: Compensatory Strategies in Distance Language Education

HEIDI HANSSON and ELISABETH WENNÖ

Introduction

Since communication is such an important aspect of language learning, opinions have been expressed that teaching languages at a distance cannot be as practicable and effective as campus-based courses. This study of a training course for future teachers of English, taught at Karlstad University, Sweden, in cooperation with Umeå University, Sweden between 1997 and 1999, charts some factors that obstruct as well as some that promote language learning at a distance. The group of students taking part in the course have been compared with students who followed face-to-face courses in the same period. The comparison is based on tests of language proficiency and correctness, analyses of student questionnaires and an analysis of the students' written work, and our research shows that the results of the distance students are equal to, or even better than those of the on-campus students. The group in question is relatively small, however, so it is not possible to draw any general conclusions about the efficacy of distance courses in languages. Nevertheless, it is possible to isolate some factors that appear to have influenced the students' results, and point to some ways in which the distance teaching of languages may be successful.

Background

The target group for the language distance programme were practising teachers of music, art, physical education, home economics, woodwork and handicraft – i.e. practical subjects – who wanted a formal qualification to teach English in addition. The course was the equivalent of 40 weeks of full-time study, but ran as a part-time course spread over two years, with extensive use of IT and two to three face-to-face meetings per term in Karlstad. We saw it as important that the distance course should not differ too much from corresponding on-campus courses, partly because the students on the different types of courses were to acquire the same formal qualification, partly to make it possible, if necessary, for the distance students to re-take exams after the distance course had finished. The course was at the level of advanced English, and the content was the same as for a regular on-campus course, with modules on phonetics, grammar, linguistics, language history, language proficiency, literature, culture and society and teaching methodology. After the trial period Karlstad University continued to offer the distance course as part of their standard course offering.

The first term of the course was evaluated thoroughly by external specialists, but this evaluation focused on the organisational, technical and social aspects of distance education as such, and gave no information about the problems and possibilities of distance language learning. We undertook the study reported here because of the dichotomy between our initial misgivings about the project, and the positive nature of the outcome. We found it difficult to believe that distance education techniques could work for languages, since the primary aim of language learning is communication. In an article about open learning, Lambert (1991: 5) points out that language teachers' experience of classroom teaching 'convinces them of how essential direct face-to-face contact is in language teaching'. Davis (1988: 547) makes a similar observation: 'To many engaged in the teaching of foreign language, the sort of distance implied here, the absence of immediate teacher–student interaction, appears inimical to our enterprise.' In a study of Australian open learning language courses Sharma and Williams (1988: 127) wonder likewise, ' ... whether or not languages, essentially tools of communication, can be taught effectively with a geographical distance between teacher and student'.

At the time when we were planning our course, there were few studies that could contradict these perceptions, especially regarding higher education courses. Ray Clifford (1990) refers to an American study of German at university level where the result shows that these students did not attain the same degree of proficiency as on-campus students (Johnson and Van Iten, 1984). In Sweden, the evaluation of national distance courses conducted by Carl Holmberg *et al.* (1996) – including English at university level – gives no further details about student results and makes no comparison with on-campus courses. This is, to be fair, rare in studies of distance courses. Lambert observes that most of the research conducted in relation to distance learning is evaluative, and mainly concerned with structural aspects, not foreign language learning:

Few studies are concerned with specific aspects of the teaching-learning process, fewer still with the pedagogical aspects of distance education, let alone with respect to foreign language instruction, and almost none with the important question of how we go beyond where we are now in both distance learning in foreign language teaching and the relationship of distance learning to the rest of foreign language instruction. (Lambert, 1991: 8)

Though the feasibility of teaching language at a distance is now established, there has been a lack of studies that focus on pedagogical rather than structural issues, and direct comparisons of distance and on-campus students have been hard to find.

Our investigation is an attempt to make these comparisons between distance and traditional learning situations. Since our misgivings before the 1997–1999 course did not materialise, we feel it is valuable to try to define and map those factors that aid or obstruct language learning at a distance. Our experiences lead us to believe that the factors important for successful distance learning are little different from those that are considered vital in any learning process. There is every reason to take Shale's (1990: 334) objection to the 'special' problems of distance learning seriously and ' . . . stop insisting that distance education is something different in kind from education as we generally understand it. [. . .] All of what constitutes the process of education when teacher and student are able to meet face-to-face also constitute the process of education when teacher and student are physically separated'. Dillon and Aagard (1990: 57) express the same attitude, claiming that we can only reject common theories about learning when research has demonstrated to the satisfaction of all that distance learning is a special case. There are, however, also advocates of the opposite view, such as Otto Peters (1998: 17) who maintains that from a pedagogical point of view, distance learning has to be considered *sui generis*, needing its own theoretical framework, interpretations and terminology to solve problems specific to the distance learning situation. In the course we gave we did not experience any *pedagogical* problems that we could relate specifically to distance learning, although there were a number of *technical and financial* problems that do not usually occur in on-campus situations.

As in traditional learning, distance learning is primarily about student motivation, teacher commitment and pedagogical interaction in the form of feedback, support and supervision. We would suggest that the kind of distance course we offered is an excellent opportunity to build up and reinforce these aspects. The problem of distance learning is not really the distance, but the available time and energy of the students and teachers involved. It is a matter of resources, in other words. We will show that what is felt to be a problem in the distance learning situation is equally problematic on campus. Conversely, our study indicates that what is beneficial in distance learning should be advantageous also in the traditional classroom. There is every reason to consider what classroom-based courses, where large student groups make it more and more difficult to achieve an optimal learning environment, can learn from the ways in which distance learning methods simulate face-to-face teaching.

Details of the Course

In all, eight teachers (six women and two men) were involved in planning and teaching the course. This group is representative of the kind of teacher collective an on-campus student might encounter: three native speakers of English, four teachers with doctorates and one experienced secondary-school teacher. None of these were experienced distance teachers, nor had they used IT in education to any great extent. The group agreed that technology should not be allowed pride of place, but that the most important aim of the course would be to ensure that the students achieved the knowledge and proficiency necessary to realise their goals of becoming teachers of English. It was also agreed that it was important to ensure that the course was the equivalent of similar teacher training programmes at the universities of Umeå and Karlstad. All the teachers were committed to planning their courses so interaction between the students would be a mandatory element. We decided to use the computer conference system First Class for messages, questions, distribution of material, discussions and other kinds of communication. In addition, the students were put into groups together with other students living in their geographical area, and these groups were to meet regularly to solve group tasks and work on group projects. The only real opportunities for oral proficiency work with a teacher present were the course meetings in Karlstad, which involved lectures and group discussions, and these meetings were therefore obligatory.

Of the 38 students accepted on the course, 16 did not come to the first course meeting or dropped out in the first few weeks, and were not counted in the study. Holmberg (1995: 199) remarks that drop-out is often regarded as a failure, but that this does not need to be the case. Considering the situation for the average distance student, it is hardly surprising that ' . . . the reasons given for discontinuation are mainly the pressures of duties, work commitments, travel, illness, lack of time, and similar circumstances'. These were the reasons our students gave us as well. Since most of the students who chose not to follow the course decided on this before or immediately after the course started, we could say that only four of our students qualify as 'real' dropouts, which amounts to 8%, instead of 42%.

Our study, then, is concerned primarily with the 24 students (20 women and four men) who followed the course to its end. Two of these were admitted after the course had started. Among the 24 there were two native speakers of English and seven who had recently studied English at university level in some form. Compared with the student population on a full-time on-campus course where the majority would be under 30 years of age, this group was considerably older and more experienced since most were over 40. Geographically, the students came from all over Sweden. Those who had the furthest to travel to course meetings dropped out at an early stage, however. A majority of the students worked full time in addition to their studies and had families or partners. Most of them had access to a computer at home, though none had any experience of communication via First Class.

To get a better idea of the students' motives for taking the course and motivation for completing it, we gave out a questionnaire in January 1999 to the 22 students present at the course meeting at the time, asking – among other things – why they had begun the course in the first place. Eighteen students answered, and of these, 17 said that they wanted to improve their future work prospects in one way or another. Interest in English is a motive further mentioned by some students. Thus, the primary motivation for study was related to the students' work situation. To sum up, the student group can be regarded as relatively homogeneous in terms of age, family situation, work experience, experience of computer-aided communication and motivation. Davis (1988: 549) observes that ' . . . distance learners, in fact, tend to be more instrumentally motivated than more traditional students'. The predominance of answers related to future work prospects in our study corroborates this, though obviously the course was designed to attract active teachers in the first place.

Nevertheless, the question as to what motivated the students to complete the course yielded more answers than the merely instrumental. These included the student's personal characteristics (stubbornness, need to finish what has been begun), the friends they made on the course, the teachers, the joy of learning, work-related goals, specific parts of the course and the course meetings. The first category – personal characteristics – seems to confirm the common view that distance learning requires a certain degree of motivation and, in particular, ' . . . maturity, self-discipline and independence' (Holmberg, 1995: 175), but apart from this and the clearly work-related goals it is clear that both cognitive and affective interaction were vitally important for the student's motivation to complete the studies. According to Holmberg (1995) personal relations and intellectual satisfaction are central to successful distance learning, and the answers from our students clearly demonstrate the importance of these factors.

Pedagogical Design

Our course was a combination of distance and on-campus education. According to Richard and Rohdin (1995) this is the most common kind of distance course at university level in Sweden. None of the four pedagogical models for distance learning that Holmberg *et al.* (1996) describe, based on discussions in Richard and Rohdin (1995), can be said to correspond to our model exactly, however. In short, these models are:

- vocational correspondence course concluded with a three-day seminar;
- alternation between distance education and on-campus education once a month;
- introductory and concluding meetings combined with televised lectures;
- introductory meeting followed by individual studies and thereafter a three-week-period taught on campus.

Our model corresponds most closely to the second type, with the difference that on-campus meetings did not occur as often as once a month. In pedagogical terms, our model can be described as a combination of what Peters (1998: 16) calls 'guided self-study' and 'indirect attendance at teaching events in a traditional university' (a third type is termed 'autonomous, self-guided learning'). Our model could be defined as 'guided self-study with elements of face-to-face teaching'.

This can be compared to the three theories of distance education as founded on (1) independence and autonomy, (2) mass education (industrialisation), and (3) interaction and communication, described by, among others, Keegan (1986). The first group of theories focuses on the individual student, whereas theories in the second group are concerned with the application of concepts from the wider context and the processes of industrialisation to distance education. Theories from the third group apply to the role that technology plays in providing facilities for interaction and communication. Today, on-line learning has probably made some of these theoretical positions obsolete, since it introduces an almost infinite range of options in terms of format, duration, access, etc., but as far as the three models are concerned our ambition resembles the third category most closely. In language education this is not only the most logical position, but also the one most likely to compensate for the lack of direct communicative interaction the distance form might entail.

To achieve communicative closeness despite the distance between students and teachers we adopted what Peters terms 'the tutor model' (based on Rowntree, 1992: 119):

> In this type of procedure, monological and expository teaching is completely abandoned. The aim of the teaching text is not to present contents but to give the impression of a conversation with an imaginary tutor. Questions are put, advice is given, opinions are expressed and correlations explained. And students are also helped not to fall into the trap of thinking that they are working in isolation from the university and in the final analysis thinking that they are alone. Proximity is simulated in this strange way as well. (Peters, 1998: 25–6)

In most cases the study guides were designed in this manner, with the teachers supplying further questions, answers, explanations, response, advice and encouragement on-line.

Completion Rate

More students than we expected completed the course. The rate of completion was, in fact, higher than for the corresponding on-campus course. This is a better result than we had anticipated, since we feared the students' language proficiency would not develop as much as in classroom learning. In other words, we feared that the students would find the distance mode unsatisfactory in terms of gains in competence and that this would prompt withdrawal from the course. We also expected the age of the distance students would lead to slower linguistic development, but this also turned out to be wrong. In comparison with on-campus students, factors like study technique, maturity and experience, and the work-related motivation of the students may have contributed to this reasonably good result. On the other hand, there were external factors that made study more difficult for the distance students, such as work and the demands of family life, the geographical distribution within and between the study groups, technical problems, and substantially fewer opportunities for face-to-face teaching.

A crucial question for distance language learning is whether it is possible to develop language proficiency when there are few opportunities for face-to-face communication. Our quantitative results, interpretation of questionnaires and analyses of the students' written production show that the distance format does not hinder such development, at least not so far as relatively advanced students are concerned. Instead, our study emphasises the value of placing the main focus on text input and content rather than formal language training, and indicates that written production that requires reflection promotes language development in general.

Quantitative Measurement of Language Proficiency

One way to measure an increased level of language proficiency is to give the students comparable multiple-choice tests at the beginning and end of the course. The test used in Karlstad and at many other Swedish universities measures grammatical correctness and the students' knowledge of idioms and stylistic nuances – VOC / MCT test. It consists of two parts: a vocabulary test with 120 English words to be matched with one of five Swedish alternatives, and a text with 90 exercises where the students have to choose the correct alternative. The maximum score is 300 (120 + 180 (90 × 2)), and a particular result is required for different levels.

To find out how our distance students performed in relation to the full-time on-campus students we compared the results of the diagnostic VOC / MCT test with the results of a similar test given after one year. We matched each distance student with a full-time student who had the same result on the first test and compared their final results to see if there were any differences in quantitative terms. The number of students is too small for any reliable conclusions, but the distance students had improved their results by at least 5 points more than their corresponding on-campus student. Since the time aspect is generally felt to be of importance in language learning, the better results of the distance students may be due to a combination of higher motivation and longer period of study, since the course ran part time. But regardless of the reasons, our study shows that the distance format has not had an injurious effect on vocabulary or language proficiency learning in this group. On the contrary, there are indications of the opposite effect.

Interaction

The purpose of the questionnaire was to find out in which ways the students felt that the distance form had obstructed or promoted learning. The questionnaire was distributed to the 22 students present at the final course meeting in January 1999. After some reminders we received 18 completed questionnaires, some signed but most of them anonymous.

One of the greatest problems in open learning is to do with bridging the gap in time and space, and this is also the aspect accentuated in literature about distance learning. The geographical distance counteracts the interaction considered vital to all education. Since our study concerns language learning, where communication is central, the issue of interaction is of special interest. As opposed to on-line chatting, interaction via First Class and similar computer conference systems does not usually take place in real-time, which means that it is removed from the demands of much authentic interaction. Our first question asked how the students experienced the contact between teachers and students, and surprisingly enough, most answers indicated that the distance format influenced contacts between teachers and students in a positive direction. The flexibility of computer communication – messages can be sent at any time – is one advantage mentioned. A disadvantage is that sending and receiving messages must be less personal than 'meeting in real life'.

The *form* of the contact – computer-aided communication – is valued less highly than the content. The accessibility and pace technology can offer do not determine students' perception of the quality of student–teacher contact. What seems to be most important is the teacher's interest and motivation. This can be understood in terms of the need for feedback and support that Holmberg (1995) views as two of three dimensions of activity in interaction. Our study appears to demonstrate that it is the teacher's availability and commitment, not technological solutions, that guarantee student–teacher interaction.

Although the medium – in our case, First Class – offered opportunities for student–student and student–teacher interaction it is doubtful whether so many students would have completed the course without the feedback and support of the study groups and the meetings in Karlstad. The students' answers indicate clearly that these opportunities for social contact were very important both for the students' *learning* and for their *motivation*, which supports the thesis that all education is fundamentally a matter of communication and that the learning process has an important social dimension (Carlsson, 1989). The comments about the meetings in Karlstad focus on the importance of *inspiration* and *exchange* for motivation or, translated into the actual teaching situation, lectures and discussions were highly valued.

To sum up, the distance format can meet students' needs for feedback and support in interaction just as well as traditional forms of education, provided the teacher is available and interested and the study groups function well. These conditions should also influence the study climate on campus. Face-to-face teaching, however, seems to be of great importance, and here the distance form cannot compete with on-campus courses. Face-to-face teaching becomes particularly important when there are *technical* problems in computer communication. When asked about the disadvantages with First Class, the students mostly answered that technical problems had caused annoyance. The advantages listed were that it is quick and that the students could receive individual feedback (which in itself has nothing to do with technology, of course). The main advantage, as we interpret the students' answers, is that First Class helps to maintain contact.

Even so, it is obvious that First Class was not used to facilitate discussion to any great extent. The opportunities for continuous discussion offered by the system ought to be of particular value in language education, but our students did not really make use of this. One reason may be unfamiliarity with computers; another could be lack of time. Since it takes longer to formulate something in writing than to take part in a classroom discussion, the students may have felt the effort involved was too great. Moreover, the written message becomes a 'published' text, available to everybody else in the group, which means many probably felt they needed to work hard to make sure their contributions were grammatically correct. This means First Class or similar communication programmes cannot replace classroom interaction, but rather can enhance the individual contact between teacher and student. Peters (1998: 62) makes a similar observation when he describes written responses from teachers: 'However, the actual significance of these written dialogues lies in the interaction of an individual student with an individual teacher, in other words in the individualization of distance education.' If individualisation is seen as an important aspect of learning, distance learning may provide better opportunities than traditional class-room teaching, given that the teacher is allowed sufficient time to communicate with the students. If, on the other hand, it is considered important that more than two parties are involved in the communication it needs to be pointed out that computer-based communication systems invite broader communication only in theory. In practice, it is mainly used for private communication.

The third dimension of activity in interaction defined by Börje Holmberg (1995) is supervision. This is clearly a teacher function, tied to the cognitive dimension of interaction, as opposed to feedback and support that can be provided by somebody other than the teacher. Moore's (1983) concept of *transactional distance*, defined as a function of the variables 'dialogue' and 'structure', is interesting in this context. Dialogue is ' . . . the extent to which, in any educational programme, learner and educator are able to respond to each other.' Physical proximity does not guarantee 'dialogue', that is, on-campus courses can also be 'distant' as Moore sees it, since he differentiates between physical and mental or communicative distance. Structure, in Moore's terms, is 'a measure of an educational programme's responsiveness to learner's individual needs' (Moore 1983: 153). A rigidly structured course must therefore also be regarded as 'distant' since it cannot be adapted to the students' needs to any great extent. Pure self-study courses and radio- or TV-courses are examples of highly structured forms that contain no dialogue (Moore, 1977: 39). Peters

(1998: 34) points out that many university courses may be characterised as 'distant' both in terms of dialogue and structure since the student groups are sometimes very large. The notion of 'transactional distance' highlights the fact that bridging the distance is a problem in all kinds of education, not specifically a problem in distance learning.

Since dialogue, as we have indicated, is not normally used to its full extent in distance learning, at least not when it is conducted via computer, the teaching structure (i.e. study guides and instructions) needs to be maximised to compensate for the distance. The effect could then be that the students' individual needs are not adequately met or that the degree of learner autonomy might be threatened. Saba (1990: 349) observes that even though ' . . . autonomy of the learner is revered, the literature is clear that distance education does not include unstructured learning'. Our study shows that the balance between dialogue, structure and autonomy can be maintained. The main advantages of the First Class system were considered to be speed and accessibility, which suggests some form of teacher–student dialogue is possible and seems to have occurred. Structure was provided through introductions at the course meetings and study guides.

Referring to Laurillard (1993), Holmberg _et al._ (1996: 108) describe ideal education as 'discursive', 'interactive', 'adaptive' and 'reflective'. And according to Holmberg _et al._ such an ideal can be achieved only when teachers and students meet in small groups or when such meetings are in some manner simulated. This ideal does not only concern distance learning, but the question is whether it is possible today to carry out teaching in this way, even on campus, where the financial situation has meant that students are taught in larger and larger groups. In such cases, a computer conference system may be a better alternative than a face-to-face meeting where the group is too large to allow two-way communication. Our distance students asked questions, replied to the teacher's comments and sent back corrected versions of their texts to a much greater extent than on-campus students normally do. One reason for this may be that when they received corrected work from the teachers they were already sitting at their computer, and could easily follow up the teacher's comments. In this case it could therefore be said that the technology creates added value, and does not serve only as a substitute.

Nevertheless, it is important to stress that even if the computer conference system helps to speed up feedback, the quality of the feedback depends on teachers' and students' willingness and practical opportunities to communicate. It is very time-consuming to send back corrected work in reasonable time, with as extensive comments as possible, especially since the teacher also needs to respond to the kind of short questions an on-campus student can ask after a lecture or lesson. If the pedagogical quality is to be maintained, mass distance education is a realistic model only if it is appropriately resourced, with an adequate student–tutor ratio.

If we support the idea that learning is not a matter of a teacher 'transmitting' knowledge to a learner in a specific place at a specific time, but assume the primary relation in learning is, as Toombs (1990: 38) expresses it, ' ... the engagement of student with subject-matter', the structured distance learning methodology appears to be superior to class-room teaching. As Beaudoin (1990: 23) points out regarding adults' learning, self-study is an attractive form, provided there are ' . . . proper resources (e.g. effective instructional guides, appropriate texts, adequate faculty communication and strong support services)'.

The Students' View of Advantages and Disadvantages in Distance Learning

In total, the students name 29 factors (several give more than one factor) that they see as the *advantages* of distance learning as compared with traditional classroom education. A great number of answers have to do with *efficient study*, where the course has required them to be disciplined and structured and to reflect (eight). The possibility to *combine* flexible study with other undertakings is important for seven. Accessibility to teachers is singled out by two, and the opportunity to gain computer skills by two. Further, two students comment on the social dimension, and one mentions better development of written proficiency. It is interesting that as many as eight people point to some form of *study quality* as an *effect* of the distance format. This calls into question the criticism often voiced about distance learning, according to Beaudoin, namely that it ' . . . fosters dependence rather than develops critical thinking and self-directed learning' and that ' . . . the chief skill acquired by the distance student is the ability to provide perfunctory answers based on readily apparent information contained in the course material' (1990: 23). Like most distance courses today, our course emphasised learner autonomy, and tried to counteract such dependence.

Of 24 answers concerning *disadvantages* in distance learning (many students give more than one factor), 11 emphasise the lack of opportunities for oral proficiency training, three would like more lectures, three mention fewer opportunities for spontaneous discussions with teachers, and three mention the few opportunities for discussions with other students. Two students point out the social advantages of studying on campus, as opposed to on a distance course. It is hardly surprising that the main disadvantage is perceived as the lack of oral proficiency training, though it is worth noting that demands for more oral practice constantly recur in evaluations of on-campus courses in English in Karlstad. It seems that neither form of education can meet this requirement.

Student Perceptions of Factors influencing Language Proficiency

Since we assume that some kind of language development takes place when you take part in a language course, we asked the students what aspects of the course they felt had been particularly valuable in improving their oral and written proficiency, and what they felt had hindered such development. Where *oral proficiency* was concerned, the students primarily pointed to the importance of the meetings in Karlstad, different types of group discussions during these meetings, and meetings in the study groups. The main disadvantage, as has been indicated, was the dearth of opportunities for oral communication. The lack of such opportunities is often commented on in studies of distance learning, and many course developers have devoted much time and effort to finding ways to ' . . . incorporate human interaction and oral language production into the distance learning situation', as Dominique Abrioux expresses it (1991: 12). A common opinion, however, is that interaction via computer cannot replace direct communication between people (e.g. Holmberg, 1990). Sharma and Williams also single out oral proficiency training as the main problem area for distance language learning (1988). As in our study, their investigation shows that oral proficiency is the area where the *students themselves* most often characterised their ability as 'poor'. Sharma and Williams conclude that it might be unrealistic to expect a comparable development of all kinds of proficiency – reading, writing, speaking and listening. It is better to concentrate on obtainable goals. It is worth noting, though, that the teachers involved in our course did not feel that there was a significant difference in the level of oral proficiency between the distance learning students and on-campus students on corresponding courses. As we have pointed out, full-time students show the same tendency to express dissatisfaction with their own level of oral proficiency.

The rapid developments in technology in recent years have led to an increased interest in the possibilities of computer-aided distance learning, but as early as 1981 Perraton pointed out that the medium is secondary; what is of primary importance is the *relevance of the course material*, the *intelligibility of the material* and the *students' motivation*. Our group was highly motivated, and the study guides were appreciated for their clarity and intelligibility. As for course material, the students mainly asked for more of the kind of material already included, which suggests they regarded the material as relevant. In pedagogical terms the course consequently provided good learning effects. Especially where advanced learners are concerned, content is of great importance. Our experiences indicate that language input with specific and relevant content combined with interaction via computer will also support the development of oral proficiency.

Another beneficial factor is the large amount of (written) language production required in distance learning:

> Swain argues that learners need the opportunity for meaningful use of their linguistic resources to achieve full grammatical competence. She argues that when learners experience communicative failure, they are pushed into making their output more precise, coherent, and appropriate. She also argues that production may encourage learners to move from semantic (top-down) to syntactic (bottom-up) processing. Whereas comprehension of a message can take place with little syntactic analysis of the input, production forces learners to pay attention to the means of production. (Ellis, 1997: 282)

Extensive opportunities for authentic writing are one of the attractions of online learning. Linnarud (1986: 23) emphasises the importance of written production for language proficiency in general: 'Although language competence seems to be partly divisible, it is clear that practice in one skill is beneficial to other skills.' In particular, the practice of writing seems to have a good effect on other parts of language performance. The answers to our questionnaire indicate the comparatively greater number of send-in tasks and the computer-based communication are what the students feel have been most advantageous for their development of written proficiency. There are reasons to conclude that these factors have also influenced other kinds of language development. None of the students mention a factor that they feel has obstructed their development of writing skills. Thus, the strength of the course as far as language development is concerned seems to be its *requirement for frequent written production.*

It is also important to consider the relationship between cognitive and linguistic processes. One explanation as to why the group developed language proficiency, despite the distance, could be that the content of the course demanded intellectual development, which in turn requires linguistic development. In their comments the students return more than once to the necessity and value of active reflection before questions or tasks were sent in. Language learning theorists agree that understanding develops faster than production, and learning takes place only when the learner is active (Wilkins, 1974). Our investigation suggests that all aspects of language proficiency are promoted not only by active production, but also by *reflective* written production based on reading.

Conclusion

It might appear obvious that the students' written proficiency is the language skill least unfavourably affected in distance learning. The old correspondence courses were based on writing, and this tradition continues both when distance courses are planned and in the students' expectations. But tasks that mainly require the student to summarise textbook material or answer factual questions contribute to their language development to only a small degree. The tasks given in the different modules of our course were problem-oriented and proceeded from the idea that academic learning is founded on dialogue. Consequently, the tasks required an active dialogue between student and texts and the *application* of new knowledge rather than uncritical learning of facts, or, in other words, the students were encouraged to show they could use their knowledge outside the learning situation. According to the students, send-in tasks and communication via computer were particularly beneficial to their language development, regardless of which module the tasks occurred in (Linguistics, Literature, Culture, etc.). Writing tasks that demand analysis and argumentation force the student to activate new vocabulary immediately, and a well-functioning interaction with textbook and reference material makes the students familiar with the style they need to apply for a satisfactory solution to the task. These opportunities also enable learners to develop more self-awareness as English language users. This is the strength of distance learning methodology. Improved written proficiency is not just the result of specific written proficiency courses, but the outcome of methods used throughout the course. There is seldom time for such continuous practice on on-campus courses, which means this is another advantage of distance learning.

The factors that seemed to be most important for the students' success were those that compensated for the deficiencies of a distance course. Thus, the lack of direct communication can be compensated for by a large input of text and frequent communication in writing between students or between student and teacher. The lack of face-to-face teaching can be compensated for by well-structured study guides and a higher proportion of individual feedback from the teacher. The lack of a study environment can be compensated for by study groups and course meetings. Finally, high motivation for study may compensate for such difficult learning conditions as may arise because of family pressures, work commitments, etc.

Many of the problems for distance language courses are actually the same as those facing traditional university courses at this time of financial cutbacks and diminishing resources. The most important conclusion reached in our study is, therefore, that the demands for compensatory structures required by the distance form emphasise those factors that should aid effective learning in general, and language learning in particular. These factors are individualisation, active interest from the teacher in the form of feedback and support, interaction between students, and well-structured supervision and guidance.

References

Abrioux, D. (1991) Computer-assisted language learning at a distance: An international survey. *The American Journal of Distance Education* 5 (1), 3–14.

Beaudoin, M. (1990) The instructor's changing role in distance education. *The American Journal of Distance Education* 4 (2), 21–9.

Carlsson, R. (1989) Tredje generationens distansutbildning. *Teldok Rapport 53*.

Clifford, R. (1990) Foreign languages and distance education: The next best thing to being there. ERIC Digests, EDO-FL–90–08 (Dec.).

Davis, J.N. (1988) Distance education and foreign language education: Towards a coherent approach. *Foreign Language Annals* 6 (21), 347–50.

Dillon, C. and Aagard, L. (1990) Questions and research strategies: Another perspective. *The American Journal of Distance Education* 4 (3), 57–65.

Ellis, R. (1997) *The Study of Second Language Acquisition*. Oxford: Oxford University Press.

Holmberg, B. (1990) The role of media in distance education as a key academic issue. In A.W. Bates (ed.) *Media and Technology in European Distance Education* (pp. 41–6). Milton Keynes: European Association of Distance Teaching Universities.

Holmberg, B. (1995) *Theory and Practice of Distance Education* (2nd edn). London: Routledge.

Holmberg, C., Lundberg, M. and Sipos-Zackrisson, K. (1996) *Det första året: Utvärdering av det pedagogiska utvecklingsarbetet inom konsortiet för nationell distansutbildning*. Linköping: Linköpings Universitet.

Johnson, M.S. and Van Iten, H.B. (1984) An attempt at televised foreign language instruction. *ADFL Bulletin* (16) 1: 36–8.

Keegan, D. (1986) *The Foundations of Distance Education*. London: Croom Helm.

Lambert, R.D. (1991) Distance education and foreign languages. *Occasional Paper 9*. Johns Hopkins University National Foreign Language Center.

Laurillard, D. (1993) *Rethinking University Teaching: A Framework for the Effecive Use of Educational Technology*. London: Routledge.

Linnarud, M. (1986) *Lexis in Composition: A Performance Analysis of Swedish Learners' Written English*. Lund Studies in English 74. Lund: CWK Gleerup.

Moore, M. (1977) A model of independent study. *Epistolodidaktia* 1, 6–40.

Moore, M. (1983) The individual adult learner. In M. Tight (ed.) *Adult Learning and Education*. London: Croom Helm.

Perraton, H. (1981) A theory for distance education. *Prospects* 11, 13–24.

Peters, O. (1998) *Learning and Teaching in Distance Education: Analyses and Interpretations from an International Perspective*. London: Kogan Page.

Richard, E. and Rohdin, B. (1995) *Modeller för distansutbildning*. Växjö: Högskolan i Växjö.

Rowntree, D. (1992) *Exploring Open and Distance Learning*. London: Kogan Page.

Saba, F. (1990) Integrated telecommunications systems and instructional transaction. In M. Moore (ed.) *Contemporary Issues in American Distance Education*. New York: Pergamon.

Shale, D. (1990) Toward a reconceptualization of distance education. In M. Moore (ed.) *Contemporary Issues in American Distance Education*. New York: Pergamon.

Sharma, P. and S. Williams (1988) Language acquisition by distance education: an Australian survey. *Distance Education* 9 (1), 127–46.

Toombs, W. (1990) Closing the loop: Distance education and the college professor. In M. Moore (ed.) *Contemporary Issues in American Distance Education*. New York: Pergamon.

Wilkins, D.A. (1974) *Second-Language Learning and Teaching*. London: Edward Arnold.

Chapter 17

PLEASE (Primary Language Teacher Education: Autonomy and Self-Evaluation)

FRANCA POPPI, LESLEY LOW and MARINA BONDI

Introduction

The last ten years have seen a major Europe-wide initiative to extend the teaching of modern foreign languages to primary age pupils, either to increase the time available for the first foreign language, or to facilitate the introduction of a second or third in the secondary stages of schooling. Generally, there have been insufficient trained language teachers available to cater for this new demand at primary level, and many countries have initiated national in-service training courses for practising primary teachers to encourage and enable them to add a foreign language to their repertoire of teaching subjects or skills. Kinds of policy, strategy and models of provision, both of foreign language teaching at primary level and types of training on offer, have varied widely across Europe, with different entry points and requirements for existing language competence. Some countries have emphasised process rather than outcome, some have focused on listening and speaking and avoided reading and writing. Some have trained specialist, peripatetic language teachers, others generalist primary teachers.

In Italy, for instance, you can find the specialist teacher, with a degree in the foreign language, who teaches in a number of different schools, or the generalist primary teacher who has been 'taught' the foreign language by taking part in one or more courses organised by the Ministry of Education.[1]

In Scotland, a national in-service programme for volunteer primary teachers has been in operation since 1993, enabling generalist teachers to add a foreign language, predominantly French, to their repertoire of skills. Teachers typically undergo 27 days of training over a period of a year, although those with prior experience or qualifications in the FL may undertake a reduced version of the course.

While the overall picture is very varied, there are several important features common to this first phase of language teaching. First, there has usually been little funding available for further training of teachers once the initial pre-service or in-service training has been provided. This is why there is a need for self-access materials for teachers who wish to further their development needs. Second, the primary foreign language teacher may be the only such teacher in his or her school, and isolation is a real possibility. Third, the nature of the initial training on offer – which may have been very concentrated, but brief, or have focused on one particular approach, model or set of materials – may have fostered dependence on a limited range of language or teaching approaches. This can act as a straitjacket on the teacher and eventually cause him or her to lose motivation. In Scotland, for example, the formalisation of foreign language teaching in the primary school within a new set of curriculum guidelines covering all four language skills and assessment and reporting on children's progress,[2] was accompanied by an acknowledgement by the First Minister of Scotland, that many teachers would not be able to implement some aspects without further training (Low, 2003).

This contribution will report on the rationale behind, and development of the PLEASE website (Primary Language teacher Education: Autonomy and Self-Evaluation), jointly developed by the Universities of Modena and Reggio Emilia, Italy, and Stirling, Scotland, as part of a Socrates Lingua Action 'A' project entitled 'Autonomy in Primary Language Teacher Education', conceived initially as a bilingual resource (English/Italian), even though it is hoped to extend it to include other European languages, subject to further funding.

This website is designed to help primary teachers recognise and overcome any dependencies they might feel and encourage them to become more active as language learners and users and agents for their own further development. In fact the website aims to provide a resource pool of ideas, activities and references, to stimulate a dynamic process of autonomous self-development for primary teachers of foreign languages, who can thus be described as both learners and teachers/facilitators, as the various sections and activities require the teachers' direct contribution and act as stimuli for group discussion and project work, under the guidance of a content Webmaster.[3]

The Project Description

The PLEASE sub-project is part of a three-year (1 September 1999–31 August 2001) – lately extended to four-year – European Co-operation Project (ECP) addressing the training needs, both initial and continuing, of primary teachers engaged in the delivery of a foreign language to their pupils.

The main purpose of the project was to foster autonomous learning and reflective teaching skills among primary language teachers and to raise awareness of their own skills and needs and of the impact of their teaching on the learners, to help their continuing professional development.[4]

As a consequence, on the assumption that the new technologies might be able to help teachers keep in touch, both with one another and with new developments in language teaching, and provide practical means whereby learners (teachers) can take a more active part in determining their own objectives and learning programmes on the basis of their actual needs, it was decided to produce a resource package for teacher self-development, including video and CD-ROM materials and a website.[5]

During the first year of the Lingua project the partners researched within and across their own countries, observing primary language classrooms and conducting surveys of teachers' views. Prototype video recordings of teaching and learning in actual primary language classrooms across Europe were also produced. This led to the drafting of two profiles,[6] one addressing language teaching skills, the other the teachers' own language proficiency.

During the second year of the project, it was decided to divide the original project into two sub-projects: one to focus on teachers' learning skills, the other on the teacher's own proficiency. The first sub-project was organised by the Universities of Münster and Granada, using video clips from actual primary language classrooms and focusing on language pedagogy and skills. The PLEASE website takes a different approach, fostering the language skills primary teachers use and need, both in the classroom and their professional self-development.

The Rationale of the PLEASE Website

Though recognising there is no shortage of teacher profiles in the various European countries, the research group felt a need for a definition of the language profile of the primary teacher that could be instrumental in highlighting the essential core of knowledge and understanding needed to underpin effective teaching, in terms of 'content' language (the language to be taught), 'management' language (the language needed to manage classroom activities and interaction), and effective professional development (cf. Bondi, 1999: 57). In addition, primary teachers are expected to be able to refer to their awareness of the language and their analytic skills to improve both their teaching and their own language learning.

In this way primary teachers will be acting as learners (checking their own knowledge and hypotheses by referring to dictionaries and grammars as well as authentic texts) and facilitators in the classroom (identifying and selecting suitable FL forms and functions to be taught, selecting materials on the basis of their appropriateness to the specific learning context and adapting them to the language level of their pupils if needed (cf. Bondi, 1999: 59).

On the basis of these issues, it was decided the website had to include:

- online grids and checklists for language assessment and needs analysis;
- online papers on classroom language;
- an exchange conferencing area.

The grids and the checklists will help teachers diagnose their language abilities, encourage them in the meantime to reflect on the accuracy of their self-assessment, and above all provide feedback on performance and advice for further improvement. In fact primary teachers are usually highly autonomous practitioners, often operating across the full range of the primary curriculum. As a consequence, there may at times be the danger of poor self-image for the primary teacher of a foreign language, partly because of the kind of training he or she has undergone (especially in the case of generalist primary teachers) but also because they may view themselves as poor relations compared with secondary school teachers, traditionally perceived to be language experts.[7]

The online papers include activities that require the reader to take an active role. Their function is to provide the teachers with some theoretically oriented background for their interaction with the learners, to stir their curiosity and interest and promote their active involvement.

Finally, the exchange conferencing area will expand on those parts of the online papers that already required the teachers' direct contribution, guiding them towards group discussion and project work. It will emphasise, above all, the importance and the advantages of collaborative learning, which can help teachers and trainees to monitor and reflect upon their own activities. This will ultimately contribute a boost to teacher confidence.

Moreover, since the research group felt the language profile of a primary teacher too wide-ranging to be defined in terms of general levels only (elementary, intermediate, advanced, etc.), it was decided to refer to the six levels of the Common European Framework of Reference (available at http://www.coe.int), assuming the required competence of an average primary language teacher should correspond more or less to the levels B1/B2 (Threshold and Vantage) of the Common European Framework (CEF).

Section 1 of the website (teacher self-assessment) is therefore based on the existing Common European Framework (CEF), as it has the benefit of not being specific to any one country or context, and has been designed with adult language learners/users and with self-assessment in mind. It consists of a series of levels across five language strands – listening, spoken interaction, spoken production, reading and writing. The Framework offers a continuum for identifying language proficiency within a self-assessment grid and as such, does not tend to highlight weaknesses – something we felt was important for our target audience of primary language teachers. In addition, we have also developed for the website, a set of specific descriptors (PLT – Primary Language Teachers) especially tailored to meet the needs of primary teachers.[8]

The Features of an Autonomous Learning Environment

One of the main aims of the project was to develop an innovative framework for ongoing support to complement rather than replace existing teacher-training programmes in the various countries. The end product was designed to enable primary teachers and trainees to acquire greater autonomy in developing their competence as foreign language teachers. Much attention has therefore been devoted to the features of the (virtual) learning environment.

On the one hand it is true that 'information systems and information technologies can promote the development of learner autonomy to the extent that they can stimulate, mediate and extend the range and scope of the social and psychological interaction on which all learning depends' (Little, 1996: 203). Nevertheless, there is a good deal of ambiguity in this relationship. In fact, the question of promoting teacher education and autonomy in a multimedia context highlights the fundamental conflict between autonomy (the notion that language learners should be encouraged to be in control) and the control exercised over them by the technological means (Esch, 1996: 35). It is the way self-access facilities are used, therefore, that determines whether independent learning takes place or not (cf. White, 1995). So in addition to the technical features we adopted, which were supposed to be designed in ways that would sustain the learners' self-motivation, we also employed a content Webmaster.

Since Nyns (1988) points out that many computer-assisted language learning programs fail to explore the educational potential of using the advanced technical capabilities of new generation computers in an imaginative way, we have tried to take into account the following pedagogical aspects in the design of the PLEASE website:

- provision of a variety of clearly identifiable links to different sections of the program to allow maximum user choice of routes through the activities proposed;
- incorporation of highlight signs in the texts to give users 'anchors' to identify quickly the new information that will be accessed;
- careful selection of visual and sound components to contextualise language forms and assist in clarifying meaning;
- incorporation of activities that encourage users to engage in conscious reflection on their behaviour, monitor the ways in which they have approached the tasks or activities, and evaluate the effectiveness of the procedures they have been using;
- the use of introductory screens that provide clear, concise and useful descriptions of program content;
- provision of interactive tasks that may cater for the needs of different styles: visually oriented (videos) aurally oriented (audio recordings). (Adapted from Watts, 1997: 5)

The Website Design

The home page introduces the PLEASE project and gives a brief description of the main topics the user will find in the different sections of the website, which can be accessed by means of a vertical menu bar on the left hand side of the page.

The main menu sections of the website are:

- test;[9]
- discussion materials;
- bibliography;
- resources;
- forum;
- chat line;
- help;
- partnerships/credits.

The test section is divided into three main parts:

- language for classroom use (teacher as a 'facilitator');
- language for professional self-development (teacher as 'language learner');
- language awareness (divided into two parts, as it includes a set of

items focusing on the teachers as a 'learner' and another set of items focusing on the teacher as a 'facilitator').

Users can choose which test to enter by means of a second menu bar, positioned at the bottom of the page, but before beginning the test, they are asked to fill in an IDENTITY CARD for statistical purposes, where they are asked about:

- status;
- years of experience in teaching;
- years of experience in foreign language primary teaching;
- if he or she is completing the test alone or with a colleague;
- if he or she is taking the test in his or her mother tongue or in a foreign language.

The READ ME button will give details about how to complete the test, which includes a total of 36 statements, covering five areas: listening, reading, spoken production, spoken interaction, and writing.

To encourage self-evaluation the website provides teachers with online checklists consisting of a series of statements. These have been specially adapted from the CEF B1 and B2 level descriptors to help teachers assess their communicative language and linguistic competences within the key contexts of the classroom and professional self-development.

For each statement the user can choose among four possible answers:

- Yes, I can
- My objective
- I don't know
- It's not relevant,

depending on whether he or she can actually master the ability described (Yes, I can); he or she would like to be able to perform it (My objective); is not sure whether he or she can actually master the ability (I don't know); thinks the ability in question is not particularly important in his or her working/personal situation (It's not relevant).

The third priority for development, namely language awareness, is addressed through a separate grid and checklist with 'I know' rather than 'I can' statements. Through engaging with these teachers should be made aware of the kinds of language proficiency needed to work in these specific contexts.

However, checklists aim to diagnose rather than merely confirm teachers' language abilities. In particular, they should encourage teachers to reflect on the accuracy of their self-assessment. The *process* is the key factor, not the award/awarding of a particular level, with teachers invited to assess their own strengths, identify their priorities and articulate the kinds of training needs or support they will need to accomplish their objectives. Teachers will, however, receive immediate feedback on 'performance' against the grids/checklists in relation to three possible levels of linguistic competence: B1, B1/B2 or B2. Moreover, more detailed feedback for each of the five areas of competence will be available by clicking on the name of the skill itself, as it appears on the screen. For more information about the navigation scheme of the site see Figure 17.1.

Two round icons will enable the teacher to compare the feedback he or she has received with the descriptors of the Common European Framework and with the adapted version of descriptors for primary language teachers (PLT descriptors). At this stage the teacher will be shown a PERSONAL DEVELOPMENT PLAN via the 'NOW WHAT' button: this personal plan summarises his or her answers to the original checklist, placing the 'Yes, I can' answers on one side of the screen (ideally making them correspond to the teacher's strengths – where he or she is now) and the 'My objective' answers on the others side of the screen (ideally making them correspond to the areas the teachers still has/wants/ to develop – where he or she wants to go, i.e. the skills he or she would like to master). This plan can be printed out or sent to the content Webmaster.

Suggestions on how to proceed (HOW TO GET THERE button) are provided by a series of pop-up windows that appear as the teacher selects the related link on the screen, and include:

- making a learning agreement;
- reviewing one's objectives;
- identifying one's priorities;
- getting some help (if the teacher feels like working towards the next higher CEF level).

The Interactive Section of the Website

Section Two of the website contains online papers on the key development area of wider ranging skills in language for classroom management. The papers contain expository sections whose function is to provide the teachers with some theoretical background for their interaction with pupils, stimulate their curiosity and interest, and promote their active involvement. Other parts of these online papers will invite teachers' direct contribution, promoting group discussion and project work, and emphasising above all the importance and advantages of collaborative

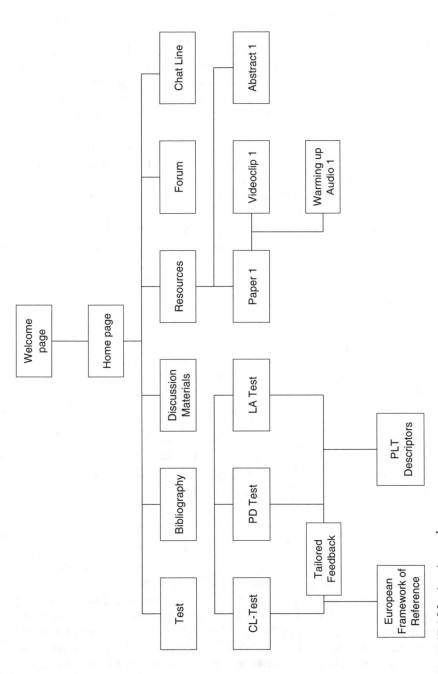

Figure 17.1 Navigation scheme

learning, seen as a vital component of the learning context for today and tomorrow (Bates, 1994).

Each paper is in English, but has been provided with a short abstract in Italian. Since these papers are meant to be accessed online (even though they are available in PDF format by clicking on the icon near the title), they have a warm-up button link to pre-reading activities and offer video clips (in Italian with an English translation and vice versa), audio texts and animations.

Section Three, the interactive section of the website, includes a forum and a chat line. The forum provides the sense of working as part of a community, as it gives access to messages from the Webmaster and other members of the group. In the forum teachers can access and download some materials (perhaps for future reference) stored in a common area on the central server, then hand in their comments via e-mail.

This common area can be used to store case studies and / or lecture presentations that demonstrate strategic behaviours, pose problems and arouse interest and discussion. Starting from a few sequences of the corpus on classroom discourse, or from one of the actual transcripts, it will be possible to show teachers several case studies, asking for their feedback. In this way teachers are asked to start from a concrete problem and to apply their problem-solving abilities to it.

The chat line will enable teachers to exchange messages in both an asynchronous and synchronous way, as they will be able – once they connect to the chat line – to discover who else is online at that particular moment and to engage in discussions with other members of the group and / or the Webmaster. This creates powerful gains, as a growing body of research on collaborative or co-operative learning has proved (cf. Kötter, 2002).

Messages exchanged in the forum and via the chat line can be sent as written text, audio recordings (to promote teachers' spoken productive skills) or a combination of the two.

Forms of Support in CMC

CMC (computer-mediated conferencing, the website, the forum and the chat line in the case of PLEASE) is beneficial to autonomous and collaborative activities because it can encourage active involvement and participation by granting the user a remarkable degree of control, and by allowing him or her to decide when to send, read, retrieve, archive and manipulate information (cf. Mozzon-McPherson, 1999: 124). Moreover, when CMC is resorted to 'the thoughts [can] be stopped and tinkered with' (Gage, 1986, in Harasim, 1990), provided there is appropriate guidance and support.

In fact, given the particular nature of the type of environment we are dealing with, it is necessary to devote particular attention and care to learner support, as the real challenge in making CMC successful consists in how to use it.

To such an extent we have, in the first place, tried to refer to 'self-motivation', that is 'a capacity that can and should be developed as an integral dimension of autonomy' (Ushioda, 1997: 38), which is of pivotal importance in optimising and sustaining one's involvement. For learners to become involved subjectively in their learning, they must be engaged in activities they can enjoy or feel good at, free from the controlling directives of the formal learning context. In short, language learning needs to cater for the learners' motivational agendas, and bring the world of their outside interests and experiences into play. This is why in the design of the PLEASE website we have tried to provide ample opportunities for teachers to raise issues, evaluate their own abilities, talk to other teachers, and so on, by referring to statements especially devised to tailor the context in which they are operating. In this way the learners will develop a particular kind of psychological relationship to the process and content of their learning that will provide the foundation for autonomous learning (Little, 1991: 4), and the experience should therefore become pleasant and rewarding (cf. Poppi, 2001: 150).

On the other hand, we felt a support role would be of vital importance. This support role, which has been identified in numerous projects as extremely useful (Esch & Makin, 1996: 48), is usually performed by advisers in language laboratories when computer-mediated learning is introduced. This adviser, who in practice takes on the role of the learner's mentor, can provide practical support and assistance aimed at encouraging the externalisation and making explicit use of metalinguistic and meta-cognitive processes that are of paramount importance as far as personal development is concerned.

However, in the case of the PLEASE website, since the various users are working entirely on their own, it was decided to have a content Webmaster who acts as a sort of online adviser/motivator. The Webmaster's task consists mainly in structuring and monitoring the online interventions by teachers, answering and directing topics, and providing answers to questions, back-up explanations and references. He also has to gather information from the chat to feedback into the forum, and to build a frequently asked question and answer page. Obviously his task involves carefully following what everyone is writing about, turning what is written into practical and constructive topics for discussion (based on teachers' own experiences), and providing some general perspectives that can be summarised and useful for all.[10]

The PLEASE content Webmaster has a wide experience with training teachers-to-be and, having piloted the use of the forum and the chat line with his students, has now started on a wider scale, with initial positive feedback from the in-service teachers involved.

Conclusions

Although the letter 'T' for teacher is missing in the PLEASE acronym for our website, the teacher is very much at the heart of the website in terms of the language learning pupils undertake at primary school. Moreover, even though the project was addressed to teachers, it was taken for granted it would inevitably influence their teaching and their learners' learning process as a whole. We therefore felt that if we were to achieve progress in the promotion of learner autonomy, we had to bring our focus of concern back to the teacher, and especially to the way in which teacher education is organised and mediated.

Moreover, keeping in mind Rogers's comment (1969: 104) (even though this refers to men, while language teachers are more often women), 'The only man who is educated is the man who has learned how to adapt and change; the man who has realised that no knowledge is secure, that only the process of seeking knowledge gives basis for security', we have attempted to devise an online instrument that we hope is easily accessible and user-friendly and also easily up-dated and therefore extremely flexible and appropriate to meet the different needs of a wide range of teachers operating in many and varied contexts.

Acknowledgements

Special thanks must go to Laura Ascari and Giulio Fregni, the two IT people who actually 'made our ideas come true'.

Notes

1. An experimental project is currently being tested in 250 primary schools in Italy. This is aimed at teachers and other members of staff in the last two years of kindergarten and the first two years of primary schools. It is e-learning based and consists of several courses and a forum that can be accessed via Internet. Two of the authors of the present contribution, Marina Bondi and Franca Poppi, have actually been involved in the development of two of these courses, one devoted to the development of early learning strategies and the other to how to establish and develop oral communication inside the classroom.
2. Modern Languages, National Guidelines (2000) Learning and Teaching Scotland.
3. The piloting phase has seen the involvement of students training to be teachers at the University of Parma (Faculty of Sciences of Education). Other target teachers have been pointed towards the website by means of meetings held at the University of Modena and letters addressed to the various primary schools of the area of Modena, Parma and Reggio Emilia. In Scotland, primary teachers

have also been introduced to the website through conferences and meetings organised by Scottish CILT. In this way a network of teachers (both in-service and student-teachers) and primary schools has been created, co-ordinated and supervised by the content Webmaster, who moderates both the forum and the chat.

4. Cf. http://www.ioe.stir.ac.uk/lingua/overview.htm
5. Cf. http://www.ioe.stir.ac.uk/lingua/overview.htm The address of the PLEASE website is: http://www.please.unimo.it
6. These profiles and the results of the project's research can be accessed at: http://www.ioe.stir.ac.uk/lingua in English, German, Italian and Spanish. Moreover, the profiles are also published in Faber *et al.* 1999.
7. Secondary teachers in fact are in a position to criticise or even ignore the work done by primary teachers in introducing the foreign language to their pupils, claiming the pupils were not properly prepared on arrival at the secondary school.
8. Basically the PLT descriptors consist in an especially adapted version of the CEF for primary language teachers.
9. The word 'test' has been used, even though, as will become clear by looking at the website, this section actually involves self-assessment activities.
10. G.M. Alessi (PLEASE website content Webmaster): personal communication to Marina Bondi).

References

Bates, A.W. (1994) *Educational Multi-media in a Networked Society. World Conference on Educational Multimedia.* Vancouver: Ottman and Tomek.

Bondi, M. (1999) Towards a language profile for the primary foreign language teacher. In P. Faber, W. Gewehr, M. J. Jiménez Raya and A.J. Peck (eds) *Effective Foreign Language Teaching at the Primary Level* (pp. 39–50). Munich: Peter Lang.

Esch, E. (1996) Promoting learner autonomy: Criteria for the selection of appropriate methods. In R. Pemberton, E.S.L. Li, W.W.F. Or and H.D. Pierson (eds) *Taking Control: Autonomy in Language Learning* (pp. 35–48). Hong Kong: Hong Kong University Press.

Esch, E. and Makin, L. (1996) La formation à l'apprentissage: Une nouvelle forme d'enseignement. In G. Aub-Buscher (ed.) *The Linguistic Challenge of the New Europe* (pp. 35–48). Plymouth: CercleS.

Harasim, L. (1990) (ed.) *Online Education: Perspectives on a New Environment.* New York: Praeger.

Kötter, M. (2002) *Tandem Learning on the Internet.* Frankfurt am Main: Peter Lang.

Little, D. (1991) *Learner Autonomy: Definitions, Issues and Problems.* Dublin: Authentik.

Little, D. (1996) Freedom to learn and compulsion to interact: Promoting learner autonomy through the use of information systems and information technologies. In R. Pemberton, E.S.L. Li, W.W.F. Or and H.D. Pierson (eds) *Taking Control: Autonomy in Language Learning* (pp. 203–18). Hong Kong: Hong Kong University Press.

Low, L. (2003) Modern languages. In T.G.K. Bryce and W.M. Hume (eds) *Scottish Education* (2nd edn) (pp. 5–14). Edinburgh: Edinburgh University Press.

Mozzon-McPherson, M. (1999) Encounters of a third kind: An analysis of the use of the computer-mediated environment in relation to learner autonomy. In D. Bickerton and M. Gotti (eds) *Language Centres: Integration through Innovation* (pp. 113–127). Plymouth: CercleS.

Nyns, R.R. (1988) Using the computer to teach comprehension skills. *ELT Journal* 42, 253–61. Online documents http://www.ioe.stir.ac.uk/lingua; http://www.coe.int; http://www.please.unimo.it

Poppi, F. (2001) Learning support systems and learning environments. In M. Mozzon-McPherson and R. Vismans (eds) *Beyond Language Teaching, Towards Language Advising* (pp. 149–60). London: CILT.

Rogers, C. R. (1969) *Freedom to Learn.* Columbus, OH: Charles E.

Ushioda, E. (1997) The role of motivational thinking in autonomous language learning. In D. Little and B. Voss (eds) *Language Centres: Planning for the New Millennium* (pp. 38–50). Plymouth: CercleS.

Watts, N. (1997) A learner-based design model for interactive multimedia language learning packages. *System* 25, 1–8.

White, C. (1995) Autonomy and strategy use in distance foreign language learning: Research findings. *System* 23 (2), 207–21.

Chapter 18

Exploring Zones of Interactivity in Foreign Language and Bilingual Teacher Education

DO COYLE

Introduction

This chapter seeks to provide a critical exploration of the development of a unique pilot network of Teaching and Learning Observatory (TLO) sites used to enhance the pre- and in-service education of foreign language and bilingual teachers. The TLO currently links a national and international hub of ten secondary schools with a training institution through innovative video conferencing facilities and interactive technology: pan/zoom/tilt cameras, six ISDN video conferencing with large screen facility, 'hot tables' and interactive whiteboards. The initial idea of the TLO was based on a pragmatic need for groups of modern language and immersion trainee teachers to observe 'expert teachers' in action, for tutors at a distance to observe and co-reflect on lessons taught by trainee teachers, as well as to provide a 'safe' environment for trainees to experiment with 'distance' micro-teaching. However, the TLO is emerging as an unprecedented powerful learning, teaching, training and research tool that currently involves key players – learners, trainees, teachers, mentors, trainers and researchers – interacting in alternative pedagogic settings. The technology facilitates interactive learning and teaching episodes in 'scaffolded zones' through the collaborative construction of dynamic learning communities. Many different 'voices' have a place in the quest for deepening professional understanding and autonomy and as such are engaged in redefining classroom boundaries and the roles played by those within and without.

The TLO concept then had its origins in a pragmatic need for over 60 trainee teachers specialising in modern languages (particularly German, Japanese and Russian but also French and Spanish) and immersion/bilingual education (Geography, History and Science to be taught through the medium of French/German), to have a greater variety of school-based experiences not readily accessible within the immediate locality of the University of Nottingham, UK. The pre-service post-graduate teacher-training programme in the UK (PGCE) has a statutory requirement for trainees to spend 24–36 weeks engaged in school-based work. Although the University of Nottingham is the main national training institution for Russian, Japanese and bilingual teaching, our local partnership of schools was not in a position to offer school-based training in all these specialised areas. In addition, as teacher educators, we also wanted large numbers of trainees to share lesson observations and participate in exemplary foreign language classroom practice focusing on challenging issues such as learner development of spontaneous language and effective use of target language with a range of learners. It was felt that shared experiences and observations would allow teachers, trainees and trainers to discuss, analyse and deconstruct observed practice, without having to spend time travelling to different schools and crowding into classrooms. There was also a need to involve foreign language trainees in statutory ICT applications through the authentic use of technologies to enhance their own training experiences and prepare them better for incorporating a range of new technologies into their future teaching repertoire.

The Training Schools Initiative, set up by the national ministry (Department for Education and Skills) in September 2000, provided the university and a state comprehensive school, Hockerill Anglo-European College in Hertfordshire, England, with an ideal platform from which to launch the first two remote sites within the TLO network. This particular school was selected not only because of its innovative approach to language teaching (it has a *'section bilingue'* and has recognised national specialist status as a Language College) and its strong links with a university, but also because of its potential as a training school as set out below:

A Training School will demonstrate and develop excellent practice across the portfolio of training, including initial teacher training (ITT) and the continuing training of teachers in schools. It will, in partnership with ITT providers and other schools:

- try out new approaches to training and developing teachers;
- carry out and use teacher research; and
- share and disseminate good practice more widely. (www.standards.dfes.gov.uk/trainingschools)

The Training Schools programme, part of the government's national diversity agenda, designed 'to support schools to develop their strengths, to contribute to other schools and the wider community' (www.

standards.dfes.gov.uk/diversity) had a focus on school-based elements of initial teacher training. The Training Schools programme, moreover, provided funding directly to designated schools that are not only promoted as 'ambitious, imaginative and influential' but also 'work collaboratively with others for the benefit of staff and pupils beyond their own boundaries'. It was against this backdrop that the first two remote pilot sites, approximately 150 miles apart, were equipped according to defined specifications in consultation with the Promethean Company, UK. Each site has two large interactive wall screens: a video stream – the 'window' for sharing each others' classrooms – where pan/zoom cameras facilitate two-way visioning teaching scenarios ranging from the whole class to an individual's work; and an interactive whiteboard, to enable different sites to share digital resources, OHTs or write on each others' white boards actively and synchronously. 'Hot tables' switch microphones to facilitate sharing and interacting in small group work between remote sites. However, each site has the power to control which interactive facilities to use as well as decide who has permission to control the site's camera. It is thus impossible for one site to access another site without mutual consent.

The Vision

The initial TLO was based on a vision common to the school and university, rooted in an articulation and realisation of constructing a 'learning community', encompassing our shared values implicit in the learning process. At the core of the TLO community lay creative and quality interactions between teachers, trainers and learners, set within an ethos of learning at all levels. The training of new foreign language teachers was thus situated in this context. The programme is now in its fourth year. Each year in excess of 60 trainees and several hundred school students are involved. Each year the network grows as more schools join and pedagogic activity evolves (ref. Table 18.1). Moreover, in working towards our vision of co-constructing a 'learning community' within a pre-service foreign-language teacher education context, the research agenda was firmly rooted in an exploration of how an interactive training tool might be embedded into the joint praxis of foreign-language teacher educators, their trainees and teachers and learners in a training school. Hence, in parallel with the development of TLO activity or practice came a growing need to make sense of and articulate its theoretical underpinning.

Adopting a Theoretical Framework for Investigating TLO Activity

Social constructivism provides a theoretical approach to learning in which students construct their own knowledge as a result of interacting

Table 18.1 Affordances and constraints of activities within multiple zones of development in the TLO

Zone of Development	Activity	Data source	Affordances	Constraints
Observing	Trainees observe expert FL/immersion teachers in a range of settings/classes. Collective post-lesson deconstruction by teachers, trainees and university tutors	Tutor field notes. Development of agreed lesson observation schedule filled in by observing trainees Interviews of trainee focus groups Video recording of lessons/debrief	Capacity for meta-talk by tutors and trainees whilst lesson is in progress (observing site can switch off own sound) enhances collective understanding of teaching in authentic contextImproved accessibility to authentic classroom contexts via non-intrusive lesson observationHighly motivating	Developing the habit and practice of working in the TLO Developing skills to use technology effectively (e.g. manipulate the cameras) Organisational skills for VC linking Dealing with issues of social presence Responding to ethical demands
Teaching and learning	Trainees observe expert FL teachers conduct lessons in trainees' 2nd, 3rd FL Subject knowledge enhancement, SKE	Focus group interviews of trainees Trainee work carried out in self-directed study programme (SKE)	Improves subject knowledge base of trainees' weaker FL at the university site while being situated in real classroom practice	Organisational, e.g. synchronising trainee SKE sessions with lesson timetablesEthics, developing the protocol re: data protection
	Teaching conducted by trainee with remote observation by tutor including collaborative post-lesson deconstruction and analysis	Video recording of interaction with supporting evidence: electronic lesson plans and lesson observations, tutor reports, field notes and target setting sheets	Remote interaction by tutor Easier access to a range of classes without having to travel long distances to observe one lesson Effective use of time Quality of debriefing and deconstruction sometimes enhanced through accessibility	Working with potential differences in student-learner behaviour in a VC lessonInteractive sequences (teaching, observing, discussing) in TLO is not same experience as in class, i.e. issues of social presence, e.g. eye contact via the cameras Post-lesson discussion not as spontaneous as in f2f, slight time lag Ethics of observing (see protocol)

Table 18.1 (*cont.*) Affordances and constraints of activities within multiple zones of development in the TLO

Zone of Development	Activity	Data source	Affordances	Constraints
Teaching and learning	Trainees carry out distance micro-teaching episodes supported by the teacher in the remote classroom and observed by tutor	As above	Remote micro-teaching. Within a 'safe' environment trainees 'try out' teaching with real learners. Developing observation, analytical reflective skills. Awareness raising concept of distance teachingInnovative and motivating-trigger for reflection	Social presence, e.g. in remote micro-teaching difficult to react with students, so need teacher in remote site to mediate. Need to establish habits and 'rules' modus operandi
Communicating (interacting and reflecting)	Virtual meetings between teachers, trainers, trainees (and sometimes technicians) to discuss, plan and reflect on activity	Electronic minutes of meetings. Video recorded meetings. Follow up web cam 121 meetings	Synchronicity, immediacy and relevanceFrequency increased	A new style of interactivity emerges (social presence), e.g. develop strategies for interruptions
	Trainee conferences with teachers and/or students to discuss issues such as use of target language/managing classroom behaviour	Video recording the conferences. Trainee focus groups	Excellent use of timeImmediacy of trainees being able to ask 'expert' practitioners as well as have tutor views	None – except co-ordinating synchronouscommunication
Developing professionally	Using and sharing digital resources but especially interactive whiteboards,e.g. use of Power Point and Internet, during lessons with trainees, teachers and learners supported by tutors	Resource bank of materials created and recycled, improved on following year and evaluated by trainees	Planning, creating, using, monitoring the effectiveness of and evaluating materials using ICT in real time during authentic lessonsEncourages creativity for trainees, studentsHighly motivating and relevant resourcesEmbedding ICT in lessons	Time to develop technological skills and understand the scope and limitations of the technology

Table 18.1 (*cont.*) Affordances and constraints of activities within multiple zones of development in the TLO

Zone of Development	Activity	Data source	Affordances	Constraints
Developing professionally	Linking interactive whiteboards use with enhance Literacy Awareness in MFL and immersion lessons	Video recording of specific lessons Observation of lessons by tutors Materials bank	Sharing materials by teachers & students at different sites. Communal resource bank set up Ever increasing involvement of learners in the interactivity which has traditionally been reserved for trainees, tutors and teachers Capacity for synchronous interactivity between two remote sites	As above
	Participation in mentor training by teachers/ mentors at school site taking place at remote university site	Field notes	Effective use of time Less expensive than incurring travel costs Teachers can extend their community	Issues of appropriateness of technology Need to plan sessions with remote teachers in mind (social presence)
	Support of beginning teacher at school site by university tutors	Observation schedules by tutor, questionnaires to students, focus group interviews and final interview with teacher	Support by experts Different 'voices' to consult from 'outside' the school	
	Creating training materials from video recordings and data collected	Resources bank of materials created and recycled	Self-directed learning library to support trainee foreign language and teaching development	Time needed to edit the videos and create training tasks in a self-access format

Table 18.1 (*cont.*) Affordances and constraints of activities within multiple zones of development in the TLO

Zone of Development	Activity	Data source	Affordances	Constraints
Researching	Researchers/tutors monitoring the development of 11-year-old beginner learners' spontaneous talk in the target language German & French throughout 1 academic year	Cycle of lesson observations video recorded analysed for critical incidents, reviewed by the teacher as well as researcher Learner questionnaires/focus group interviews Tests used to compare level of talk at end of year with national norms	Non-intrusive longitudinal observation of classroom practice Gradual involvement of learners in research process Contribution to the research intelligence in this crucial field Involvement of teachers in the research process had 'knock-on 'effect for professional development. Teachers researched practice alongside the researchers Motivating, empowering use of TLO to support teacher development, student learning, recycled into training programme Virtual relationship develops between researchers and class Breaks down traditional classroom barriers	Ethics of using videoed classroom data Vast quantity of data collected Analysis requires transcription of data to gain a coherent picture

with their environment and of mediating their understanding through meaningful cultural and social contexts contained within. Based on the contributions of theorists such as Vygotsky (1978) and Bruner (1990), social constructivism posits that learning and development is a social collaborative activity in which the community plays a central role in assisting learners to 'make meaning'. In contrast, working within the zone of actual development (ZAD) (Vygotsky, 1978), learners alone can construct only an individual and limited view of the world. However, if they are to share ideas and understanding with knowledgeable others this will lead to further developments in understanding and 'knowledge construction' (Dwyer, 1996) as learning in this case takes place within the zone of proximal development (ZPD), (Vygotsky, 1978). Social constructivism, therefore, supports a context-based communicative perspective on learning and teaching which foregrounds two crucial elements: learning though communication in a meaningful context and the need for scaffolded environments to help co-construct and negotiate meaning (McLoughlin & Oliver, 1998).

Reviewing the guiding principles underpinning the TLO suggests that building on the notion of collaborative learning and co-constructed understanding elevates the ZPD to a pivotal position. The ZPD implies that learning through, with and in the TLO is a coordinated activity with all participants responsible for contributing to creating meaning. Moreover, according to Smith (1999) 'It is not so much that learners acquire structures or models to understand the world, but they participate in a community of practice.' In this sense, TLO activity aligns itself to the work of Lave and Wenger, where '[learning is an] evolving, continuously renewed set of relations' (Lave & Wenger, 1991: 50). This would suggest that collective learning situated within our TLO learning community results in the construction of:

> practices that reflect both the pursuit of our enterprises and the attendant social relations. These practices are thus the property of a kind of community created over time by the sustained pursuit of a shared enterprise. It makes sense, therefore, to call these kinds of communities 'communities of practice'. (Wenger, 1998: 4)

and that 'new knowledge and learning are properly conceived as being located in communities of practice', (Tennant 1997: 77). However, what is distinctive about the TLO 'community of practice' is that this community is both virtual and real since it is founded upon interaction and learning mediated in, with and through ICT. Certainly, the question as to whether the technology or the participants determine how the community functions in terms of affordances and constraints within virtually constructed zones of development is a crucial one. To make sense of the complex web of activity operating within the TLO during the initial phase, it was decided to investigate the multiple 'scaffolded' and interactive zones within our community of practice. Whilst the boundaries between zones are fluid, activity within the zones may overlap, or be dependent, yet the synergy generated is likely to influence the extent and the quality of learning within the community. There was therefore a need from within to evaluate the efficacy of our practice to understand it better and to explore the potential for richer and deeper construction of knowledge.

Within the overall social constructivist framework of the research, five zones emerged from the foreign language teacher education setting/TLO community. These are identified as zones for observing, teaching and learning, communicating (interacting and reflecting), developing professionally and researching. A sample of activities within each zone is provided as follows:

Observing

- non-intrusive lesson observations in real time of expert modern languages or immersion teachers in their classes by large groups of trainee teachers;
- observation of lessons conducted in a foreign language that is not necessarily the trainees' first foreign language: this allowed trainees to update their skills – especially in terms of classroom language and giving instructions – in their third language in preparation for their practicum.

Teaching and learning

- individual remote support by tutors and observations of lessons taught by trainees during their teaching practice based at the remote school site;
- trainees experimenting with and carrying out micro-teaching activities in French and German for school students based at the remote site.

Communicating

- virtual meetings between teachers, tutors, trainees and technicians;
- trainee video conferences linking learners, teachers and trainees to discuss learning and teaching issues, lesson organisation and management issues.

Professional development

- sharing interactive whiteboard applications between the two sites, e.g. trainees creating and using digital teaching materials (especially using power point, web-quests and internet sites) with remote classes;
- trainee-teacher experimentation with interactive whiteboard use in order to enhance literacy awareness;
- teachers at one site participating in mentor training taking place at the other site;
- newly qualified teacher (NQT) support for History/Geography taught in German with a challenging class of 14-year-old learners;
- using edited video recorded lessons and related data to create training materials for foreign language trainees.

Research

- observation and longitudinal research into the development of foreign language strategic classrooms, e.g. focusing on spontaneous talk in a class of beginning 11-year-old French learners and a similar class for German during one school year;
- observation and analysis of the use of the TLO by a team of researchers.

Inquiry into the zones was centred around a variety of data collection methods depending on the nature of the activities. These included tutor-researcher field notes, VC observation notes, trainee logs or diaries, trainee focus groups for discussion, school learner interviews, teacher interviews, teacher stimulus recall techniques and video recording VC activity. To co-construct the TLO with the reader, a sample of the data collected between 2001 and 2003 and analysed from the zones is presented here.

Co-constructing the zones: Multiple voices tell their stories

Extract One: The Observing Zone

Trainee Teacher Reflective Log (RW2)

Observing classes which are taking place far from where we are at the time is a less intrusive way of observing classes and being able then to discuss the lesson immediately afterwards. It is clear that such technology will prove to be very useful for PGCE students in the future and any collaborative work which the School of Education wants to do with schools wanting to advance bilingual education.

Extract Two: The Teaching and Learning Zone

University Tutor Report/Field Notes (AF1) written after a discussion and observation of a lesson given by a trainee and one of his tutees.

An 'affordance' of the use of the TLO was that I could jointly observe the lesson with a colleague; we were able to discuss the unfolding lesson in a way that would not have been possible if we had been present in person ... I wondered if the debrief was rather more focused and business-like ... It was certainly shorter than debriefs undertaken when present in person ... I also noted there were 'efficiency' gains in terms of avoiding the need for a 250-mile round trip.

Extract Three: The Teaching and Learning Zone

Trainee Teacher Log (PR4)

The Teaching Observatory is a tremendous resource which has allowed me and other PGCE students who are interested in bilingual education to experiment with teaching classes at a distance and to analyse the associated strengths and weaknesses of this kind of teaching. Teaching lessons where we have used some of the new technologies such as shared Power Point and interactive whiteboards has made us familiar with what are the strengths and weaknesses of these teaching methods as well.

Extract Four: Overlapping Professional Development and Research Zones

Transcript of TLO lesson during research into monitoring and recording teacher strategies for promoting spontaneous talk

The following classroom scenario observed in the TLO by researcher and tutor, was selected as one in a series of 'critical' incidents for research purposes, since it demonstrates the scaffolding of learners by each other as well as by the teacher; the recycling of new language and its transference to student-initiated contexts; whole class contributions to constructing the phrase needed in order to say what they wanted; and examples of self-regulation and interactivity. It makes teaching and learning strategies accessible and available to the community. The students had been learning German for only one month. The extract takes place entirely in German.

T: *Tom? [xxx?]*
L1:   *Ich bin tot.* [I am dead].
T: *Oh! Schade. Du kannst nicht die Prüfung machen.* [Oh. What a shame.
         You can't do the test then]
L: *Jaaaaa!* [Yeah!]
Ls: *Juhu! Jaa!* [Many voices] [Yipee. Yeah!]
T: *Tom ist tot!* [Tom is dead].
L2:   *Wie sagt man 'Party'?* [How do you say 'Party'?]
T: *Das ist ganz einfach. 'eine Party'* [That's very simple. 'a party.']
Ls: *eine Party.* [many voices][A party.]
L3:   *Wie sagt man 'Can I throw him out of the window' auf deutsch?* [How do
         you say 'Can I throw him out of the window' in German?]
T: *Das kannst du sagen. OK. Schschsch. Wer kann . . . wer kann Paul
         helfen? Wir beginnen. . . . Also: Fenster. Wir haben 'Fenster'. Also, gut,
         was können wir sonst noch sagen? Ja?* [You can say that. OK. Shush.
         Who can . . . who can help Paul? We start . . . So: window. We have
         'window. OK, what else can we say? Yes?]
L3:   *Kann ich . . . ?* [Can I . . . ?]
T: *Kann ich . . . Fenster . . . wer ist das?* [Can I . . . window . . . who's that?]
Ls: *Tom.* [many voices] [*Tom*].
T: *Also: 'Kann ich Tom Fenster . . . mmmm?'* [The *mmm* is a sound the
         teacher often makes to indicate placing the next word / verb][So:
         'Can I Tom window . . . mmmm?']
L4:   *ausziehen.* [Take off clothes]
T: *ausziehen?* [T gesturing as if taking off clothes] [Take off clothes?]
Ls: –laugh [whole class laughs here at their misunderstanding of the
         teacher's gesture]
T: *Hört zu? Hört zu: 'werfen'* [accompanied by throwing gesture] [Lis-
         ten? Listen. 'throw']
Ls: *werfen.* [many voices][throw]
Ls: *Kann ich Tom werfen die Fenster?* [many voices][Can I throw Tom
         out of the window?]
T: *Kann ich Tom aus dem Fenster werfen? . . . Oh, ich möchte kein Englisch
         hören da. Gut, Tom. Tom, du machst die Prüfung. Ja? Du bist nicht tot.
         Sonst werfen sie dich aus dem Fenster.* [Can I throw Tom out of the
         window? . . . Oh, I don't want to hear any English there. Good,
         Tom . . . Tom, you do the test. Yes? You are not dead. Otherwise,
         they're going to throw you out of the window.]

This extract was reviewed on video after the VC lesson and subsequently discussed using stimulus recall techniques with the teacher along
with a trainee, tutor and researcher. Whilst the trainee was able to 'see how

the strategies were unravelling in front of her very eyes, without needing teaching materials and other stuff – just the teacher's use of her own classroom language' – the teacher (KR1) was engaged in the process of articulating her own practice and reflecting on what she did explicitly and implicitly.

> I think I respond to a set of principles which I have in my head which are (a) you've got to get as much out of the kids as possible without giving it to them, (b) you've got to encourage them and help them . . . they are quite simple principles and you kind of apply them to whatever situation . . . getting them to use what they've got, encouraging them – I think the scaffolding comes from encouraging principle.

Extract Five: Research Zone

School Student Interviews

I = interviewer
L1, L2, L3 = three student interviewees (12-year-old learners) at end of first year of secondary school, having worked in the TLO for one year.
I: This year, you've been involved in helping to train teachers in Nottingham, because they've been watching some of your lessons. What does that feel like to know that you're training teachers?
L1:   [. . . , it's fun.
I: Why?
L1:   [..] Errr, it's sort of weird, because you expect teachers to teach you and then like 'Wow' you can teach a teacher. So, . . .
I: So, if you had some recommendations to make that I could pass on to my student teachers, what would you say is important for them to be good languages teachers?
L1:   To . . . I think what Mr X does is really good that he always speaks in French and, errr, just to make sure that you understand before . . . that everyone understands before you carry on. [. . .]
I: Anything else? What's that felt like?
L2:   Errr, a bit nervous, but then you just get used to it . . . because you feel like you're helping someone, but you're also very nervous, because you can see all the people on the thing [screen] watching you, but then when they turn it off, so it's like a normal lesson, it's alright. I'm not nervous anymore.
I: No. How do you think it's helped the student teachers? How do you think it's helped the trainee teachers?
L2:   Errm, because . . . 'cause they can see how you . . . we're being taught and they can see what they need to improve on and im-

prove on that. And then the teachers can tell them while they're watching what they've done wrong and they can improve on that.

L3:   Errm, we just sort of, like, try and ignore the cameras, 'cause otherwise then you get a bit sort of nervous and it's, like, 'Oh, what if I say the wrong thing?' and ... but it's not too bad, 'cause you know once you get used to it, like the first lesson was a bit 'Arrgghh', but once you get used to it it's OK, so you don't really notice.

I: What does it feel like to know that you're helping to train teachers?

L3:   It's quite a big responsibility,'cause if you say the wrong thing ... you know you might sort of give the school a bad reputation and if things ... and it's quite hard at first, but it's OK once you learn new things, so you can actually talk in French more.

Affordances and Constraints of Working in the TLO Community

The data analysis along with collective experiences of working in the TLO clearly gave rise to articulating and reporting affordances and constraints brought to the surface through redefining our working practices (see Table 18.1). In listening to different voices speaking in different tongues within the TLO community, an emerging discourse begins to take shape that has at its very core interaction and a sense of co-constructing 'shared meanings' with alternative boundaries. Certainly the theoretical framework adopted promotes 'learning' as an interactive and social activity that is substantiated by evidence based on TLO activity. However, the voices tell stories that lie outside the more traditional conceptualisation of 'foreign language teacher training' processes, where trainees observe expert teachers before practising their own teaching, supported by experts. Through facilitating interaction and the co-construction of different aspects of learning to teach within the five zones, the technology enables and mediates professional activity so the definition of learner, teacher, tutor and researcher roles becomes more fluid and responsive.

The articulation of practice by the TLO teachers has made the classroom interaction situated in a particular setting with a particular class both explicit and transparent. This is fundamentally different from a prescriptive *quick fix* approach to understanding teaching using broad brushstrokes, since the involvement of trainees, learners and their tutors in complementary discourse has led to shared ownership and deeper understandings. The very core of TLO activity has been transformed through extending the observation of foreign language lessons into a highly participatory process and opening classroom activity and interactivity to analysis, discussion and collaborative reflection by large groups of trainees based on genuinely communal experiences. Learners are also involved in that process and, having had their own awareness raised about what it is to learn to teach, become more aware of their own learning. Moreover, the analysis of lessons through joint selection of 'critical incidents' by researchers, tutors, trainees and the teachers who conducted them, has turned the complexities of progression in learning over a period of time into a video repertoire of events telling their own story. They can be identified, described, revisited, evaluated and transformed. A year-long sequence of chapters or 'critical incidents' from targeted classes, tracks events in student learning and teacher input alongside a teacher commentary. The teachers' commentaries make the implicit explicit (e.g. teaching strategies that were deliberate and those that were intuitive) and involve the teachers in researching their own practice while trainees interpret and share this very practice synchronously with the learners and the teachers. Hence the TLO provides the means for 'shared inquiries into practice' (Hargreaves, 2002). The interactivity is dialogic and multi-layered, using foreign languages as well as mother tongue, constructing classroom talk and professional dialogue, negotiating shared meanings and teaching-learning discourse.

However, while 'new technologies give us opportunities to rethink educational relationships' (Pouts-Lajus & Riche-Magnier, 2000), I would not wish to give the reader the impression that 'rethinking' has been straightforward. Using technology in alternative ways has been uncertain and complex. Certainly, responding to technical, social and ethical constraints and challenges that emerged from working in 'uncharted territory' has been demanding. Alternative technical demands have required all those involved in the TLO to work with and through the technology – without the exclusive support of technicians. Trouble-shooting and managing VC links are time consuming. Addressing issues such as broadband links or ISDN connectivity is complex. Driving one's own professional development not only to develop skills in the use of the technology but to use it effectively brings with it shared but very 'real' responsibilities.

In terms of social behaviours an understanding of alternative sets of strategies has developed over time to try to overcome medium-related communication problems and counterbalance a potential loss of interactivity and spontaneity (Sellen, 1995). Moreover, if the quality of interaction, collaborative learning and learner satisfaction is linked to 'social presence' (White, 2003) then the TLO community in its early stages had to heed Tammelin's (1998) warning:

> Teachers who have little or no prior personal experience in telematically mediated learning environments may experience some

difficulty in coping with them unless they are aware of the existence and potential significance of *presence* in such mediated environments. (http://www.hkkk.fi/~tammelin/MEP8.tammelin.html)

The construct of 'social presence' defined by Garrison (1997) as 'the degree individuals project themselves though the medium both verbally and non-verbally', has led to an evolving *modus operandi* through strategies that seek to acknowledge and address problems such as time delays, interruption, turn-taking, eye contact, conversational cues and control during VC-mediated interactivity in all the zones. In particular, a protocol has developed within the community to manage the transition between observation mode (where one site is non-participatory) to interactive (where both sites communicate), using an invitation procedure during a VC link. Sensitivity about the ethics of learner awareness in classrooms as to whether or not learners were being observed from a remote site or were required to interact with 'distant' others was crucial to the community in order to dispel fears of CCTV and 'Big Brother'. The protocol that was developed, establishes two-way contact at the start and end of every VC link – even if the objective is for one site to engage in non-intrusive observation. The process is transparent for all participants at all times. Working within the professional development zone, for example, requires individuals to invite other members of the community to engage collaboratively in joint work (e.g. supporting a beginning teacher). All members of the community must be 'willing' participants in any TLO activity – it is not an assessment mechanism. The TLO is based on the principle of shared ownership where all members of the community must agree on the outcomes and uses of TLO work, e.g. video recorded lessons to be edited for training purposes. Other ethical questions concerning permission to video record VC activity, using VC work for research purposes and legally protecting those involved in the TLO activity have also had to be resolved between schools and the university.

Pause for Reflection

Learning to accept that innovative practice can be uncomfortable and to balance realism with vision in terms of what can be achieved, has in fact knitted the community more closely together. Ultimately, according to Doolittle, Hicks and Lee (2002), 'technologies should be used as engagers and facilitators of thinking and knowledge constructors' for which they propose:

- Learning and instruction are facilitated when teachers, learners and trainees are prepared to use technology as a tool for inquiry.

- Learning is enhanced when technology is used to create authenticity within the classroom or training setting.
- All those involved in the learning process acquire multiple perspectives on issues when technology is used to enhance social interaction with other learners, learners in remote locations, and experts.

Doolittle *et al.* summarise as follows:

> Technology must serve to facilitate the creation of meaning and disciplined knowledge within each student, and not to serve as a substitute . . . for 'teacher talk' . . . technology must be used to create authentic experiences that link new knowledge to prior knowledge, in a socially interactive environment where questions being pursued are relevant to the student . . . (Doolittle *et al.*, 2002: 14)

It could be argued that the evolving TLO activity described in this chapter goes beyond the creation of meaning and knowledge 'within each student' since interaction and teacher talk are extended so that, in effect, knowledge constructed is knowledge shared by and for the TLO community. These outcomes appear to coincide with what Holmes *et al.* (2001) described as 'communal constructivism', a construct that:

> Conveys a meaning that captures specific elements of the additional value that various forms of ICT bring to learning environments, specifically the different forms of virtual and community building, as well as the different ways in which knowledge is constructed and shared and reconstructed. (Holmes *et al.*, 2001: 3)

As the TLO evolves from its early conception as a non-intrusive observation instrument and the two pilot sites have grown into the current 'innovative practice hub' comprising ten institutions, as the complexity of inter-site communal understanding of learning and teaching grows and TLO capability extends to include new activity that is reshaping classroom boundaries, the potential of the TLO as a powerful conduit and facilitator for community building rooted in real life contexts also evolves (Jacobs & Rodgers, 1997; Laurillard, 1993). The story continues.

References

Bruner, J. (1990) *Acts of Meaning*. Cambridge, MA: Harvard University Press.
Department for Education and Skills (DfES) – Online document: www.standards.dfes.gov.uk/diversity
Department for Education and Skills (DfES) – Online document: www.standards.dfes.gov.uk/trainingschools

Doolittle P.E., Hicks D. and Lee, J. (2002) Information technology, constructivism, and social studies teacher education. Paper presented at *13th International Conference of the Society for Information Technology and Teacher Education (SITE 2001) March 2002* (pp. 3112–119). Nashville, USA.

Dwyer, D.C. (1996) The imperative to change our schools. In C. Fisher, D. Dwyer and K. Yokam (eds) *Education and Technology: Reflections on Computing in Classrooms* (pp. 15–33). San Francisco, CA: Jossey-Bass.

Garrison, D.R. (1997) Computer conferencing: The post-industrial age of distance education. *Open Learning, June 1997*, 311.

Hargreaves, A. (2002) *Teaching in the Knowledge Society.* Maidenhead, England: Open University Press.

Holmes, B., Tangey, B., FitzGibbon, A., Savage, T. and Mehan, S. (2001) Communal Constructivism: Students constructing learning for as well as with others. In J. Price, D. Willis, N.E. Davis and J. Willis (eds) *Proceedings of the 12 International Conference of the Society for Information Technology and Teacher Education (SITE 2001) March 2001* (pp. 3112–119). Orlando, USA.

Jacobs, G. and Rodgers, C. (1997) Remote teaching with digital video: A transnational experience. *British Journal of Educational Technology* 28 (4), 292–304.

Laurillard, D. (1993) *Rethinking University Teaching.* London: Routledge.

Lave, J. and Wenger, E. (1991) *Situated Learning: Legitimate Peripheral Participation.* Cambridge: Cambridge University Press.

McLoughlin, C. and Oliver, R. (1998) Maximising the language and learning link in computer learning environments. *British Journal of Educational Technology* 29 (2), 125–136.

Pouts-Lajus, S. and Riche-Magnier, M (2000) New educational technologies, an opportunity to rethink educational relationships. *Observatory of Technology for Education in Europe* – Online document: *http://home.worldnet.fr/~ote/text0008.htm* (28/11/2000).

Sellen, A.T. (1995) Remote conversations: The effects of mediating talk with technology. *Human-Computer Interaction* 10, 401–44.

Smith, M.K. (1999) Online document – www.infed.org/biblio/learning-social.htm

Tammelin, M. (1998) From telepresence to social presence: The role of presence in a network-based learning environment. In S. Tella (ed.) *Aspects of Media Education: Strategic Imperatives in the Information Age.* Media Education Centre, Department of Teacher Education. University of Helsinki. *Media Education Publications 8* – Online document – http://www.hkkk.fi/~tammelin/MEP8.tammelin.html

Tennant, M. (1997) *Psychology and the Adult Learner.* London: Routledge.

Vygotksy, L.S. (1978) *Mind in Society.* Cambridge, MA: Harvard University Press.

Wenger, E. (1998) *Communities of Practice: Learning, Meaning and Identity.* Cambridge: Cambridge University Press.

White C. (2003) *Language Learning in Distance Education.* Cambridge: Cambridge University Press.

Notes on Contributors

Nwabisa Bangeni is currently a lecturer in the Department of English at the University of the Transkei in South Africa, specialising in the field of distance teaching and learning.

Uwe Baumann has worked as a lecturer for the German Academic Exchange Service (DAAD Lektor) at Manchester Metropolitan University in the UK. He joined the Open University in Milton Keynes in 1995 and is now Head of German and Senior Lecturer in the Department of Languages – part of the Faculty of Education and Language Studies. His research interests are the development of intercultural competence, knowledge gain, attitudinal change and learning outcomes in language courses taught at a distance.

Sigrun Biesenbach-Lucas teaches ESL/EFL methodology and second language acquisition at American University in Washington, DC. Her research focuses on how technology affects language use, and pragmatic differences between native and non-native speakers of English in student–teacher interaction. She is also investigating the effectiveness and usefulness of asynchronous interaction in higher education. She has presented papers at numerous international, national, and local conferences and has published in *Language Learning & Technology, Computer Assisted Language Learning* and the *Journal of Asynchronous Learning Networks.*

Marina Bondi teaches English at the University of Modena and Reggio Emilia in Italy. She has published on various aspects of discourse analysis and English for Academic Purposes, with particular reference to the argumentative features of political and scientific discourse. In addition, she has also published several works on the organisation of classroom discourse, and its features.

Do Coyle is Senior Lecturer, Vice Dean and Director of Learning and Teaching in the School of Education at the University of Nottingham in the UK. She has worked in the field of foreign language and bi-lingual (CLIL) teacher education for 14 years, with a special interest in spontaneous talk, learner autonomy, thinking skills, learning strategies and subject teaching through a foreign language. Her recent innovation – the Teaching and Learning Observatory Network – embeds the use of new technologies in foreign language settings.

Leah Davcheva manages intercultural training and education projects for the British Council in Bulgaria. She previously taught English as a Foreign Language in secondary schools and was involved in teacher education. Recently she has co-ordinated the setting up and development of a Helpdesk for Intercultural Learning Materials. Her interests include the intercultural dimensions of school education, distance learning and the intercultural emphasis in translation and practices of cultural representation.

Alex Ding works at the Centre for English Language Education at the University of Nottingham in the UK. Here he is involved in technology enhanced language learning and teaching, and creating virtual self-access centres for EAP students. He is currently studying for a PhD at the University of Nottingham, investigating collaborative student autonomy in online learning environments. For a number of years he worked in French universities where the main focus of his work was setting up self-access centres and the promotion of learner autonomy.

Carisma Dreyer is a professor in the Graduate School of Education at the University of Potchefstroom in South Africa. She is responsible for teaching courses in learning and motivation as well as research methodology. She has published 30 refereed articles in national and international journals and presented papers at national and international conferences. She specialises in distance teaching and learning, educational technology, ESL teaching and learning, individual learner differences, reading instruction and statistics.

Richard Fay is a lecturer in education in the Faculty of Education at the University of Manchester in the UK. He has worked in the field of English language teacher education for ten years with special interests in the development of appropriate learning methodology for international language teacher education courses and the development of an intercultural paradigm for the teaching of English as an international lingua franca.

Cecilia Garrido has extensive experience of teaching languages, both in South America and the UK. She had the responsibility for the development of the Spanish programme at the Open University in the UK. Her main research interests are related to the development of intercultural competence and its implications for teachers, students, syllabus and curriculum design. She is currently Associate Dean (Course Production) in the Faculty of Education and Language Studies at the Open University.

Regine Hampel is a lecturer in German at the Open University in the UK. Her current research focuses on theoretical and practical issues around online tuition and the use of technologies, such as audio-graphic conferencing or instant messaging in language courses. She regularly presents her research at national and international conferences and has published a number of studies on online language learning and teaching. More recently her research has focused on the significance of meta-cognitive knowledge acquisition and meta-cognitive strategy use in virtual language learning contexts.

Heidi Hansson is a senior lecturer at Umeå University, Sweden. She has been involved in several distance education projects at Umeå University, and is also interested in how to develop supervision strategies in postgraduate education. Her other main research interest is women's literature, and she has published in the fields of postmodern romance, and Irish women's writing. She is also running a project on foreign visitors' travel narratives from the north of Sweden.

Mirjam Hauck joined the Open University in the UK in 1996. She is a lecturer in German in the Department of Languages and is involved in the production and presentation of several second- and third-level language courses. She has worked on fictional autobiography, narrative and literary theory. Her current research focuses on theoretical and practical issues around online tuition and the use of related technology in language courses.

Börje Holmberg is a linguist by training who has led the field in the development of central theories relating to distance learning and teaching. He has held senior posts at Hermods, a leading distance teaching organisation in Sweden and the FernUniversität in Germany, and was most recently vice-chancellor of the Private Distance-Teaching University of Applied Sciences in Darmstadt, Germany. He is on the Roll of Honour of the European Association of Distance Learning and has been awarded the prize of Excellence of the International Council for Open and Distance Education. He holds honorary doctorates from Deakin University in Australia and the OU in the United Kingdom. His many publications include *Growth and Structure of Distance Education* (1986), *Theory and Practice of Distance Education* (1995 2nd edn) and *Distance Education in Essence: an overview of theory and practice in the early twenty-first century* (2001).

Stella Hurd is a senior lecturer in the Department of Languages at the Open University in the United Kingdom, where she has contributed to French materials at a variety of levels. She taught French and managed languages provision in adult education before moving to higher education in 1992. She has edited and published in the area of adult open and distance language learning for many years. Her chief research interests are autonomy and learner differences, and their impact on second language acquisition at a distance.

Lesley Low is a lecturer in the Institute of Education at the University of Stirling, working with modern languages students on a concurrent programme of Initial Teacher Education. Previously, she was research fellow at the Scottish Centre for Information on Language Teaching and Research, working on a range of funded research projects, mainly in relation to language teaching in primary schools, and on two collaborative European-funded projects on monitoring and evaluation of primary language teaching and autonomy in primary language teacher education.

Christine Foster Meloni teaches English as a Foreign Language at The George Washington University in the USA. She has also taught EFL in Italy. Her primary academic interest is in the use of the Internet in the teaching of foreign languages. She is co-author with Warschauer and Shetzer of *Internet for English Teaching* (2000) and writes two regular columns 'Wandering the Web' (*TESOL Matters*) and 'Christine Meloni's Networthy' in *ESL Magazine*.

John Milton has taught English as a First, Second and Foreign Language in Canada, Mainland China, Bahrain and (currently) Hong Kong. His research interests are the empirical analysis of learners' English and the development of language tools and web-based resources for Second Language Acquisition. He has published and presented widely on these subjects and holds the post of Director of Language Courses at the College of Life-long Learning in the Hong Kong University of Science and Technology.

Linda Murphy has been a member of the regional academic staff of the Open University in the UK, based in Oxford, since 1996. Prior to this she worked in teaching, teacher training and educational management posts in Adult and Further Education in the areas of adult learning, language learning and English as an additional language. Her research interests are in the development of learning strategies, self-direction and learner autonomy.

Charl Nel is currently a lecturer in the Department of English in the Faculty of Education Sciences in Potchefstroom University in South Africa. He has presented papers at national and international conferences and published papers in national and international journals. He specialises in the field of ESL teaching and learning, educational technology and reading instruction.

Franca Poppi teaches English at the University of Modena and Reggio Emilia in Italy. She has published on various aspects of teacher–learner interaction, focusing on learner autonomy and advice in self-directed learning. She has contributed to the development of two projects involving computer-mediated language learning: DIAPASON (Distributed Interactive And Personalised Audiovisual Study Over Network) and MISSILE (Military Service Special Initiative in Language Education) and has edited a book *Percorsi assistiti nell'auto-apprendimento*, which includes several contributions focusing on the use of ICT in autonomous language learning.

Cristina Ros i Solé is currently Head of Spanish in the Department of Languages at the Open University, UK, where she has worked since 1996. She has also previously taught Spanish in various Higher Education institutions in the UK. Her main research interests are assessment and feedback, online language learning and the cultural and linguistic identities of second language learners.

Andreas Schramm teaches in the Second Language Teaching and Learning Program in the Graduate School of Education at Hamline University, Minnesota, USA. He was instrumental in re-creating the K–12 English as a Second Language licensure program on the web. Andreas has taught Linguistics for Language Teachers and the History of English on the web, and Sociolinguistics by email. His interests within linguistics lie in the social and psychological dimension of language and in expository writing.

Monica Shelley worked as a teacher and translator of German before joining the Open University in the UK as a lecturer in Community Education. She subsequently worked there as a lecturer in Modern Languages and a lecturer in Knowledge Resources Management. She has edited and published work in the field of foreign languages and distance education. Her research interests focus on the language learning needs of distance learners, on the design and structure of language courses taught at a distance and the development of intercultural competence. She is currently Visiting Research Fellow in the Systems Discipline of the Centre for Complexity and Change at the Open University.

Mike Truman is a lecturer in Spanish in the Department of Languages at the Open University in the UK. He has worked in the Spanish programme since 1998, where he has been closely involved in the development of the Department's assessment strategy. He has also co-authored several course books for students of Spanish in higher education. His research interests include assessment, feedback and translation.

Vincenza (Enza) Tudini is Convenor of Italian and Program Director for Languages at the University of South Australia. Her research interests and publications in the Computer Assisted Language Learning (CALL) field deal with multimedia computer software, synchronous and asynchronous Computer Mediated Communication (CMC). She is currently leading the oral interaction strand of a Cassamarca Foundation-funded project on the development of an online Italian programme in the School of International Studies in the University of South Australia.

Donald Weasenforth works as an instructor of English as a Second Language and as Chair of Developmental Reading, Developmental Writing and ESL at Collin County Community College in Texas, USA. One of his primary instructional and research interests is the use of computer-based instructional technology for language instruction, on which he has published a number of articles.

Elisabeth Wennö is Director of Studies at the English Department of Karlstad University in Sweden, and senior lecturer in English. She has long experience of teaching English language and literature at university level, as well as of curriculum design and course development. She has published a number of articles in literature-related fields, and a book-length study, *Ironic Formula in the Novels of Beryl Bainbridge* (1993).

Cynthia White is Associate Professor in the School of Language Studies at Massey University in New Zealand, where she has worked in the field of distance education at the tertiary level for 20 years. She has also worked in Thailand and China as a language teacher and project adviser. Her primary research areas are language learning in self-instruction contexts, learner autonomy and distance education. In 1997 she received the DEANZ (Distance Education Association of New Zealand) award for excellence in research in distance education. She has published extensively in journals such as *Open Learning, Distance Education, Educational Media International* and *System*. In 2003 her book entitled *Language Learning in Distance Education* appeared with Cambridge University Press.

Index

Authors

Subjects